YALE STUDIES

IN POLITICAL

SCIENCE, 20

COLOMBIA:

THE POLITICAL DIMENSIONS
OF CHANGE

Robert H. Dix

Yale University Press

NEW HAVEN AND LONDON

Originally published with assitance from the Louis Stern Memorial Fund.

Copyright © 1967 by Yale University.

Second printing July 1969.

Designed by Beverly Kruger,

set in Caledonia type,

and printed in the United States of America by

The Carl Purington Rollins

Printing-Office of the

Yale University Press,

New Haven, Conn.

Distributed in Great Britain, Europe, Asia, and

Africa by Yale University Press Ltd., London; in

Canada by McGill-Queen's University Press, Montreal; and

in Mexico by Centro Interamericano de Libros

Académicos, Mexico City.

Library of Congress catalog card number: 67-24495

To Mary
and to the people of Colombia

both, in their own way,
inspirers of this book

PREFACE

Perhaps the most important source for this study, though one to which it is impossible to give adequate citation, was the three years, from 1957 to 1960, that the author spent at the United States Embassy in Bogotá. These were years that witnessed significant developments in Colombian political life. In particular, they saw the fall of the military-based dictatorship of General Gustavo Rojas Pinilla in the wake of popular demonstrations and the advent of the National Front, an institutionalized coalition of the country's two traditional, warring political parties. It is my belief that the facts and interpretations that follow can be buttressed from the sources cited in the footnotes. Much, indeed, has been gleaned exclusively from them. Yet there unquestionably remains a residue that stemmed originally from other forms of research, including perusal of the official papers which crossed my desk at the Embassy. Most important, my years as a diplomat instilled a curiosity to go beyond day-to-day events in order to seek a deeper understanding of what has made Colombian politics take their particular form.

I subsequently returned to Colombia as an academician during the summer of 1963 to gather additional material, to bring my observations up-to-date, and especially to conduct a series of interviews with political leaders, social scientists, clergymen, military officers, businessmen, and other Colombians whose knowledge and opinions were germane to my inquiry.

Needless to say, neither officials of the United States government, nor those Colombians of various political leanings and professional occupations with whom I have talked or corresponded bear a whit of responsibility for the facts or interpretations presented. Whether Colombians or North Americans, they shall for the most part remain nameless in order in no way to be identified with what is said here. Suffice it to state that I am sincerely grateful for their assistance.

Doubtless few Colombians will agree with all that I have said concerning their country. Nevertheless, I found them unfailingly hospitable and courteous to the importuning foreigner. I can assure all of them that what they have said to me, and the materials they have kindly provided me, have been taken seriously into account. In the last analysis, this book would provide its greatest personal dividend to the author if it helped to stimulate the interest of Colombians in the objective study of their own political life, and if it contributed in some small measure to the understanding of Colombia on the part of those who are her citizens as well as those who are not.

Among those to whom this book and I owe a particular debt are John N. Plank, now of the Brookings Institution, who was my adviser when the book first took form as a doctoral dissertation at Harvard; Albert Berry of Yale University, who lent invaluable advice and materials on Colombian economics; Fernando Cepeda Ulloa, of the newly formed Institute of Political Science at the Universidad de los Andes in Bogotá; and the following institutions in Bogotá, all of which were generous with their facilities and with the time of their personnel: the Centro de Investigaciones of the Facultad de Sociología at National University; the Centro de Investigaciones Sociales; the Centro de Investigación y Acción Sociales; and the Centro de Estudios sobre Desarrollo Económico of the Universidad de los Andes.

I would also like to extend my thanks to Yale University for providing funds for summer research; to the Yale Concilium on International Relations, which supplied travel money; to the Social Science Research Fund of Yale University for financial aid in preparing the manuscript; to Ruth Davis and Edward White of the Yale University Press for the application of their editorial talents; to Lavon Saunders, who typed the manuscript; and to Violet Kordak, Claudia Carter, and Cynthia Meehan, who also assisted with portions of the manuscript. Not least, it remains profoundly to thank my wife—who shared the Colombian experience, typed the manuscript in its original form, and helped to edit the final version—for her indispensable assistance and encouragement.

R. H. D.

August 1966

CONTENTS

PREFACE   vii

LIST OF TABLES   xiii

PART I. INTRODUCTION

1. SCOPE AND PURPOSE   3
    The Dimensions of Change   3
    The Political Study of Colombia   10

PART II. THE SETTING OF POLITICS

2. THE ECOLOGICAL FOUNDATIONS OF POLITICS   21
    The Geographic Basis of Politics   21
    The Economy: Agriculture   24
    The Economy: The Non-Agricultural Sectors   31
    Population: Racial Composition and Demographic Trends   36

3. SOCIAL CLASS AND POLITICS   42
    The Elite   42
    The Middle Sectors   55
    The "Popular" Classes   63

PART III. THE REGIMES OF MODERNIZATION

4. THE REVOLUCIÓN EN MARCHA—MODERNIZATION
    BY AN ELITE   77
    The Precursors of Change   77
    The Revolución en Marcha   82
    The Decline and Fall of the Liberal Republic   91

5.   REFORM, REACTION, AND MILITARY RULE   99

     Jorge Eliécer Gaitán: Charismatic Reformer   99
     The Legacy of Gaitán   105
     The Conservative Counterrevolution   107
     The Military in Power   115
     Military Rule—A Balance Sheet   121
     The Transition to Constitutionalism   126

6.   THE NATIONAL FRONT   129

     The Origins of Bipartisanship   129
     Intraparty Factionalism: Problem for Coalition   136
     The National Front: Modernization   147
     Leadership under the National Front   158
     The National Front: Consensus and Modernization   164

          PART IV.   THE DYNAMICS OF CHANGE

7.   THE GOVERNMENT   171

     The Administrative Tradition and the Weak State   171
     The Spoils System   179
     The Electoral System   184
     The National Front and the State   192

8.   THE TRADITIONAL PARTIES (I)   203

     Party Organization   203
     The "Hereditary Hatreds"   211
     Variations on the Two-Party System   216
     The Traditional Party System—Stability and Change   221

9.   THE TRADITIONAL PARTIES (II)   231

     The Question of Political Dualism   231
     Ideology and the Parties   232
     The Social Bases of the Parties   239
     The "Colony" versus the "Republic"   245
     Why Two Parties?   248
     Change and Political Dualism   252

10. THE OPPOSITION   256

    The Opposition as Counter-Elites   256
    The Movimiento Revolucionario Liberal (*MRL*)   257
    The Revolutionary Left   269
    The Non-Leftist Opposition   281
    The Failures of Opposition   289

11. TRADITIONAL INSTITUTIONS   294

    The Military   294
    The Church   305 ✓

12. INTEREST ASSOCIATIONS   322

    Interest Groups and the Political System   322
    Organized Labor in Politics   330
    Students in Politics   341
    Interest Groups and Political Change   351

13. LA VIOLENCIA   360

    The Origins of La Violencia   360
    The Dynamics of La Violencia   370
    The National Front and La Violencia   376
    The Implications of Violence   382

PART V.   CONCLUSION

14. MODERNIZATION BY AN ELITE—SUMMARY
    AND IMPLICATIONS   389

    Process and Problems   389
    Causes   399
    The Road Ahead   412

BIBLIOGRAPHY   419

INDEX   435

LIST OF TABLES

1. Departmental Distribution of Total Factory Employment, 1953–1959   23
2. Rate of Growth of Gross Domestic Product (GDP)   32
3. Percentage of Urban Population Living in Communities of Varying Sizes, 1938–1965   39
4. Popular Vote for Chamber of Representatives, 1958–1966   140
5. Political Composition of Congress, 1958–1966   142
6. Results of Presidential Voting, May 1962   144
7. Results of Presidential Voting, May 1966   146
8. Per Cent of Those Registered Actually Voting in Elections, 1946–1966   162
9. Party Voting in Cities Casting More than 25,000 Votes, March 1962 Senatorial Election   243
10. Ecological Distribution of the MRL Vote in Selected Departments, March 1962 Senatorial Election   263

LIST OF MAPS

Colombia: Political Divisions   28
Colombia: Major Rivers and Mountains   29

LIST OF TABLES

LIST OF MAPS

PART I

Introduction

I

SCOPE

AND PURPOSE

Forces both foreign and domestic are transforming the traditional societies of much of the world, moving them in a direction we have come to call "modern." After generations of relationships based on highly stratified rank distinctions, and personal ties confined to family and village, men are imbibing ideas of equality and of a broader community where relatives or neighbors have not the sole claim on their loyalties. Ascribed status begins to give way to achieved. Economically, modernization entails an increase in productivity through the adoption of new technologies and the more effective mobilization of resources of land, capital, and labor. The market is less and less the village; more and more the nation, or even the world. In the realm of politics and government, the process is marked by an expansion in the numbers of the politically relevant; at any rate a much broader segment of the population increasingly influences, or is influenced for, political ends. Institutions such as political parties are formed as links between rulers and the ruled. Meanwhile government itself becomes more highly differentiated and functionally specific, as well as more "rational" and impersonal.

The Latin American nations share with those of Africa and Asia a concern with the modernization of their societies. All governments feel called upon to devote substantial energies to questions of policy whereby modernization may be advanced or, in some cases, resisted. Partly, such attention is a response to demands emanating from the society through the channels of political movements and parties, and groups such as business organizations, labor unions, and peasant leagues. Relevant, too, are the ideologically conditioned goals of the nation's leadership, and the felt imperatives of foreign challenge. But whatever the continent, and whatever the posture toward modernization itself—whether to promote it wholesale, to foster its gradual and cumulative progress, or to attempt to contain certain of its effects—the rulers and would-be rulers of the majority of the nations of mankind have come to address themselves to the implications of modernization.

Such concerns are not, of course, exclusive to the nations we term developing. Most nations, even the most developed, seek to enhance economic productivity. Yet the challenges of modernization do have a particular acuteness for the developing nations, and do tend especially to characterize those nations as a group in contrast to those we customarily designate as modernized or advanced. Whether one speaks of Ghana or Ceylon, Brazil or Iraq, those persons engaged in policy formulation and administration, as well as those who seek to become the government, must perforce direct their efforts toward problems raised by the impact of modernization on traditional societies, economies, and polities. If other tasks interpose—preserving the community in the face of foreign attack or natural disaster, or pacifying rival factions in the face of imminent civil war—direct involvement with questions of modernization may momentarily cease. But in the end the latter remains, almost by definition, the focus of attention in most developing societies.

This is even likely to be true of individuals or groups opposed to change. Less and less does politics *exclusively* resemble a game among rival personalities or clans within an elite. More and more does it become necessary for ruling groups to heed the implications of change—whether in order to resist it altogether, or to promote (and hopefully to control) it under their own auspices.

The countries of the underdeveloped world may differ in the specific problems of modernization they confront. For some, the heart of the matter may be the coexistence of separate linguistic and cultural communities within the same national state; for others a more central difficulty may be the wide disparity among caste-like social classes. Rates of economic and social change vary widely among the "third world" countries. The historical experiences of peoples are dissimilar, as are the characteristics of their traditional, now modernizing, societies. Still there is no escaping, for any of them, the impact of ideas, of economic and social forces, of the actions of individuals or of organized groups of men within their own societies, and even of the policies of other nations, which together impel those who hold or who would assume the mantle of authority to take into account the issues and dilemmas posed by modernization.

It therefore seems possible to say that all of the developing nations— either actually, or surely in the near future—face in a general way a common set of tasks. They are moving, or there are insistent pressures on them to move, their societies from poor to richer; from few to greater opportunities and rewards for the many; from territorial states to nations in the full sense; and from rule by tribal chieftain, landed aristocracy, or colonial power to polities in which greater numbers, in some way, both participate and are reached by the administrative arm of government.

So far relatively little attention has been paid in the growing literature on modernization to the variety of political ways that nations can meet this broadly common set of challenges. Yet, as Daniel Lerner writes, "The values of modernity have infused . . . a new perception of a desirable future; the conflict now turns upon *power*. The question is who shall control the direction and tempo of modernization and under what banners?" [1] Put another way, what sorts of political regimes will the developing countries evolve to deal with change, and how successful will varying political approaches to modernization be in accomplishing their objectives? The question itself divides into two clusters of related sub-questions.

In the first place, what kinds and what degrees of change in the traditional locus of power will occur in the face of modernization or at given stages of that process? Will the traditional elite prefer palliative reforms, changes designed to alleviate strains in the system while retaining the essentials of the existing order? Or will the response on the part both of elites and potential counter-elites be to reach a mutual accommodation on the sharing of power between the two without wholesale destruction of the old order? Or will change be accomplished by the overthrow of the existing power configuration and its substitution by a new elite which had not found a place in the previous system?

Secondly, by what political means will change be approached? By

1. Daniel Lerner, *The Passing of Traditional Society* (New York, The Free Press, 1958), pp. 405–06 (Lerner's emphasis).

means of traditional forms of domination? Under the aegis of a mass
revolutionary party? Through the instrumentality of military rule? Within
the framework of a functioning constitutional democracy? Or in some
other way?

In sum, what sorts of regimes will arise in the developing nations as
they confront the tasks imposed on their political systems by the challenges of modernization? How will a particular nation view change, who
will lead the process, and what political methods will be developed to
carry it out? How effective will given solutions be and what further problems will they raise for the political system?

James Coleman, following Edward Shils, has proposed a typology of
regimes of modernization in developing areas that includes the following
categories: political democracy, tutelary democracy, modernizing oligarchy, traditional oligarchy, terminal colonial democracy, and colonial
or racial oligarchy.[2] David Apter has proposed a threefold distinction
among modernizing autocracies, reconciliation or "consociational" regimes, and mobilization regimes.[3] A. F. K. Organski, including in his
compass the experience of the already developed nations, has depicted
three alternatives within the stage of the "politics of industrialization":
bourgeois politics, stalinist politics, and "syncratic" or fascist politics.[4] All
three typologies have their uses (and we will have occasion to refer to
Organski again at a little length), but each has shortcomings for our purposes. Coleman's scheme was developed with Africa and Asia primarily
in mind and is inadequate for Latin America. The Apter and Organski
categories fail, by virtue of their limited number, to make some distinctions which are important in the Latin American context.

We suggest instead the following categories of modernizing regimes
for Latin America:

1. The totalitarian mobilization regime, which crushes all opposition and seeks to politicize all groups and organizations in order to
mobilize them for the transformation of society (e.g. Castro's Cuba).

2. Gabriel Almond and James Coleman, *The Politics of Developing Areas* (Princeton, Princeton University Press, 1960), pp. 559–76.
3. David Apter, "Political Religion in the New States," in Clifford Geertz, ed., *Old
Societies and New States* (New York, The Free Press, 1963), pp. 57–104.
4. A. F. K. Organski, *The Stages of Political Development* (New York, Alfred A.
Knopf, 1965).

2. The democratic single-party mobilization regime, in which one party dominates the political scene, and seeks to mobilize the society for the ends of modernization, but does not eliminate all opposition or criticism or attempt to politicize the entire society (e.g. Mexico).

3. The populistic authoritarian regime, in which an authoritarian leader or group, representing a coalition of traditional and modern interests and orientations, acquires a genuine mass following (e.g. Perón's Argentina).

4. Constitutional democracy, which assures both majority rule and minority rights and effects cumulative change by consent (e.g. contemporary Chile).

5. Rule by a modernizing elite, whereby limited modernization is carried out by an elite that holds a virtual monopoly of political, social, economic, educational, and other resources but which does not exclude a measure of intra-elite political competition (e.g. Colombia).

6. Corporate military rule, or limited modernization carried out under the auspices of the military acting essentially as a corporate institution, even though one individual may hold the title of chief of state (e.g. contemporary El Salvador).

7. Dictatorship, or limited modernization carried out under the rule of one man (though he may be allied with specific groups or parties), usually a military man but not necessarily so (e.g. Pérez Jiménez' Venezuela).

All Latin American nations whose leaderships have more or less committed them to sustained modernization would seem to fit into one of these categories, which imply something both about the political structure of a regime and the degree and mode of change which it seeks to enact. All have empirical referents in contemporary or recent Latin America. The categories should, at the same time, be taken as ideal-types into which no given regime necessarily fits perfectly. It is also true that a nation may, at different times, pursue different political routes to modernization. Moreover, within a given nation men may well disagree over who should carry out change, and to what degree and at what pace. It would also be theoretically possible, for example, for the military to effect a social revolution instead of confining itself to a program of limited modernization. Nonetheless, the above categories would seem to represent the major possible ideal-types of modernizing regimes in twentieth-century Latin America. We shall attempt to place our analysis within the context of the questions that have evoked this kind of classification.

It is not enough, however, for the student of comparative politics to confine himself to the study of the processes and institutions which evolve in the course of the development of various nations, or to an analysis of the varying effectiveness of different political approaches to resolving the dilemmas of modernization. The question remains: what factors—historical, economic, social, political, cultural—have brought about one type of political response to the challenge of modernization at a particular time in a particular country, and what other factors have produced a quite different result in another time and place. Some, like James Coleman, who have discussed the varieties of modernizing politics, have gone beyond typologies to pose such questions. However, most such attempts have taken a global perspective, concerning themselves primarily with broad-gauged correlations between social and economic indices and the degree of competitiveness or democracy evinced by a wide array of political systems.

The principal exception is the pathbreaking work edited by Robert Ward and Dankwart Rustow, which attempts to compare the process of modernization in Japan and Turkey and to account for the differences between the two.[5] Experts on the two countries explore such topics as the nature of traditional society, environmental and foreign factors, education, the civil bureaucracy, the military, and political leadership. The editors conclude with a list of types of problems or crises which presumably all nations confront during the process of modernization. Differences in the specifics of the problems or crises confronted, and in the way they are handled, are held to explain the contrasts between countries.

The central interests of the contributors to *Political Modernization in Japan and Turkey* are in comparative *rates* of modernization and in the *timing* of the origins of the modernization process. The principal focus of our attention is on the somewhat different, though obviously related, question of comparative political *approaches* toward change. For this and other reasons we do not follow precisely their otherwise useful checklist. We do, however, make use of some of their categories, or of categories quite analogous to theirs.

5. Robert E. Ward and Dankwart Rustow, eds., *Political Modernization in Japan and Turkey* (Princeton, Princeton University Press, 1964).

Thus among the causal aspects of the dimensions of change it seems possible for our purposes to distinguish the following:

1. The ecological base of the political system(s) in question, that is, the geography, the dynamics of the economy, and the size and distribution of the population. Germane to this area of concern are of course such phenomena as rates of industrialization and urbanization.

2. The pattern of social stratification, the changes taking place therein, and the attitudes toward change of the various groupings in the social structure.

3. The political culture of the society, that is, the beliefs, values, and symbolic attachments toward political persons and institutions which in turn condition such things as the propensity to resolve conflict through violence and the willingness to trust one's fellows in the community.

4. Established or pre-modern institutions and their own adaptations to change, including the governmental framework itself, traditional political parties, and such politicized structures as the military and traditional religious organizations.

5. Potential counter-elite groups, whether they take the form of system-opposition political parties, an organized labor movement, student organizations, or guerrilla bands, with particular attention to factors affecting their cohesion and their orientations toward the existing structure of power.

6. The impact and timing of forces and events external to the political system itself, including foreign models and ideologies of change and the efforts of foreign nations to encourage one or another political route to change (by means of an Alliance for Progress, for instance).

7. The timing and sequence of a series of historical "crises" which presumably every nation tends to confront during the course of modernization. Such crises include:

a. the crisis of identity, by which the boundaries of the nation are established, as well as a sense of identification with the national unit and its symbols;

b. the crisis of legitimacy, or the essential agreement of most major groups in the society on the appropriateness of a given set of political institutions and myths;

    c. the crisis of integration, involving the creation of a sense of community and trust among the diverse ethnic, cultural, or other groups in the society;

    d. the crisis of penetration, or the process by which the bureaucratic arms of governmental control penetrate the society;

    e. the crisis of participation, that is, the process of extending voting, and other forms of participation in the political system, beyond the confines of a narrow elite;

    f. the crisis of distribution, or the way in which the political system resolves demands for it to take an active role in the distribution of goods and services in a society.[6]

Societies tend to differ in the sequence in which they are confronted by such crises, and in the timing of them. For example, is the working class admitted to political participation before it comes to demand a fuller share of society's material rewards, or simultaneously? Does the church-state issue persist politically into the era of class struggle and thus complicate, exacerbate, or moderate the latter?

In short, taking into account all the above categories of causal factors, it should be possible to assess—in quite broad terms admittedly—the probable political route that a country will take in the face of the challenges of modernization, or to appraise the factors that have worked to produce an outcome which is already evident.

Our general area of inquiry, then, is that posed by Lerner—who shall control the direction and tempo of modernization and under what banners? Our corollary concern is to account for the different routes to development "chosen" by particular nations.

THE POLITICAL STUDY OF COLOMBIA

In a Latin American world where the twentieth century has brought three social revolutions resulting in one-party regimes (in Mexico, Bolivia, and Cuba, the first two quasi-democratic in form, the latter totalitarian); several significant instances of populistic authoritarian regimes (most notably, Perón's and that of Vargas in Brazil); governments of democratic

    6. In addition to Ward and Rustow, see Lucian W. Pye and Sidney Verba, eds., *Political Culture and Political Development* (Princeton, Princeton University Press, 1965), pp. 555–60.

reform in Chile, Venezuela, Costa Rica, and elsewhere; periods of modernization by the military in El Salvador and Brazil, among other countries; and dictators who sought to promote at least the economic dimensions of modernization, Colombia has remained in a relatively unique position. It is not the only case, but it is the outstanding one, at least in contemporary Latin America, of an effort by an elite which is substantially traditional in its origins to transform a nation within limits that will enable the ruling class to retain for itself the essential levers of power. Argentina and Chile during the late nineteenth and early twentieth centuries might fit this category of our typology, but they faced a rather different set of challenges, especially in the political realm. Brazil, at various points since 1945, and Peru within the last few years, might also fit into the description of rule by a modernizing elite. But such regimes are of recent creation (not until at least 1956, and in a sense not until 1962, could it be said that the Peruvian elite, long dominant in the country, had committed itself to modernization). Or they have been subject to frequent interruption and the competition of significant alternatives (as was true of Brazil under Vargas [1930–45 and 1950–54] and Goulart [1961–64] and today under a substantially military regime). Colombia, it is true, experienced a partially military interregnum during the years 1953–57, when a dictator with military and some civilian support tried half-heartedly to imitate Argentina's Juan Perón. But it was brief in duration and did no permanent damage to elite rule.

As a matter of fact, except for a short period in the mid-1940s, and with some qualification within the last few years, Colombia has lacked any serious *challenge* to elite rule on the part of an opposition political party or movement. Potential counter-elites such as labor and student groups have likewise been quite weak politically and relatively unradical. Even the Communist party has been weaker and less effective than the relative size of the country, or its relative rank on the standard indices of modernization, might suggest.

Instead of moving, in Gino Germani's terms, from a phase of limited participation politics to one of expanded participation, and subsequently to a politics of total participation, Colombia has remained essentially in the former stage, despite profound changes in its society and economy.[7]

7. Gino Germani, *Política y Sociedad en una Epoca de Transición de la Sociedad Tradicional a la Sociedad de Masas* (Buenos Aires, Paidos, 1962), chapter 6.

True, the vote is now accorded substantially to all adult Colombians. Yet the posts of leadership, the key decisions, and the principal social, economic, cultural, and political resources of the society remain mainly in elite hands. It is true, too, that the Colombian elite has become a modernizing one. However, it has sought to carry out its modernizing role by emphasizing the economic and by trying to avoid paying most of the social and political costs that have been incurred in other countries during the course of development.

A frequent political outcome of such an attempt among Latin countries in both Europe and Latin America has been what K. H. Silvert has called "Mediterranean syndicalism." It entails the construction of an ideology, and an institutional ordering, which subsumes class to hierarchy. "The good society pictured by the syndicalist would have the individual firmly rooted in his institutional place . . . Public decisions would then result from the interplay of the institutional oligarchs, and not from the deliberations of groups and men elected at large from a citizenry escaping its occupational bonds in an act of political selection and decision formally and somewhat substantially indicative of equality. The secular state could not become supreme in its area; mass man would be tamed by being herded into institutional kennels, safely under the tutelage of the leader." [8] Examples would be Franco's Spain and Perón's Argentina. Organski, in categorizing an approach to development which involves a compromise between a declining agrarian elite and a rising industrial elite in the face of the "danger from below," has called it "syncratism" and noted that it has so far occurred only in Latin countries (he has in mind Spain, Argentina, and Mussolini's Italy).

During the 1950s Colombia inclined to this approach, first under President Laureano Gómez and, subsequently, in a modified sense, under the government of General Gustavo Rojas Pinilla. Yet both before and after the decade of the '50s Colombia's modernizing elite has not sought out the governmental forms or ideology of either Silvert's syndicalism or Organski's corporatism. If it has pursued *objectives* similar to those of syndicalist or syncratic regimes it has done so in a rather different way. In fine, the political path to development which Colombia has most consistently followed has been that of a modernizing social elite working within the forms and some measure of the reality of representative government.

8. K. H. Silvert, "The Costs of Anti-Nationalism: Argentina," in Silvert, *Expectant Peoples* (New York, Random House, 1963), p. 360.

Colombia's political attempt to meet the challenge of change we date, a bit arbitrarily, from 1934. It is, of course, true that modernization has no certain starting point and no well-defined end. Long before any concerted governmental effort to modernize, Colombia possessed a number of the characteristics customarily associated with that term. Politically, it had a functioning Congress and judiciary, a chief executive chosen in competitive elections, and the rudiments of a rationalized bureaucracy. Colombia likewise had a functioning party system, and a political culture which somewhat more than nominally embraced the norms of representative government. Economically, the country—though not the majority of Colombians—was substantially involved in the international market, notably via the coffee trade. Many of its leaders were oriented to the goals of economic progress: there were an appreciable number of Colombians familiar with such modern undertakings as the export-import trade, banking, commercial agriculture, and industrial entrepreneurship. Culturally, the elite, at least, considered itself without equivocation to be a part of Western civilization. It looked to the European, North American, and other Latin American centers of that civilization for its cultural nourishment and the education of its sons. Social change had also made significant advances. Notable were a slowly accelerating rate of urbanization, and unrest in some parts of the countryside. Finally, while the mass of Colombians certainly had only the poorest sense of identity with their nation, the country was unified: no one contested its boundaries and few its ultimate authority. Although the majority of Colombians were effectively barred from important areas of the national life, only in the case of a few remote Indian tribes was that exclusion founded primarily on ethnic, linguistic, or religious divergences. The problems relating to the effective integration of the majority into the nation were still very great, but they did not threaten the state with dissolution.

In many other respects, however, Colombia was in 1934 a distinctly unmodern nation. Its economy was still relatively primitive and agricultural, and the state had never truly adopted as a goal of government policy the promotion of economic development. Though social mobility was not wholly absent, status was still mainly founded on birth and privilege, not merit. Equitable distribution of the material products of the society had received almost no attention; nor had protection of the underprivileged, despite the existence of some legislation concerning such matters as workmen's compensation. Education was still the province of the few:

well over half the nation was illiterate, and there was as yet little conception of education as a means to augment the pool of skills available to the society. The nation, though its legitimacy seemed established, was a vague and distant entity to the masses and a subject for underlying contempt to the elite who looked abroad for "real" culture. Lastly, political participation was limited. In the highly competitive election of 1930 only 824,462, or about a third of the adult male population, had voted for president, and this was an increase of some 150,000 over the previous high, recorded in 1922. Moreover, the genuineness of even this degree of participation may be questioned in view of coercive expedients used to get voters to the polls in some instances and the undoubted fraud in some localities.[9] Meanwhile admission to the ranks of political leadership was largely restricted to the sons of the landed, commercial, and industrial elite.

It is, then, with 1934 and the accession to the presidency of Alfonso López Pumarejo that we date Colombia's "take-off" on the road to modernization—social, economic, and political.[10] For it is from about that date that Colombian leadership groups become irrevocably confronted with the issues and dilemmas posed by the modernization process, and at least partially committed to their resolution. Beginning roughly in 1934 a significant proportion of the Colombian elite becomes conscious of the need to adjust old habits and institutions in the face of the challenge of change, and in the interests of its own survival. Groups that have previously had almost no share of important political, social, or economic resources simi-

9. Election figures are taken from República de Colombia, Registraduría Nacional del Estado Civil, *Organización y Estadísticas Electorales, Marzo y Mayo de 1962* (Bogotá, 1962), p. 209. The population of 1930 may be roughly estimated at 7,250,000, extrapolating from data on pp. 21 and 39 of Juan Luis de Lannoy and Gustavo Pérez, *Estructuras Demográficas y Sociales de Colombia* (Bogotá, Centro de Investigaciones Sociales, 1961). Of that number, some 30 per cent were under voting age; and of the remainder about 50 per cent were women and excluded at that time from the vote. It should be noted that the estimate of one-third participation on the part of adult males (many of whom were denied the vote by literacy and property restrictions) is very rough indeed. Census figures, for example, are questionable (the census of 1928 which showed a population of 7,851,110 being generally regarded as inflating the true numbers) and I have accepted the qualifications of them introduced by Lannoy and Pérez. Voting in 1934 exceeded 922,000. Given the interim increase in population, voter participation thus remained at about the same rate as in 1930. However, Alfonso López had no opposition in 1934 and many Conservatives abstained from voting at all. The potential, or extrapolated, rate of participation would therefore be somewhat higher for 1934.

10. Cf. Ward and Rustow, p. 435, concerning the concept of the modernization "take-off."

larly begin in the 1930s to come into a new awareness of their position and to force themselves onto the attention of those that govern. It is likewise during this period that the cumulative impress of twentieth-century economic and political events, and foreign ideologies and models of development, first impinges markedly on the Colombian political system.

Throughout the sequence of efforts since 1934 to deal politically with the implications of change, the Colombian upper class has yielded up its power to control the nation and to direct (and contain) the process of modernization only for fleeting moments and in a partial way. This has continued to be true, despite conflict within the elite itself over the pace of modernization, sporadic challenges to elite rule, and serious rural violence in the decade after 1948.

We are interested, then, in mapping out Colombia's road to modernization over the last thirty-odd years, and in the vicissitudes of the journey. But we also wish to weave into our discussion an examination of the reasons that have propelled Colombia in that direction rather than—at least as yet—toward revolutionary totalitarianism, constitutional democracy, populistic authoritarianism, or some other regime of modernization.

It should be said at the outset that there is at least no immediately obvious reason for Colombia's deviance that is apparent from the standard measurable indices of social and economic modernization. Within the Latin American sub-universe of the developing nations, Colombia ranks generally just above the mean. Its gross national product per capita of $263 per annum places it eighth among the twenty Latin American nations. On an index of urbanization, Colombia is in seventh position, along with Panama, with 22 per cent of its people living in cities of more than 20,000 persons. Colombia is eighth (in a tie with Costa Rica and Paraguay) in the percentage of persons employed in non-agricultural pursuits and eighth also in the percentage (62) of those over 15 years of age who can read and write. It is in eleventh position (tied with Ecuador) on an index of the degree of exposure of its populace to the mass media as measured by the number of daily newspaper readers per 1,000 population.[11]

Explication, therefore, cannot end here. We will be obliged to search

11. For the above figures and comparisons see Bruce M. Russett, and Hayward R. Alker, Jr., Karl W. Deutsch, Harold D. Lasswell, *World Handbook of Political and Social Indicators* (New Haven, Yale University Press, 1964), passim. There are, of course, problems in the adequacy and comparability of data, as the authors duly acknowledge. The rankings are used here to indicate rough approximations only.

elsewhere for the causes of Colombia's political "choice" of a modernizing elite. We must revert instead to the causal categories outlined earlier, although these will be treated in the course of our discussion of process, leaving to the Conclusion a separate and fuller elaboration. Thus influences external to the system (those of the United States government, Castro's Cuba, and the Vatican, for example) will receive mention at various places but not in a separate chapter. We do the same for political culture. Many of the elements of the analysis are so interwoven in any case, and the causal categories themselves so overlapping, that it would be unnecessarily repetitious to do otherwise.

This introductory chapter has been designed to set the inquiry in something of an analytical framework and to clarify the author's aims in pursuing the study. Part II will treat the environmental background of Colombian politics, in the belief that an investigation into the nature of a particular polity cannot be concerned solely with the traditionally political but must scrutinize, even if briefly, the relevant aspects of geography, economics, demography, and social structure.

Part III, essentially an historical analysis, will explore Colombia's political efforts to meet the problems arising from the country's encounter with the mid-twentieth century. It will begin with President Alfonso López' "revolution on the march" and the conditions that led to its emergence, pass on to the partial breakdown of the traditional Colombian political system under the impact of modernization, and conclude with the "re-creation" of the traditional system under the National Front.

Part IV then undertakes to analyze the dynamics of change in Colombia, group by group and institution by institution. The objective will be to outline the nature of the Colombian political system, to portray the way in which elements of the traditional political order are altering their orientations toward politics, and to depict the new forces emerging in challenge to the old order. Hence we will center our attention on the changing role of government, on the party system and the nature of the opposition, on the political role of such traditional institutions as the army and the Catholic Church, on the entry into the political arena of newer groups such as labor unions and agricultural and industrial pressure groups, and on that peculiarly Colombian manifestation of change, *la violencia*.

In conclusion, we shall try to draw together the threads of the foregoing analysis as regards both the process and the causes of Colombia's political approach to modernization. We shall also try to make explicit some of the implications of our analysis for the process of change in other developing nations, and in other Latin American polities in particular.

Colombia is therefore our universe for inquiry into the questions we have set ourselves concerning the political dimensions of change. Concretely, this study is an effort to assess the dynamics of a particular political route to development, that of a traditional elite which, because of changes internal to itself and changes in its society, has become a modernizing one within the limits it has set for its own survival. It is therefore an investigation into the adaptation of traditional institutions and structures of power to the conditions posed by the demands and pressures for modernization. Our focus is both on the attempt itself, and on its prospects for success, as well as on the crucial variables that have led Colombia as a nation to give preference to one political route to modernization rather than some other.

Finally, this study obeys the logic that Latin America taken as a whole (despite the very wide differences among the nations of the area) clearly places somewhere between the countries of the developed world and most of the so-called new states of Asia and Africa in its relative degree of social, economic, and political modernization. In this, as in other ways, Latin America "would seem to constitute a perfect connecting link between Western and non-Western political experience." [12] Moreover, as we have noted, Colombia ranks in the middle range of the Latin American countries, at least by some crude quantitative measures of modernization. Insofar as the study of a particular political system can have implications for the understanding of others, the study of Colombia may therefore prove especially useful for an investigation into the political dimensions of modernization.

In the end, it is frankly recognized that "The study of a single country . . . can lead to conclusions which are valid for it alone and do not in themselves warrant a wider application. But such conclusions will [hopefully] suggest hypotheses for testing in other contexts, so that, when these are checked by a comparative method, a reliable body of argument can be pieced together." [13]

12. Dankwart A. Rustow, "New Horizons for Comparative Politics," *World Politics,* 9 (1957), 546.

13. Leslie Lipson, "The Two-Party System in British Politics," *American Political Science Review,* 47 (1953), 338.

PART II

The Setting of Politics

2

THE ECOLOGICAL FOUNDATIONS
OF POLITICS

THE GEOGRAPHIC BASIS OF POLITICS

Rather well-defined socioeconomic regions, rooted in such topographical facts as the division of the country three times over in a roughly north-south direction by parallel spurs of the Andes mountain chain, came into being in Colombia during the colonial period and persisted under the republic. Most population centers were located on isolated plateaus and in remote valleys and, as in many of the other countries of Latin America, regionalism proved a highly divisive force during the nineteenth century. Although the struggle between centralism and federalism is no longer a focal issue of politics, regional differences and regional loyalties continue to be strong.

Today at least four principal regions are significant in terms of population and resources. Each also has a major urban center. These regions are: the eastern cordillera, centered on Bogotá; the department of Antioquia and its southern extension, Caldas, centered on Medellín; the Valle del Cauca in southwestern Colombia, formerly focused on Popayán, now on the economically and demographically burgeoning Cali; and the Atlantic coastal region, once with Cartagena as its principal city, but with Barranquilla now dominant. Some would add, with considerable justice, the region around Bucaramanga in the northeast, and another comprising the departments of Caldas and Quindío. There are also areas of lesser substance, and subregions within regions, all with some claim to individuality and importance. Several include cities of 100,000 or more inhabitants.

The result is that Bogotá is less important economically and demographically, relative to the rest of the country, than are the capitals or major cities of most Latin American countries. Peru, with a population about three-quarters that of Colombia, has a capital city of approximately equal size, and only three other cities with more than 100,000 population (one of which, Callao, is in effect part of Lima). Colombia, by contrast, has two cities other than Bogotá with well over half a million population (Medellín and Cali), and another of almost 500,000 inhabitants (Barranquilla). At least nine others, dispersed throughout the country, have more than 100,000 persons.[1] In Colombia, there does not prevail the "Goliath's head" condition of a capital or other major city dominating a dependent interior demographically, economically, culturally, and politically. Colombian regionalism is rather one of multiple balances: "A functional map of Colombia would not resemble a wheel with all the spokes leading to Bogotá (as Venezuela is dominated by Caracas, for example) but a series of wheels with complex interrelations between them."[2]

With rapid urbanization under way there is indeed some tendency toward an increasing concentration of population in the departments which already contain the largest urban centers. However, in 1962 the three largest departments together still held only 41 per cent of the population, compared to 38 per cent in 1951.[3] There is likewise some evidence of an increasing concentration of industrial production, especially in the Bogotá area. The two departments of Cundinamarca and Antioquia have more than half the country's factory employment (see Table 1). Nevertheless, dispersion remains quite wide, with both the petroleum industry (Santander and Norte de Santander) and the steel industry (Boyacá) located outside the four departments which lead in factory employment. Meanwhile agricultural production is beginning to move from the slopes of the Andes to the lowlands of the Magdalena River valley and the Atlantic coast. Despite some indications of growing centralization, Colombia continues to have the geographic, economic, and demographic bases for a genuinely multiregional society and politics.

During the nineteenth century, the existence of several powerful re-

1. Information on cities was taken from *The South American Handbook, 1963, passim.*
2. John M. Hunter, *Emerging Colombia* (Washington, D.C., Public Affairs Press, 1962), p. 10; see pp. 4–10 for a succinct description of the geographically conditioned contrasts and divisions within Colombia.
3. Percentage calculated from estimates in República de Colombia, Departamento Administrativo Nacional de Estadística, *Anuario General de Estadística, 1962* (Bogotá, 1964), p. 10 (hereafter cited as *Anuario de Estadística, 1962*).

TABLE 1

DEPARTMENTAL DISTRIBUTION OF TOTAL FACTORY EMPLOYMENT, 1953–1959 [4]

Department (and Principal City)	1953	1959
Cundinamarca (Bogotá)	24.9%	28.9%
Antioquia (Medellín)	24.6	24.9
Valle del Cauca (Cali)	14.5	16.1
Atlántico (Barranquilla)	9.5	10.0
All others	26.5	20.1
	100.0	100.0

gional centers undoubtedly contributed to civil disorder. Today, by permitting a pattern of development diffused among several parts of the country, it may be an economic asset. Politically, the relative dispersion of the population and of economic resources may cause difficulties for the coherence of the government's modernizing programs and tend to dilute them through concessions to the many regional claimants. Yet the relatively balanced nature of Colombian regionalism and the decentralization of economic and political initiatives may at the same time provide a greater degree of pluralistic access to the political process, and help to mitigate the separation that exists in many developing countries between a capital where power and decision-making are concentrated and "other" sections of the country.

The improvement of the road network in the last decade, and the completion of the railway from the interior to the Atlantic coast in 1961, have for the first time created a single national market for both industrial and agricultural products. This should both spur further growth and foster the development of regional economies of specialization. By increasing interdependence and communication, it may also help to modify some of the more divisive political manifestations of regionalism. Colombia's unusual multifaceted regionalism nevertheless persists and continues to have important implications for the country's political development, particularly in the geographic dispersion of the centers of economic, social, and political power.

4. República de Colombia, Consejo Nacional de Política Económica y Planeación, Departamento Administrativo de Planeación y Servicios Técnicos, *Colombia. Plan General de Desarrollo Económico y Social* (2 vols. Bogotá, 1961–62), Part II, p. 16 (hereafter cited as *Plan General de Desarrollo*).

THE ECONOMY: AGRICULTURE

Any discussion of the Colombian economy must begin, although it obviously cannot end, with coffee. Actually, tobacco was the first crop to dominate Colombia's export trade, in the years after 1850. Also during the nineteenth century cinchona bark, indigo, and other products enjoyed brief booms.[5] But by the late nineteenth century coffee production had begun in earnest on Colombia's congenial shaded slopes. Since the early years of this century, as coffee has gone so has the Colombian economy, including its international balance of payments. In most recent years coffee has provided between 66 and 83 per cent of Colombia's foreign exchange.[6]

Several facts about Colombian coffee stand out, other than its importance for the economy, its dependence on international markets, and its excellent quality. The first is that although coffee depends on foreign markets, particularly that of the United States, its production and trade have always been substantially in Colombian hands. Moreover, coffee has provided Colombia with a domestic source of capital, located in the hands of private merchants oriented to the maximization of profits through commerce and the production of cash crops. It seems hardly accidental that Colombia's principal coffee-growing region was also the center of the country's initial industrial growth.

A second significant fact about coffee in Colombia is that much of it is produced by the small, independent farmer. It is true that there are some large coffee plantations employing agricultural labor; it is also true that most of the international trade in coffee is controlled by the Coffee Growers Federation, which is in turn dominated by large growers and merchants. Yet, some 78 per cent of the coffee farms have less than 20 hectares of land [7] (1 hectare = 2.471 acres). The optimum topographical and cli-

5. See Luis Eduardo Nieto Arteta, *Economía y Cultura en la Historia de Colombia* (2d ed. Bogotá, Ediciones Tercer Mundo, 1962), chapters 17 and 18, for the booms and busts in Colombia's nineteenth-century export trade.

6. *Plan General de Desarrollo,* Part I, p. 309.

7. República de Colombia, Departamento Administrativo Nacional de Estadística, *Directorio Nacional de Explotaciones Agropecuarias (Censo Agropecuario) 1960. Resumen Nacional* (Bogotá, 1960), Part II, p. 51 (hereafter cited as *Censo Agropecuario*). It should be noted that the number of "exploitations" and the number of owners do not exactly correspond. However, the figures are close enough to be useful for our purposes.

matic conditions for growing Colombia's particular varieties of mild coffee are conducive to the small hillside plot. So, too, were the "internal frontier" conditions of the late nineteenth century (discussed below) when coffee production was taking hold in Colombia. In any case, the nation's principal export crop is grown not on a few plantations or haciendas but on several hundreds of thousands of individually owned plots.

Finally, coffee is a cash crop. One might suppose that this would have a positive effect on national integration by tying significant sectors of the rural population to a market of national and international scope. On the other hand, involvement in such an economic nexus can create dependence on factors outside the control of the growers and thus act as a destabilizing influence.

It is true that while some 429,000 families make their living from coffee production,[8] the majority of rural Colombians are engaged in subsistence farming or in the production of food staples such as maize, yucca, and potatoes for local markets. This is the case in many places both in the Andean highlands and along the Atlantic and Pacific coasts, but it is especially characteristic of the departments of Cauca and Nariño in southwestern Colombia and of Boyacá in the east. At the same time, many Colombians other than some growers of coffee are engaged in large-scale agriculture for a wider market. Sugar, cotton, rice, cattle, and bananas are among these other products. Yet only in the case of bananas, which for decades were grown for export in the Atlantic coastal region under the aegis of a United Fruit Company affiliate, have these been in foreign hands. However, United Fruit now owns but 18 per cent of all banana-producing land; most Colombian bananas are grown by independent producers under contract to sell to the company.[9]

In fine, Colombian agriculture is characterized by a substantial infusion of cash-crop farming, often carried on by small independent producers, notably in coffee. Moreover, the participation of foreign ownership and control is minimal in the sector of the economy on which the majority of Colombians depend for a living and on which the country depends for most of its export earnings.

Colombia is self-sufficient, or nearly so, in many agricultural products,

8. Ibid., p. 51.
9. Stacy May and Galo Plaza, *The United Fruit Company in Latin America* (New York, National Planning Association, 1958), pp. 175–80.

and its variety of climates, terrains, and soils prompts optimism regarding the country's agricultural potentialities. True, agricultural productivity is low: agriculture engaged the labor of some 47 per cent of the economically active population in 1961, but its contribution to the gross national product was only 35 per cent.[10] Yet there remain substantial portions of the country which are fertile, or potentially so, but are still virtually unoccupied. In itself the availability of such vacant lands does not solve Colombia's agrarian problems. The agricultural laborer who wants land, or the small owner who wants more than he now has, is not necessarily eager to uproot himself and his family and move to the new frontier. Nor does he usually have the capital or the credit to begin anew in an unknown place. Yet, contrasted with other countries where pressing agricultural problems also exist, but where there is little new land of any kind, Colombia would appear fortunate.

Meanwhile the modernization of Colombia's agriculture along capitalistic lines has made rapid strides, notably since the late 1950s. Lush valley land formerly used for cattle-grazing, or new lands in areas like the lower Magdalena Valley, are in many instances being turned to the raising of commercial crops such as cotton and sugar-cane, often complete with mechanization. Lauchlin Currie, who studied Colombian agriculture in the early fifties, at that time emphasized the underutilization of the country's best lands. Yet by the end of the decade Currie (perhaps overoptimistically, as Hirschman suggests, but none the less symptomatically) was speaking of a silent "agrarian revolution" that was taking place in the direction of mechanization and improved land use.[11] The implications for the undermining of traditional patterns in the Colombian countryside are likely to be profound.

Central to the matter of agricultural productivity, as well as to other aspects of Colombian economic and social life, is the pattern of landownership and the size of landholdings. The large estate—the *latifundio* or

10. For figures on the sectoral breakdown of the economically active see *Plan General de Desarrollo*, Part I, p. 276; for agriculture's contribution to the GNP see *Cuentas Nacionales* for 1961 (Bogotá, Banco de la República).

11. Albert O. Hirschman, *Journeys toward Progress* (New York, The Twentieth Century Fund, 1963), pp. 130–31. The number of tractors used in Colombian agriculture is in fact greater than in any other Latin American country except Uruguay and the much larger countries of Argentina, Brazil, and Mexico. *Statistical Abstract of Latin America, 1963* (Center of Latin American Studies, University of California, Los Angeles, 1963), p. 46.

the *hacienda*—continues to dominate the pattern of land distribution, as it does throughout most of Latin America, in terms both of the value of the land and the percentage of arable land it comprises.[12] Today the hacienda may be found in virtually every part of the country, but it has retained a particular hold in those areas suitable to tropical or semi-tropical plantation agriculture and to cattle-raising. Such areas include the Valle del Cauca, the savanna of Bogotá, and the interior of the Atlantic coast departments. The slopes of the department of Cundinamarca between Bogotá and the Magdalena River are also predominantly owned in large blocks and by 1920 had been mostly converted into coffee plantations. In all, properties of more than 500 hectares comprise less than 1 per cent of agrarian holdings but 31 per cent of the arable land. Another 3 per cent, those between 100 and 500 hectares in size, cover 33 per cent of the land.

In contrast, almost a third of Colombian farm properties are an uneconomic two hectares or less. Another quarter are between two and five hectares. Thus more than half of the country's agricultural holdings are parcels usually designated as *minifundia,* or plots normally too small for adequate subsistence. Even the 28 per cent of the farms assigned to the "family-size" category of 5 to 20 hectares often do not afford more than a minimum standard of living for their owners because of poor location, soil, or terrain.[13] Today the minifundio is most prevalent in the departments of Boyacá and Nariño, the former in eastern, the latter in southwestern, Colombia.

In other areas the small holdings are closer to a size that is economically viable. This has been true of parts of the departments of Santander and Norte de Santander in northeastern Colombia since pre-independence times. Today, such family-sized farms—farms adequate to provide the

12. The *latifundio* generally refers to any large landholding. The *hacienda* refers somewhat more concretely to a large estate worked by tenants or sharecroppers and forming a kind of community unto itself.

13. The figures on land distribution are from Economic Commission for Latin America, *Analyses and Projections of Economic Development. III. The Economic Development of Colombia* (Geneva, United Nations Department of Economic and Social Affairs, 1957), pp. 194–95 (hereafter cited as *ECLA Report*). This report tends to consider all farms under five hectares as minifundia as a matter of convenience. Technically, the term refers to those farms which are uneconomic because of their smallness (whether over or under five hectares), with factors such as soil and terrain taken into consideration.

COLOMBIA

Political Divisions

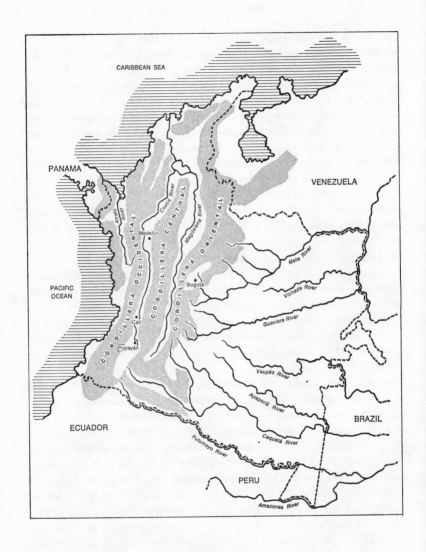

COLOMBIA

Major Rivers and Mountains

owner with a modest living without having to hire himself out, as many minifundio owners do, for labor on a neighboring large estate—are to be found primarily in southern Antioquia and in the departments of Caldas and Quindío, mainly as a result of "internal colonization" of unoccupied lands during the nineteenth century. It may be pertinent to note, with Hirschman, that the very period of internal colonization and the proliferation of small farms in Colombia saw in Mexico (under the regime of Porfirio Díaz) the concentration of land ownership in a small number of huge latifundia. In Mexico there soon followed the Revolution of 1910 in which the landless *campesino* played a leading role.[14]

Thus a striking feature of Colombian agriculture is that, despite a manifestly unequal pattern of landownership, a large number of campesinos own at least some land, however small or unproductive the plot. To be sure, in most economic, social, and political respects the minifundio owner has little more affluence or independence than he who tills but does not possess any land. But he does *own land*. In addition, there are quite a few Colombian farmers who, if hardly prosperous, do at least own and operate farms that are economically viable. In all, 755,000 Colombians own some land. Of these, some 309,000 own more than the 5 hectares commonly used to designate the upper limit of the minifundio.[15] It seems reasonable to speculate that in such facts as these may lie one cause of the slowness with which a class consciousness has developed among rural Colombians. Moreover, there exist in the countryside the rudiments of a rural middle class on the basis of which a new agrarian structure—political and social, as well as economic—might in the future be constructed.

At the same time, the persistence of the large estate in some areas, plus the prevalence of the minifundio, keep the rural economy at low levels of productivity and help to create the kind of social and political tensions which, beginning in the late 1940s, produced the phenomenon known as *la violencia*. Finally, the highly stratified rank distinctions of Colombian society and the traditional structure of Colombian politics have rested above all on the base of an agrarian property structure in which the hacienda and the plantation have been, in the last analysis, the dominant institutional forms.

14. Hirschman, p. 100. I use campesino throughout as a generic term to indicate the members of the rural lower class. Some are landless; some are tenants or sharecroppers; others are squatters; still others may own a small plot of land.

15. *Censo Agropecuario*, Part II, p. 42.

THE ECONOMY: THE NON-AGRICULTURAL SECTORS

It was about the turn of the century when modern industry made its appearance in Colombia, although artisan-type industries had existed as far back as pre-Conquest times. What is today the largest single industrial enterprise in the country, the Bavaria Brewery, established its first plant in 1891. An industrial exposition was held in Bogotá in 1899. The first modern sugar refinery, the first modern textile plant, and the first cement factory all date from the initial decade of the twentieth century.[16] By 1925, 7.6 per cent of all goods and services were produced by the manufacturing sector, not including artisan industries.[17]

Colombia's subsequent industrial development was stimulated by several factors. Among them were high coffee prices during the 1920s, the profits of which were partly invested in industry; the opening of the Panama Canal in 1914, with the resulting benefits for the development of western Colombia; the $25 million paid Colombia by the United States in 1921 as indemnity for the role played by this country in effecting the independence of Panama; foreign investments, chiefly at first in petroleum, plus a rash of foreign private loans during the late 1920s, many of them to municipalities and departments for the construction of public works and other infrastructure facilities; and a series of international events— World War I, the depression of the early 1930s and World War II—that forced the country to fall back on its own resources for many of the manufactured items it was accustomed to obtain from abroad. In addition, the change from subsistence agriculture to the farming of the cash-crop coffee may have helped to create capital by reducing disguised unemployment and by opening new lands to cultivation.[18]

In the years 1925–53 the proportion of the gross national product derived from industry, transport, electric power, and public utilities doubled three times: once between 1925 and 1936, again between the latter year and 1945, and once more from 1945 to 1953. Also during the years 1925–53 the percentage of economically active persons employed in manufacturing

16. American University (Washington, D.C.), Foreign Areas Studies Division, *Special Warfare Area Handbook for Colombia* (U.S. Department of the Army, 1961), p. 498 (hereafter cited as *Special Warfare Handbook*).

17. *ECLA Report*, p. 16.

18. See for this point the article by Carlos Lleras Restrepo in *Cultura y Economía en: Colombia, Ecuador, Venezuela* (Bogotá, Oliverio Perry, 1956), pp. 12–13.

nearly doubled. Fields such as construction, mining, and transport likewise showed increases.[19] Today slightly more than 15 per cent of the work force is engaged in either artisan-type industry or in manufacturing.[20] Industry has been growing at a faster rate than the total economy ever since the early 1930s, with a significant trend toward larger firms as well.[21]

The tertiary sector of the economy has also shown a rapid increase. Whereas it employed 16.8 per cent of the economically active population in 1925, the comparable figure in 1958 was 26.3 per cent. The expansion of both the secondary and the service sectors has been paralleled, of course, by a marked decline in the percentage of the economically active engaged in primary occupations (agriculture, fishing, mining, etc.), from 70.1 in 1925 to 46.6 in 1961.[22]

The long-term growth of the economy has meanwhile been substantial, despite periodic lags. Table 2 shows the average annual growth rate in the gross domestic product for various periods since 1925. Between 1960 and 1965, inclusive, it averaged over 4 per cent a year.[23] Most of these gains

TABLE 2

RATE OF GROWTH OF GROSS DOMESTIC PRODUCT (GDP) [24]

Years	Average Annual Rate of Growth
1925–29	7.3
1930–38	4.1
1939–44	2.2
1945–49	6.2
1950–55	5.0
1956–58	2.4
1958–59	6.2

19. See *ECLA Report*, pp. 14–15, for the above figures.

20. *Plan General de Desarrollo*, Part II, p. 19.

21. Ibid., p. 41; and *Boletín Mensual de Estadística*, 9 (Nov. 1961) (Bogotá, Departamento Administrativo Nacional de Estadística), 7.

22. *Plan General de Desarrollo*, Part I, p. 276; Lannoy and Pérez, p. 93. Between 1938 and 1951 the percentage annual decline of those employed in agriculture in Colombia was among the highest in the world. Cf. Russett et al., *World Handbook*, pp. 180–81.

23. 1960–64 figures taken from *Cuentas Nacionales*. The 1965 figure was a rough estimate provided the author by Professor Albert Berry of Yale University. See below, p. 149.

24. *Plan General de Desarrollo*, Part I, p. 7. Individual years show somewhat greater variation but the rate of growth has been generally quite steady.

have taken place in manufacturing, and today Colombia is largely self-sufficient in such consumer goods as beverages, processed foodstuffs, textiles, footwear, and cigarettes. The 1950s saw the rise of such new industries as chemicals, rubber, and steel. Today the country manufactures most of its requirements in pharmaceuticals and tires, while its steel production amounts to about a third of domestic needs.[25]

Thus, despite extensive civil violence during much of the 1950s, and despite recent balance of payments problems caused in part by a weakening of the international coffee market, the rate of economic growth, especially in the manufacturing sector, has been reasonably good. As the report of a study commission headed by Father Louis Lebret concluded, Colombia has "exceptional potentialities, absolute as well as relative, compared with a great number of the countries in the process of development," although it also warned that enthusiasm concerning rates of growth should not "obscure the incompatibility of an out-of-date social structure with a really healthy economic development."[26] There is, then, something of an economic margin to work with which may help to assuage the impact of change by permitting expectations to be matched in some degree by real opportunities for economic advance.

Colombia's advantages in this respect are nevertheless by and large those of the long run. They are at least in part gainsaid by such immediate problems as continuing poverty, economic inefficiency, inflation, and scarcity of foreign exchange. Nor has the country's growth in the last few decades made Colombia an industrialized nation. Small factories and artisans' shops comprise a large segment of Colombian industrial establishments,[27] and manufacturing still contributes only about a sixth of the nation's gross domestic product.[28] Moreover, the manufacture of heavy machinery and machine tools and of such durable consumer goods as automobiles and appliances is at best in the beginning stages.

The most obvious, and probably the most significant, single economic difficulty that Colombia faces is its great dependence on coffee exports for the foreign exchange it requires for development. There are some signs

25. *Special Warfare Handbook,* p. 519.

26. Misión "Economía y Humanismo" (Louis J. Lebret, O.P., Director), *Estudio sobre las Condiciones del Desarrollo en Colombia* (Bogotá, Aedita, 1958), pp. 9, 10.

27. Of 11,082 "manufacturing establishments" only 471 employed more than 100 persons, although these same firms employed 144,033 of the 276,159 engaged in "manufacturing." *Anuario de Estadística, 1962,* pp. 768–69.

28. The 1959 figure was 13.8 per cent. *Plan General de Desarrollo,* Part II, p. 7.

that diversification—both industrial and agricultural—is gaining ground, but the pace is slow. The substitution of domestic products for imports, and the diversification of exports to reduce dependence on coffee, are therefore high on the agenda of those who would further Colombia's economic development and long-run economic stability.

Colombia's substantial rate of growth has not eliminated poverty or unemployment; in some ways it may have accentuated them. The gross national product per capita, though slowly rising, stands at a low $263.[29] Rates of unemployment were estimated at about 7.5 per cent in Bogotá during 1963 and 1964; in Medellín at 11 to 13 per cent.[30] Meanwhile, it was generally conceded that in Cali, and probably in Barranquilla, unemployment rates were considerably higher. Such figures do not take into account the substantial rates of underemployment in marginal service occupations such as lottery-ticket selling and shoe-shining that have proliferated in the cities, although it is questionable whether the degree of disguised unemployment so caused is any greater than that resulting in rural areas from such factors as the seasonal nature of crops.

Inflation has become a persistent problem. In only three different years between 1942 and 1964 has the cost-of-living index for blue-collar workers gone up by less than five per cent over the previous year. Increases of well over ten per cent have been registered in 9 of those 23 years.[31] Interestingly enough, real wages do not seem to have suffered, at least recently. In fact between 1955 and 1963 they showed an increase of more than fifty per cent, according to government figures.[32]

Nevertheless, this does not take into account the adverse effects of in-

29. This is the figure used by Russett et al. Other published figures for Columbia's GNP place it anywhere from $200 to more than $300 per capita.

30. Universidad de los Andes, Centro de Estudios sobre Desarrollo Económico, unpublished figures. A 1961 survey of 3 representative districts of Bogotá put the percentage of unemployed at 14.6; cf. Miguel A. Antequera Stand, *Ocupación y Desocupación en Bogotá,* Monografía No. 14 (Bogotá, Universidad de los Andes, Centro de Estudios sobre Desarrollo Económico, 1962), p. 3.

31. Figures taken from *Boletín Mensual de Estadística* and *Revista del Banco de la República* (Bogotá).

32. Estimate based on figures from annual editions of the *Anuario General de Estadística* and from the monthly *Boletín Mensual de Estadística.* Between 1938 and 1954, however, real wages, while fluctuating from year to year, remained about the same at the end of the period as they were at the beginning. It should be noted that post-1955 figures are for the nation as a whole; those before 1955 are for northeastern Colombia, including Bogotá.

flation on the incomes of the poorly organized, who are less able to come to their own economic defense than some elements among unionized labor. Furthermore, the wage increases which have followed price rises have frequently been achieved by the socially and politically disruptive process of strikes or other forms of protest action directed, in the last analysis, against the government. An added problem is that urban wage rates have risen at a proportionately more rapid pace than rural wages, thus increasing the disparities between the modernizing and more traditional sectors of Colombian society.[33] On the other hand, as Hirschman suggests, inflation, by calling attention to underlying structural problems which require resolution, and by alleviating social tensions through wage and price concessions granted successively to competing groups, may at least in the short run contribute to stability. In this sense inflation becomes the moral equivalent to class-based civil war.[34]

A final notable feature of Colombia's industrial development has been that it has depended for the most part on domestic capital sources. In comparative Latin American terms, Colombia ranks ninth, behind all the other major countries, in the amount of United States direct investment in the economy, and more than half of such investment is in petroleum.[35] With this exception, United States or other foreign investments do not dominate entire industries in Colombia, and there is relatively little foreign capital in such politically sensitive enterprises as public utilities. Even petroleum, though it is important to the economy, is by no means the major earner of foreign exchange and employs rather few workers. Entrepreneurship is largely Colombian, and Colombian economic progress has in large measure been the consequence of the operation of domestic trends and forces. Thus entrepreneurial talents and motivations have to some extent been incorporated into the Colombian experience and into the Colombian system of values. This should spare Colombia the disruption that often attends the effort to reduce direct external economic control. The relative lack of such a target for aggressive nationalism may indeed be an important factor in having so far prevented the coalescence of otherwise diverse groups in a major effort to dethrone the reigning elite.

33. Lauchlin Currie, *Ensayos sobre Planeación* (Bogotá, Ediciones Tercer Mundo, 1963), p. 53.

34. Cf. Hirschman, pp. 220–23, concerning this phenomenon in Chile during the 1950s.

35. *Statistical Abstract of Latin America, 1963*, p. 83.

It is true that the country's economic growth has increased the demand
for foreign capital, and that foreign firms have in turn found Colombia a
relatively attractive field for investment. The amount of foreign, primarily
United States, capital invested in Colombia has increased markedly in
recent years. If the trend continues, we may expect a heightened sense of
economic nationalism, although the fact that most new foreign investment
is in manufacturing rather than in the politically more sensitive mines,
plantations, and public utilities may keep such a response to a minimum.

When, in sum, one looks at the factors in the non-agricultural sectors of
the economy which potentially affect Colombian political development,
one faces a paradox: conditions of quite acute instability (inflation, balance of payments difficulties, unemployment) and continuing underdevel-
opment confronting promising growth rates, impressive advances in industrial production, and a relative absence of foreign enclaves.

POPULATION: RACIAL COMPOSITION AND DEMOGRAPHIC TRENDS

Colombia, like its neighbor Venezuela, differs from the Andean nations
to the south of it in not being an "Indian" country. Colombia today has
few Indians, and most of them live in jungle areas and on reservations in
isolated pockets in the Andes. In all, they number perhaps 2 per cent of
the population. The majority of Colombians are, instead, mestizos, the
result of the admixture of Indian and white blood during the several centuries subsequent to the Spanish conquest. There has also been an infusion
of Negro genes, the result of the importation of African slaves during the
colonial period to work the plantations of the coast and some of the lower-
lying valleys, as well as some of the early mines. In all, about three quarters of the Colombian people are accounted as mixed-bloods, with another
20 per cent listed as white, and 4 per cent as Negro.[36]

While Colombia can broadly be termed a country where the mestizo
predominates, this simplistic description ignores several things. One is the
seeming infinity of racial types, including all degrees of white, Negro, and
Indian intermixture. Another is the diversity of racial and cultural origins

36. *Statistical Abstract of Latin America, 1963*, p. 23. Figures on Colombian ethnic
composition are to be treated with particular caution, since not only statistical accu-
racy but matters of definition are in question. Cf. e.g. the breakdown in *Special
Warfare Handbook*, p. 60, which distinguishes among different categories of mixed-
bloods.

among those three broad categories: whites from many parts of Spain, plus a scattering from Great Britain, Germany, the Near East, and elsewhere; Negroes from many parts of Africa and many different tribes; Indians of different cultures and degrees of civilization at the time of the arrival of the Spaniards. Use of the generic term mestizo to describe Colombians likewise ignores the fact that the distribution of racial types is not uniform, either by geographic region or by social class. For example, Negro-white, rather than Indian-white, is the predominant racial mix in the Atlantic and Pacific coastal areas. Furthermore, the farther up one goes in the social scale the likelier one is to encounter persons of white or nearly white racial ancestry. Racial prejudice in the North American sense is not great, although it exists, and caste-like barriers founded primarily on racial criteria are by and large absent. Rather, the historic alignment of low status with the Negro slave and with the Indian servant and agricultural laborer has persisted in the form of a general identification of darker skins with lower social status. It is life-style as much as ethnic origin per se that perpetuates such gradation.

Since colonial days immigration into Colombia has been quite small, despite sporadic attempts to encourage it. The massive flow of immigrants to countries such as Argentina, Uruguay, and Brazil, or even the smaller but appreciable rate of recent immigration into Venezuela, has been absent. In another sense, however, immigration has had some importance, since most Europeans and the few North American immigrants almost automatically take their places in the middle or upper classes and bring with them skills and attitudes which have an influence beyond the number of persons involved. Besides the immigrants, colonies of temporary residents also exist, especially North Americans in several of the larger cities, but their total is probably less than 10,000. While their technological and management skills contribute to the development of the Colombian economy, the effect of their presence on the social structure and on politics is marginal.

Colombia, then, does not have an Indian subculture of any appreciable size. No massive European immigration has posed the problems of assimilation faced by Argentina, for example. Nor have Negroes retained the degree of separate cultural identity characteristic of some other Latin American countries.[37] Virtually all who reside within the boundaries of

37. Cf. *Special Warfare Handbook*, p. 74.

the Colombian state speak Spanish and are a part of the broad mestizo
racial and cultural patterns of the society. While racial factors play a real
part in accentuating the distinctions among social strata, they do not pose
entirely rigid barriers to social mobility. Yet there remains the problem of
integrating millions of campesinos and recent migrants to the cities into
the effective nation. A wide cultural gap yawns between the wealthy landowner or industrialist, often educated in Europe and the United States,
and the illiterate farm worker. Real kinds of separateness do therefore persist within Colombian society, but they are based more on distinctions of
social class than on ethnic grounds.

In the last several decades Colombia's population has been growing
rapidly, almost entirely as the result of natural increase. Between 1900 and
1925 the population increased from 4.1 to 6.6 million. By 1950 it had
reached 11.1 million, thus nearly doubling in 25 years.[38] By the end of
1963 it was estimated at about 16,000,000 persons with an annual growth
rate of some 3.2 per cent.[39]

The effects, linked to but distinct from those of economic growth, have
been multiple. The larger potential market has probably been a stimulus
to economic development, but the close race between the rates of economic and population growth has made any substantive advance in the
per capita standard of living difficult to achieve. Too, the population remains a young one, with 43 per cent of Colombians estimated in 1958 to
be under the economically active age of fifteen.[40] The population explosion has therefore greatly increased the demand for such facilities as
schools. It has also been instrumental in augmenting the social dimensions
of the land problem, with more and more people pressing on the readily
available land—a factor that has contributed to migration from the rural
areas to the rapidly growing cities.

Internal migration has in turn had consequences for the economic, social, and political orders at least as great as the absolute increase in population itself. The very rapid rate of urbanization that has characterized
Colombia for more than three decades is only in part a response to indus-

38. See *Plan General de Desarrollo,* Part I, p. 46.
39. Cited by Eduardo Wiesner in *Boletín Mensual de Estadística, 13* (June
1964), 5.
40. Lannoy and Pérez, pp. 87–89.

trialization; it has, in fact, tended to outrun the capacity of industry to absorb the migrants. Population pressures in the countryside, and the spread of modern communications, with their emphasis on the attractiveness of urban living, have both contributed, as has the violence that has prevailed in some regions of the countryside. Whatever the causes, the urban population has been growing at a striking pace. During the years 1918–53 the proportion of the Colombian people living in communities of 1,500 persons or more doubled, from 21 to 42.8 per cent.[41]

Still more significant is the growing concentration in the largest cities, as Table 3 graphically illustrates. Thus there has been a precipitate de-

TABLE 3

PERCENTAGE OF URBAN POPULATION LIVING IN COMMUNITIES

OF VARYING SIZES [42]

1938–1965

Size of Community	1938	1951	1955	1960	1965 (est.)
1,500–20,000	55.8%	41.0%	37.5%	31.5%	27.6%
20,000–100,000	19.7	19.9	20.2	19.1	18.0
100,000–500,000	24.5	24.5	27.6	25.1	15.6
Over 500,000	—	14.6	15.2	24.3	38.8
	100.0	100.0	100.5	100.0	100.0

cline in the percentage of the urbanized population living in the smallest communities, relative stability in the 20,000–100,000 urban category, a corresponding stability but anticipated decline in cities with over 100,000 but less than half a million inhabitants, and a marked increase in the very large cities. Using cities of more than 20,000 as a definition of urban, the Economic Commission for Latin America estimated that 26.9 per cent of Colombians were urbanized in 1955 and that almost 36.5 per cent would be so by 1965.[43]

The consequences of urbanization for the Colombian economy, society, and polity are incalculable. Economically, the prospective market for

41. Misión "Economía y Humanismo," pp. 23–24.

42. Adapted from Economic Commission for Latin America, Division of Social Affairs, *Some Aspects of Population Growth in Colombia* (ECLA, Division of Social Affairs, 1960), Part I, p. 27. The 1965 figures represent projections. Note that communities of 1500 or larger were defined as urban. 1955 figures exceed 100% due to rounding.

43. *Plan General de Desarrollo*, Part I, p. 256.

manufactured goods is increased and made more accessible while the tertiary sector of the economy expands to meet urban needs. Entire new districts of jerry-built slums, sometimes erected by squatters on public or even privately owned lands and lacking the elementary urban services of water, electricity, and transportation, have grown up on the cities' fringes, most notably around Cali.[44] Many of the new arrivals to the city are unemployed or underemployed, yet their proximity to urban amenities and urban communications raises their aspirations. Politically, potential discontent is more concentrated as a result of urbanization, while at the same time the poor are released from some of the old forms of domination and control by the *patrón* and the cacique. The gap between city and countryside is another of the potentially explosive consequences of rapid urban growth and one of the principal bottlenecks in the development process. Whether it is a matter of literacy, wage levels, or political participation, the city dweller is far ahead of the campesino and is likely to become more so in the years ahead. The question could well become, indeed is already, whether a nation half-modern and half-traditional can evolve stable institutions.

Increasing numbers of Colombians are in any case becoming involved in the world of urban life and becoming available as participants in the political process. The way in which they express that participation will presumably depend in large measure on the degree to which the aspirations they bring to the city are met eventually by some genuine degree of vertical social mobility and economic opportunity. There is evidence from separate studies of two important urban groups—businessmen and students—that at present Colombians regard their future in this respect with some optimism. The businessmen generally expected to improve their standard of living over the ensuing decade. Of the students questioned, more than half expected upon graduation to hold a socioeconomic position better than that of their parents.[45]

Given sustained economic growth and the tendency of real wages to

44. Cf. John P. Powelson, "The Land-Grabbers of Cali," *The Reporter* (Jan. 16, 1964), pp. 30–31.

45. Aaron Lipman, *El Empresario Industrial en América Latina. 4. Colombia,* (Naciones Unidas, Comisión Económica para América Latina, 1963) p. 45; and Robert C. Williamson, *El Estudiante Colombiano y sus Actitudes,* Monografías Sociológicas No. 13 (Bogotá, Universidad Nacional, Facultad de Sociología, 1962), pp. 16–17.

advance, the fact that urbanization (which may be seen as a very crude measure of aspirations) tends to outrun the capacity of industry to absorb the migrants from rural areas may not be crucial to the stability of the social and political systems. A great deal therefore probably depends on the future performance of the economy, at least if the assumption holds that greater wealth eases the struggle over its distribution.[46] The capacity of the political system to absorb the new aspirants to participation—to provide channels of expression for their newly articulated demands—will also be critical. As Lerner has posited in *The Passing of Traditional Society*, "Where the increase of desirous individuals and the growth of opportunities are in balance, there the psychosocial conditions for stable growth are good. Where personal desires greatly exceed institutional capacities, there the prospects are for instability of a sort which impedes rational and cumulative modernization." [47]

46. Cf. Seymour Martin Lipset, *Political Man* (New York, Doubleday Anchor ed., 1963), pp. 50–52.
47. Lerner, *Passing of Traditional Society,* p. 401.

3

SOCIAL CLASS AND
POLITICS

THE ELITE

Very wide differences in income, occupation, education, and life-style—
differences which show a significant degree of correlation [1]—suggest that
social class is a crucial determinant in the lives of Colombians. Such distinctions are not merely a matter of objective observation but are reflected
in the subjective identifications of Colombians as well. A study of the community of Cereté, in the department of Córdoba, comments: "Within the
municipio of Cereté, . . . the interrelationship among the community members is almost completely regulated by social class groupings . . . social
classes . . . are readily recognized by the inhabitants of the municipio. The
present study indicates that social class is the major source of identity for
the community members." [2] Although social rankings in the cities may be
more fluid, the consciousness of class distinction likewise permeates much
of urban social behavior.

The social rank-distinction of greatest significance and longest standing
for Colombians, as for Latin Americans generally, has been that between
the upper class or elite and most of the remainder of the population. Until
quite recently one could with considerable justice look at Colombia's social system in terms of just such a bifurcated class structure. This is no
longer an accurate portrayal and never was literally the case. Neverthe-

1. Cf. e.g. Antequera Stand, *Ocupación y Desocupación*, p. 3.
2. A. Eugene Havens and Michael Romieux, *A Socio-Economic Survey of Cereté,
Córdoba: an Area of Latifundio*, Typescript draft (Bogotá, Universidad Nacional,
Facultad de Sociología, 1963), p. 22. See also Andrew H. Whiteford, *Two Cities of
Latin America* (Beloit, Wis., Beloit College, 1960), passim.

less, most forms of social power, along with control of the political system, have primarily rested in the hands of the upper class. As such the composition of the social elite, the accessibility to its ranks, and the degree to which it is answerable to the rest of society for its actions are matters of prime importance in our inquiry.[3]

Colombians have in recent years frequently used the word *oligarquía* (oligarchy) to designate their ruling class. The term was popularized by Jorge Eliécer Gaitán, the late leftist political leader, and has since been employed as a term of opprobrium by the political Left and even, on occasion, by Conservatives, who have sometimes meant by it the rule of Liberal capitalists. In the more technical, non-pejorative sense of the word, the term oligarchy is a justifiable one to the extent that the Colombian elite is substantially a self-perpetuating minority in control of the key power resources of the society, without any real accountability to the rest of the community.[4]

Power tends to be cumulative. Those in possession of one kind of power resource, such as large landholdings, are likely also to hold or acquire others, such as higher education. By the same token, those excluded from one form of power are not very likely to have access to another. Thus, in a nation where only five per cent of those over school age have completed secondary education and only one per cent higher education,[5] a study of owners and managers of large businesses in Bogotá indicated that 52 per cent of those questioned had at least attended a university, and only 6 per cent had not completed their secondary education.[6] Another area of congruence is that between economics and politics. Members of both party hierarchies have been officers of the powerful, semiofficial National Federation of Coffee Growers, which tends to be dominated by

3. Cf. Harold D. Lasswell, Daniel Lerner, and C. Easton Rothwell, *The Comparative Study of Elites* (Stanford, Stanford University Press, 1952), p. 1.

4. In English the term oligarchy tends to be a purely political term; in Latin American usage it refers more broadly to the control of politics, economics, and cultural life by a self-perpetuating minority.

5. Figures cited in United States Department of Labor, Bureau of Labor Statistics, *Labor Law and Practice in Colombia* (Washington, D.C., 1962), p. 6.

6. Cf. Lipman, *El Empresario Industrial*, pp. 41–42. Lipman notes that, after a certain point, education and income are not correlated in Colombia. Similar patterns are evident in the United States. However, the crucial dividing line in this country tends to be between those with only a secondary school education and those who have gone to college. In Colombia that line lies between those with secondary school education and those with primary training only.

the large growers and exporters. Former Conservative President Mariano Ospina Pérez, whose interests extend to cattle, real estate, mining, and the tobacco industry, was for four years its manager. Carlos Lleras Restrepo, elected president in 1966, has been a member of the Federation's national committee, as well as an officer of various important business enterprises. The family of former President Alfonso López was prominent in the coffee trade. A perusal of Colombia's *Quién es Quién* (*Who's Who*) confirms the large degree of fusion among the elites of property, social standing, education, and political power.[7] Within certain limits, it is therefore legitimate to speak of Colombia's upper social stratum as a ruling class or oligarchy, membership in which "is a virtually indispensable prerequisite of eligibility for induction into a major political role."[8]

Some have used the term caste to describe the elite's relationship to other social strata. The Lebret mission, which completed its study on the social context of Colombian development in 1956, concluded that "Colombian society, taken as a whole, still appears more as a 'society of castes' than as a 'society of classes'."[9] Although denoting the real social distance among classes in Colombia, this puts the matter rather too strongly. Mobility both into and out of classes, including the upper class, is by no means unknown, even if it is not easily accomplished. Aaron Lipman's study of Bogotá businessmen (at least some of whom would presumably rank as members of the elite), shows that while none had working class origins, an appreciable percentage considered themselves to stand at least slightly ahead of their fathers on the social scale.[10] A study by Robert Williamson of students at the National University in Bogotá similarly points out that only 20 per cent of the students' fathers had had a university education and that, following their graduation from the university, 52.6 per cent of the students expected to have a higher socioeconomic position than their families.[11] The existence of a new upper class based on wealth, even in some of Colombia's more traditional communities, is another indication that the social order is not frozen.[12] There is also scat-

---

7. See *Quién es Quién en Colombia* (3d ed. Bogotá, Oliverio Perry, 1961).

8. George I. Blanksten in Almond and Coleman, *Politics of Developing Areas*, p. 513.

9. Misión "Economía y Humanismo," *Estudio sobre . . . Colombia*, p. 109.

10. Lipman, *El Empresario Industrial*, chapter 4.

11. Williamson, *El Estudiante Colombiano*, pp. 13 and 17.

12. See Havens and Romieux, p. 24. Undoubtedly it was more so in the past, however, and is still relatively fixed in some parts of Colombia. Cf. the study of Popayán

tered evidence in the literature and from personal observation that *down-ward* mobility occurs.[13]

In fact, there seems to be a somewhat greater degree of both access to and egress from the ranks of the Colombian oligarchy than there has been in the case of the Peruvian, for example. Latin America's quasi-feudal society has always had something of the unstructured frontier about it, without an array of courts and titles to sustain it. In Colombia the fortunes of the many civil wars, as well as the vagaries of economic cycles affecting such boom-and-bust export crops as tobacco, undoubtedly further contributed to social fluidity.

The extent of such mobility should not be exaggerated. Access to the upper class is possible, but difficult, and then generally only from the ranks of the relatively small middle class. While individual families may have risen or fallen in status over time, the elite as a whole has been maintained intact and has never been effectively challenged by any competing group.[14]

On what is the supremacy of such a class founded? Traditionally, in the first instance, on ownership of large tracts of land. Landownership gives economic power, social prestige, and the means of domination over those who work the land or otherwise depend on its patrón (owner or boss). The ownership of land in Colombia is quite highly concentrated: less than four per cent of the farm properties contain about two thirds of the readily available and cultivable land. Most of those who are today numbered among the upper class have current or at least recent roots on the hacienda.

Historically one's family name or ancestry (*abolengo*) has been closely associated with landownership, but abolengo has acted as something of an autonomous source of upper-class status as well. For example, White-

---

in Whiteford, and Whiteford's comments in *Land Reform and Social Change in Colombia* (Land Tenure Center, University of Wisconsin, Discussion Paper 4, Nov. 1963), p. 15.

13. See e.g. Orlando Fals Borda, *La Transformación de la América Latina y sus Implicaciones Sociales y Económicas,* Monografías Sociológicas No. 10 (Bogotá, Universidad Nacional, Facultad de Sociología, 1961), p. 6; Havens and Romieux, passim; and my discussion (see below, pp. 60–61) concerning the Colombian middle class.

14. Perhaps the best brief description of the Colombian elite may be found in Vernon Fluharty, *Dance of the Millions* (Pittsburgh, University of Pittsburgh Press, 1957), pp. 183–86. For a characterization of the Colombian elite by one of its members see the novel by Alfonso López Michelsen, *Los Elegidos* (Mexico City, Editorial Guaranía, 1953).

ford notes its indispensability as a condition for membership in the upper class in Popayán, that most traditional of Colombian cities where it is customary for the upper class to have the family crest carved in stone over the doorway.[15] Abolengo is not a certain guarantee of elite status, however. Pearse and Rivera note of the community of Tenza in the department of Boyacá that the correct *apellido* (surname) is a necessary but by no means the sole requisite for the status of *principal*.[16] Even in Popayán, while abolengo appears to assure one of membership in the upper class, it is money and the consequent ability to validate one's social position by having the right kind of house, clothes, club memberships, and education that determine whether one falls into the upper or lower division of that class.[17] In the larger cities, where one's ancestry is not personally known to most, abolengo would seem to play somewhat less of a role, although there is little solid evidence to support such a conclusion.

Associated with abolengo, but not identical to it, is a certain racial basis to elite status. Most of those who would be identified as upper class are predominantly of white European descent. The emphasis placed on genealogy by families of the traditional elite is not only to prove descent from notable forebears but to prove racial purity (even though there are relatively few Colombian families without at least a trace of remote Indian ancestry). A dark complexion is not in itself an insurmountable barrier, especially in certain parts of the country, nor is a light skin a sure passport. But if one possesses other criteria of elite status, a white skin is one of the outward manifestations that one belongs.

Still another source of elite status has been education. Intellectual and professional pursuits have always been honored in Colombia. Doctor, lawyer, and writer have been among the preferred occupations in a society which has looked down on commerce and manual labor. The sons of the

15. See Whiteford's comments in *Land Reform and Social Change*, p. 14. The tracing and affirming of genealogy is a persistent preoccupation of traditional upper class Colombians. However, it is probably true that only in a few of the older Colombian cities such as Popayán, Cartagena, and Mompós, do the origins of today's elite go back beyond the establishment of the vice-royalty of Nueva Granada in 1717. Cf. Gerardo Reichel-Dolmatoff, "Notas sobre la Clase Media en Colombia," *Ciencias Sociales* (Unión Panamericana), 3 (Feb. 1952) 2–4.

16. Andrew Pearse and Salomón Rivera, *La Tenencia de la Tierra y sus Implicaciones Socio-Económicas en Tenza, Colombia. Un Estudio de Minifundio*, Typescript draft (Bogotá, Universidad Nacional, Facultad de Sociología, 1963), p. 109.

17. Whiteford, p. 46; and *Land Reform and Social Change*, p. 14.

landed elite have generally been educated to one of the professions. As a matter of fact, many of Colombia's *hacendados* are in the first instance professional men, even while they continue to derive much of their income from the land and retain an interest in its management.

Until quite recently Colombian education has been largely education for the sons of the elite, or for those who entered the latter's service. Both secondary schools and universities have concentrated on producing men of culture rather than men who could contribute by their skills or their outlooks to the building of a modern society. Philosophy, the arts and letters, and the traditional professions have been given precedence. Science, technical subjects, and the experimental approach to knowledge—all basically alien to traditional values and potentially dangerous to traditional society—have played but a small part in the curriculum.[18]

There has been a hesitancy to appropriate funds for public education, while the whole weight of economic and social circumstances has tended to discourage those not born into the upper class from effecting their advance on the social scale by means of education. Despite the honor accorded leading intellectuals and professional men, such attainments in themselves are only rarely sufficient to win an individual high social status. Increasingly, it is true, members of the growing Colombian middle class attain secondary or university educations and subsequently enter the professions. And a new group of technocrats is emerging, men whose principal claim to recognition is their technical or administrative skill. The most important of them might be placed in the upper ranks of Colombian society. Yet without some other claim to social position—unless, for example, he is able to use his education or professional reputation to acquire wealth, or unless he can marry into the upper class—the man of intellect will seldom acquire elite standing. Those who base their social status solely on membership in a profession belong as a rule more appropriately to the middle sectors.

Above all, education, or rather the lack of it, has constituted more of a barrier to upward social mobility than a channel for advancement. Approximately 37 per cent of Colombians 15 years of age and older are illiter-

18. See Orlando Fals Borda, *La Educación en Colombia, Bases para su Interpretación Sociológica*, Monografías Sociológicas No. 11 (Bogotá, Universidad Nacional, Facultad de Sociología, 1962) for a discussion of the nature and history of Colombian education.

ate. Despite a gradual but steady decrease in this percentage since at least the turn of the century, the absolute number of illiterate Colombians has risen since that time. Moreover, many of those accounted as literate are only barely so, having had only one or two years of primary schooling. More than half of Colombian primary schools, including the overwhelming majority in rural areas, do not go beyond the second year.[19]

In general, the effective denial of even a secondary education to the vast majority of Colombians has been one of the important underpinnings of a social and political system founded on a relatively closed elite. Compared to 1,948,772 Colombians matriculated in primary school in 1962, there were only 174,966 in secondary school, and 27,410 in universities. Entry does not guarantee graduation, however, with many forced to drop out for economic reasons. At the university level, of every 100 entering almost half fail to matriculate for the second year, while less than ten per cent finish the full six years.[20] Such denial of education restricts access to both prestige and skills, including those necessary for politics at the departmental or national levels. The availability of education to the upper class, on the other hand, provides it with the intellectual tools and cultural attributes to complement its reliance on land and abolengo. Education, the communication with the world beyond Colombia that it makes possible, and the wealth to travel, also create a highly cosmopolitan elite whose members may be as much at home in New York or Paris, or with the ideas and events of those places, as they are with matters Colombian.

Once serving as the almost exclusive basis for admission to upper-class status, land, abolengo and culture must now share that position with wealth derived from capitalistic pursuits. Important merchants, especially those engaged in the export of coffee and other agricultural products, have always been part of the upper class. In the last several decades their numbers have expanded as both exports and imports have grown. Their ventures in commerce and banking have meanwhile been supplemented by the growth of a substantial number of industrial entrepreneurs. Capitalism

19. Data on literacy and schools taken from *Anuario de Estadística, 1962*, pp. 206, 210, 220. Note that there is a one per cent difference in the literacy figure from that used for comparative purposes by Russett et al. in *World Handbook*. See above p. 15.

20. *Anuario de Estadística, 1962*, pp. 232 and 298; and Fals Borda, *La Educación*, pp. 27–28. Although there are variations, primary school is generally five years in Colombia, secondary school (leading to the so-called *bachillerato*) six years, and university (leading to the so-called *doctorado*) either four, five, or six, depending on the field of study.

has even entered the formerly sacrosanct precincts of the hacienda and is opening new lands to the mechanized production of cotton, sugar, and other crops.

Among Colombia's capitalists power is highly concentrated. In 1954 the five largest banking institutions in the country allegedly accounted for more than three quarters of the capital, reserves, and profits of all Colombian banks. As of 1952, seven large industrial firms held 30 per cent of the capital in manufacturing enterprises owned by Colombian nationals.[21] A 1960 study of managers, presidents, and members of boards of directors of firms listed on the Bogotá stock exchange, showed a high degree of concentration of economic power in a relatively few hands.[22] Still other figures show that 4.6 per cent of the Colombian population receives 40.6 per cent of the national income.[23]

In part, the agent of Colombian domestic capitalism, and of change within the Colombian elite, has been the self-made man, risen from the middle class (especially its artisan element), and the foreign immigrant. The claims of either to upper-class status are based exclusively on wealth, or on the marriage of the man of wealth with the daughter of abolengo. In many communities they fill the ranks of a new upper or lower upper class, which may lack the lineage, the cultural refinements, and the landed connections of the traditional upper class, but which nonetheless regards itself as the equal of that class (though it is not so regarded by the latter or by others below it on the social scale). Its members tend to be less paternalistically concerned for the community and for their social inferiors than the more traditionally based elite.[24]

At the same time a large percentage of Colombian capitalists of both industry and agriculture have their origins in families of the traditional elite. There has been a partial metamorphosis of an aristocracy of abolengo into an aristocracy of money. Very often elite families have shifted to urban commercial or industrial pursuits while maintaining strong rural ties. As one consequence the bonds of the extended family, and the habits

21. Mauricio Torres, *La Naturaleza de la Revolución Colombiana* (Bogotá, Editorial Iqueima, 1959), chapter 4.

22. Eduardo Wiesner Durán, *Control Personal de la Economía Colombiana*, Monografía No. 6 (Bogotá, Universidad de los Andes, Centro de Estudios sobre Desarrollo Económico, 1960). Whether this is a higher degree of concentration than in other nations Wiesner does not pretend to say.

23. Gustavo Pérez Ramírez, *El Campesinado Colombiano* (2d ed. Bogotá, Centro de Investigaciones Sociales, 1962), p. 89.

24. Cf. Havens and Romieux, p. 24.

and attitudes of paternalism characteristic of the landed elite, have been to a large extent transferred to an urban and business context. A reverse process is also at work. Some of the younger sons of families that visited their haciendas only occasionally, living in the city as absentee landowners, are beginning to take a real interest in their properties and in their increased productivity. Often, also, those not of the traditional elite who have made their money and their name in industry are investing in land for prestige and other reasons; they bring to the countryside a greater interest in productivity than has been true of the traditional landowners.

One of the results of this interpenetration of traditional and modern interests and values is that achievement and wealth are increasingly coming to supplement, or even to replace, family name and the inheritance of landed estates as criteria for elite membership. Thus the answers to a questionnaire distributed in 1962 to 61 Bogotá businessmen who were members of the National Association of Manufacturers (*Asociación Nacional de Industriales*—ANDI) indicated that they considered factors such as hard work and education to be more important for business success in Colombia than such traditional considerations as familial and political connections.[25] At the same time, a large measure of paternalistic behavior and a desire to retain ties to the land continue to characterize the urbanized members of the upper class.

Another consequence of changes in the composition and orientations of the Colombian elite is a new kind of diversity of interests within it. Frequently the interests of industrialists, or of commercial agriculturalists, conflict with those of the more traditional landowners. For example, the Cauca Valley Corporation (CVC) has been supported by the former groups while being vehemently opposed by the regional Cattlemen's Association (*Asociación de Ganaderos*).[26] It becomes increasingly difficult for the government to satisfy elite demands as they grow more complex and conflicting, and as they run counter at points to the national interest in development.

The Colombian elite is far different from what it was thirty years ago. Its values and its goals have to an important extent become modernizing ones and the sources of elite power have become more pluralistic. Yet it is also true that despite such changes much of the traditional value system and of the ancient pattern of social distinctions has been preserved. The

25. Lipman, *El Empresario Industrial*, pp. 27–30.
26. Cf. *Land Reform and Social Change*, p. 3.

Colombian elite has evolved, but it has neither been destroyed nor even effectively challenged by any group or class that might become its successor.

A notable illustration of elite change within the framework of continuity has been the growth of a dynamic entrepreneurial element centered in the department of Antioquia. We have previously noted the largely self-generating nature of Colombian economic growth and it is the *Antioqueño* who has been responsible for much of it. Brazil has a comparable group in the *Paulistas* of the state of São Paulo. Other Latin American countries, notably Mexico since the Revolution of 1910, have also witnessed the growth of entrepreneurial groups. But as a rule it has taken a social revolution to unleash the required economic energies, or, as in the case of Brazil, there has been a significant admixture of recent immigrants with the native entrepreneurial group. Neither of these things has been true of the Antioqueños. Of course, by no means all Colombian entrepreneurs come from Antioquia, and foreign firms have indeed contributed to Colombian economic development. Yet much of the country's economic growth has originated internally, promoted by Antioquians who derive from generations of native-born families. Everett Hagen has found that of 110 large enterprises started by Colombians in the three leading industrial regions of the country more than two thirds were founded by Antioquians, even though they comprised less than 40 per cent of the population of the respective areas. "In proportion to population, more than three times as many Antioqueños became entrepreneurs as Old Colombians of non-Antioqueño stock." [27]

Hagen has examined the reasons for the development of entrepreneurial talents and energies within a national culture which has tended to disdain those who possess them. He concludes that the economic advantages of Antioquia are not the answer, although it should be pointed out that as the principal coffee-exporting region Antioquia was readily able to accumulate the capital necessary for investment. [28] Rather, Hagen finds the explanation in differences in personality structure between Antioqueños and other Colombians. "The successful economic innovators of Antioquia . . . were so different in personality structure from a group of equally promi-

27. Everett E. Hagen, *On the Theory of Social Change* (Homewood, Illinois, The Dorsey Press, 1962), p. 365.
28. Cf. e.g. Lannoy and Pérez, *Estructuras Demográficas*, p. 136, concerning the economic advantages of Antioquia.

nent community leaders elsewhere in Colombia who were interviewed and studied that they may be thought of as a different breed of men." [29] The Antioqueño typically interpreted pictures shown to him in a thematic apperception test as portraying problems which could be solved if worked at. Other Colombians tested usually saw the pictures in philosophical or historical terms and gave formula solutions, involving little sustained effort, for any conflicts they perceived. Fantasies and reveries not closely connected with reality tended to characterize their interpretations.

The question remains, of course, why there should be such differences among Colombians. Hagen explores several possible causes: the Basque origin and cultural inheritance of many Antioqueños; the early importance of mining in the region which apparently led to the formation of some non-family risk enterprises; the difference in post-1900 investment opportunities for affluent Antioquian traders as compared with those from other parts of Colombia; and a deep-rooted feeling of social rejection and status deprivation relative to the rest of the country which in time brought its own reaction in the form of an orientation toward business achievement. Hagen concludes that all these factors may have played a role, although he looks with greatest favor on the latter.

Other explanations include that of Charles Savage, who points to the limited amount of land available for haciendas in Antioquia. This circumstance forced settlers themselves to engage in work and even induced cooperation among families for productive purposes. Fernando Guillén attributes the distinctiveness of Antioquia to the fact that here were best preserved the municipal institutions of medieval Spain, remote from the stultifying bureaucratic centralism that plagued the rest of the country, and indeed most of Latin America. The resulting freedom and community spirit, the relatively wide property distribution, and the preservation of artisan traditions contributed to the forging of a distinct Antioquian regional character. Finally, the fact that the Antioqueños became involved in the development of an internal frontier may have played a part in the evolution of their uniqueness.[30]

Of greatest significance for our purposes is that such a group or region

29. Hagen, p. 368.

30. See Charles H. Savage, Jr., *Social Reorganization in a Factory in the Andes* (Ithaca, N.Y., Cornell University Press, 1964), p. 3. See also Fernando Guillén Martínez, *Raíz y Futuro de la Revolución* (Bogotá, Ediciones Tercer Mundo, 1963), pp. 57–58.

does exist which has taken the lead in the industrialization of the country; which is wedded to the capitalistic system; and which is imbued in marked degree with traits usually associated with the "Protestant ethic." These men dominate a region of Colombia that is important not only economically, but demographically and politically as well, and their influence has spread to other parts of the country.

Paradoxically, this pool of entrepreneurial energies and abilities exists within both a national and regional social framework whose overall patterns and values are still basically Hispanic. It is to be expected that some traditional values would continue to infuse Antioquian entrepreneurship. For example, family-owned firms are still much more common than in North America, and paternalistic attitudes toward employees remain strong.[31] More surprising is the fact that in some ways Antioquia is the stronghold of Colombian conservatism. The department has traditionally been Conservative in politics, though this seems to be changing somewhat. Its social customs—with respect to the place of women in society, for instance—remain among the most tradition-bound in the country. Antioquia is also, by most available measures, the most Catholic of Colombian regions. It is here that the number of priests per inhabitant is highest, and here the proportion of religious vocations among its people exceeds that of other parts of the country.[32]

Not only does this raise some interesting questions concerning the relationship between religion and capitalism, but it has great potential significance for our immediate concern—Colombian politics. For although a Colombian who is not an Antioquian may tend to look at the Antioqueño brand of businessman with a mixture of disdain and envy, the latter is not placed in a position where he feels he must openly challenge the basic institutions and mores of Colombian society in order to vindicate himself. In many instances the Antioquian entrepreneur has sprung out of the old landed, mercantile, and mining elite of the region. In any case, he has succeeded economically and has won for himself a solid place among the nation's elite. Colombia's dispersed regionalism may have played its part by permitting the Antioquian entrepreneur to win his spurs

31. For the nature of early industrial paternalism in Antioquia and the strains imposed on it by industrial expansion, see Savage.

32. Gustavo Pérez Ramírez, *El Problema Sacerdotal en Colombia* (Bogotá, Centro de Investigaciones Sociales, 1962), p. 16 and chapter 4.

regionally without direct challenge to the more tradition-minded elites of other areas. In any case, the Antioquian capitalist has attained his position without seeking to destroy the elites of other regions, attacking religious institutions or dogma, or allying himself with other, lower classes. He has worked through the devices of the marketplace, as well as by fusion or in association with old groups, traditional values, and long-standing institutions. He has sought his political outlet within the traditional elite-dominated party system, and the positions he takes toward the social problems created by industrialization tend to be in word, and sometimes in deed, those of the papal encyclicals. Accordingly, that segment of the Colombian elite which has taken the lead in industrial innovation is in key respects a chief support of traditionalist Colombia.

A final comment or two can be made concerning the Colombian elite. One is that there is little question that in many ways the Colombian upper class has provided the country with able direction. Vernon Fluharty, a foreign critic of the Colombian elite, has listed among its qualities culture, industry, tenaciousness, vision in certain regards, gentility, and many-sided comprehension. He has the following words of praise for the abilities of its members: "This upper-class Colombian has made his mistakes, but he has also done a first-class job of building the national economy and the national culture into a respectable edifice worthy of admiration. In brief, he is quite a fellow." [33]

These capacities have within the last two or three decades brought Colombia well along the road of industrialization, and for more than forty years prior to 1948 gave the country a political stability which was the envy of most other Latin American nations. Even the great depression produced no more than a peaceful change of governing parties. More recently Colombia's ruling class has constructed the impressive political edifice of the National Front.

Yet the Colombian upper class has been subject to a weakness which has characterized such elites almost everywhere, namely, that it "tends on the whole to disregard excluded classes or groups and to treat them as beings of an inferior order." [34] An English observer has written of the Colombian elite:

33. Fluharty, pp. 185–87; cf. also M. Torres, *La Naturaleza de la Revolución,* for brief words of praise from a Marxist for the ability of the oligarchy.

34. Carl J. Friedrich, "Oligarchy," *Encyclopedia of the Social Sciences,* 9 (1937 ed.), 464.

They point with pride to the new skyscraper for a bank, while its doorman suffers from hunger and is uneducated. They talk about commercial conditions, of devoted servants, of their cousin in the Embassy in Washington, of their nephew studying at Oxford, while the tragedy of disease is there to be seen by all. The foreigner ends by feeling oppressed by the injustices which the people suffer; but many Colombian gentlemen apparently do not see them, or they don't matter to them, or they simply don't believe that they exist, or possibly they prefer not to discuss them with foreigners.[35]

Tangent to this attitude has been the tendency of the upper class to scorn the autochthonous and to look abroad for everything from its fashions in clothing and its literary tastes and themes, to its political ideologies. There is a certain propensity, declining perhaps but persistent, for members of the Colombian upper class to regard themselves as part of a cosmopolitan elite of "civilization" and culture over against the "barbarism" and lack of culture of the lower-class and somewhat darker-skinned members of their own society. Such "foreignizing" attitudes cut the elite off from the real roots of Colombian nationality and to that degree incapacitate it to lead the people of its own country in creating a truly national community.[36]

THE MIDDLE SECTORS

Despite long-standing allegations to the contrary, there *is* a meaningful middle class in Colombia.[37] There was always such an element in Colombian society—the shopkeeper, the overseer, the government clerk. But it was restricted in number and little more than an appendage to the tradi-

35. James Morris in *The Manchester Guardian*, quoted in Belisario Betancur, *Colombia Cara a Cara* (Bogotá, Ediciones Tercer Mundo, 1961), p. 109.

36. With respect to this point see the following: Mario Laserna, *Estado Fuerte o Caudillo* (Bogotá, Ediciones Mito, 1961), pp. 45–46 and 236–37; José Gutiérrez, *De la Pseudo-Aristocracia a la Autenticidad* (Bogotá, Ediciones Tercer Mundo, 1961); and Alfonso López Michelsen, *Los Elegidos*, and "Economía y Sociedad en Colombia" in *La Nación ante la Universidad*, Curso Académico, Organizado por la Universidad Nacional de Colombia (Bogotá, Fondo Universitario Nacional, 1957 [?]), pp. 36–46.

37. Or, as John Johnson would have it, middle sectors, or groups, or elements, to indicate the internal disparity and the lack of self-consciousness of that "class." John J. Johnson, *Political Change in Latin America* (Stanford, Stanford University Press, 1958).

tional upper class. In the last two or three decades the middle sectors have grown into numerical significance. The Lebret report of 1958 estimated the size of the middle class at about 15 per cent of all Colombians, while the study of Cereté placed its percentage of that community at 25.4.[38] That the middle class is recognized as such by its own members and by others in the social system is clearly indicated by community studies such as those of Popayán and Cereté. Williamson found that more than 80 per cent of university students identified themselves as middle class.[39] The political importance of the Colombian middle sectors meanwhile remains more potential than actual, a fact pointing up one of the prospective areas of strain in the Colombian polity.

Who, then, may be said to comprise the middle sectors in Colombia? Above all, white collar employees, both government bureaucrats and the clerks, technicians, sales and managerial personnel of private firms; professional people and intellectuals, including lawyers, teachers, journalists, and doctors who do not possess the criteria for upper-class membership; the majority of merchants and businessmen; most military officers, commissioned and noncommissioned; much of the clergy; and the middle level of farm owners.

On what depends their common identity as components of the middle sectors? Centrally, it is their occupations. The middle groups are those not of the elite who, generally speaking, do not engage in manual labor or, if they do, own their own shops, businesses, or farms and employ others to assist them. They tend also to occupy a middle level with respect to such things as income and education. Their life-styles correspond. The lack of some combination of abolengo, land, money, and culture mark them as not of the upper class; the fact that they are not "those who cook, serve, clean, run errands, bow and scrape, and perform the hard and menial tasks of the society," [40] distinguish them from the lower class. Clearly, the lines are not easy to draw. Whiteford uses the following example to illustrate the difference between lower middle class and lower class in Popayán:

We have two bakers; one of them puts on his coat when he goes out

38. Misión "Economía y Humanismo," pp. 36–37; Havens and Romieux.
39. Williamson, *El Estudiante Colombiano,* p. 16.
40. Fluharty, p. 183.

on the street, possibly even his hat, and he wears shoes all the time. He has the proper parties for his children on the occasion of their first communion, and so on. His son is going to the *liceo* [secondary school], and he is planning to send him to the university. He sees that his wife also wears shoes and is always neat and clean. The second baker wears *alpargatas* [sandals] even on the street and goes down to the corner *tienda* [store] in his undershirt and with his apron tied around his middle. He takes his son out of school after five years because he needs him to help in the bakery. The first baker is lower middle class and the second is lower class, even though their incomes may be the same. This is a question of their attitudes towards life and society.[41]

There are several characteristics of these middle groups that deserve our particular attention because of their implications for politics. They demonstrate that it is a mistake to assume that any middle class, in any time or place, will necessarily resemble the classic picture of the European bourgeoisie or the North American middle class.

First, whatever the attributes impressed on the middle sectors by their particular situation in the social system, they have also been socialized to those values and behavior patterns that apply generally in the culture. They are not only middle class, but Colombians. Gillin lists among the values subscribed to by Latin American middle classes: personalism, that is, a variety of individualism which stresses the uniqueness and dignity of the person, tends to scorn collaboration with others, and stresses personal relationships in business and politics over impersonal confidence in a corporation or an institution; familism, the emphasis on kinship ties, including ceremonial kin or godparents; hierarchy, especially the emphasis on a stratified society of patron-client relationships; the high valuation placed on the aesthetic compared to the material; and a sense of fatalism.[42] None of these would be regarded as typical of an Anglo-Saxon middle class. The continuing onrush of modernization will undoubtedly modify some of them, as to an extent it already has. But the process will be a gradual one. It further seems likely that there will remain a very

41. *Land Reform and Social Change,* p. 16.
42. John P. Gillin, "Some Signposts for Policy," in Council on Foreign Relations, *Social Change in Latin America Today* (New York, Harper, 1960), chapter 1.

distinct admixture of traditional Latin American culture. Such circumstances will make of the Latin American middle classes, including that of Colombia, a quite unique social phenomenon, with political consequences not wholly predictable from the experience of other countries.

Secondly, the Colombian middle sectors have fewer entrepreneurial elements, plus a higher proportion of white collar employees and non-self-employed professionals, than at a comparable stage of middle class development in the United States or Western Europe. A large percentage of them are *empleados,* dependent on an employer, rather than independent farmers, lawyers, and merchants. In the same way, the Colombian middle groups are highly dependent on the state, and notably the central government, both for employment and for policies favorable to their economic success and social advancement. The government is more involved in the Colombian economy and society, and absorbs a larger proportion of the nation's resources, both of money and personnel, than was true in western Europe and the United States at a comparable stage of economic growth. With even the entrepreneurial groups among the middle sectors more reliant on state policy and administration than their forerunners of other nations, their concern with opportunities for individual initiative may well be less; while their direct claims on government and the political process will be correspondingly greater.

A third factor attesting to the special nature of the middle class is that those who have elsewhere provided its economic power, and often its political leadership—the "upper bourgeoisie"—are in Colombia frequently found in the upper class. This group, which in Europe was often indeed in the middle—on the one hand struggling for power against the nobility and on the other defending itself against a burgeoning working class—has tended instead in Colombia to fuse economically, socially, and politically with the traditional elite. This is not wholly the case: many of Colombia's self-made men would more appropriately be designated middle class than upper class. Moreover, a clash of interests and values between traditional and capitalistic elements within the elite is by no means lacking. There is nonetheless something of a tendency for the traditional elite and the more important among the bankers, merchants, and industrialists to form one fusional upper class. This has meant that much of the potential strength and independent basis of power of the Colombian middle class has been absorbed instead into the existing elite. Here may lie one of the principal causes of the continuing political weakness of the Colombian middle sectors, despite the recent increase in their numbers.

Fourthly, a special word must be inserted concerning Colombia's rural middle class. According to the Economic Commission for Latin America (ECLA), 12.4 per cent of Colombian farms fall into the category of medium-sized (20–100 hectares).[43] Such holdings, without being latifundia, are adequate to provide the farmer with the economic basis for a middle-class standard of living, to hire others to work for him, to buy a house in town, and to educate his children. Some, but by no means most, of the farms that ECLA has termed family-sized (5–20 hectares) may also provide the basis of a middle-sector level of living, especially if they are turned to cash-crop agriculture. The increase in such farming in recent years is probably augmenting gradually the dimensions of the rural middle class.

It would be a mistake to call the peasantry the firm foundation of Colombia's middle class and "the principal force of the nation in the maintenance of democratic ideals." [44] A rural middle class exists in strength only in the departments of Antioquia and Caldas. Furthermore, a rapid growth in population has tended to turn many of these small coffee farms into minifundios through the process of subdivision.[45] The small coffee cultivators are to a considerable extent at the mercy of the larger coffee growers and the coffee traders and exporters, who together dominate the policy aspects of coffee production and trade. In recent years many cultivators have had to mortgage their farms on terms making their ownership illusory. Even so, in certain parts of the country there is something of a rural middle class whose outlook and interests might be expected to diverge from those of their urban counterparts.

Disparate in their aspirations and identifications, the Colombian middle sectors have been largely lacking in self-awareness and in unity as a social and political force. The dispersal of the middle sectors among Colombia's relatively numerous large urban centers works against ready cohesion. The dependence of the clergy and the officers of the military on their superiors, plus the special nature of those callings, have militated against

43. *ECLA Report,* pp. 194–95.

44. Reichel-Dolmatoff, "Notas sobre la Clase Media," p. 4.

45. See Horst Mendershausen, "Economic and Fiscal Problems of a Colombian Department," *Inter-American Economic Affairs,* 6 (1953), 48–89, passim; on the other hand, the Misión "Economía y Humanismo," p. 134, tends to regard coffee minifundia as "acceptable" in view of their relative productivity.

class identification on their part.[46] The wide rural-urban gap has had
something of the same effect on independent farmers.

The presence of a diverse social stratum which places some of its members virtually on the lower fringes of the upper class and others barely
above the proletariat in terms of income and standard of living distinguishes Colombia. The difference between a successful entrepreneur who
may lack only the proper abolengo for full acceptance into the upper
class and the clerk in his firm is vast, yet both may be deemed middle-
class. The social gradations among those who make up that class are
accordingly infinite, based on such things as employment, income, education, and style of living which, of course, do not always link consistently.
However, broadly speaking, observers have tended to divide the Colombian middle sectors into two halves. By and large these divisions correspond to the familiar upper and lower middle classes of other societies
and may be distinguished generally in terms of such criteria as income.
Yet in a more meaningful sense the categories of upper and lower middle
class in Colombia might rather be called the traditional and the new middle classes, where the crucial marks of differentiation are those of the outlooks and the origins of their members.[47] It is here that the diversity
among the Colombian middle sectors has its deepest meaning for politics.

The traditional middle class is comprised primarily of professional people and managerial personnel, medium-sized landowners, governmental
bureaucrats, and entrepreneurs. Some are impoverished descendants of
families that once stood at the apex of the social pyramid and who still
hold a nostalgia for their families' former aristocratic status. They strive
to emulate elite behavior patterns and, if possible, regain their foothold
in the ruling class.[48] Others, possibly of a similar origin but at a more

46. However, it should be noted that some military officers, who now commonly
have middle group origins, have shown signs of an awakening class consciousness.
ɔee below, chapter 11.

47. Cf. Havens and Romieux; see also, with regard to the analysis that follows,
Fals Borda, *La Transformación*, p. 6; Whiteford, passim; and *Land Reform and Social
Change*, p. 16.

48. According to T. Lynn Smith, writing in 1949, the Colombian middle class com-
prised little more than such "hangers-on" of the elite. See Smith, "Observations on the
Middle Classes in Colombia," *Materiales para el Estudio de la Clase Media en
América Latina*, 6 (Washington, D.C., Unión Panamericana, 1951), 1–14. Cf. also
Ralph Beals, "Social Stratification in Latin America," *American Journal of Sociology*,
58 (1952–53), 337.

remote period in time, are those whose ancestors have for centuries filled such social space as existed between the traditional elite and the masses of those who lived by their manual labor. The members of this upper or traditional middle class tend to have in common a concern for *fachada* (appearance, or façade) and for "culture." They are characterized by strong social control and the women, especially, give strong support to church activities. They tend in short to be socially and politically more conservative than their fellows in the lower middle class and even, perhaps, than many in the upper class.

The new middle class, on the other hand, derives mainly from the upwardly mobile, such as rural migrants newly arrived in the city, who have taken advantage of new opportunities afforded by rapid industrialization and urbanization. Their skins tend to be a shade darker than those of the traditional middle class, reflecting their origins lower on the social scale. Many, such as small shopkeepers, some small farmers, artisans, and lower-level government employees, are precariously perched only a rung above the urban proletariat. On the whole they tend to imitate elite preoccupations less; to be less concerned with fachada and culture and more with making money; to place less emphasis on social control and to participate less in church activities; to have less scorn for work with one's hands; and to exhibit a degree of political nonconformity. Numerically, the bulk of the Colombian middle class lies here.

As with all social classifications, there are overlappings and inconsistencies when one attempts to generalize. The task is made more difficult by the fact that the few extant studies of the Colombian middle groups are not of very large cities; that observers have not been in entire agreement on terms and categories; [49] and that there are regional and other differences among the middle strata of the various communities studied. Nevertheless, if the broad pattern that we have set forth holds for Colombia, it implies an inherent disunity within the middle sectors with respect to their political perspectives. It suggests, above all, that the two wings of the middle class may have different orientations toward social and political change.

Unfortunately, opinion surveys are lacking to confirm this, and electoral and census statistics as now compiled do not permit the kind of study based on aggregate data which might provide a substitute. Working then

49. Cf. Beals, pp. 327–39, for a discussion of this point.

mainly on the basis of impressions and inferences, it would appear that the traditional middle class has tended to support the Conservative party or the more conservative wing of the Liberal party, while the lower middle class may be found somewhat to the left, supporting such movements as those of Jorge Eliécer Gaitán during the 1940s. What seems crucial in the final analysis is that, facing Colombia's crisis of modernization, the country's strategic middle sectors are disunited and lack a consciousness of class concerning the desirable degree and direction of change or their political role in the nation's development.

In Colombia the elite has so far done more than the middle sectors to spur modernization. Alfonso López Michelsen, son of former President López and current leader of the principal left-of-center political force in the country, the Liberal Revolutionary Movement (*Movimiento Revolucionario Liberal*—MRL), has in some disgust termed the Colombian middle class apolitical. He has blamed its failure to follow his movement— and its own interests—for the MRL's defeat in the large cities in the election of 1962.[50] Whiteford, comparing the middle class of a very traditional Colombian city to one of comparable size and tradition in Mexico, found the middle class of Popayán, Colombia, to be more conservative and imitative of the upper class, and less prideful and self-conscious, than the middle class of Querétaro, Mexico.[51] Hirschman has noted an enhanced tendency of the Colombian middle groups to seek alliance with the hacendados on agrarian issues once they began to invest widely in land beginning in the fifties.[52] And Fluharty has said of the political role of the Colombian middle sectors: "The Colombian middle class acts neither as a liberalizing nor a stabilizing element in the nation's social struggle. It has gained no political competence of its own, for it has traditionally equated its interests with those of the oligarchy. In a general way, its function has been to sharpen the conflict, by tending to increase the numerical strength of the 'enemies' of the masses."[53]

Yet the middle sectors are expanding, and there are some signs of a growing self-consciousness and self-assertion on their part. Within the past several years there have been several strikes by middle-sector ele-

50. Interview with Alfonso López Michelsen, Bogotá, Aug. 21, 1963.
51. Whiteford, p. 76.
52. Hirschman, *Journeys toward Progress*, pp. 124–25.
53. Fluharty, p. 191.

ments such as bank clerks and teachers; a Central Committee of the Middle Class, composed of groups such as small businessmen, accountants, and lawyers, has formed branches in several Colombian cities; and a Popular Colombian Association of (Small) Manufacturers (*Asociación Colombiana Popular de Industriales*—ACOPI) has been established. López Michelsen, as well as other political leaders, are trying seriously to appeal to such groups. Reformist movements such as those led by Gaitán during the forties, and Alfonso López during the 1930s, were both based to some extent on middle-class support. Inertness and conservatism do not entirely characterize the political role of the Colombian middle sectors, even though to date they have constituted the dominant themes.

How a group or class first enters into full political participation may well be crucial for its subsequent political attitudes and allegiances. The fact that Argentine labor was first effectively incorporated into the political arena by Perón has had profound repercussions both for various Argentine parties and politicians, as well as for Argentine democracy and political stability. The Colombian elite still has the opportunity to grant the Colombian middle sectors a larger share of political leadership, with little likelihood of endangering its own social and economic status.[54] Most members of the middle sectors are undoubtedly more concerned with an extension of opportunity than with an equality that might narrow the gap between them and the lower classes of Colombian society. At the same time, in view of their continuing relative weakness, it seems probable that if the middle sectors are to wage effective political battle for their own interests they will have to seek alliance with other groups or classes. One of the important questions for the maintenance of the existing Colombian social and political system is with what class the middle sectors will ally.

THE "POPULAR" CLASSES

The overwhelming majority of Colombians are of course neither of the upper class nor of the middle sectors. Approximately 75 to 80 per cent constitute what are euphemistically called the "popular" classes. This mas-

54. This is Federico Gil's judgment of what has occurred in Chile, for example. See Federico Gil, *Genesis and Modernization of Political Parties in Chile,* Latin American Monograph Series No. 18 (Gainesville, University of Florida Press, 1961), pp. 46–47.

sive lower class, also referred to as "*los pobres*" (the poor), is defined by its lack of those attributes of occupation, education, income, manners, dress, and housing which mark the middle and upper classes. Whiteford notes: "In Latin America generally, if anything is lifted, pushed, pulled, or carried, it is done by members of the lower class. If one does any of these manual tasks, it is almost impossible to be classified as anything but lower class. Of course it is also almost impossible to do these things and earn enough money to acquire any of the characteristics by which anyone could possibly mistake you for a member of another class." [55] The chief exceptions would be those farmers and artisans who work with their hands but are able to hire others to assist them, or who have adopted, like one of our bakers earlier, middle sector patterns of behavior.

Traditionally, los pobres have been primarily campesinos, whose position in the social system has been conditioned above all by their relationship to the land. They fall into five principal categories: the *minifundista*, or owner of a minifundio; the *colono*, or semipermanent squatter on land he does not own but which in other respects is usually similar to a minifundio; the *arrendatario*, or tenant who pays rent for the land he works; [56] the *aparcero*, or sharecropper, who is allowed to till a small plot on an hacienda in return for part of the crop or for labor on the lands of the owner; and the *jornalero* (*peón*), or landless agricultural day-laborer.

On the whole, the level of living of the minifundista (and the colono and arrendatario) is higher than that of the aparcero, who in turn is better off on the average than the jornalero.[57] In some places such differences in material circumstances among the campesinos seem to have some significance for local social relations. Yet at least several students of agrarian Colombia tend to agree that the potential for social distinctions among the campesinos based on property relationships is not in the main realized. In the first place, the practice of dividing land among all the heirs militates, at least at this level, against social distinctions based on its concentration. In addition, when one member of a family owns land, a close relative frequently does not, thus making more difficult the formation of

55. *Land Reform and Social Change,* pp. 16–17.

56. Some of those who rent land do so on a relatively large scale and engage in commercial agriculture; others do so to supplement their own meager holdings by cultivating a few extra hectares.

57. Lannoy and Pérez, p. 181.

rigid social lines. The institution of ritual godparenthood (*compadrazgo*) meanwhile creates bonds of reciprocity among potentially different social levels.[58]

Most important, minifundistas are for most practical purposes on the same economic and social plane as those who squat, rent, sharecrop, or are totally landless. Most of their properties are extremely small and uneconomic, are located on the poorer, often mountainous lands, and feed numbers of mouths far in excess of their capabilities. This places the minifundio owner at a near-subsistence level about equivalent to that of most other campesinos. Despite the fact that he owns a plot of land, the minifundista is often not much more independent economically than the aparcero or the jornalero. He frequently lives, as they do, in economic symbiosis with the latifundio, offering his part-time or seasonal labor to supplement the meager income from his own plot. Like them he may well be in debt to the local moneylender or merchant, or to the latifundista himself, and he may be dependent for his water supply on the neighboring hacienda.[59]

The uneconomic size of his plot, or the lack of any land at all, has kept the campesino economically at the mercy of the moneylender, the middleman, and the hacendado. Little provision has been made by society for the education of his children, and he often lacks the incentive or the wherewithal to see that they get more than a rudimentary one.[60] Because of his precarious economic situation he has had difficulty in obtaining credit. The courts have often been rigged against him, with a much higher percentage of campesinos convicted of crimes than the accused of urban localities.[61] The police and other authorities can frequently be found in collusion against him. It is no wonder that the inferior economic and

58. For illustrations of some of the above points see Pearse and Rivera, p. 120; Universidad Nacional, Facultad de Sociología, "Factores Sociales que Indicen en el Desarrollo Económico de la Hoya del Río Subachoque," Typescript draft (Bogotá, 1963), p. 88; and Havens and Romieux, passim.

59. See Gerardo and Alicia Reichel-Dolmatoff, *The People of Aritama* (Chicago, University of Chicago Press, 1961), pp. 220–23, for a good description of the precarious situation of the small coffee grower in one region of Colombia.

60. Thirty per cent of Colombian children of primary school age are not in school at all and most of those who are not live in rural areas; *Plan General de Desarrollo*, Part I, p. 229.

61. Pérez, *El Campesinado*, pp. 111–12.

social position of the campesinos has left them "subordinates in public affairs, passive pawns in the great chess game of power which the elites and groups of large landowners have enacted." [62]

Coercion, economic and sometimes physical, looms large in a situation of this kind. However, like all enduring social and political systems, this one has been based largely on its acceptance as being right, or at least unchangeable, by those who are the "subordinates." "The feudal attitude, skillfully managed by those who have workers at their service, prevents the latter from taking cognizance of the common good . . . [T]he masses, especially the campesinos, are impermeable to ideas and movements designed to make effective their own rights for fear of 'losing credit' with their particular patrón and consequently with the other patrones." [63] The campesino has been trained to accept the prescribed patterns of behavior at an early age and his contact with the larger social system is very limited throughout his life. There is some desire for change on the part of the campesino. However, channels of mobility are on the whole effectively blocked. The degree of change aspired to is in any case low, usually amounting to a wish to add an hectare or two to his current holding. "They live the life of their class and rarely question [it]." [64] The result is a static, in-bred, traditional rural community [65] in which the majority leave public affairs in the hands of those who manipulate the system from superior positions on the social scale. As the Lebret report put it, "it is in agriculture where the least autonomous social levels are found." [66]

Much of rural Colombia still conforms to this pattern. But the forces of change are beginning to enter even this most traditional sector of Colombian society. Orlando Fals Borda, who has been studying the community of Saucío in the department of Cundinamarca since 1950, notes that it was toward the turn of the century when new forces appeared that began to challenge the existing social system of Saucío, although the impact was

62. Orlando Fals Borda, *El Hombre y la Tierra en Boyacá* (Bogotá, Editorial Antares, 1957), p. 215.

63. Centro de Investigaciones Sociales (cis), *Estudios sobre Desarrollo, Informe No. 1. Condiciones de Desarrollo y Reconstrución en el Municipio de Sonsón (Antioquia)* (Bogotá, CIS, 1963), p. 216.

64. Havens and Romieux, pp. 40 ff.

65. For a case study of this kind of community, see Pearse and Rivera.

66. Misión "Economía y Humanismo," p. 36.

limited until about 1930. Starting with the decades of the 1950s the pace has accelerated.[67]

Pearse and Rivera have noted the impact on the municipio of Tenza of wage payments to highway workers. Up to 30 years ago the roads were maintained locally; now they are maintained by the department, which pays in wages—something new to Tenza—at rates higher than the salaries of any municipal employee, and as high as that of the mayor. Sources of income outside of the community are thereby opened up to its members, along with new opportunities for earnings and for social status.[68] Another innovator has been the automobile and its variants, the truck and the tractor. As Fals Borda notes of Saucío, many of the youth now aspire to be drivers. For those who are, the effect has been to further the process of liberation from parental control and from the agricultural routine, as well as to promote business and recreational contacts outside the neighborhood.[69]

A force for change of another sort has been agricultural innovation. Gerardo and Alicia Reichel-Dolmatoff's study of a community in the semi-tropical lowland region of northern Colombia cites a trend toward an aggressive self-assertion in the form of more active participation in community affairs, politics, and economic efforts. They comment, "There can be no doubt that the factor that has most strongly influenced the local culture during recent years is the replacement of subsistence farming by cash crops, cattle, and wage labor." The Reichel-Dolmatoffs ascribe the ready acceptance of such changes to the fact that the new agricultural activities have provided money to buy the status symbols of the traditional culture.[70]

The actions of government and politicians have also stirred Colombia's traditional rural society. Promises of agrarian reform, the political cam-

67. Orlando Fals Borda, *Facts and Theory of Sociocultural Change in a Rural Social System,* Monografías Sociológicas No. 2 Bis (2d ed. Bogotá, Universidad Nacional, Facultad de Sociología, 1962), p. 34. Paul J. Deutschmann and Fals Borda note in *La Comunicación de las Ideas entre los Campesinos Colombianos,* Monografías Sociológicas No. 14 (Bogotá, Universidad Nacional, Facultad de Sociología, (1962), passim, the strategic role of the mass media as a form of change-inducing communication in the Colombian countryside.

68. Pearse and Rivera, p. 112.

69. Fals Borda, *Facts and Theory,* pp. 30–31.

70. Reichel-Dolmatoff, *People of Aritama,* pp. 450–55.

paigns of the late Jorge Eliécer Gaitán, and legislation such as Law 200 of 1936 and Law 135 of 1961, which have both resulted in some campesinos obtaining land, have helped to raise expectations for further change in the countryside.

The campesino's aspirations and outlooks are thus slowly being transformed in ways significant for the social system and for politics. Where once the campesino looked almost exclusively to investment in more land, he now may prefer to save to educate his children [71] so that they can aspire to an urban occupation, or he may invest in a truck with which to haul his produce to urban markets. Attitudes of rationality are beginning to erode those of fatalism, traditionalism, and isolation. The peasant belief that "When God decrees that a person should be rich, everything helps him along" is gradually giving way to one that affirms "God helps those who help themselves; my garlic was saved because of the fertilizer I used." [72] As Fals Borda concludes of Saucío, "The local ethos is losing its passivity and Hispanoid characteristics. The peasant seems to be readier for change, as the focus of his culture is shifting from the nucleus of religiosity and passivity handed down by the colonial society, to a fulcrum of rationality and action with a clearer awareness of the national whole and the world." [73]

There have also been alterations in the class structure and in class relationships. A new orientation toward economic success has enabled some farmers to achieve a higher standard of living and to enter the rural middle class. At least some of the peasants are increasingly able to defend themselves from abuse and exploitation; there are signs that the old subservience is starting to erode; and in places there is a growing aggressiveness toward the upper class. Attitudes evident among the campesinos of some localities, such as Subachoque in the department of Cundinamarca, indicate that if their land hunger is not soon assuaged, "the leap which they will take will carry them from the 18th century in which they are to the 20th to which they aspire, in a form very similar to that of the Bolivians who, in doing so, left a wide path of blood in their wake." [74] It may be, too, that the years of violence have helped to radicalize the

---

71. Fals Borda, *La Transformación,* p. 14.
72. Fals Borda, *Facts and Theory,* p. 35.
73. Ibid.
74. Universidad Nacional, *Factores Sociales,* p. 107.

Colombian campesino. So far, though, this increasing inconformity on the part of the Colombian rural dweller lacks ideology and organization. On the whole, changing attitudes have not as yet found their political expression.

Accompanying these changed perspectives is evidence that a new kind of leadership is beginning to emerge among the campesinos themselves. This is in part an informal leadership, based in considerable measure on the ability to establish rapport with public opinion. Such leaders are characterized by slightly higher levels of education, somewhat greater ability at the articulation of ideas, and wider contact beyond the immediate community than are non-leaders. In some cases, the formation of co-operatives or rural unions is absorbing this informal leadership and opposing to the traditional hierarchical patterns institutionalized "rational" patterns of direction. The end result of the development of such leadership, both informal and "rational," is the weakening of the power of the hacendado and of the seignorial style of domination over the campesino. As yet, however, the new leaders have shown themselves to be quite conservative, perhaps because most are between 40 and 65 years old.[75] The real test for the system may come when a new generation is at the helm.

One final form of change in the Colombian countryside, though of a different order, has been migration, sometimes to other rural areas in search of higher wages, more often to the towns and the cities. At least one study has shown that it is those campesinos with more land who tend to emigrate,[76] probably because it is they who have the wider perceptual horizons and because they have an economic margin which they can fall back on if the risk of emigration fails. Some apparently contradictory evidence indicates that those regions with the lowest agricultural wages have the highest number of vacated houses. However, it is not clear whether the poorest in those areas are the ones who have left.[77] The extent of the impact of migration on the individual rural community, an aspect which is sometimes lost sight of, is indicated by the fact that in the municipio of Subachoque 39 per cent of the families had at least one relative in Bo-

75. Orlando Fals Borda, "El Liderazgo Rural y La Reforma Agraria," (Paper prepared for first National Seminar on Agrarian Reform, Bogotá, Nov. 1962), pp. 4–7.
76. Pearse and Rivera, pp. 131–32.
77. Pérez, *El Campesinado*, p. 96.

gotá.[78] Migration has loosed contradictory forces in the rural community. Whereas the departure of the young and ambitious tends to breed rural stagnation, the ties which urban emigrants retain with their families in the countryside—not to mention all the other influences of new technologies and new economic, social, and political relationships—work at the same time in the opposite direction to stimulate change.

The rural still outnumber the urban lower class in Colombia, but the percentage of the economically active population engaged in agriculture has been declining steadily since at least 1925 and in the not-too-distant future the proportions will be reversed.[79] As among the campesinos, there is diversity within the urban lower class. Speaking in broad terms, there is one threefold distinction of particular significance: *obreros* working in medium- and larger-sized industries; persons engaged in artisan-type manufacture; and what might be called the sub-proletariat.

The first category includes those most commonly thought of in industrialized countries as the urban working force. Its members have regular employment; their wages are relatively high, sometimes placing them above individual members of the lower middle class in earnings; and their employers are large enough to come under the provisions of labor laws granting sickness and vacation benefits, severance pay, and the like. They form a kind of privileged group compared to the working classes as a whole. More cohesive and better organized than the others, industrial workers are able to exert a certain amount of pressure to effect their demands, both on their employers and in the political arena and often at the expense of consumers generally.

The second group, those who work in household or small-scale industries, or who operate such establishments by themselves, lack many of the advantages of the factory worker in terms of security, welfare benefits, and wages. They are less well organized on the whole and less able to improve their situation through concerted action. To be sure, some artisans who own their own shops fall more properly into the middle sectors, but many others are best placed in the popular classes by their style of life. The percentage of those employed in "non-factory manufacturing" is diminishing progressively with the years in relation to those working in

78. Universidad Nacional, *Factores Sociales*, pp. 14–15.
79. *ECLA Report*, p. 17.

factories, but artisans still comprise almost two thirds of those engaged in "manufacturing." [80]

The final category of the urban popular classes comprises the habitually unemployed, the underemployed, as well as domestic servants and porters. Most unskilled non-factory workers, such as those in construction, would also be classified here. Their common characteristic is the generally marginal or transient nature of their employment. A large percentage of them are migrants from the rural areas who lack the skills for urban life and work.

Removal to the city has done little to change the relative social position of most migrants, particularly the more recent ones. They often exchange rural poverty and underemployment for the urban counterparts. Their mobility in many cases is purely geographical and horizontal, not vertical.[81] Job opportunities for the unskilled and the virtually illiterate are scarce. Housing for the migrant (and for some not so recently arrived in the city as well) is frequently a shack on a hillside in a district which lacks running water and other municipal facilities. Nutritional levels, too, remain low.[82]

Despite such facts, most among the popular class of the cities seem to have hopes of improving their condition, or that of their children. Whiteford has remarked of Popayán's poor that, "Life frequently seemed to be nothing but an endless trail strewn with sharp rocks, but there were very few who did not hope and expect that the future would be better for the next generation." [83] Public education, for one thing, is more accessible in the city. Statistics show that the majority of industrial workers have attended school for one to five years (few for longer), whereas many agri-

80. *Plan General de Desarrollo*, Part II, p. 12. To be considered industrial as defined in this document an enterprise must have either 5 or more employees or an annual value of production which exceeds 24,000 pesos; otherwise it is considered "artisan."

81. However, urban-ward migration may actually represent a kind of upward mobility. Cf. Pearse and Rivera, p. 120.

82. Camilo Torres Restrepo, *La Proletarización de Bogotá*, Monografías Sociológicas No. 9 (Bogotá, Universidad Nacional, Facultad de Sociología, 1961), passim, compared the nutritional standards of the working and middle classes in Bogotá, although his study did not differentiate recent migrants from long-time residents.

83. Whiteford, p. 118; see also p. 123; see also *Land Reform and Social Change*, p. 17. See Pat M. Holt, *Colombia Today—and Tomorrow* (New York, Praeger, 1964), p. 18, for two individual case examples of upward social mobility.

cultural workers are illiterate or have had less than a year of schooling.[84] The level of living is also somewhat higher for the urban poor than for the rural.[85]

Aspirations run high, and where unfulfilled, breed frustration. This is undoubtedly one reason why, in revisiting during the summer of 1962 the city he had known since 1947, Whiteford found "considerably more tension, frustration and expressed antagonism toward the status quo than I ever encountered before." [86] The continuing movement to the cities means that the human fuel for the kind of explosion exemplified by the riots of April 1948 is at hand at the principal centers of government. It transfers certain rural problems, such as the occupation of private property by squatters, to an urban setting. The urban lower class is, like the rural, still too close to the margin of subsistence to be able to act independently as a major cohesive force in politics; the entire weight of the economic, social, and political systems has so far prevented a real change in its subordinate role. Still, the urban context frees its members from some of the subtle forms of coercion, and from some of the bonds of traditionalism prevalent in the countryside. Lacking property, education, and other assets on which the elite, and to some extent the middle sectors, have built their own positions, power for the popular classes will depend in large part on the degree to which they can translate their numerical predominance into unified action. It is in the city that this becomes more possible. It is, in fine, migration from the countryside to the city or town that constitutes the ultimate dimension of change for the Colombian campesino.

The lower classes, the middle sectors, the elite, all have been cast within a mold of values and group relationships largely derived from a past which, for the sake of a shorthand designation, may be called quasi-feudal. Its principal marks have been a rather rigid class system based on ascribed social roles, and close dependence of the many on the few. The last several decades, however, have witnessed changes in the composition and attitudes of the elite itself, an expansion and variegation of the middle sectors, the emergence of new outlooks among the rural lower classes,

84. U.S. Dept. of Labor, p. 8.
85. Pérez, *El Campesinado*, pp. 91–92.
86. *Land Reform and Social Change*, p. 17.

and the rise of a large urban lower class. Social structure, relationships among the classes, and the perspectives of Colombians throughout the social hierarchy all show the effects of the traditional past adjusting to a modernizing present. How those adjustments continue to be made will go far toward determining the future of Colombia's political response to change.

PART III

The Regimes
of Modernization

4

THE REVOLUCIÓN EN MARCHA—
MODERNIZATION BY
AN ELITE

THE PRECURSORS OF CHANGE

Nineteenth-century Colombia experienced warfare among rival *caudillos* —generally aligned with one or the other of the two historic parties, the Conservative and the Liberal—of a dimension and intensity unparalleled in the majority of the other Latin American republics. In the years 1899–1902 there occurred the most extensive and costly of all of Colombia's civil wars up to that time, the so-called War of the Thousand Days. Yet the end of that conflict, which terminated in a negotiated peace but with the Conservatives essentially victorious, marked the beginning of roughly forty-five years of relative political peace. To be sure, localized violence sometimes occurred at election time; there were one or two abortive military coups; and following the transfer of power from a Conservative to a Liberal administration in 1930 rather extensive rural violence broke out in two of Colombia's eastern departments. However, there was no generalized violence, and no forcible overturn of the government, from 1902 until about 1948. Peaceful transfers of power took place twice between the two traditional parties, once in 1930 and again in 1946, as the result of reasonably free elections.

These four and a half decades corresponded to that stage of Latin American political development that Gino Germani has termed one of "limited participation," or rule by the liberal (not Liberal) oligarchy.[1] It

1. Cf. Germani, *Política y Sociedad,* chapter 6.

78   *The Regimes of Modernization*

had its analogies elsewhere: in Brazil in the years 1891–1930; in Argentina in the decades before 1916; and in Chile prior to 1920. It was an era in which the government and the parties almost exclusively represented the interests of a small upper class; in which mass participation in politics was limited by property and literacy restrictions on the vote and by the dependence of a largely rural population on powerful landlords; and during which material growth usually did not narrow the gap between the elite and the masses of the population. Assuming the exclusion of the majority from politics, and from the benefits of material growth, something resembling democracy nevertheless took place within the upper class. Civil liberties were respected, elections were regularly held, and the opposition had at least some opportunity to win political office. "Colombia became something like an aristocratic republic, in the style of Rome, Venice, or the Athens of Pericles, with a responsible patriciate, formed by the . . . leading . . . families, whose own interests were confounded with the general interest of the state, [thus] producing the health of the nation." [2]

Yet Colombia's "Athenian" politics rested on certain false and tenuous foundations. The issues around which the strife of the nineteenth century had revolved, especially that of the place of the Church in politics, in education, and in other aspects of the national life, were not entirely dead, but rather lying dormant. Secondly, the reigning consensus had been evolved during a period when the unspoken assumption was that the Conservatives would remain dominant. In keeping with the outcome of the War of the Thousand Days, the Liberals were to resign themselves indefinitely to a role which, if assured, was nonetheless secondary. The election of 1930, from which the Liberals emerged victorious, appeared to indicate that Conservative hegemony was no longer a prerequisite for political peace. Yet when a post-election coalition gave way in 1934 to a "Liberal Republic," the tensions of "ins" versus "outs" began once more to mount. The apparent consensus within the elite had not been a fundamental agreement on how to settle differences by peaceful means; it had rather been a freezing of a political status quo by the exhausted adversaries of civil war. In the third place, there had been no lasting change in Colombian political culture to admit of a bargaining ethos, or a real

2. Rafael Azula Barrera, *De la Revolución al Orden Nuevo: Proceso y Drama de un Pueblo* (Bogotá, Editorial Kelly, 1956), p. 490.

possibility of appreciating a rival's point of view, at least when highly emotional or ideological issues were involved. The apparent consensus was therefore by its very nature a fragile thing; it had not sent down deep roots into the national mores.

Most important, political agreement among the rival segments of the elite, as symbolized by a series of constitutional amendments adopted in 1910, was implicitly based on the exclusion of the majority from political life and from any great share in the emoluments of social status or economic gain. It was founded on the assumption that an elite would rule— politically, socially, economically, culturally. It rested on the further premise that a nation progressed through the greatest possible freedom for powerful individuals or firms, both foreign and domestic, and through the most rapid possible accrual of foreign loans to promote the building of public works. The system paid little attention to the social effects of economic growth; little to the political demands of interest groups whose presence reflected that growth, and who were becoming influenced by new ideologies emanating from such places as Soviet Russia; and little to the possibility that the state might need to take a hand at some point in controlling the excesses of economic greed or in meeting the difficulties posed by world depression. The consensus attained within the Colombian elite in the years after the turn of the century had not yet been called upon to stand the test of rapid change. The challenge of modernization simultaneously exposed and exacerbated the flaws in the political system of the forty-five year peace.

The processes of change were beginning to undermine the "idyllic" Colombian political order as early as the 1920s. It is in this period that began what Antonio García has called "the crisis of the traditional order." [3]

Economic growth was one facet of the transformation taking place. The gross domestic product increased at an average annual rate of 7.3 per cent in the years 1925–29,[4] mainly as the result of investments in public works and transportation financed by a boom in coffee exports and by foreign loans. A steady rise in coffee prices during the twenties had meanwhile encouraged thousands of farmers to turn to coffee growing as a way of

3. Antonio García, *Gaitán y el Problema de la Revolución Colombiana* (Bogotá, 1955).

4. *Plan General de Desarrollo,* Part I, p. 7.

life. The trend to cash-crop farming greatly increased the dependence of many Colombian campesinos on markets national and international. When the depression brought a 60 per cent drop in coffee prices, growers found themselves in economic trouble. Their investment in coffee trees already planted made it difficult to shift readily to other crops.

In addition, the rate of growth of the population between 1912 and 1929 was the most rapid in the history of the republic up to that time. The number of Colombians increased from about five million to slightly under eight million in those years.[5] Such growth augmented the pressure on land resources and spurred migration to the cities and larger towns.

Overt manifestations of the undercurrents at work were evident in the Colombian countryside. Squatters moved in on public, and even private, lands in some areas. Others decided that they were the rightful owners of lands which they had settled but whose titles were unclear. In some instances tenants on large estates tried to assure their permanency on the land by planting long-maturing coffee trees on their subsistence plots. Violent incidents between squatters, settlers, and tenants on the one side, and landowners on the other, occurred frequently during the late twenties and the early thirties. The landowner could as a rule count on the support of the authorities, and police actions resulted in a number of evictions in the departments of Cundinamarca and Tolima, and in the Cauca Valley.[6]

Labor, too, began to flex its muscles. The workers of the American-owned Tropical Oil Company went out on strike in 1924, in 1926, and again in 1927. On the last occasion the strike was forcibly suppressed. A strike of banana workers near Santa Marta on the Atlantic coast in 1928— also against an American company, United Fruit—resulted in a massacre by army troops.[7]

5. Cf. Jesús María Henao and Gerardo Arrubla, *History of Colombia,* trans. and ed. J. Fred Rippy (Chapel Hill, N.C., University of North Carolina Press, 1938), p. 535; and Misión "Economía y Humanismo," *Estudio sobre . . . Colombia,* p. 19.

6. See Hirschman, *Journeys toward Progress,* pp. 101–06, for the best brief discussion of agrarian unrest in this period. See also República de Colombia, Cámara de Representantes, *Informe de la Comisión que investigó los sucesos sangrientos de Paquilo, Municipios de Pandi y San Bernardo, y estudió el problema de los colonos de Sumapaz* (Bogotá, Imprenta Nacional, 1932).

7. For an account of the strike see J. Fred Rippy, *The Capitalists and Colombia* (New York, Vanguard Press, 1931), pp. 182–88. For a Conservative commentary and some relevant documents, see José María Nieto Rojas, *La Batalla contra el Comunismo en Colombia* (Bogotá, Empresa Nacional de Publicaciones, 1956), pp. 75–80. Also cf. Hirschman, p. 101n.

A process of political fermentation was likewise underway. The "postwar generation," the sons of those who had laid the foundations for Colombia's forty-five year peace, was not immune to the impact of the Bolshevik Revolution nor to the shadow of the Mexican Revolution. Discussion circles, political clubs, even new parties, were signs of a new ebullience. For the most part the new groups were short-lived, and their sphere of influence narrow. In its test of fire after 1930, when the Liberals assumed power, the post-war generation largely succumbed to the temptations of office. For many of them the "socialism" of their youth gave way to the political realism of maturity and, perhaps, to closer examination of the new doctrines. Their enduring importance was to launch on their way several varieties of Colombian leftist thought, from Communism to a rather mild reformist Liberalism.[8]

On the political Right, what was later to be termed the counterrevolution had its first stirrings. In 1924, a group of "nationalist" Conservatives, also called the "Leopards," issued a manifesto warning against the anarchic manifestations of the nascent urban proletariat and extolling the "spirit of the earth" of the campesinos. The Leopards at first based their philosophy on that of Charles Maurras and *Action Française;* they were later to look to victorious Spanish Falangism for their inspiration. Such doctrines were the counterparts within Conservative ranks to those which were to find their principal Colombian homes in the left wing of the Liberal party and in the Communist party.[9]

Meanwhile the Liberal party was showing signs of change from within. Rafael Uribe Uribe, one of its heroes of the War of the Thousand Days, had declared as early as 1913 that the party must socialize or perish, by which he meant it must sponsor a certain amount of state intervention in the social and economic fields. The party's convention of 1922 adopted a program incorporating a concern for social justice. By the time the Conservatives left office in 1930 many Liberal intellectuals, as well as many among the Liberal masses, expected, if not a social revolution, at least important new departures in social and economic policy. However, the coalitional nature of the regime of President Enrique Olaya Herrera (1930–34) was not propitious for such measures on any very extensive

8. See A. García, *Gaitán,* pp. 32–97, for a discussion of the post-war generation.
9. See ibid., pp. 80–81; and Azula Barrera, pp. 295–296, for brief treatments of the Leopards.

scale, and a brief undeclared war with Peru in 1932–33 diverted attention to foreign affairs. Some Liberals felt defrauded by their party's unwillingness to make a "revolution" after 1930. They embarked for a time on a movement called the Revolutionary Leftist National Union (*Unión Nacional Izquierdista Revolucionaria*—UNIR), but it failed to gain support and collapsed when its leader, Jorge Eliécer Gaitán, returned to the Liberal fold.

The accession to power of the Liberals and President Olaya Herrera in 1930 was in some measure a response to the stirrings of the 1920s. The Olaya government adopted some measures of electoral reform and introduced higher tariff schedules for the benefit of the country's manufactures and its depression-bereft agriculture. The initial steps toward an agrarian reform were taken during this administration, and some legislation was passed for the benefit of urban labor. But the whole hardly added up to a concerted program of reform. It would be incorrect to say that prior to 1934 Colombia had addressed itself systematically to the manifold implications of rapid societal change. It was instead the government of Alfonso López Pumarejo (1934–38) which first did so in a substantial way.

THE REVOLUCIÓN EN MARCHA

Much of Latin America in the early 1930s lived under some form of military-backed dictatorship or was just emerging from a period of turbulence and military rule. Among Colombia's nearest neighbors on the South American continent, Venezuela in 1934 was approaching the end of the quarter-century dictatorship of Juan Vicente Gómez; Peru was ruled by a military dictatorship; and Ecuador had acquired her seventh president in four years. Among the major Latin American countries elsewhere, Mexico was about to embark on a period of the most far-reaching change since the Revolution of 1910 under the leadership of President Lázaro Cárdenas. Brazil was deep into the Vargas era with a regime that was soon to become a full-fledged dictatorship pursuing nationalist and reformist goals. Argentina had seen the overthrow in 1930 of the Radical party, oriented to the middle class, and its replacement first by a military regime, then by a decade of essentially Conservative rule, backed by the military. Chile had emerged in 1932 from a period of unwonted political disturbance and was in 1934 making strides toward recovery from the depression under the leadership of the formerly reformist, now conservative, Arturo Alessandri.

The peaceful demise of the Conservative regime in 1930, and the absence of the military from overt intervention in politics, therefore made Colombia something of an exception. The onset of a period of reform in 1934 under the auspices of the freely-elected regime of President Alfonso López made Colombia still more exceptional at this moment in Latin American development.[10]

Ideologically, the López reforms drew on many sources for their inspiration. The Mexican constitution of 1917 was clearly one. It had been the first in Latin America to set forth systematically a body of provisions relating to social welfare, the protection of labor, state responsibility in the economic and educational fields, and the social function of property. The ideas of the Peruvian *Apristas,* whose ideology of change had achieved some currency throughout the hemisphere by the early thirties, were another influence. López and some of his aides had also evidently been impressed by the actions of the New Deal of Franklin D. Roosevelt, especially in the fiscal and economic fields. Meanwhile socialist thought had attracted some Colombian intellectuals during the previous decade; as a result, some diluted Marxian strains were among the well-springs of the new regime. Finally, the fact that traditionalist mother Spain had embarked on a liberal republic in the early 1930s provided an example for liberals in her former New World colonies.[11]

When one turns to the social roots of the López reforms, it should be noted that the Liberal party had always tended to be urban-oriented, at least compared to the Conservatives, even though many large landowners and campesinos were counted in the Liberal ranks. The party was therefore potentially more receptive to modernizing proposals than was its rival. The Liberal party incorporated more of the urban working class; probably more of the campesinos in those areas of the country where un-

10. These political facts may have some relation to other, economic facts, namely, that real income per head seems to have dropped less in Colombia than in at least some other Latin American countries at the time of the depression, and that Colombia made an especially rapid economic recovery.

11. For a discussion of the diverse strands of influence on López, see Peter C. Maffitt, "Colombia, The Revolution on March 1934–1938" (unpublished Scholar of the House essay, New Haven, Conn., Yale University, 1963), Part II, chapter 1, pp. 10–14.

rest was greatest; and probably, too, a somewhat higher percentage of the upwardly-mobile and of the "empathic," that is, of those able and willing to see other horizons than the traditional ones and other points of views than their own.[12] Also behind certain of the López reforms were some of the new industrialists, although many of them subsequently opposed key elements of his program. Mainly, however, those who supplied the leadership for the revolution on the march were intellectuals and politicians, members of elite families whose economic base rested on large-scale commerce, coffee growing, and similar enterprises. Many of them were young, members of the post-war generation of the 1920s. They carried with them new ideas, energy in pursuing them, and a certain impatience with the Liberals of a previous generation whose memories were those of the War of the Thousand Days and who thought primarily in terms of the spoils of office and the clarion calls of the Liberalism of the past century. While members of the middle sectors were represented in the councils of the administration, that class was still too weak to provide the leadership for reform shown by its counterpart in Chile under the Popular Front of the late 1930s or earlier in Uruguay under José Batlle y Ordóñez.[13] The López reforms were essentially directed by the modernizing segments of the Colombian upper class, although they had the support of such groups as urban labor and the middle sectors.

As impressive as any specific ideological, class, or generational thrust for the revolution on the march was its pragmatism in reacting to the problems that faced Colombia and the problems and opportunities that faced the Liberal party. Along with many other Latin American countries, Colombia had been confronted in the early thirties with a drying up of the sources of foreign loans and with a sharp decline in income from its principal export, coffee. The nation's balance of payments, its economic health, and even its budget largely relied on those sources of support. Hence there was considerable impetus to free the country from economic cycles, at least partially, by using government policy to stimulate the growth of industry and agriculture. An inchoate desire to modernize Colombia, to bring it out of its backwardness and out of its dependence

12. See below, chapter 9, for a discussion of the differences between Conservatives and Liberals in their sources of support. For the concept of empathy as employed here see Lerner, *Passing of Traditional Society*, pp. 49–50.

13. Cf. Johnson, *Political Change*, chapters 4 and 5.

on forces not under its control, seems to have taken shape at this time. This was particularly true of the small group that was to provide the leadership for the López administration, although it was true of some Conservatives as well. Besides, by the 1930s important segments of the elite recognized that there was an incipient crisis of the old order. Agrarian and labor unrest clearly had had an impact, and the government saw itself being increasingly forced into the dangerous position of overt defender of the claimed rights of large landowners and foreign companies. Evidences of internal political stirrings, such as Gaitán's UNIR, as well as numerous examples of the potential explosiveness of social forces elsewhere in Latin America and around the world, helped to prod the Liberals in the direction of reform.

Finally, there was recognition on the part of López and his associates that if the Liberal party were to consolidate its hold on power, it would have in some degree to meet the demands and aspirations of groups which could serve as political counterweights to Conservative strength in the army and the Church, and among the more traditionalist-oriented of the campesinos. Thus it would have to reduce the influence of the Church in education and on the electoral process, organize urban labor as political battalions for the party, and promote a rate of economic growth which would wed to it the interests of the new industrialists.

López himself symbolized the philosophy and approach of the revolution on the march. The son of a coffee merchant, he later studied finance in England, worked for his father's firm in New York, then in 1904 returned to Colombia to take part in the management of the family business. He became one of the founders of a commercial bank, and in 1933 represented Colombia at the London Economic Conference. López therefore entered the presidency with considerable experience in the world of business and international trade. He was less the man of letters than many members of the Colombian elite (in fact, he had not completed his university education) and more the practical man of affairs. He had resided in England and the United States on several occasions and had travelled widely in Europe, North America, and Latin America. As the consequence of his family and occupational background, his schooling, and his periods of travel and residence abroad, Alfonso López had acquired a desire to modernize his country, an acute awareness of his country's relationship to international economic forces, and something of a pragmatic, almost Anglo-Saxon approach to change. As Hirschman says of him, "he seems . . . to have had a realistic understanding of the combination of pressures and promises needed to push through measures that went against the class or immediate pecuniary interests of those who were called upon to vote for them."[14]

Some of the López administration's policies sought to fulfill long-standing Liberal demands. One of these was the expansion and purification of the suffrage. The constitutional codification of 1936, which supplied the legal foundation for a number of the reforms of the López era, struck from the constitution the literacy and property qualifications which up to then had been required in the voting for president and for the Chamber of Representatives.[15] López and the Liberals likewise set out to limit the power of the Church. Symbolically, the new codification omitted mention of Roman Catholicism as the religion of the nation, as well as the clause of Article 38 which had stated that "the authorities will protect [the Church] and see that it is respected as an essential element of the social order." The new amendments reduced religious associations to legal status equal to that of other voluntary associations, excluded priests from political office, and opened the possibility of taxation of religious buildings. Nor did the constitution any longer require that "Public education will be organized and directed in accordance with the Catholic religion."[16]

Yet the revolution on the march would not have constituted a period of

14. Hirschman, p. 108. Most of the above biographical information on López was taken from *Quién es Quién en Venezuela, Panama, Ecuador, Colombia* (Bogotá, Oliverio Perry, 1952), p. 792. For a précis of López' career and a characterization of him see Maffitt, Part II, chapter 1, pp. 7–9.

15. The constitutional changes in 1936 were technically amendments to the Constitution of 1886. Because of their extent, and because other amendments had been passed since 1886, a new document called a codification was drawn up incorporating all the changes. Another codification took place in 1945. Translations of both may be found in William Marion Gibson, *The Constitutions of Colombia* (Durham, North Carolina, Duke University Press, 1948).

16. For statements by the Church and the Conservative party concerning the proposed constitutional reforms see República de Colombia, *La Opinión Nacional ante la Reforma de la Constitución* (Bogotá, Imprenta Nacional, 1936), pp. 6–13. For López' policy toward the Church see pp. 15–33 and *Mensajes del Presidente López al Congreso Nacional, 1934–1938* (Bogotá, Imprenta Nacional, 1939), pp. 214–18. Proposals were made at the time in Congress for the legalization of divorce, but they came to nothing.

significant innovation if it had limited itself to traditional Liberal goals such as electoral reform and diminution of the power of the Church. The López government moved on to new departures in the social and economic fields. As a beginning, the state was accorded a new role in economic life. The codification of 1936 gave the state a constitutionally guaranteed role in economic development and diversification and provided it with the legal means to protect domestic industry and consumers. It became official policy to promote economic growth through the strengthening of credit institutions, the development of Colombia's frontier regions, and a program of road construction.

A graduated income tax was made effective for the first time; and an excess profits tax was introduced, as well as a patrimony tax, that is, a tax on the total value of one's property and other holdings, aimed at those with wealth but not high incomes. The government likewise succeeded in improving tax collection procedures. The overall effect of such changes was that the tax burden was shifted somewhat from consumers to investors and from indirect to direct taxation. In the process the government's budgetary reliance on such sources of revenue as customs receipts was measurably reduced. The reforms thus obeyed both distributive and fiscal purposes.[17]

The new administration also turned its attention to labor. Article 40 of the constitutional codification declared that "labor is a social obligation, and it shall enjoy the special protection of the state," while Article 44 affirmed that "the right to strike is guaranteed except in the public services." Moreover, the López administration actively sought to improve the conditions and status of labor. A series of laws gave unions firmer guarantees in the negotiation and enforcement of labor contracts, and granted workers sick pay, paid vacations, and an eight-hour day. Under the twin umbrellas of the Liberal Republic and of the new amendments to the constitution the unionization of urban workers waxed as it never had before.

Potentially the most revolutionary tack taken by the regime of Alfonso López was the conception of property embodied in the codification of 1936. Contrary to long years of constitutional tradition, private property was no longer to be an absolute right. It was to have a social function

17. *Mensajes del Presidente López,* pp. 132, 136, 221–27; cf. also Maffitt, Part II, chapter 6, pp. 1–9.

which entailed obligations: "For reasons of public utility or social interest, as defined by the legislature, property may be expropriated by judicial decree with prior indemnification. Nevertheless, the legislature, for reasons of equity, may deny indemnification by means of an absolute majority vote of the members of both Houses" (Art. 30).

Agrarian reform, although not explicitly provided for in the constitution, found its legal foundation in these clauses. The heart of López' agrarian policy was Law 200 of 1936. The aims of the law were basically two: to clear up prevailing uncertainty about existing land ownership and titles; and to give legal application to the notion that ownership of land carried the obligation to use it productively. It was thereby hoped to bring security of tenure to squatters with uncertain titles, to improve the lot of the rural lower classes, and to reduce the number and intensity of conflicts in the countryside. The first article of the law established the principle that a presumption of ownership exists in favor of those who occupy the land and make economic use of it. Evictions of squatters already on the land was made difficult unless the owner could prove title prior to the year 1821. The other major provision of Law 200 was contained in Article 6, which stipulated that, with certain exceptions, all privately owned lands that remained uncultivated for ten consecutive years were to revert to the public domain. Thus by 1946 all privately owned lands were either to be cultivated, or expropriated and made ready for distribution to would-be settlers.[18]

Colombian education at every level felt the impress of the reforming spirit. Federal expenditures on education increased more than fourfold between 1935 and 1938,[19] although the number of schools and teachers expanded at a lesser rate. Primary education was nationalized to a significant degree by bringing many schools formerly financed and controlled at the municipal or departmental level under jurisdiction of the government at Bogotá. The constitutional revisions of 1936 made primary education obligatory. A reorganization of the National University granted it a degree of autonomy by enhancing the role of both faculty and students in its governance. A modern university city was constructed in the capital.

18. Concerning Law 200 see Hirschman, pp. 96 and 107–13; cf. also *Política Oficial: Mensajes, Cartas y Discursos del Presidente López* (5 vols. Bogotá, Imprenta Nacional, 1935–38), *1*, 67–72, and *2*, 59–60.

19. *Mensajes del Presidente López*, p. 224.

The government introduced teacher training schools; by 1938 there were nineteen. Efforts were made to modernize both curricula and educational techniques throughout the school system.

The revolution on the march contained a nationalistic strain, though López' nationalism was hardly aggressive or xenophobic. No effort was made to exclude foreign capital or to expropriate foreign properties. But the government did affirm a policy of "Colombia first for the Colombians." Some of the special privileges accorded to foreigners were to end; in such matters as taxation and employment foreigners were to be on equal footing with Colombian nationals. The government also worked toward a more effective integration of the country. Steps were taken to make the army an instrument for building communication and transport networks in remote areas. The police, formerly organized into separate departmental forces, were nationalized. Remaining tariff barriers among some of the departments were eliminated.[20]

As fundamental as some of these reforms appear in the context of the Colombia of the 1930s, closer examination casts considerable doubt on the efficacy and permanence of many of them. The attempt to eliminate fraud and to perfect democracy was partly nullified by the inability of the López administration to control the actions of Liberal party officials at the local level. The extent to which the Church's role was actually curbed is also open to question. In practice, clerical influence on textbooks and other aspects of Colombian education was hardly diminished. All schools were still required to retain religious instruction. In most respects, in fact, "the . . . period of Liberal rule did little to alter the essential position of the Church in Colombia." [21] Although the López government had established the legal foundations to permit state intervention in the economy, and in the field of labor-management relations, it often failed to make effective use of them. The potentially sweeping provisions concerning the confiscation of property were never really invoked, tax rates in the upper income brackets remained very low, while state intervention hardly amounted to state planning or any very real limitation on business or industry. Despite the new labor laws, wages remained low, many workers

20. Cf. *Mensajes del Presidente López* and *Política Oficial*, passim, concerning these aspects of López' nationalism.

21. Ben G. Burnett, "The Recent Colombian Party System: Its Organization and Procedure" (unpublished Ph.D. dissertation, University of California, Los Angeles, 1955), pp. 58–59.

were still unorganized or were exempt from the laws' protection, and unions remained dependent on a favorable political climate. Increases in the
cost of living, prompted by the coming of World War II and the strains
of industrialization, soon made most of the workers' economic gains
illusory.

Meanwhile, the article of Law 200 which envisaged the reversion to
the state of all uncultivated land after a period of ten years remained
virtually a dead letter; practically no redistribution of land took place as
a result of it. Law 200 did legalize the titles of many squatters, but this
occurred after a certain redistribution had already taken place through
unlawful invasions. It would have required a major display of force by
the government to undo these, and such action would probably have
resulted in a condition of chronic strife in the countryside. In any case,
it was previously uncultivated lands that had been invaded and occupied
in the main. The position of the large estate which was already under
cultivation was not really touched by Law 200.[22]

Despite the hopes and aims of the educational reforms, religious influences on public education remained strong, few of the traditional methods
of teaching gave way to modern, and the quantitative expansion of the
school system barely kept pace with the growing population.

Changes in other areas were similarly quite modest. The influence on
the country of foreign markets, foreign investments, and foreign technicians remained great. The integration of Colombia's rural areas and of
some of the nation's more remote departments and territories advanced
at only a slow pace. The army did not fully take to its role as modernizer.
And the attempts to create a bureaucracy in tune with the requirements
of a modern state proved limited for various reasons, including the continued virulence of the spoils system.

In most respects intentions and legislation outran their practical effects
by a considerable distance. The revolution on the march had not trans-

22. Hirschman tends to discount certain alleged adverse effects of Law 200 with respect to the expulsion of squatters, and one must agree that the claims of the critics
somewhat outrun the supporting evidence. Concerning the controversy over the effect
of Law 200, see Hirshman, pp. 108–13; Orlando Fals Borda, *Peasant Society in the
Colombian Andes: A Sociological Study of Saucío* (Gainesville, Fla., University of
Florida Press, 1955), footnote p. 66; Fals Borda, *El Hombre y la Tierra*, pp. 103–05;
and Nestor Madrid Melo, "Génesis y Ineficacia de la Reforma sobre Tierras," *Universidad Nacional de Colombia, 1*, 399–420.

formed Colombia overnight from a developing to a developed nation; it had barely begun the task. Still, the accomplishments should not be underestimated. Probably of greater importance than any specific enactment was the fact that the leaders of the state had injected into Colombia's traditional game of politics the adrenalin of conscious modernization. This Colombian New Deal helped to train a generation of politicians and administrators in the intricacies of reform; it helped to accustom some segments of the Colombian elite to the existence of new social forces and conditions which would increasingly demand solutions from government; and it helped to lay down precedents for further reform at another time.[23] For all its limitations, the revolution on the march proved the first concerted Colombian response to the implications of twentieth-century change.

THE DECLINE AND FALL OF THE LIBERAL REPUBLIC

Opposition to the López reforms within both parties was stubborn and vehement. By the time of the congressional elections of April 1937, a real and lasting internal Liberal division had developed. So serious was the opposition from his own party in the new Congress that López threatened to resign in May 1937. With the election of the moderate Liberal Eduardo Santos to the presidency in 1938 it was clear that the revolution on the march no longer would march, although neither did it retreat. Santos' administration (1932–42) was a "businessman's era." The new president shunned the reliance which López had placed on labor and on reformist intellectuals and even took Conservatives into his government.[24] In a sense the breach was between those historic or old-line Liberals to whom civil and political freedoms, administrative decentralization, laissez faire, and the Church question were still central; and the reformists, akin to the Radicals of Chile, who envisaged a larger and more positive role for the state in the economic and social spheres.

The Conservatives, too, were soon disenchanted with López. In a mani-

23. Cf. Hirschman, passim, for the importance of this consideration in effective "reformmongering."

24. See Alfonso López Michelsen, *Cuestiones Colombianas (Ensayos)* (Mexico, D.F., Impresiones Modernas, 1955), p. 232, for a somewhat different interpretation of Santos' government. Eduardo Santos, *Una Política Liberal para Colombia* (Bogotá, Editorial Minerva, 1937), is a good source for Santos' philosophy of government.

festo issued on March 17, 1936, the Conservative National Directorate
accused the Liberals of embarking on constitutional reforms which struck
at the very foundations of Colombian institutions, and of doing so in a
unilateral and partisan manner. The Church hierarchy, led by the archbishop of Bogotá, felt equally endangered and issued a protest on the
same date and in a similar tone to that of the Conservative party: "This
declaration is not a menace nor an instigation to rebellion . . . but when
the moment comes to fight for justice, neither we, nor our clergy, nor the
faithful will remain defenseless and passive." [25]

Unquestionably in the late 1930s "a new note appeared in Colombian
politics," [26] induced by growing Conservative impatience with being out
of power, by ideological influences wafting in from Europe, and by opposition from various quarters to the reforms of the revolution on the march.
Marxism, or rather what seemed like it to some among the Colombian
upper class, had entered the picture in the form of the constitutional
amendments and laws of 1936. Property and the Church were being
directly challenged, or so it appeared, and in the eyes of many Conservatives it was now Christ against Lenin. Politics began to polarize, with the
moderate Liberals, upholding nineteenth-century liberal principles, and
the moderate Conservatives, adhering to the republican traditions of their
party, caught uncertainly in the middle. Coupled with the attacks on the
reforms was disparagement by some Conservatives of rule by "the one-
half plus one," which was seen as destroying what was "right" and "best"
and established. The apparent death-throes of Western democracy in the
decade after 1936 amid the rise to world power of nations embodying the
doctrines of Fascism and Communism gave added meaning and urgency
to the battle. Some saw the possibility of a reenactment in Colombia of
the Spanish Civil War.

A great many politically aware Colombians did not, of course, see the
situation in these terms, exaggerated as they were by the ideologism in
which Colombian politics had always been couched. It was mainly that
faction of the Conservatives dominated by Laureano Gómez, and some
Liberals of the far left influenced by Marxist doctrine, who tended to view

25. *La Opinión Nacional*, p. 11.
26. Abelardo Patiño B., "The Political Ideas of the Liberal and Conservative
Parties in Colombia during the 1946–1953 Crisis" (unpublished Ph.D. dissertation,
American University, Washington, D.C., 1954), p. 52. López himself recognized that
his reforms were having this effect: cf. *Mensajes del Presidente López*, pp. 144–45.

the issues so intensely. But by the time of the elections of 1942 the Liberals had become deeply divided over the question of how far modernization should go. The Conservatives, led by Gómez and more and more susceptible to a spirit of "intrepid action," waited in the wings, not merely this time for an opportunity to regain public office or to modify slightly one or another policy, but to effect the "counterrevolution."

Reelected in 1942, López was faced from the beginning by a Congress dominated by opposition Liberals and Conservatives. Furthermore, scandals involving influence-peddling, corruption, and the private lives of López' official and personal families gave his enemies a series of openings which they exploited to the full in the press, in Congress, and on the hustings.

The president might nevertheless have lasted his full four-year term but for the impact of the economic and political currents he himself had helped to loose by the reforms of his first term. By 1942 Colombia's burgeoning economic development had witnessed the concomitant rise of a new group of industrialists who wished to preserve their gains and felt that reform had gone far enough. Since many of them depended heavily for their success on opportunities shaped by tariffs, government credit facilities, government contracts, and other instrumentalities of public assistance and control, their reliance on official policy and on the more personal favor of politicians and officials was substantial. To establish a factory was now a business, not an adventure, and it was a business that entailed the continuation of certain economic policies.[27] Although at first the interests of such groups and those of other urban elements often coincided—in the diminution of the powers of large landowners and of the Church, for instance, and in the promotion of economic growth—the time had come when it appeared impossible to sustain both the developmental and the welfare policies of the first López administration. Seeking favorable tax policies and protection from labor's demands, the industrialists now tended to side with the landowners in a common resistance to reform. Together they helped to block key parts of López' program in Congress, which was still overwhelmingly Liberal. Thus the reformist impetus of the Liberal party was forced to capitulate before those within the party who opposed further change.

27. Luis Ospina Vásquez, *Industria y Protección en Colombia 1810–1930* (Medellín, 1955), p. 411.

Then, too, the attitude of the government itself had altered. Inflationary and supply difficulties caused by industrialization and the Second World War had impelled the government to concentrate on increasing production by every possible means. The administration had also become incrusted with political and economic vested interests that preferred to gather the fruits available through the manipulation of import licenses, exchange controls, and the confiscation of German properties rather than to embark on further unsettling reforms. In any case, the second López administration felt that the time had come to put the brakes on the demands of workers for increased social benefits. The same approach characterized the regime's agrarian policy. The principal legislation of the period, Law 100 of 1944, evidenced the government's intention of enlisting the collaboration of the landowners instead of coercing them by threats, again with the presumed goal of increasing production. This new law extended for another five years the period of compliance with that part of Law 200 of 1936 regarding uncultivated lands. It also forbade the planting of trees or other perennials by a tenant or sharecropper without the explicit permission of the landlord. The hope was to encourage the contracting of tenants and sharecroppers by easing the landowners' suspicions that their residency might later be turned to claims of permanent rights to the land.[28]

The government's new attitude was characterized as "treason to leftist ideas" by some Liberals; others on the Left, not necessarily Liberals, depicted López as an "unscrupulous demagogue who deceived the revolutionary hopes of the people!" [29] Many of those who had supported López in the past had expected the resumption of the revolution on the march after the hiatus of the Santos presidency. To the discontent caused by the halt in the "revolution" were added the inflation and economic dislocation of the early forties. In fact, some of the very policies of development, such as credit expansion, helped to aggravate inflation and hence the income inequalities and balance of payments problems that such policies had been designed to remedy.

At last, opposed from both Right and Left within his own party, and subjected to continuing virulent attacks by the Conservatives, López resigned in August 1945 in favor of the *designado,* Alberto Lleras Cam-

28. Concerning Law 100 of 1944 see Hirschman, pp. 114–15.
29. A. García, *Gaitán,* p. 230.

argo.[30] López apparently hoped that such a move would mollify the contending spirits and enable his own party to consolidate its forces and seek bases of mutual tolerance with the Conservatives.[31] Though a long-time associate of López, Lleras was in no way tarred with the brush of scandal. He proceeded to form a government of National Union by taking three Conservatives into his Cabinet, despite the fact that the Conservative National Directorate disavowed its members' participation.

Lleras made a further effort to quench the flames of partisanship and political turmoil by pledging his government's neutrality in the presidential election of 1946. The Liberal convention nominated Gabriel Turbay, but Gaitán, declaring—correctly—that the convention was unrepresentative, launched his own candidacy. Gaitán was confident that his popularity among both the Liberal and Conservative masses would lead him to victory over Liberal and Conservative "oligarchs" alike.[32] However, when the returns were in, Mariano Ospina Pérez, the Conservative candidate, had some 565,849 votes, Turbay 441,199, and Gaitán 358,957.[33]

The rivalries among the party's ambitious politicians contributed to the Liberal debacle. But in the last analysis the defeat was born with the reforms of 1936, which some Liberals could never fully accept and which many Conservatives regarded as an assault on the Colombian social order. The political tensions thus engendered, and the additional stresses created by inflation and by the unrest of groups who in the second López administration wanted to march again with their "revolution," led in 1946 to the dethronement of the Liberals.

Nonetheless, Lleras' National Union, which was at the outset continued in expanded form by his Conservative successor, plus the transfer of power between the parties in 1946 (the second peaceful one in less than

30. The *designado*, or designate, acts in lieu of a vice-president in the Colombian governmental system. Chosen every two years by the Congress, he may fill any other position, public or private, during his tenure. His only duty as designado is to fill the office of president should it fall vacant.

31. In a speech on May 4, 1959, the former president averred that his resignation had signaled a surrender to reaction and had been a mistake; *El Tiempo,* Nov. 21, 1959.

32. See Alberto Niño H., *Antecedentes Secretos del 9 de Abril* (Bogotá, Editorial Pax, 1949 [?], pp. 2–3.

33. *Revista de la Controlaría de la República,* Separato de Anales de Economía y Estadística. Supplement to Nos. 17 and 18 (Bogotá, May–June 1946). This publication contains data on the 1946 presidential election.

two decades), seemed at the time sufficient to contain the mounting waves of social unrest on the one hand, and counterrevolution on the other. Imperceptibly the country was slipping into a state of chronic political and social crisis. Yet it was still not clear that, as President López had phrased it, Colombians were "living the last days of a political Arcadia." [34]

Looking back, it seems clear that the first López administration was an effort to meet the challenge posed by a set of economic, social, and political conditions new to Colombia. By the time of López' resignation in 1945 it had become quite evident that the response to the challenge had proven not only inadequate in itself, but also unable to overcome the strong reaction against the attempted incursion on old or newly won prerogatives. Under the impact of the conflicting forces traditional political passions experienced a revival of a kind unknown for several decades, and the political forms and procedures which had given Colombia her vaunted era of peace and stability showed signs of increasing strain.

Several points stand out clearly in an assessment of the era of the Liberal Republic that began in 1934 and came to its end in 1946 with the election of the Conservative Mariano Ospina Pérez to the presidency.

The first is that the Liberal Republic, even in its halcyon early years, was not an era of revolution. Despite the designation that was sometimes given it of the revolution on the march, the Liberal Republic did not attempt to destroy an old order and to erect a new one on its ashes. Real, though limited, change did take place as the result of governmental initiative. Non-elite groups such as urban labor and the colonos did improve their material lot, at least temporarily, as well as their security of status. Yet even such reforms did relatively little in practice to grant new groups a real share of economic, social, or political power. Palliative rather than genuine reform—certainly not revolution—may thus be the more accurate description of the Liberal programs of the period.

The period of the Liberal Republic meanwhile saw the beginnings of a movement of vast proportions in the bedrock of Colombian politics. The ground was shifting underneath, even though the surface features—in the form of the traditional parties—retained much of their original form and appearance. In the past the contest between the parties had taken place within the Colombian elite over the spoils of office, or over such

34. *Semana*, No. 677, p. 29.

issues as the status of the Church and centralism versus federalism. Now it was no longer possible to disregard the interests of the urban and rural masses. They were beginning, even though hesitantly and often ineffectually, to enter political life. Colombia's politics was showing the first indications of shifting its axis from one of intra-elite competition to one founded on antagonisms among social classes.

Perhaps the salient aspect of the first self-conscious response of the Colombian polity to the challenge of the twentieth century was that the pressures and initiatives for reform came fundamentally from within the Colombian elite itself. There were signs, in the form of labor and agrarian unrest, that the excluded Colombian majority was beginning to awake from centuries of political apathy. Yet there was little direct, articulate political pressure on López and his associates to carry out the program of 1934–38. A number of the younger and more far-seeing in the Liberal party, some of middle-class origin but for the most part sons of the Colombian upper class, instead took it upon themselves to modernize their country while simultaneously building a more secure base for continued Liberal political domination. It was a case of initiative taken at the top, rather than a response to any overriding mass demand for action.

Furthermore, with the possible exception of that part of Law 200 of 1936 which legalized what had in any case been accomplished de facto by the colonos, the López reforms did not essentially endanger the superior position of the Colombian elite. Indeed it might well be argued that the elite acquiesced in the reforms precisely because this seemed the best way of heading off any real frontal attack on its position, or even any real sharing of its power with other groups. As long as the elite continued to control the principal levers of social, economic, and political power, it could make certain concessions to change. Of course, the Colombian elite was by no means a monolith; some among it stood to benefit from certain of the policies of the revolution on the march. Yet it was clear even before the end of López' first administration that the thrust of change was being quite effectively parried by resistance from within the Liberal party itself and from some of the very groups that had initially benefited from reform.

The very process of containing and bringing to a virtual halt the revolution on the march points up the difficulties inherent in reform from above. Since the extent and continuation of reform depend on the continued good will of those who may at some point see further change as destructive of their own interests, change is likely to be limited. The issue will then confront the political system of whether reform has been sufficient to damp down a potential social explosion, or whether the resistances and the hopes that it has engendered have not on the contrary created new problems with which the polity may be unable to cope.

The López reforms brought just such problems in their wake. The measures were enacted by a Congress and by an administration homogeneously Liberal, and many Conservatives looked upon them as laying waste the foundations of Colombian institutions. The procedural and substantive consensuses that had prevailed since the turn of the century were thereby broken. Several of the principal assumptions on which the forty-five year peace had been founded were shattered: namely, that both parties were to be represented in government and were to agree to any major constitutional changes; that the Conservative party would be the dominant political force, with the Liberals guaranteed a role, but a minority one; and that the social and economic status quo was to be maintained. Above all, the Liberals had fostered the organized articulation of popular demands, and encouraged the expectation of their satisfaction, without having the will or the political strength to confront fully the implications.

5

REFORM, REACTION, AND
MILITARY RULE

JORGE ELIÉCER GAITÁN: CHARISMATIC REFORMER

The disintegration of the Liberal Republic during the second López
administration and its fall in 1946 brought with them an increasing polarization of Colombian politics, despite the fact that the new Conservative
president continued and expanded the National Union inaugurated by the
Liberal Lleras. From the Right, there were accusations that the incumbent Congress had been fraudulently elected and that the Conservatives
had been deprived of their rightful majority by the machinations of the
Liberal administration. For their part, the Liberals continued to regard
themselves as the true majority in the country, only temporarily deprived
of the presidency by an unfortunate split in their own party. "The Liberals refused to admit they had lost anything, while the Conservatives
would not admit they had not won everything." [1]

Yet there were more than the traditional partisan antagonisms involved.
The Conservatives, or at least some Conservatives, under Laureano
Gómez—first as party leader and after 1950 as president of the nation—
were moving increasingly in the direction of a quasi-authoritarian attempt
to freeze the social order under a Conservative hegemony with corporatist
overtones. A segment of the Liberal party meanwhile looked to Gaitán,
the candidate who had run third in the presidential race of 1946, to advance the cause of reform (some of his supporters hoped it would be
genuine revolution) by means of a direct appeal to the lower and middle
classes.

1. Former President Rafael Urdaneta Arbeláez, quoted in Azula Barrera, *De la
Revolución,* p. 277.

Gaitán was no ordinary Liberal leader; nor did his movement originate
within the elite as had that of López.[2] Gaitán's route to political prominence had been somewhat exceptional. For although he had obtained a
university education and had become a well known lawyer, he derived
neither from the aristocracy of land and abolengo nor from that of money.
His social station and physical characteristics marked him as an intruder
in realms usually reserved for the better born. That he could reach the
top rung of the Liberal party was an indication of fluidity in that party's
pattern of leadership recruitment. Yet both traditional parties had always
been fairly effective at cooptation of individual non-elite elements into at
least the lower reaches of their party hierarchies. Gaitán's attainment of
high political position, an isolated occurrence, would hardly of itself have
disturbed the moorings of Colombian political life.

What is truly significant about the rise of Gaitán was that to date he
has been the only Colombian to have attained major political stature by
challenging the position of the elite and appealing to the Colombian
masses. Hence his actions threatened to erode the tacitly understood
boundaries of Colombian political contention and indeed to destroy the
whole framework of that "Athenian democracy" within whose limits
Colombian politics had theretofore been conducted.

It was only in the biennium preceding the fateful election of 1946, and
with the beginning of his campaign of outspoken opposition to a president
of his own party, that Gaitán came fully into his own. He had been
among those Liberals who had opposed the reelection of Alfonso López
in 1942. Now, in a political atmosphere poisoned and embittered by apparent corruption in the administration, by the increasingly vitriolic oppo-

2. The sources for the following discussion of Gaitán and his ideology are primarily
Jorge Eliécer Gaitán, *Las Mejores Oraciones de Jorge Eliécer Gaitán 1919–1948*
(Bogotá, Editorial Jorvi, 1958); A. García, *Gaitán;* Azula Barrera, *De la Revolucion,*
esp. pp. 54–65 and 257–62; *Colección Jorge Eliécer Gaitán—Documentos para una
Biografía, 1* (Bogotá, Concejo Municipal de Bogotá; 1949); Jorge Eliécer Gaitán, *Las
Ideas Socialistas en Colombia* (Bogotá, Editorial América Libre, 1963); Antolín Díaz,
A la Sombra de Fouché; Pequeño Proceso de las Izquierdas en Colombia (Bogotá,
Editorial ABC, 1937), pp. 64–68; *La Nueva Prensa,* Nos. 95 and 132; Fluharty, *Dance
of the Millions,* passim; Niño H., *Antecedentes Secretos,* passim; José María Córdoba,
Jorge Eliécer Gaitán, Tribuno Popular de Colombia (Bogotá, 196?); and J. A. Osorio
Lizarazo, *Gaitán: Vida, Muerte y Permanente Presencia* (Buenos Aires, Ediciones
López Negri, 1952). Surprisingly enough for such a controversial figure, there is a
rather wide area of agreement among those of differing political persuasions concerning the character and political role of Gaitán.

sition of the Conservatives, by the disappointment of those who sought once more to march with a López "revolution," and by the social dislocations prompted by economic development and World War II, Gaitán launched his attack.

It was a campaign that for the first time in Colombian history sought to pit the masses against the so-called oligarchy, which in Gaitán's view was composed of both Liberals and Conservatives. Gaitán depicted the oligarchy as divided into three distinct organs: the brain, which controlled the others and was made up of the powerful and the rich; the voice, which received and communicated orders and was composed of "men of intelligence who have souls of secretaries"; and the arms, which carried out orders and were represented by the political bosses in the village, the city district, or the regional political committee.[3] Gaitán was fond of distinguishing between this "political country" and the "country" of real national concerns: "In Colombia there are two countries: the political country which is concerned with its jobs . . . and its power, and the national country which thinks about its work, its health, its education, things which are neglected by the political country. The political country follows a different course from that of the national country. What a tremendous drama in the history of a people!"[4] His battlecry was "For the democratic and moral restoration of the Republic. *A la carga!* (to the attack!)."

Gaitán's appeal was frankly charismatic: the "tribune of the people" employing his assets as an orator and as a man of humble origin. Many have commented on the impassioned speeches—the gestures, the voice, the cadence. "He began to speak in a low voice, almost inaudible, and slowly became transfigured as the Liberator in battle, and from his throat came the roaring voice of the people, with apocalyptic accents and thundering imprecations; and the burning passion of his imagination cast over the audience brilliant shafts of eloquence, flames of passion which fired the multitudes into a sublime frenzy."[5]

Denunciation of the oligarchy, and a messianic identification with the masses ("I am not a man, I am a people") were twin aspects of Gaitán's

3. Gaitán, *Las Mejores Oraciones,* pp. 361 and 370–71. Cf. also Osorio, *Vida,* pp. 245–46.

4. Gaitán, *Las Mejores Oraciones,* p. 370.

5. Milton Puentes, *Historia del Partido Liberal* (2nd ed. Editorial Prag, 1961), p. 615.

appeal. The third and probably the least in importance was the program which he offered to better the lot of those who would follow him. His strength did not lie in the elaboration of an ideology or a concrete program and it would be a mistake to try to read into either an undue coherence or specificity. For the most part, the changes he advocated were moderate. "We are not enemies of wealth," he said, "but of poverty." [6] The stress was less on the wholesale redistribution of wealth or on a reordering of the structure of social power than on such things as increased educational opportunities, programs to improve the health of the Colombian people, measures to increase the role of the state in the development of the economy, the elaboration of administrative machinery to promote economic development, an improved tax system which would penalize speculation and unproductive wealth, electoral reform to ensure a more democratic suffrage, the granting of titles to squatters on lands not otherwise cultivated and the extension of social benefits to those working cultivated lands, defense of the rights of labor, limited profit-sharing, and the nationalization of electric, water, and telephone services. It was a program of reform, not of revolution, despite the aggressive language Gaitán sometimes employed on the hustings. [7]

The Gaitanista program was nationalistic, with elements of non-Marxian socialism, and there was considerable affinity to the approach of the Peruvian Apristas. Yet it was likewise infused with much of the traditional Liberal spirit, even while Gaitán vaguely talked of the supersession of the historic parties by a union of the masses of them both. In the last analysis, Gaitán's philosophy was informed by no consistent ideology; it was a composite of many strands. "The ideology of Gaitán was confused. Trained in Fascist Italy, it was difficult to establish, in Gaitán, where the sympathizer of Mussolini ended, the Liberal chief began, and the leftist leader had its roots." [8]

Undoubtedly some of Gaitán's popularity in the years subsequent to his electoral defeat was not primarily a matter of class but constituted the emotional support of the Liberal rank-and-file in the face of the fall of

6. Cf. José Gutiérrez, *La Rebeldía Colombiana* (Bogotá, Ediciones Tercer Mundo, 1962), p. 70.

7. *La Nueva Prensa,* No. 132, contains the 1947 Platform and other documentary materials on the Gaitanista program.

8. Raúl Andrade, *La Internacional Negra en Colombia y Otros Ensayos* (Quito, Editora Quito, 1954), p. 47.

their party from power. Still, it seems evident that much of his following did represent the awakening of a class feeling, at least in the negative sense of feelings of hatred directed against the elite. In the election of 1946 Gaitán ran best in the departments along the Atlantic coast and in Cundinamarca, in which Bogotá is located. In the country as a whole, he did somewhat better in urban than in rural areas.[9] To the extent that we can identify Gaitán's supporters, they seem to have come disproportionately from the urban lower classes and from the lower middle class from which he himself had sprung.

Many of the members of his own party, as well as the Conservatives, opposed Gaitán's program of reform. Yet it was less his proposals for legislative or administrative action which aroused their fears than the sources of his strength and the manner in which he couched his appeals. Not the other party primarily but the oligarchy was the target; not the elite and their minions but the masses were the foundations of his support.

The other Liberal candidate in the presidential election of 1946 had been Gabriel Turbay, who was identified with the Liberal elite even though some of its members referred to him derisively as a *turco* (denoting that one branch of his family was of Near Eastern origin). After the election Turbay left for Europe, where he shortly died. The Liberal leadership thereupon devolved on Gaitán, who had amassed some forty-five per cent of the Liberal vote in 1946 despite the fact that he had lacked the support of the official party organization. Clearly, he had become the hero of the Liberal rank-and-file. Just as clearly, it would ensure Liberal defeat in future elections if the party continued to reject him.

The pressures on Gaitán in his unaccustomed role as both chief of the Liberal party and hero of the Colombian masses were intense. The refusal of the Liberal majority in Congress to pass the program of legislation proposed by its own leader caused resentment among his followers against the whole pattern of politics as it was. Amid an atmosphere of increasing social and political tension, Gaitán was shot down by an assassin on April 9, 1948. There immediately followed mass riots in downtown Bogotá (hence their subsequent designation as the *bogotazo*) which destroyed many public and ecclesiastical buildings and resulted in several thousand

9. See *Revista de la Contraloría,* Separato, supplement to Nos. 17 and 18.

deaths. Accusations as to the authorship of the assassination and the instigation of the riots that followed have been laid at the door of almost every conceivable domestic and international source. What evidence there is suggests that the murder was the work of a demented individual with a personal resentment against Gaitán and that the riots—although various leftist political groups and leaders attempted unsuccessfully to direct them toward the overthrow of the government—were in the main a spontaneous reaction by avenging mobs.[10]

Some have called the bogotazo a social revolution. But even had the government of President Mariano Ospina Pérez been toppled, it is unlikely that it would have meant more than the usual change of the party in power, followed probably by all-out civil war as the Conservatives reacted to their loss. Any prospect that the riots would turn into real revolution was eliminated by the poor organization of the forces of the Left, by the strength among the urban masses of traditional ties to the elite-dominated Liberal party, by the attitude of the Conservative-dominated army, and by the cool-headedness of the president, who stood his ground throughout.

Rather than a planned attempt at revolution, the bogotazo "was the earthquake of a people moved by the assassination of their own voice." [11] The extent of the pillage and the fury of the mob is in part explicable by Gaitán's preaching of hatred for the oligarchs, that is, as an "atavistic rebellion of castes." [12] The riots were a severe jolt to the forms and traditions of Colombia's vaunted democracy. From April 1948 forward Colombia's elite would have the memory of this brief, sudden upsurge of the people's frustration with their condition. Ironically, by making the reactive strengthening of authority seem indispensable to the continuity of

10. Accounts of the bogotazo and analyses of its implications and the responsibility for it may be found in Niño H., passim; Azula Barrera, pp. xix–xxiii and 303–465; Andrade, *La Internacional Negra*, pp. 47–98; Enrique Cuéllar Vargas, *13 Años de Violencia* (Bogotá, Editorial SIPA, 1960), pp. 15–78; Fluharty, pp. 84–107; Carlos Lleras Restrepo, *De la República a la Dictadura* (Bogotá, Editorial ARGRA, 1955), pp. 241–49; López Michelsen, *Cuestiones Colombianas*, pp. 20–23, 33, 47, 93–95, 273, 289, 349–51; John D. Martz, *Colombia, A Contemporary Political Survey* (Chapel Hill, N.C., University of North Carolina Press, 1962), chapter 4; Nieto Rojas, *La Batalla contra el Comunismo*, chapters 7–8; Osorio, pp. 279–317; and Julio Enrique Santos Forero, *Yo Sí Ví Huir al Verdadero Asesino de Jorge Eliécer Gaitán* (Bogotá, Gráficas Atenas, 1959).

11. A. García, *Gaitán*, p. 19.

12. Gutiérrez, *Rebeldía Colombiana*, p. 71.

social life, the bogotazo contributed to at least the short-run reinforcement of elite rule.[13]

THE LEGACY OF GAITÁN

Colombia was closer to a prerevolutionary situation in the years 1946–48 than it ever had been before or than it has been since. It was during this period that agitation for change was at its peak and that the Colombian Left both found and lost its principal champion.

Gaitán's death in April 1948 of course makes it impossible to know whether he would have been elected president in 1950 or, perhaps more to the point, permitted by the Conservatives (quite possibly allied with some Liberals) to run in the first place, and to take office if he had won. It may be that a fear of mass revolt would have prevented such interference; yet the events of subsequent years make it seem unlikely that Gaitán, had he lived, would ever have been allowed to assume the presidency.

The events of April's "black Friday" prevent any sure knowledge of what Gaitán's policies would have been even had he reached the pinnacle. Some things, however, are reasonably clear. One was the difficulty he had in reconciling his leadership of the Liberal party, which was still dominated in the main by the elite groups that had always controlled it, with his leadership of the Colombian masses in their quest for social and political justice. His brief tenure as mayor of Bogotá further suggests that in office he might well act differently toward strikes and other mass actions than he did in opposition. Moreover, it seems that Gaitán had more than one opportunity to take part in a plot to overthrow the Ospina government and that he refused. The "revolutionary" of the hustings became the republican legalist when faced with the responsibility for revolutionary action. Gaitán's shifting back and forth over the years between cooperation with Liberal governments and with the official party organization on the one hand, and opposition to them on the other, suggests opportunism. Finally, Gaitán's talents—and they were great—did not, to all appearances, lie in the executive and administrative arts. Given such factors, it seems exceedingly doubtful that the presidency, had Gaitán attained it,

13. José Gutiérrez, *La No-Violencia en la Transformación Colombiana* (Bogotá, Ediciones Tercer Mundo, 1964), p. 38.

would have proven to be other than a Pyrrhic victory, either for himself as a political leader or for the cause of the Colombian Left.

Gaitán's importance does not rest, however, with such might-have-beens. For he was the only leader of national stature who in the years after 1942 carried the torch of social consciousness and who saw—in an instinctive as much as in a rational way—that the traditional parties and the elites who dominated them must bend to the forces of change.

"Populist" may ultimately be the best designation for him, in that he sought, through direct identification with the people, to express their resentment against the privileged who governed Colombia and their hopes for a greater measure of social, economic, and political democracy. As such he short-circuited the traditional avenues for the expression of political demands through the machinery of the traditional parties. As a matter of fact, it might be said that he evoked such demands for the first time. He also called into question the recruitment of the nation's political leadership from the ranks of cultivated aristocrats and the latter's tendency to deprecate the national and the autochthonous.[14] In such respects, more than in any specific proposals for reforms, Gaitanismo represented for Colombia a unique political response to change.

Gaitán had succeeded in stirring the masses without providing them with any channel for the expression of the emotions he had quickened other than through identification with his person. He might have done so had he had more time, and it may have been his goal to accomplish this by remaking the Liberal party in his image. In the light of his experience as party leader in 1947–48, prospects for the success of such an undertaking would seem to have been dubious. Gaitanismo also failed to establish an enduring mass base in the labor movement. In all, no strong Gaitanista organization survived his death. Gaitán had helped to undermine the old order but was not to have a full opportunity to demonstrate whether he could build as well. He was proof of Max Weber's dictum that, "In traditionally stereotyped periods, charisma is the greatest revolutionary force," as well as of the difficulty of translating such a force into something which outlasts the person of the leader.[15]

14. See Gutiérrez, *La Pseudo-Aristocracia*, pp. 39–40.
15. Talcott Parsons, ed., *Max Weber: The Theory of Social and Economic Organization*, trans. A. M. Henderson and Talcott Parsons (New York, The Free Press of Glencoe, 1964), pp. 333–34.

What survives is a name and a mystique, which continue to be invoked on suitable occasions by Liberal leaders, including many who were Gaitán's opponents while he was alive, and by virtually all parties and factions on the Colombian political Left. What survives, too, is the memory of the bogotazo, that great anomic explosion which expressed the fury of the people at the loss of their idol. Part republican legalist, part populistic demagogue; at times verbally revolutionary, at heart a reformer and moralizer; Gaitán offered what to date has remained the most direct challenge to the continued rule of the Colombian elite. "Had he lived," as John Martz has adjudged, "the bloodshed and heartache of the following decade might have been avoided or at least lessened." [16]

Possibly. But what to this writer stands out in the long sweep of Colombia's political development is less Gaitán's achievement, or any probable achievement had his assassination not taken place, than the reasons for his ultimate failure. One cause was his own inability to translate charisma into a mass-based political movement which could survive him. But above all, the collapse of Gaitanismo was mute evidence of the continued strength of the Colombian elite, and of its control of the two traditional parties. In the end, Gaitán's failure may have lain less in his own inadequacies than in the overpowering challenge that he faced: the strength and resilience of the traditional institutions of Colombian society and politics. Gaitán had, in a way, come too early. He may yet prove to be the precursor of a Colombian social revolution (one Colombian has indeed compared April 1948 to the Russian 1905),[17] but he was not to be its embodiment. The bogotazo, and the political reaction to it, were to produce not revolution but counterrevolution: an attempt to delay change through the invocation of traditional Hispanic values and the importation of some of the political devices of European corporatisms.

THE CONSERVATIVE COUNTERREVOLUTION

The electoral triumph of the Conservative Mariano Ospina Pérez in 1946 was not merely a minority victory over the two candidates put up by a divided governing party, as Olaya Herrera's victory had been in 1930. For the alternation of the parties in 1930 carried forward and was

16. Martz, *Colombia*, p. 44.
17. Gutiérrez, *La Rebeldía*, p. 61.

expressive of new forces and trends in Colombian society. In 1946 Conservative victory signified an attempt to clamp the lid on change, and indeed to reverse advances made by such groups as urban labor. To many Liberals the subsequent collaboration of their party with Ospina in a government of National Union appeared to mean an end to Liberal militancy; it looked like a coalition between the parties to squelch popular aspirations.

There was a second difference between 1946 and 1930. When the Liberal majority of 1946 was confirmed by the congressional elections of 1947 and 1949, both held under conditions of Conservative control of the central government, it became clear to most Conservatives—although it was still not always publicly admitted—that they were a *permanent* minority in the country. They would therefore surely lose the presidency in 1950, and with it their control of governmental posts at all levels, the more so since the Liberals had apparently taken their defeat to heart and unified their previously serried ranks. Besides, Gaitán, the prospective Liberal candidate, was a popular hero, even among some Conservatives. How could he be defeated in a free election?

Lastly, Gaitán's elevation to the leadership of the Liberal party confirmed the worst fears of some Conservatives that the Liberal party was at bottom "red," "radical," in the hands of "Communists."

The final rupture of the National Union inaugurated in 1946 by the Liberal Lleras occurred in May 1949, amid mounting rural violence between Liberals and Conservatives. The coalition collapsed partly because it was never envisaged by President Ospina as a coalition of equal partners, but rather as a Conservative government with Liberal cooperation. It failed, too, because of the fundamental antagonism between the parties, because of forces within both that preferred either total opposition or hegemony to collaboration with the partisan enemy. For the Liberals, those forces tended to be the Gaitanistas; for the Conservatives, Colombia's "radical Right," led by Laureano Gómez, the man who since the early 1930s had been the party's principal caudillo.

Although another Conservative had in 1946 become president of Colombia, it had long been true that "to the average Colombian, Laureano Gómez, wealthy, impressive, intensely Catholic, cultured, implacably reactionary, [was] the Conservative Party." [18] Gómez seemed

18. Russell H. Fitzgibbon, "Colombian Gadfly," *The Inter-American,* 4 (1945), 15.

born for opposition, often assuming the role of critic of Conservative presidents in the pre-1930 period, and later becoming the scourge of Liberal administrations. He was known for his iron rule of his party, his skill in parliamentary in-fighting, his oratorical ability, and his vitriolic denunciations of opponents. "Heresy," whether within or outside his own party, seemed to obsess him. He became "the sincere counter-revolutionary Inquisitor who would be capable, in defense of his orthodoxy, of condemning Christ to the scaffold." [19] Amid the political and moral degeneration of Colombian life he saw himself in the role of purifying knight.

By 1937 Gómez was clearly coming under the influence of Spanish Falangism: "Spain, marching forward as the sole defender of Christian civilization, leads the Western nations in the reconstruction of the empire of *Hispanidad,* and we inscribe our names in the roster of its phalanxes with unutterable satisfaction." [20] Gómez came to view majority voting and universal suffrage contemptuously as the rule of "the one-half plus one." Authority, order, hierarchy were instead the principles on which a government should be founded. To Gómez the era of the Spanish colony was the golden age; Franco's Spain its proximate modern embodiment. Hispanic values were to be honored and fostered in contradistinction to imported Anglo-Saxon ones. The Church was to be the foundation stone of such a society, with close ties to the state.

It would be a mistake to view Gómez as a Fascist, however, despite some of his vocabulary and some of his methods. What Gómez offered was a curious blend of traditional Conservative republicanism (in the retention of parliamentary forms, for example) and modern European corporatism. Although his wing of the Conservative party did have some middle-class suport, it did not primarily represent the reaction of small businessmen, artisans, and independent professionals to the growth of big business and big labor, as did European fascism. Gómez' adherents tended rather to come from the traditionalist elements in Colombian society, including the campesinos and the clergy, and, initially at least, from the Colombian elite. Gómez' object was to change political institutions in order to conserve traditionalist values and the extant social structure, while at the same time promoting economic development. He

19. A. García, *Gaitán,* p. 230.
20. Quoted in Germán Arciniegas, *The State of Latin America,* trans. Harriet de Onís (New York, Alfred A. Knopf, 1952), p. 163.

was therefore closer to the Austrian Dollfuss, to Portugal's Salazar, and to Spain's Generalissimo Franco than to Hitler or Mussolini, although even at that he never wholly succeeded in translating his philosophy into institutional practice.[21]

Amid mounting rural violence, and the attempts of Liberals in Congress to investigate the conduct of the president, Ospina Pérez imposed a state of siege and closed Congress on November 9, 1949. The Liberals meanwhile announced their intention of abstaining from the presidential elections scheduled for November 27, charging that they lacked guarantees for their partisans and that a free election was impossible. As a consequence Laureano Gómez was elected without a contest for the 1950–54 presidential term.

Not only Conservatives, but some Liberals as well, looked on Gómez as the strong arm that might put an end to the violence between Liberal guerrilla bands and Conservative police and civilians that now amounted to virtual civil war in the countryside.[22] Perhaps Gómez could guarantee the status quo against another eruption such as the one experienced in 1948, even at the cost of public liberties. Many in the Church hierarchy looked on the accession of Gómez as a prospective contribution to rural peace and national unity. They also looked forward to a continuation and a strengthening of Ospina's favorable policies toward the Church.

Meanwhile, business flourished and the country took some important strides toward sustained economic development as the consequence of government action. Expanding export markets for coffee, Colombia's principal cash crop, provided a major stimulus for such advances. So did an end to some of the war-stimulated economic dislocations and controls. Austerity measures helped to improve the government's fiscal position. Foreign investment was encouraged by such means as decrees permitting both the free importation of capital in either currency or equipment and

21. Cf. on this point Lipset, *Political Man,* chapter 4. For characterizations and interpretations of Gómez and his doctrines see Arciniegas, *State of Latin America,* pp. 160–64 and 190–91; Azula Barrera, pp. 31–34; Ernesto Bedoya Cardona, ed., *De Desterrado a Presidente* (Medellín, Tipografía Estile, 1950); Fitzgibbon, "Colombian Gadfly"; Fluharty, pp. 49–51 and 61–64; A. García, *Gaitán,* pp. 301–03; Martz, passim; and Felipe A. Molina, *Laureano Gómez, Historia de una Rebeldía* (Bogotá, Librería Voluntad, 1940). See also the various writings and speeches of Gómez himself, including *El Cuadrilátero* (Bogotá, Editorial Centro, 1935, *Comentarios a un Régimen* (Bogotá, Editorial Minerva, 1934), and Gómez' paper, *El Siglo.*
22. See below, chapter 13, for a full discussion of the violence.

its re-exportation at any time. The government also acted to implement certain parts of the report on economic development drawn up by an international mission headed by Lauchlin Currie during the Ospina years, and loans for various developmental projects were obtained from the International Bank for Reconstruction and Development and the Export-Import Bank.[23] Despite the rural violence and other political difficulties, the annual rate of economic growth (gross domestic product) was a reasonably high 3.1 in 1951, 6.3 in 1952 and 6.1 in 1953.[24]

At the same time, the regime moved further toward the authoritarian hegemony of the Conservative party. Censorship was tightened. A number of the departmental authorities previously chosen by departmental assemblies were to be chosen by the presidentially appointed governors; similarly, certain posts previously filled by municipal councils were now to be dependent on appointment by the mayors, who under the constitution were themselves chosen by the departmental governors. The effect was to bypass Liberal majorities in many departmental assemblies and municipal councils and to strengthen the central government's, and with it the Conservative party's, control of the nation. Gómez likewise seized upon a constitutional loophole to manipulate the position of designado. In November 1951 he was able to place his own choice, Roberto Urdaneta Arbeláez, in the office. Immediately thereafter, with Gómez ill, Urdaneta assumed the presidential duties for most of the remainder of Gómez' term.

The Gómez-Urdaneta regime also carried further the labor policies of the Ospina administration. Legal and administrative weapons were used to weaken the Confederation of Colombian Workers (*Confederación de Trabajadores de Colombia*—CTC) and to promote its rival, the Union of Colombian Workers (*Unión de Trabajadores de Colombia*—UTC), which had been founded in 1946 under Jesuit auspices. The law prohibiting the formation of parallel unions within given plants or industries was repealed, thus opening the way for the fragmentation of labor's strength and encouraging the creation by employers of docile company unions. A number of union leaders were blacklisted, and the police were sometimes used to break up union meetings. There was some extension of social security and other benefits, but generally speaking the restraint of labor

23. See Martz, pp. 111–15 for further details.
24. See *Cuentas Nacionales* for the respective years.

or other lower-class demands and the promotion of economic growth was the philosophy of the Conservative governments of this period.

Gómez, acting through his alter ego Urdaneta, also moved to provide Colombia with the legal basis for the kind of state he envisaged and to expurgate from Colombia's basic law certain of the amendments of 1936. The reform was to be approved by a National Constituent Assembly (ANAC) composed of persons elected by Congress, the president, and by various corporate groups. The office of the presidency was to be considerably strengthened by extending the president's term to six years, by granting him decree powers in case of economic crisis, and by eliminating Congress' impeachment powers. Both the Senate and the departmental assemblies were to be elected indirectly, with the Senate chosen in part by departmental electoral colleges and in part functionally. The qualifications for senator were to be tightened. Other proposals would subject the "spoken press" to a new form of censorship; eliminate the clause of the 1936 codification that permitted the Congress to bypass the requirement of prior indemnity for expropriated property by majority vote of both houses; stipulate that arbitration procedures be exhausted before the right to strike was exercised; and require public education to be directed in accordance with the Catholic religion. The final decision on these changes, however, was to be up to the ANAC, whose convocation was several times postponed.[25]

Gómez' real difficulties in the presidency lay as much with members of his own party as with the Liberals. He and Ospina had had their differences certainly as early as 1948. Ospina was at heart a republican and his ambitions to return to the presidency in 1954 did not fit with Gómez' plans for the construction of a Colombia along semi-Falangist lines. In addition, a large percentage of the members of the Congress elected in 1951 were followers of Gilberto Alzate Avendaño, a right-wing Conservative perhaps even closer to Falangism than Gómez and ambitious for party and national leadership. The *Alzatistas* caused considerable difficulty to the government forces in Congress, which were led by Alvaro Gómez Hurtado, Laureano's son.

25. For the text of the proposed reform see República de Colombia, Ministerio de Gobierno, *Estudios Constitucionales* (2 vols. Bogotá, Imprenta Nacional, 1953), 2, 391–429. Concerning the reform see also Laureano Gómez, *Los Efectos de la Reforma de 1953* (Bogotá, Imprenta Nacional, 1953); and Martz, pp. 150–54.

There seems also to have been a growing feeling on the part of those among the Colombian elite who had previously supported Gómez that his methods were not adequate to put down the civil strife and that as a result the economy of the nation would eventually be damaged. Attacks condoned by the authorities on the homes of López and Carlos Lleras Restrepo, fellow members of the upper class although Liberals, helped to crystallize this sentiment. Such actions broke the tacit rules of the game that the violence was not to strike directly at members of the elite and was to be principally confined to areas outside the major population centers.

Nevertheless, the crucial element in the equation was the army. As the year 1952 advanced, the military became increasingly dissatisfied. The futility of repression as a means of ending the civil conflict became daily more apparent, and the army's revulsion at its part in the slaughter of its fellow Colombians grew apace.

It seems probable that Lieutenant General Gustavo Rojas Pinilla, the commander-in-chief of the armed forces, had reached an understanding with the *Ospinistas* to prevent Gómez from resuming active charge of the chief executive's office. In any case, on May 22, 1953, Rojas stated in a speech that the destiny of the nation was in the hands of the armed forces and that it would back the *acting* president until his successor had been elected. At the patent challenge to his presidential title, Gómez attempted to have Rojas sent abroad; that failing, he sought to have him arrested. The army remained loyal to Rojas, however, and on June 13 Rojas assumed the presidency with the backing of the armed forces.[26]

President Ospina and the moderate wing of the Conservative party had in the late 1940s attempted to slow the process of change and bring order out of what they regarded as incipient political anarchy. But Gómez and those in the Conservative party who had become imbued with the ways and ideas of Franco's Spain wished to turn history *back*

26. For the events of June 13 and their background see *Rojas Pinilla ante el Senado, El Gobierno Militar ante la Historia* (Bogotá, Editorial Excelsior, 1959); Gonzalo Canal Ramírez, *Del 13 de Junio al 10 de Mayo en las Fuerzas Armadas* (Bogotá, Editorial Antares, 1958); *Contrapunto*, June 17, 1965, which contains accounts by Rojas and by Jorge Leyva, Gómez' newly appointed Minister of War; and the interview with Acting President Urdaneta published in *La República*, June 3, 1959.

—certainly to a point prior to the reforms of 1936, if not, in spirit at least, to that time when society was divided into corporate entities rather than individual atoms; when the Church and the spirit of tradition held sway instead of materialism and the rule of the "one-half plus one"; and when representative bodies, where they existed, did not dare to test their power against the reigning executive.

The virtual dictatorship of Gómez could not give guerrilla resistance its quietus. The counterrevolution therefore failed in its primary mission —the preservation of order and authority. The repressive methods often resorted to gave an opportunity to those in Gómez' own party who were ambitious to escape from under the wing of the caudillo, and engendered the opposition of those who saw in the Conservative party's republican traditions the best guarantee of a consensual order for Colombia. Efforts to combat Liberalism by military means led to the defection of the military from an enterprise which they had come to regard as both futile and disruptive of national unity. Nor could the sending of Colombian troops to Korea reforge those bonds through the nation's involvement in such a distant place.[27] The result was the reentry of the Colombian army onto center stage of the political arena, in alliance with dissident elements of the Conservative party, after many decades of being relegated to the sidelines.

Nevertheless, the broader significance of Gómez' counterrevolution does not lie in its failure. Its deeper meaning for Colombia, and the deeper meaning in the rise of Gaitán and in the bogotazo, which together must be seen in tandem with the Gómez regime, is that when political processes do not keep pace with social change and with demands for increased popular participation, politics is likely to take the extreme courses: on the Left, "to the streets," on the Right, "via the knife."[28] The fact that the late '40s and early '50s helped awaken some Conservatives to this fact has had important consequences for subsequent Colombian political development. Laureano Gómez' own "reconversion" to republicanism at Benidorm, Spain, in July 1956, may in part be ascribed to the experience of these years.

27. Colombia was the only Latin American nation to send troops to Korea. One motivation in sending them was undoubtedly to get certain officers out of the country.

28. Cf. Robert A. Scalapino and Junnosuke Masumi, *Parties and Politics in Contemporary Japan* (Berkeley, Cal., University of California Press, 1962), p. 153.

THE MILITARY IN POWER

The public response to the coup of June 13, 1953, was instantaneous and enthusiastic. Crowds gathered at the presidential palace to cheer General Rojas Pinilla. The Liberal press gave the new government its support and Darío Echandía, a prominent Liberal leader, termed the act a *coup d'opinion.* Most Conservatives, as well as the few Socialists, announced their wholehearted adhesion. The Church hierarchy, too, gave its blessing, pronouncing the new regime as Christian and legitimate.[29]

Only a few opposed the move. The last-ditch followers of Laureano Gómez were among them. From New York and later from Spain Gómez cried out against the "usurping boot" and against his "betrayal" by his Conservative copartisans and by the Colombian clergy.[30] Though no friend of Gómez, the Communist party of Colombia (*Partido Comunista de Colombia*—PCC) likewise saw little gain from its standpoint in a military takeover.[31]

Yet for most Colombians, the advent of the Government of the Armed Forces meant that "the terrible night had ended." Hopes rose for an end to the five years of bloody undeclared civil war. Echoing General Herrera's phrase of 1902 on the occasion of the armistice ending the War of the Thousand Days, the new government was to be one of "The Fatherland above the parties": "The Armed Forces call on all Colombians of good will, who are not corrupted by vile sectarian passions, nor by petty private interests, to join in the crusade which, faithful to the traditional mandate of the Fatherland, puts the latter above the parties and the common good above the interests of castes or groups."

In this his first speech as president General Rojas also promised social justice, on the grounds that "The Fatherland cannot live in peace while it has children who are hungry or without clothing." Concerning the dura-

29. *Laureano Gómez y la Jerarquía Eclesiástica* (Bogotá, Ediciones "La Unidad," 1954[?]), pp. 4–6.

30. Ibid.; see also Gómez' manifesto of August 31, 1953, reprinted in Fidel Blandón Berrío (pseudonym for Father Ernesto León Herrera), *Lo Que el Cielo no Perdona* (Bogotá, Editorial Minerva, 1955), pp. 322–27.

31. Reading between the lines of Communist publications over the next few years, however, one gets the impression that for a time the Communists felt Rojas was some improvement over Gómez.

tion of his government, he declared: "The Armed Forces will be in power for the time necessary to organize the conditions propitious for pure elections from which may derive, through genuinely democratic systems, the magistrates, the legislators, and the judges which the Colombian people wishes to give itself in full liberty." He emphasized that before taking power he personally had exhausted all other possibilities in a search for a solution that might save the country.[32]

The assumption of power by the Colombian army in June 1953 reversed the pattern of more than four decades during which the military had played little overt part in determining the destinies of the nation. True, the army had become rather closely identified with the foregoing Conservative governments. Yet the onus of warfare against the Liberals had fallen on the police, and on numerous occasions the army had moved to contain the latter's excesses. It was therefore still able to pose as something of a political neutral. At the same time the intrusion of the military into politics may be traced in an important degree to intrigues arising from factionalism within the Conservative party. The coup of June 13 was carried out with the active connivance of the Ospinistas. In a real sense the Colombian military did not intervene in politics on its own initiative; instead, it had politics thrust upon it.

To call the new regime military is accordingly somewhat of a misnomer. Rojas himself was of course an army officer,[33] as were many of his Cabinet ministers, governors, and other officials, and in the final analysis the government depended on its military backing. On the other hand, civilians (mainly Conservatives) comprised the majority of most of the series of Rojas Cabinets. Indeed it seems that General Rojas' initial intention was to "purify" the Conservative party and ensure its continued rule on a "nationalist," rather than on a narrowly sectarian, basis. This implied a policy of tolerance toward the Liberals on the theory that

32. For the above speech see Gonzalo Canal Ramírez, *El Estado Cristiano y Bolivariano del 13 de Junio* (Bogotá, Editorial Antares, 1955), flyleaf. Five months later Rojas reaffirmed that he would leave power "when concord and democratic procedures have been established." See *El Tiempo*, November 15, 1953.

33. For Rojas' career and character see Tad Szulc, *Twilight of the Tyrants* (New York, Henry Holt, 1959), chapter 6; and *Rojas Pinilla ante el Senado*, pp. 460–63, 547–56.

"the Liberals also are sons of Colombia." [34] It further entailed adopting measures in the social and economic spheres which would further national development.

The ideology of the new regime was vague. Beyond the objective of instituting political peace by means of a moratorium on partisan politics, its program was not very concrete. Rojas declared that his was a government based on an "indestructible union" between the armed forces and the people. It was to be infused with Bolivarian and Christian principles —Bolivarian in that Bolívar was seen as the military hero acting to place the nation over all lesser considerations; Christian in that the principles of Catholic social justice and respect for the religious traditions of Colombians were to be given an important place. Rojas himself at an early point characterized his rule as the "National Christian Movement of the 13th of June"; it is perhaps the best description in a few words of what in his own mind he was trying to achieve.[35] As time passed, however, his interpretation of what that term meant tended to shift. Instead of the mere restoration of peace founded on a "nationalized" Conservative party and tolerance for Liberals, it came to include the creation of a "New Order."

The new regime took immediate steps to bring an end to civil strife.[36] In return for an amnesty and government aid in their rehabilitation many of the guerrilla bands ceased fighting. An effort was made to depoliticize the national police force by removing it from the jurisdiction of the Ministry of Interior and making it into the fourth branch of the armed forces. Political prisoners were freed and press censorship relaxed.

34. General Rojas, quoted in Pedro Belmonte, *Antecedentes Históricos de los Sucesos del 8 y 9 de Junio de 1954* (Bogotá, Imprenta Nacional), p. 43; see also the speech of Rojas' Minister of Government, Lucio Pabón Núñez, in Belmonte, pp. 119–28.

35. Canal Ramírez, *El Estado Cristiano,* passim, is the best available discussion of the "Christian" and "Bolivarian" ideology of the regime. It includes excerpts from some of Rojas' speeches. See also the speech by Lucio Pabón Núñez in Belmonte, pp. 121–23.

36. Sources on the Rojas regime include *Rojas Pinilla ante el Senado;* the several books by Gonzalo Canal Ramírez; Belmonte; Hirschman, *Journeys toward Progress* (on the regime's agrarian program); Fluharty; Martz; and Szulc. The latter three attempt overall assessments of the regime. Fluharty's is highly favorable, based on events up to the middle of 1956; Martz and Szulc dismiss Rojas as little more than a bungling tyrant.

The government also undertook an extensive series of public works and social welfare projects; imposed higher assessments on land for taxation purposes; improved the system of credit for small farmers; decreed measures designed to protect small businesses against monopolistic practices on the part of larger firms; and, for the first time in Colombia, enacted a tax on dividends from corporate stocks and bonds. The government also sponsored the creation of the Cauca Valley Corporation (cvc), a regional development agency patterned after the Tennessee Valley Authority. Subsequently, the leading national airline (AVIANCA) was nationalized, and a government-owned petroleum corporation (ECOPETROL) was established. In the area of political participation women were accorded the vote for the first time in 1954 (although neither they nor other Colombians were to be given the opportunity to exercise that right as long as Rojas remained in power).

The Government of the Armed Forces was therefore an effort to restore political peace while at the same time confronting the tasks of modernization. It was not long, though, before it also took on the outlines of a full-blown dictatorship. Press censorship was once more tightened until, in August 1955, *El Tiempo*, the country's leading newspaper, was ordered closed for allegedly having insulted the president. A series of violent incidents revealed the regime's increasingly heavy-handed and arbitrary nature. In June 1954 police and army troops opened fire on student demonstrators, killing several. Again, in February 1956 spectators at a bullfight in Bogotá who failed to show the requisite enthusiasm in cheering Rojas were beaten or thrown down the steps of the grandstand. Political opponents of the regime suffered harassment; a few disappeared or were imprisoned; still others were forced into exile. Guerrilla warfare had meanwhile been renewed, although on a lesser scale than before. An attempt by government troops at a scorched earth policy in the affected area only intensified opposition to "pacification."

Rojas did not stop at repression to consolidate his hold on power. He showered the military with favors and increased its share of the budget. He also went out of his way to prove his government eminently "Christian," and declared himself an advocate of church-state relations along pre-1936 lines. As a result the Church found him, in March 1954, "a man convinced that the principles of the Gospel are the ones which must give life to our Society." [37] Significantly, and as somewhat of a departure from the rule of the classic Latin American strong-man, Rojas tried to build other bases of support for his dictatorship. Here the imitation of the Perón regime in Argentina was evident.

One step was the creation in late 1954 of the National Secretariat of Social Assistance (*Secretariado Nacional de Asistencia Social*—SENDAS). It gathered virtually all social welfare functions of the government into one office under the directorship of Rojas' daughter. One of its principal tasks was the rehabilitation of campesinos displaced by the violence. Another was the dispensing of largesse for political purposes. Though it may have been the regime's most effective mechanism for generating popular support, it never reached the dimensions, or achieved the success, of a similar agency headed by Eva Perón in Argentina.

Rojas also sought to organize a pro-government labor federation, in design another leaf from Perón's book. Several attempts were made, the last being the conversion of what remained of the CTC after Conservative persecution and its own internal splits into an arm of the regime. Yet, although there was considerable support for Rojas among the ranks of labor, he was never able to develop a large, disciplined organization which could be called into the streets as a political weapon. Rojas likewise attempted in 1956 to create a Third Force, a political movement "above the parties." It stressed the bonds that united the armed forces and the people against the "oligarchs." However, its patently official nature, the attachments of Colombians to the traditional parties, and opposition from both the Church and some within the military caused its early demise.

Finally, Rojas tried to give his rule a façade of legality by inducing Gómez' National Constituent Assembly (ANAC) to confirm his rule for the remainder of Gómez' term, then to elect him for another four-year term beginning in 1954. When in 1957 he maneuvered to have himself chosen for still another term, however, the opposition against him crystallized. There ensued the so-called "days of May" when student demonstrations, a civic strike involving the voluntary closing of banks and businesses, the declared opposition of the Church hierarchy, and finally the

37. *Laureano Gómez y la Jerarquía*, p. 31. Cf. also *Rojas Pinilla ante el Senado*, pp. 729–30.

defection of the military leaders forced him out of power and into exile on May 10, 1957.

The Liberals first, then the Ospinista Conservatives, had become disaffected as it gradually became clear that they would not come into the political inheritance of a transitional military regime, and as the regime came to seem less and less transitional and more and more inclined to construct a political base independent of the parties. The Church, originally Rojas' ally, looked with deep suspicion on his efforts to construct Peronista-style political and labor organizations. Businessmen resented the regime's tax policies, the lavish expenditures on the army and on public works, and the emergence of a new group of businessmen, granted special privileges by the regime at the expense of those previously accustomed to receiving them. When on May 1, 1957, the government placed under house arrest in Cali Guillermo León Valencia, the man chosen less than a month earlier by the leaders of the traditional parties to be their joint candidate to succeed Rojas in 1958, the spark was ignited which produced the events of the "days of May."

The demise of the dictatorship came more peacefully than many had supposed possible. One reason the rebellion kept within the bounds of moderation was the attitude of the army when it came to the final test— it deserted the dictator. A second was that the movement which led to the overthrow of Rojas Pinilla was largely controlled by those who had most to lose by violence. For the "days of May" were not engineered by the same urban lower classes and refugees from rural violence who had assaulted the bastions of political authority on April 9, 1948.[38] The clubs, the Church hierarchy, the business associations, and the leadership of the two parties were its principal authors. When it came to street demonstrations in Bogotá students from the Jesuit university were prominent among the leaders, not just those of the more "radical" universities. On the morning of May 10 those who poured into the streets of the capital came in the first instance from the northern districts of the city, not from the south where resides the *"chusma"* (riff-raff). Nor did the guer-

38. For the arrest of Valencia and the development of the civic strike in Cali see José Berardo García, *La Explosión de Mayo* (Cali, Imprenta Departamental, 1957). For similar events in Bogotá, and particularly for the adhesion of various groups to the movement, see *El Tiempo,* December 29, 1957, Literary Supplement; and *El Independiente* (the substitute version of *El Espectador* during the dictatorship), May 10, 1957. See also *Rojas Pinilla ante el Senado,* pp. 34, 60–61, 358, 372–78, 732–42.

rillas "come over the mountains" as some euphoric souls believed they would. The small Communist party, which had combatted Rojas for several years, was hardly even the tail of the revolutionary kite.[39] All these facts helped to determine both the nature of the revolution and the identity of those who would be its inheritors.

Still another factor which accounts for the relatively pacific tenor of the uprising was that it was a lineal descendant of a series of political agreements previously reached between the traditional parties, including the selection of a joint candidate to succeed Rojas. The aims of the revolution were concrete, limited, and articulated by the recognized leaders of the parties. Neither social revolution nor interparty warfare had a place among those objectives. Rather, the anti-Rojas movement (generally referred to as the *Frente Nacional* or National Front) "was an alliance of traditionalisms to free the country from the process of revolutionary annihilation to which it was submitted."[40]

Moreover, the Rojas dictatorship had in the final analysis been a rather mild one. There had been repression, most notably of the press. Nor are incidents such as those of June 1954, that of the bullring, or the deaths of several students and others during the demonstrations of May, to be overlooked. Yet Conservative and Liberal leaders were able to meet in order to conclude the very pacts which resulted in Rojas' downfall. Besides, the dictatorship had lasted less than four years. Had it endured longer or been more ruthless in its methods, the hatreds, the tensions, and the frustrations might have been greater and the consequences might have been more explosive than they proved.

MILITARY RULE—A BALANCE SHEET

If a balance sheet were to be drawn up, the Government of the Armed Forces, led by its Supreme Chief, Lieutenant General Gustavo Rojas Pinilla, would impress more with its failures than with its achievements.

Violence, though brought more or less to a permanent end in the

39. Cf. Anteo Quimbaya, *Los Tres Partidos Colombianos* (Bogotá, Ediciones Suramérica, 1959), p. 58.

40. Alvaro Gómez Hurtado, "El Derecho a la Continuidad," in *La Nación ante la Universidad,* p. 146.

eastern plains and for a time terminated in most of the rest of the
republic, flared up again, and when Rojas fell in May 1957 there were
still guerrilla groups active in southern Tolima.

Large budgets for the armed forces and for public works, manipulation
of import licenses, extravagant purchases abroad, and an unlucky drop
in coffee prices helped to deplete Colombia's foreign exchange reserves
and to accentuate the long-term rise in the cost of living.

The government that was supposed to be above the parties and to
lead Colombia back along the road to constitutional order and democracy
instead tried to suppress opposition and resorted to measures of highly
dubious constitutionality in order to perpetuate itself. The Rojas dictatorship also failed in its efforts to create a solid basis of popular support as
Perón had successfully done in Argentina. By its attempts to do so it
managed to alienate the Church and elements of the military.

Despite declamations against the "oligarchs" in the latter years of his
rule, Rojas brought no substantial changes in the Colombian social order.
One observer, in most respects laudatory in his judgment of Rojas,
regards this as his major shortcoming: "He failed to carry out the revolution in depth which the country needs. That was his great historic error,
and perhaps the principal cause of his fall. When revolution is not carried
to its logical conclusion, counterrevolution results. And today [1959] we
have government of the oligarchy in all its splendor, such as is not seen
in any other place in America." [41]

Even some of the concrete measures Rojas did take against the established elite accomplished little. The evidence seems to be that his agrarian
taxation policies did little to alter the undervalued assessments of the
latifundios despite the apparently radical nature of those policies. One
reason for this may well have been that many among Rojas' cohorts—
originally from the lower middle class—were themselves ambitious to
become landowners. Hence the matter of land taxation was not pushed
further.[42] Although Rojas *talked* against the oligarchy, and although some
of his policies were genuinely reformist and hurt the interests of the
elite (for example, the end to the exclusion of dividend income from the

41. *Rojas Pinilla ante el Senado*, p. 32; cf. also Canal Ramírez, *Del 13 de Junio al
10 de Mayo*, pp. 123–28.
42. Hirschman, *Journeys toward Progress*, p. 124. Other tax measures appear to
have been somewhat more effective, however.

income tax), on balance his administration effected relatively little lasting change in the country's economic or social structure. Rojas proved more adept at generating opposition to himself than at forging a new order for Colombia.

Yet there were also accomplishments. Although the dictatorship did not put an end to violence, it did manage to reduce it, especially during its initial months in office. The programs of rehabilitation, carried out in large part by the army itself and through SENDAS, were a blessing to a distraught people. Many of the public works projects were of permanent value for the development of the country. Perhaps most important for the long run was the degree to which Rojas contributed to the awakening of the Colombian masses, and to some extent to their welfare, by his tirades against the oligarchy, his tax and land reforms, the attention he gave to the expansion of credit to small farmers, and the scorn and discredit which he heaped upon the old methods and leaders of the political parties and upon their spokesmen in the press.

In its initial stages, the regime had not been a dictatorship in Robert MacIver's sense that it severed the state from the community, invoking its own will as its only legitimating authority.[43] If anything, Rojas' coup brought the state and the community closer. Its real legitimation lay not in the farce of the ANAC but in the popular support which it initially received from almost all quarters. For a time Rojas' popularity was by no means so mythical as some of his detractors later claimed; nor was it entirely dissipated among the masses by the time of his fall. But it had soon become clear that measures designed to pave the way for a return of the parties to the front of the political stage were taking second place to the efforts of the government to consolidate its hold.

The parties themselves bore a share of the responsibility for this development; for after a lull of a few months in 1953 political violence began to pick up, with Conservatives and Liberals once again the protagonists. Seeing that the parties showed few signs of moderating their bitter partisanship in the national interest, Rojas seems to have acquired a true sense of mission. He apparently came to believe that he was the second Bolívar, and that he had come to save his country from destruction at the hands of the self-seekers and parasites of the old order. He seems

43. Robert M. MacIver, *The Web of Government* (New York, Macmillan, 1948), p. 225.

genuinely to have felt that the directors of the traditional parties were responsible for Colombia's plight, and that only by putting aside mutual hatreds and integrating all Colombians into the national life could Colombia be made whole again.

As it proved, those sentiments were only poorly articulated into concrete programs, and the leadership and organization which were to carry them into effect were too weak and inept to carry the day in face of vested interests, among which were the historic parties and the Church. A basic difficulty was that the administration never found its bearings in the Colombian political maze. It began almost as an instrument of one Conservative faction against another, and of that faction which is ordinarily representative of big business and a moderate approach to politics. But the regime also had corporatist and nationalist elements: a few in its ranks looked to Fascist Italy, Hitler's Germany, or Nasser's Egypt for inspiration.[44] Still another strand of support, composed of some of the old Gaitanistas, reached its apogee during the dying days of the regime when a desperate Rojas accepted its plan to carry out various social and economic measures of a more radical nature than his government had hitherto undertaken, including the nationalization of the banks.[45] Not proving a ready tool of the traditional elite, the regime lost its initial backing; failing to establish an independent power base broader than the army, it was unable to act as the vehicle for national revival; unwilling to act as the engine of social change until too late, it did not reap the advantages possibly to be gained from such a stance.

An important element that must enter into any explanation of the regime's turn toward dictatorship, as well as of its ultimate collapse, is the personality of Rojas himself and the ambitions of those, both civilian and military, who fastened themselves to his star. The man who evidently had been reluctant to assume the role of chief executive (though ambition may not have been wholly absent even before June 13, 1953) soon found that he was enjoying it. He gloried in the adulation of the crowd, and his picture and name began to be conspicuously displayed as a matter of official policy. Meanwhile good political sense was thrown to the winds in face of an obsessive sensitivity to criticism.

44. Cf. e.g. Colonel Carlos Sus Pacheco, *Presente y Futuro ante el Nuevo Orden* (Bogotá, Editorial Antares, 1956), pp. 77–97 passim.
45. *Rojas Pinilla ante el Senado,* p. 838.

Rojas' vanity and ambition gave those who saw in the administration an opportunity for personal gain a wide field for flattery and for a weaving of the webs of corruption. A coterie formed whose connections permitted its members to establish economic empires. None were anxious for steps to be taken that might bring an early end to their preferment. Rojas himself was not immune to temptation. As one of his erstwhile supporters put it, Rojas might in fact have been his country's second Bolívar if he had not been so anxious to be its first rancher.[46]

Any real sense of mission on the part of Rojas or the army, though it existed, was in the final analysis forced to play a role subordinate to the private interests of the hangers-on of the regime and was vitiated by the personal ambition and self-glorification of the Supreme Chief himself. Surrounded by flatterers and sycophants, he lost touch with the people and with reality. In fine, all else was made subordinate to continuation in office. A government that might have instituted reform, albeit by essentially authoritarian methods, became instead not very much more than another Latin American dictatorship, doing little to find the answers to Colombia's dilemmas of change.

Lacking both ideological direction and mass support, the single attempt at a "populistic authoritarian" solution to Colombia's crisis of the traditional order thus proved abortive. In smaller, less complex countries, or for shorter periods or lesser tasks, the military alone may be a sufficient instrument of political rule. But where there is a diversity of articulate interests, a moderately complex economy, and strong loyalties to traditional political groups something more is needed. Rojas recognized this in his futile efforts to create government-run labor unions and a Third Force. But the efforts were clumsy and halfhearted and succumbed to opposition from the Church and from within the military itself. To succeed in the future, the military would have to ally itself with a political party or mass movement having some degree of organization and popular base or, alternatively, be adept enough to create its own. Both the military, and Gómez before it, had learned that in politics, in a country like Colombia, simply to command is not enough.

46. Canal Ramírez, *Del 13 de Junio al 10 de Mayo,* p. 49. This is a reference to Rojas' cattle interests. The best source concerning corruption and influence-peddling during Rojas' administration is *Rojas Pinilla ante el Senado,* passim, which contains the charges against Rojas during his trial before the Senate as well as his defense.

Yet the Government of the Armed Forces constituted a challenge—however feeble—to the traditional Colombian social and political order. It was the flouting of the historic forms of oligarchic democracy, and the apparent danger to the social foundations and economic policies on which the position and prosperity of the traditional ruling groups depended, that at long last brought together the two elite-dominated parties in an institutionalized coalition which would try to bring its own version of political peace to Colombia. Their unity was forged by the overriding desire to purge the country of a dictator. In that rather negative respect Rojas may have rendered his best service to his country. It may in the long run prove a more substantial contribution to the political development of Colombia than a continuation of the hegemonic party regimes, complete with political violence, into which Colombia's vaunted "Athenian democracy" had fallen. Essentially failing in its efforts to impose a consensus on Colombians, and failing in turn to move the country toward sustained modernization, the Government of the Armed Forces helped to create the conditions for a new effort of a different kind to attain those elusive ends.

THE TRANSITION TO CONSTITUTIONALISM

It was not the civilian leaders of the opposition, however, but a military junta who were the immediate heirs of the "days of May" and the accords reached between the parties. For it had been to a group of his erstwhile colleagues-in-arms that Rojas had "agreed" to turn over power on May 10. It was to depend on them, as well as on the mutually suspicious politicians and on the relationships between the latter and the military, whether the proffered coalition of the traditional parties would ever be put to the test.

Plural executives had existed in Colombia for very brief periods in 1810 and in 1863, and had on other occasions been proposed as a device to provide for the participation of the minority party in the executive branch.[47] A purely military junta was new for the country, however, as were the circumstances which had brought it into being. Its members

47. See e.g. Vicente Laverde Aponte in *Cromos*, No. 2219, p. 90; Henao and Arrubla, *History of Colombia*, pp. 484–85; and the letter of Sergio Camargo in Jorge Cárdenas García, *El Frente Nacional y los Partidos Políticos (Análisis e Interpretación de una Política)* (Tunja, Boyacá, Imprenta Departamental, 1958), p. 93.

were all high-ranking officers and all had held prominent positions in the Rojas government. Yet, on balance, the real direction of the state during the fifteen months of junta rule rested with the politicians of the National Front coalition, with the military acting as guarantor. Paradoxically, it would seem, the military stood behind changes which resulted in curtailing its own political influence. However, for the Colombian army this did not represent an abandonment of its traditional political role, as it did for the armed forces of certain other Latin American countries at about the same time. It evinced rather a return to the course which had been customary for it since the end of the nineteenth century. The members of the junta were the front men for this return. Some officers still savored political authority, but on the whole the armed forces seemed glad to leave to the civilians the task of government which they had found not entirely to their taste.

The remnants of Rojista sentiment constituted the main test of the mettle of the junta and of the genuineness of its intention to complete the transition to constitutional government. During the early morning hours of May 2, 1958, just two days before the election which was to choose a new president, elements of both the military police and the national police garrisons in Bogotá arrested four of the five members of the military junta, plus candidate Lleras. The fifth junta member escaped detention, and Lleras was shortly released when his abductors encountered loyal troops. The fact that the coup did not fully attain its immediate objectives helped to defeat it, but it collapsed on the very day it had begun primarily because the expected support among the armed forces was not forthcoming. The so-called "visible" head of the brief revolt, Lieutenant Colonel Hernando Forero of the military police, claimed at his trial that there were "invisible" heads as well who had backed down at the last moment. Forero cited in particular two members of the junta and the commanders of the army and the air force.[48]

Here the government adhered to a policy it was again to follow when Rojas himself was put on trial less than a year later: that of placing the responsibility on the immediate culprit while refusing to look beyond. True, implications of involvement in the events of May 2 were denied by the junta and the latter was absolved publicly by Lleras. But the facts of

48. For the facts and charges concerning the abortive coup see the report of the military tribunal which tried its authors, in *El Espectador* (P.M. edition), Dec. 7, 1959; and Forero's accusations in *Semana*, No. 672, p. 16.

the case were never really pursued. The whole affair reflected the tacit agreement between the civilian and military leadership not to examine too closely the behavior of the military, past or present, in exchange for military guarantees of an early restoration of constitutional order.[49]

Despite the flurry, the election was duly held on May 4. Lleras, with the support of both parties, was the overwhelming victor. The only opposition came from Jorge Leyva, a former Cabinet minister under Gómez. Calling himself an independent Conservative and objecting to the selection of a Liberal as the National Front candidate, Leyva polled some twenty per cent of a vote of 3,108,567.[50]

True to its word, on August 7 the "government by military committee," still technically operating under the state of siege declared by President Ospina Pérez in November 1949, turned over the reins of authority to an elected president. It had acted to prevent the return of disgruntled Rojistas to power and had refused to take part in plans which might have kept one or more of its number in office beyond the scheduled interim period. Like the military governments led by General Pedro Aramburu in Argentina following the fall of Perón and by Vice-Admiral Wolfgang Larrazábal in Venezuela after the overthrow of Marcos Pérez Jiménez, the Colombian junta constituted another example in the late 1950s of a Latin American military establishment serving to guarantee a transition from dictatorship to constitutional government. It is distinctly within the realm of possibility that, had the government been entrusted fully to the politicians on May 10, without additional time to translate opposition to dictatorship into the construction of a future government, Colombia might have witnessed a sundering of the still-fragile bonds of coalition, and even a return to power on the part of the Rojistas. To act the constitutional midwife had become a military function. It was now up to the parents to determine whether the National Front could survive its infancy.

49. Cf. Lleras Camargo's speech to a group of officers of the armed forces on May 9, 1958, one week after the conspiracy, in Alberto Lleras Camargo, *Sus Mejores Páginas* (Bogotá, Compañía Grancolombiana de Ediciones, 1959[?]), pp. 207–20; see also the letters exchanged between Lleras and General Navas Pardo in December 1959 as published in *El Tiempo*, Dec. 30, 1959.

50. *Memoria del Ministro de Gobierno al Congreso Nacional de 1958* (Bogotá, Imprenta Nacional, 1958), p. 63.

6

THE NATIONAL FRONT

THE ORIGINS OF BIPARTISANSHIP

Coalition between Colombia's two historic parties was by no means new. In 1869 an agreement between one faction of the Liberal party and the Conservatives stipulated that the two were to cooperate "with the goal of adopting a policy to assure peace and the consolidation of republican institutions and to achieve the reconciliation of Colombians." Public posts were to be shared equally between Liberals and Conservatives. Instances of other short-lived coalitions abound during the nineteenth century.[1] Rafael Núñez, writing in 1882, noted that there had been three periods of complete political peace in Colombian history, all of which had been characterized by toleration of the other party and even joint participation of the parties in the administration. Núñez went on to say that "Politics is an experimental science . . . and if the same manner of governing tried, in different circumstances, three times, has produced an identical result, that of the preservation of order, we might rightly deduce that that manner of governing is precisely that which suits the Republic."[2]

The Republican Union of 1909, formed in the wake of the War of the Thousand Days and a brief dictatorship, President Olaya's National Concentration regime of 1930–34, and the National Union of the late 1940s were all twentieth-century examples of the temporary coalescence of

1. Cf. Guillermo Hernández Rodríguez, *La Alternación ante el Pueblo* (Bogotá, Editorial América Libre, 1962), pp. 162–63. The agreement of 1869 was never put into practice since the coalition's candidate, General Tomás C. Mosquera, lost the election.

2. Rafael Núñez, *Los Mejores Artículos Políticos de Rafael Núñez* (Bogotá, Ministerio de Educación Nacional, 1936), pp. 43–46.

leaders of the Conservative and Liberal parties to effect a political truce, or the transfer of power from one to the other by gradual stages. Nevertheless, these earlier coalitions had brief life-spans and were at bottom intended to be temporary. They also lacked a constitutional basis. Most important, in all such instances one or the other party was the clearly dominant partner, or it was tacitly understood which one would emerge as such after a period of transition.

There were precedents as well for formally guaranteeing a role for the opposition party. In 1905 President Reyes had decreed that in all popular elections for legislative bodies the right of the minority to be represented would be recognized. This was shortly translated into legislation which gave to the majority two thirds, and to the party winning the second largest number of votes in a given electoral jurisdiction one third of the seats at issue (the so-called "incomplete vote"). This provision was retained until 1929, when straight proportional representation by means of the electoral quotient replaced it. Elsewhere in Latin America the Sáenz Peña Law adopted in 1912 in Argentina had contained a clause guaranteeing the second party a third of the seats at stake, and Uruguay has provided for assured minority party participation in the executive most of the time since the second decade of this century. Like those laws, the Colombian was designed to eliminate one of the alleged curses of Latin American politics: the hegemony of the victorious party to the virtual exclusion of the opposition from any representation in government. The system of the incomplete vote may well have contributed to the maintenance of political peace in Colombia while it was in effect. Yet under its aegis the parties did not really share power, and it did not touch the all-important presidency.

The National Front was to venture beyond all previous arrangements. In conception it was more than just an "agreement from above" as a convenient political tactic, more than a device to reëstablish by constitutional fiat a role for both contending parties, more than an instrument of the elite to resist change and combat "leftist" ideas. The National Front was all these things, and a good deal more. In its extent and in its purpose it was a new departure without real precedent, either in Colombia or elsewhere.

In the first place, it was a design for obviating all political struggle between Colombia's two bitterly antagonistic parties by forcing them to share power and office at all levels (including, as it proved, the presidency) for a period of a decade and a half. Secondly, it was genuinely seen by some of its originators as a means for educating Colombians in the arts of political compromise and for inculcating that most difficult part of democratic political culture—the acceptance of the legitimacy of opposition. Thirdly, the National Front was to be the instrumentality for retaining real power in elite hands *while at the same time* carrying forward Colombia's economic development, and instituting those changes in the social order which would both advance elite material interests and ward off social revolution. Finally, the Front was conceived by a few as the political expression of a great national enterprise of development. By setting aside ancient political hatreds, it would permit the country to move toward the goals of greater social justice, real national independence, and an enhanced measure of political participation for the majority of Colombians.

The inspiration for the National Front came from Alfonso López, the very leader who had forged the hegemonic Liberal Republic of the 1930s. As his second administration staggered to its rather inglorious end, President López had become convinced that Colombia could not retain its political health if one party was all-powerful and the opposition was more or less forced to take an intransigent position. He declared that the time had come to provide for minority representation in the administration.[3]

The National Union government of Alberto Lleras Camargo, López' successor, was the only immediate consequence, and it was merely a coalition along traditional lines. Under President Mariano Ospina Pérez the policy of National Union received such refinements as the "cross-over" plan of appointing the governor and secretary (or minister) of government in each department from opposite parties. Shortly before the election of November 1949, Ospina proposed that elections be suspended for four years and that for the period of the next presidential term there be four presidents, two from each party and each acting for one year. During this time electoral reform was to be enacted and violence brought to an end. The Liberals, after first rejecting this scheme, did give their assent, but the intensity of political antagonisms prevented its final adoption.[4]

3. *Semana*, No. 677, pp. 27–28.
4 Cuéllar Vargas, *13 Años de Violencia*, pp. 98–100; Lleras Restrepo, *De la República a la Dictadura*, p. 297.

In 1954, with military rule in full swing but the dictatorship not yet full-blown, former President López issued a statement which is sometimes accorded the honor of originating the National Front idea. It repeated concepts he had put forward earlier calling for a constituent assembly, in which the two major parties would be equally represented, to reform Colombia's constitution along lines which "the experience of the last 25 years vociferously advises." [5] Indeed, talk of the necessity for alterations in Colombian political institutions in order to ensure representation of both parties in government was in the air during this period. But what shape such reform should take, and how the outcome might differ from the coalitions of the past, were by no means evident. It required the catalyst of resistance to a military dictator for both parties to see mutual advantage in a plan which would go beyond mere temporary expediency.

The first concrete step toward the creation of what was to become the National Front was taken in March 1956 when the Liberals, with López as instigator, proposed the formation of a bipartisan opposition. The Liberal party thereupon gave its Director, Alberto Lleras, a mandate to seek an understanding with the Conservatives concerning the organization of a government, or a series of governments, based on the principle of coalition. In pursuit of this objective, Lleras went to Spain in July 1956 to explore the possibilities of such an agreement with Gómez, who remained the outstanding Conservative leader and who apparently had let it be known that he was thinking along similar lines. [6] The result was the Declaration of Benidorm, signed by Lleras and Gómez on July 24, 1956. It pledged the two parties to work together for a restoration of constitutional government and embodied the concept of one or a series of coalition governments after the presumed end of Rojas' term in 1958. [7] This was the real origin of the Civil (later to be termed the National) Front.

Early in 1957 the armed forces announced their support for Rojas'

5. *Por qué y cómo se Forjó el Frente Nacional* (Bogotá, Imprenta Nacional, 1951), pp. 9–10. Carlos Lleras Restrepo claimed in 1959 that the idea of the National Front first appeared in a plan presented by a Liberal parliamentary commission to the Conservative party in March 1949. Cf. M. Torres, *La Naturaleza de la Revolución,* p. 122.

6. See *El Frente Nacional, Síntesis Doctrinal e Histórica* (Bogotá, Ediciones Laguram, 1958), p. 16.

7. The text is contained in *Por qué y cómo se Forjó,* pp. 12–16.

reelection for the 1958–62 presidential term. The response of the parties was a manifesto subscribed to by their respective directorates in Bogotá on March 20. It explicitly opposed Rojas' reelection and called for free elections to choose his successor. The two parties further pledged themselves to present a single candidate, with Liberals backing a Conservative for the purpose. In addition, the constitution would be amended to embody the principles of coalition government, including "equity in the representation of the parties." [8]

Some two months after the downfall of the Government of the Armed Forces, with fissures beginning to show in the coalition, Lleras traveled once again to Spain to meet with Laureano Gómez. There the two leaders subscribed to the so-called Pact of Sitges on July 20, 1957. By its provisions bipartisan cooperation was to continue for twelve years, the two parties were to have parity in Congress and in the public administration during that time, and the Colombian people would be called upon to certify their adhesion to this rather drastic alteration in their political institutions by exercising their primary constituent power in a plebiscite. A Bipartisan Commission of Institutional Readjustment was appointed to advise the government on the return to normalcy and to incorporate the National Front agreements in formal proposals for constitutional reform.

The first major concrete step in this direction, following upon the Pact of Sitges and the preparatory work of the Bipartisan Commission, was a plebiscite held on December 1, 1957, to gain formal popular assent to the National Front reforms. Being the first plebiscite in Colombian history, it perhaps befitted the unique political experiment it was designed to inaugurate. Only the alternatives of acceptance or rejection were posed, and approval was advocated by all major factions of the Conservative and Liberal parties. The final tally showed 4,169,294 in favor, with only 206,864 against, plus 20,738 blank ballots.[9] The vote reflected a carry-over from the euphoria of the "days of May," although it is highly probable that many did not understand for what they were voting. Indeed, Rojas Pinilla was later to claim at his trial before the Senate that many campesinos voted "yes" under the illusion they were casting a ballot for *Don Plebiscito* (Mr. Plebiscite).[10]

Nevertheless, the vote constituted an overwhelming endorsement of

8. For the text see ibid., pp. 16–29.
9. *Memoria del Ministro de Gobierno . . . 1958*, p. 55.
10. *Rojas Pinilla ante el Senado*, pp. 726–27.

the proposed constitutional amendments. Their principal features were as follows:

1. For a period of twelve years beginning in 1958 seats in all "public corporations" in the nation (the Senate and the Chamber of Representatives, departmental assemblies, and municipal councils) were to be divided equally between the Liberal and Conservative parties and only those parties. Within each party seats were to be allotted by proportional representation to lists which might be presented by different factions.

2. All Cabinet offices (with the exception of any military appointees), as well as positions on the Supreme Court, were to be distributed according to the proportion of seats held by the parties in the national legislature (that is, equally divided).

3. All government officials and all employees in the various branches of the public administration were to be appointed on the basis of parity between Liberals and Conservatives. The exceptions were those falling under career service regulations and military personnel.

4. The approval of nonprocedural measures within all elective bodies was to be by two-thirds vote. However, also by a two-thirds vote, Congress could stipulate that a majority would be sufficient on particular issues for periods of not more than two years at a time.

Other significant provisions of the plebiscitary reforms, less directly related to the functioning of coalition government, affirmed that the Roman Catholic religion was that of the nation and was to be protected by the state "as an essential element of social order"; stipulated that members of the Supreme Court were to be appointed for life; gave women political rights equal to those of men; prohibited participation of civil service employees in partisan political activity other than voting; declared that beginning with January 1, 1958, no less than ten per cent of the nation's general budget must be spent on education; and legalized the rule of the military junta until August 7, 1958.[11]

The next step on the road to the new constitutional order was the election of legislative bodies and a president. Because of a reopening of the old rift in the Conservative party between Laureanistas and Ospinistas

11. The text may be found in *Por qué y cómo se Forjó,* pp. 42–44. The provisions concerning the Church were something of a reversal of the codification of 1936, which had in turn modified the provisions of the 1886 constitution. With regard to the vote for women, Rojas' ANAC had accorded them this right in 1954 and they had exercised it in the plebiscite itself.

subsequent to the tenth of May, the presidency posed a dilemma. Further-more, Guillermo León Valencia, the agreed coalition candidate, was iden-tified with the Ospinistas and with earlier support for Rojas. Hence he proved unacceptable to Laureano Gómez, who had been in Spain when Valencia was selected by the party directorates. Gómez, in poor health and seemingly aged well beyond his sixty-eight years, had returned to Colombia and to political battle in early October 1957. He threatened to disrupt the coalition if Valencia were to remain its nominee.

It was finally agreed to leave the matter of Valencia's candidacy up to Congress and to this end to hold the voting for that body prior to the balloting for president.[12] In the ensuing elections held in March 1958 the Liberals outdistanced the total Conservative vote, 58 per cent to 42 per cent, although of course, under the parity system, the seats in Congress were to be equally divided between the two parties.[13] The crucial con-test took place within each party, where proportional representation pre-vailed. There was no real battle among Liberals but among Conservatives the supporters of Gómez won an overwhelming victory over the Ospi-nistas and a third, anti-National Front, faction. Valencia's candidacy was thereby quashed. The Liberals, caught between their pledge to back Valencia and the obvious practical necessity of working with the major-ity faction of the Conservatives if the National Front were to have any meaning, decided to work with the Laureanistas.

The problem became one of selecting a new Conservative candidate acceptable to the Liberals. After a period of tortured interparty negotia-tions and intra-Conservative discussions, Gómez came up with the stun-ning proposal that the candidate not be a Conservative at all but a Liberal, Alberto Lleras Camargo. The condition was that the Liberals agree that the president to follow Lleras would be a Conservative. The Liberals then proposed that the coalition agreement be extended from twelve years to sixteen and that the presidency alternate between the parties every four years during that period. Thus the president to follow Lleras would have to be Conservative under the constitution, the follow-ing one Liberal, and the last one under the National Front agreement,

12. This was the so-called Pact of San Carlos, signed at the presidential palace in Bogotá on November 22, 1957. See ibid., pp. 89–91, for the text.
13. Each department's representation was adjusted to an even number for the purpose.

for the term 1970–74, Conservative. Both parties shortly accepted both the Lleras candidacy and the amended plan.[14] They further pledged themselves to support the latter's passage in two consecutive ordinary sessions of Congress, which was the regular method for constitutional amendment, the plebiscite having been strictly exceptional and not provided for in the constitution.[15] One signal advantage of *alternación*, beyond its obvious expendiency, was purported to be that over a period of a decade and a half it would accustom Colombians to seeing the presidency shift between the parties and thus perform a service in education for democracy.[16] In view of the constitutional strength of the Colombian president, this was a key addition to the National Front accords. Though opposed by minority segments of both parties, alternation was duly approved by Congress and appended to the constitution in 1959.

With its adoption, and with the simultaneous extension of the term of the National Front to sixteen years, the constitutional basis for Colombia's experiment in institutionalized coalition government was essentially complete. Its three pillars, constituting a unique form of bipartisanship, were to be: *parity* in all public elective bodies and in all executive departments and administrative posts (with the previously mentioned exceptions of the civil service and military appointees); *alternation* in the presidency every four years; and the requirement that decisions made by public corporations be by *two-thirds vote*, thus presumably forcing bipartisan cooperation on all legislation.

INTRAPARTY FACTIONALISM: PROBLEM FOR COALITION

The success of the National Front depended on agreement not only between, but also within, the two political parties. Yet from the outset factionalism was the most persistent difficulty facing the government of Alberto Lleras, accentuated as it was by an electoral system which froze competition between the two ancient antagonists while according proportional representation within each party's allotted one half of legislative seats to intraparty groups who ran separate slates. Divisions first arose in

14. See *Por qué y cómo se Forjó*, pp. 46–62, for the relevant documents.

15. Ibid., pp. 62–66; and for the text of the amendment embodying alternation, see pp. 117–18. Alternation, like parity, had precedents, notably President Ospina's proposal that the four members of a bipartisan governing committee each hold the principal executive power for one year during their four-year term.

16. See Lleras Camargo, *Sus Mejores Páginas*, pp. 192–93.

the Conservative party, where the Ospinista-Laureanista dispute was reopened shortly following the overthrow of the common enemy, General Rojas. Other, lesser factions led by Jorge Leyva and Gilberto Alzate Avendaño also became involved in the internecine warfare. Several attempts were made to patch up the quarrel but success invariably proved temporary and superficial. President Lleras at first hoped to deal with the Conservatives on the basis of proportional representation of the factions in his government, but when the Conservatives failed to agree among themselves on such a plan, Lleras turned to cooperation with the majority wing of the party as the only feasible means to make coalition work. On the basis of the congressional elections of March 1958 that wing was the Laureanistas. The excluded Ospinistas took the position that they supported the National Front agreement but objected to the way in which it was being executed, and in particular to the exclusion of their faction from a share in the government at the insistence of Gómez.[17] In late 1959 the *Alzatistas* and Ospinistas, drawn together by their opposition to Gómez, formed an alliance, thus constituting what was for a time an *Alza-Ospinista* faction.

By mid-1959 the Liberals were showing signs of internal schism as well. A group led by Alfonso López Michelsen, a son of former President López, denounced the constitutional amendment instituting alternation in the presidency. The *Lopistas,* or *Alfonsistas,* affirmed their support of a sharing of both parties in government and of the need for an understanding between them to moderate Colombia's traditional political warfare. But they objected that the Liberals were the majority in the country and that to give that majority an opportunity to be heard through the free election of the president was essential to democracy. "What ought to happen is that the responsibility of government should rest with a single party, with the administrative and political collaboration of the other." [18] As the Liberal split developed, the faction led by López Michelsen elaborated an economic and social program which enhanced both its appeal and its significance. It also adopted the designation Liberal Recovery Movement (*Movimiento de Recuperación Liberal*—MRL), later renamed the Liberal Revolutionary Movement.

17. One cause of Gómez' intransigence was undoubtedly the circumstance that Laureanistas still held the majority of administrative jobs in the government. Martz, *Colombia,* p. 259.

18. Alfonso López Michelsen, interview in *El País* (Cali), Jan. 13, 1960.

In view of the divisions within both parties, the congressional elections of March 1960 loomed as a clear-cut test for the coalition agreement. The results showed striking gains for the "opposition" factions. In this, its first electoral test, the MRL won 20 of the 76 Liberal seats in the Chamber of Representatives with about 21 per cent of the Liberal vote, whereas only five members of the Liberal half of the previous Chamber could be counted as supporting its factional position. Among Conservatives the Alza-Ospinistas and the Laureanistas each won 37 seats, with adherents of Jorge Leyva winning two. For the Laureanistas this represented a distinct decline from the 45 seats out of 74 they had hitherto held and deprived them of a majority among Conservatives in the Chamber. More-over, the Alza-Ospinistas had won a clear majority of the Conservative popular vote (57 per cent) over the other two factions put together.[19]

The consequences were far-reaching. First, after a period of equivoca-tion, the Laureanistas forbade participation of their members in the Cab-inet, Gómez declaring that he had been discharged of all governing responsibility by Conservative voters. Lleras therefore found himself col-laborating exclusively with the Alza-Ospinistas, just as he had once had to work only with the Laureanistas.[20] Heretofore bitterly critical of the National Front, the Alza-Ospinistas proved to be cooperative partners once they shared in the administration.

Secondly, since opposition factions now held some 26 per cent (in the case of the MRL) and more than 50 per cent (in the Conservative case) of their parties' seats in the Chamber, and the Laureanistas still held the Conservative majority in the Senate, Lleras' problems in dealing with Congress were considerably magnified, particularly in view of the two-thirds rule for the enactment of legislation.[21]

19. For figures on this and other elections under the National Front see Table 4. It should be noted that the number of seats in the Chamber had been increased from 148 to 152 since the March 1958 election.

20. The reasons were different, however. When the Laureanistas were in the majority they demanded exclusion of the Ospinistas as a price for cooperation; when in the minority they ultimately refused participation in the Cabinet on a basis of pro-portional representation of the factions even though the Alza-Ospinistas were agree-able to such an arrangement.

21. Senate seats were not at stake in the 1960 election. It should be noted that factions opposed to the National Front as a *system* so far have not held as many as one third of the seats in the Senate or Chamber. At least in general, Ospinistas, Laureanistas, and Alzatistas have battled over the political composition of the govern-ment, not over its existence or the constitutional provisions on which it is founded.

Thirdly, the election made quite clear that there were important segments among the faithful of each party who subscribed less than wholeheartedly to the idea of joining forces with their ancient enemies and instead longed again for predominance. The Alza-Ospinistas, though afterward cooperating in the government, conducted their campaign in 1960 to appeal to this sentiment, as did the MRL; both made sizable inroads into the pro-National Front vote.

In the fourth place, the results greatly sharpened the problem of choosing a candidate for president (necessarily Conservative according to the alternation amendment of 1959) for the election of May 1962. From whichever faction he were chosen he would directly represent only one segment of what was in any event the country's minority party.

Finally, in view of Conservative division and the anti-alternation views of the MRL, there arose the outside chance that a candidate opposed to one of the key features of the National Front could be elected president in 1962. True, the constitution forbade a Liberal's assuming the presidency for the next term. But if each Conservative faction ran its own candidate, López Michelsen, campaigning under the designation Liberal, might conceivably win even if the "official" Liberals supported one of the two Conservatives. The government could prohibit his running, or deny him office if elected, but it would thereby openly go counter to its vaunted democratic nature and base the legitimacy of the next four-year period of the National Front on shaky ground indeed. If López were victorious and were allowed to take office (which was unlikely), it might drive the Conservatives to civil war; at the least it would mean the rupture of the laboriously constructed National Front.

The possible victory of a Laureanista candidate in 1962 posed a less serious problem. Although at the time vociferously critical of the factional complexion of the National Front, the Laureanistas still claimed allegiance to the coalition of which Gómez was a principal author and to its central institutions. Furthermore, the Laureanistas were Conservatives, and a victory for a candidate of their choosing would comply with alternación.

As 1961 brought the presidential election closer, "unity conferences" were called to find a candidate acceptable to official Liberals, and to both Alza-Ospinistas and Laureanistas. The hope was to prevent collapse of the National Front and a possible reentry of the army into politics, although military leaders rejected such an idea and admonished the politicians to solve their own problems. The Laureanistas refused to participate in the

TABLE 4

POPULAR VOTE FOR CHAMBER OF REPRESENTATIVES, 1958–1966 [22]

	1958	%	1960	%	1962	%	1964	%	1966 [a]	%
LIBERALS										
Oficialistas	2,105,171	(100)	1,100,000	(78.5)	1,081,103	(64)	738,437	(64)	1,117,692	(72)
MRL	—		300,000	(21.5)	601,926	(36)	381,847	(33)	351,500	(23)
Linea Blanda [b]	—		—		—		284,952	(25)	351,500	(23)
Linea Dura	—		—		—		96,895	(8)	—	
ANAPO	—		—		—		16,495	(1)	81,984	(5)
MIL (Liberal Left Movement)	—		—		—		7,129	(0.6)	—	
CONSERVATIVES [c]										
Ospinistas (Unionistas)	340,106	(22)	600,000	(55)	794,688	(57)	794,000	(72) [d]	521,547	(40)
Laureanistas (Alvaristas)	915,886	(59)	400,000	(37)	487,733	(35)	}		333,973	(26)
Independents (incl. [e] Alzatistas in 1958)	287,760	(19)	—		—		—		—	
ANAPO	—		85,000	(8)	115,587	(8)	293,183	(28)	436,754	(34)
TOTAL VOTE [f]	3,650,606		2,500,000		3,090,203		2,261,190		2,843,450	
Liberals	2,105,171	(58)	1,400,000	(56)	1,685,531	(55)	1,157,998	(51)	1,551,176	(55)
Conservatives	1,545,435	(42)	1,100,000	(44)	1,402,786	(45)	1,095,465	(49)	1,292,274	(45)

See notes on following page.

conferences, Gómez likening the idea of Conservatives' negotiating with the Liberals regarding the selection of a Conservative candidate to the witches' brew in Shakespeare's *Macbeth*.[23] The Laureanistas instead put forward various formulas for the selection of a Conservative candidate which in turn were rejected by the opposing faction. At last an accord was reached between Liberals and Alza-Ospinistas whereby the latter would submit a list of five names, from which the Liberals would select one as the joint nominee of the two government factions.

The choice of the Liberals, and hence the National Front nominee, was none other than Guillermo León Valencia, the original candidate of the coalition formed in 1957 to oppose Rojas Pinilla and the man vetoed by Gómez for the presidential term beginning in 1958. From the Liberal point of view Valencia was the safest Conservative candidate, solidly committed to the National Front idea, and one who as president they might be able to manage. However, prior to the presidential election of May, which would test whether Liberals would vote for a Conservative for president, there was the hurdle of the congressional elections of March. The MRL hoped for significant gains that would discredit alterna-

a. Figures for the 1966 elections are unofficial, with about 97 per cent of the vote included. Totals for the *Línea Dura* of the MRL, for Independent Conservatives, and for such slates as those of the UTC, the Christian Democratic Party, and the Communists, which ran under one or the other major party label, were unavailable but in any case small in number. The MIL evidently ran no candidates in 1966. The total ANAPO vote—both Conservative and Liberal—was 518,738.

b. By 1964, the MRL had split into a *Línea Blanda* ("soft line") and *Línea Dura* ("hard line"), the principal difference being that the Línea Dura was further to the left. Both lines opposed the National Front, as well as each other. By 1966 the Líea Dura was virtually moribund.

c. In 1960, the Laureanista Conservatives were pro-National Front, and the Ospinista Conservatives were anti-National Front. Since 1962, these roles have generally been reversed.

d. By 1964, the Laureanista and Ospinista Conservatives had coalesced in support of the National Front and did not put up separate slates. They split again later in the year.

e. The Independents were a dissident Conservative, anti-National Front group, composed of followers of Jorge Leyva, who had been Laureano Gómez' Minister of Public Works. This group did not field a slate in 1962 or 1964, and entered only a token slate in 1966.

f. Votes for others, or null, or in blank have been omitted from the calculation. Few in any case, they account for certain minor discrepancies in vote totals.

22. The 1958 figures were taken from Martz, p. 267; the 1960 figures from Holt, *Colombia Today*, pp. 56–57; the 1962 and 1964 figures from the respective editions of Registraduría del Estado Civil, *Organización y Estadísticas Electorales;* and the 1966 figures from *El Tiempo*, March 28, 1966.

23. *The New York Times*, July 2, 1961, p. 13.

TABLE 5

POLITICAL COMPOSITION OF CONGRESS, 1958–1966 [24]

	1958	1960	1962	1964	1966
SENATE					
Liberals					
Oficialistas	40	40 [a]	37	37	46
MRL	—	—	12	12	7
Línea Blanda	—	—	—	(9) [b]	(7)
Línea Dura	—	—	—	(3) [b]	—
Conservatives					
Ospinistas (Unionistas)	10 [c]	12 [c]	31	31	21
Laureanistas (Alvaristas)	26	28	16	16	14
Independents (incl. Alzatistas in 1958)	4	—	—	—	—
ANAPO	—	—	2	2	18
Total Membership	80	80	98	98	106
Liberals	40	40	49	49	53
Conservatives	40	40	49	49	53
CHAMBER					
Liberals					
Oficialistas	74	56	59	59	70
MRL	—	20	33	31	21
Línea Blanda	—	—	—	(23)	(21)
Línea Dura	—	—	—	(8)	—
ANAPO	—	—	—	1	4
MIL (Liberal Left Movement)	—	—	—	1	—
Conservatives					
Ospinistas (Unionistas)	17	37	50	⎰65	38
Laureanistas (Alvaristas)	45	37	36	⎱	24
Independents (incl. Alzatistas in 1958)	12	2	—	1	1
ANAPO	—	—	6	26	32
Total Membership	148	152	184	184	190
Liberals	74	76	92	92	95
Conservatives	74	76	92	92	95

a. Senate elected in 1958 before MRL existed.

b. No new Senate election had been held since 1962 but the MRL had divided in that year. Due to fluctuating affiliation figures are approximate.

c. Alzatistas and Independents had generally become identified with the major factions by 1960. Conservative factional figures for 1958 are approximate.

tion and even presage an upset of Valencia by López Michelsen in May. Among Conservatives a comeback by the Laureanistas might well force the reconsideration of the Valencia candidacy in favor of someone more acceptable to that faction.

The results of the congressional elections indeed showed a gain for the MRL, which increased its percentage of the Liberal votes from 21.5 to 35; its seats in the Chamber from 20 of 76 Liberals, to 33 of 92; and its Senate seats from none, to 12 of 49 Liberals. The Laureanistas, on the other hand, were badly defeated. They won only 36 of 92 Conservative seats in the Chamber as against 37 of 76 held previously. They also lost their preeminence among Conservatives in the Senate. At the same time, while the Independent Conservatives, or *Leyvistas,* won no seats in either House (losing the two they previously held in the Chamber), a new faction of supporters of former President Rojas Pinilla won six seats in the Chamber and two in the Senate.

Taking into account the seats won by the pro-and anti-government factions of both parties, the coalition about held its own in the elections of March 1962. It maintained a two-thirds majority in the Senate, though it did slightly less well in the Chamber. Since the Laureanistas opposed the government but not the National Front system itself, the lack of a two-thirds majority in the Chamber was less decisive than it might have been. Moreover, within a year of the elections the two main factions of the Conservative party had achieved a temporary union. Nonetheless, significant for the longer term was the augmented support for the two groups that opposed major features of the system itself: the MRL among Liberals, and the supporters of Rojas Pinilla, organized into the National Popular Alliance (*Alianza Nacional Popular*—ANAPO), among Conservatives.

Once again in May, factionalism within the parties whose "official" wings were cooperating in the National Front made the presidential elections in effect a plebiscite concerning the Front's very continuation. The results are shown in Table 6. The votes for both López and Rojas were,

24. Martz, p. 267; Holt, *Colombia Today,* pp. 56–57; Registraduría del Estado Civil, *Organización y Estadísticas, 1962, 1964; El Tiempo,* March 18, 23, 1958, April 20, 1966. The 1958 figures are distillations of those of Martz and *El Tiempo.* Figures from various sources concerning the factional distribution of seats sometimes differ since factional allegiance is not always clear, or may change.

TABLE 6

RESULTS OF PRESIDENTIAL VOTING, MAY 1962 [25]

	Votes	Percentage of Total
Guillermo León Valencia	1,636,081	62.1
Alfonso López Michelsen	625,630	23.7
Jorge Leyva	308,992	11.7
Gustavo Rojas Pinilla	54,562	2.1
Others	9,575	0.4
Total	2,634,840	100.0

for different reasons, declared null by the Electoral Court.[26] López' total, though disappointing to his supporters, was quite impressive in view of the known fact that it would be unconstitutional for him to take office. Impressive in another way was the poor showing of those Conservatives who campaigned against the Front. Leyva, though not officially a candidate of the Laureanistas, did receive some support from them. Even so, he ran far behind, perhaps because the candidate of the coalition was on this occasion a Conservative. As for Rojas Pinilla, he got a bare two per cent of the total vote.

The next electoral test of the National Front, and of the effect upon it of intraparty factionalism, was the congressional elections of March 1964, during the presidency of Guillermo Valencia. For the moment the major Conservative factions were united. The MRL's share of the Liberal votes and of the Liberal seats in the Chamber remained about the same as before. The ANAPO, essentially opposed to the National Front and all its works, won 27 seats (one of them Liberal). Those opposed to the system as such therefore constituted nearly a third (60 seats out of 184) of the Chamber of Representatives.[27] To complicate matters further, the tenuous

25. Registraduría del Estado Civil, *Organización y Estadísticas, 1962*, pp. 206–07. "Others" includes a scattering of votes for other candidates, votes in blank, and nullified votes (other than those for López Michelsen and Rojas Pinilla which technically also were null).

26. Rojas had been deprived of all political rights by the Senate following his trial; the votes for López were void because he was a Liberal. The curious fact is that either was allowed even to be a candidate.

27. 23 of the Línea Blanda of the MRL, 8 of the Línea Dura, 27 of ANAPO (1 of them a Liberal), 1 of the Liberal Left Movement (*Movimiento de Izquierda Liberal—* MIL), and 1 Independent Conservative.

unity between Alza-Ospinistas and Laureanistas that had been forged early in 1963 and had lasted through the 1964 elections was broken later in the year, with the followers of the late Gilberto Alzate now generallly aligned with the Laureanistas, led by Laureano's son, Alvaro Gómez Hurtado.[28]

Two years later, in the March 1966 elections, the ANAPO made striking gains, winning 18 seats in the Senate and 36 in the Chamber. Meanwhile, the MRL percentage of the Liberal vote fell off considerably. Hence the ANAPO became the principal political group opposed to the National Front system. Together, the ANAPO and the MRL now held 25 of 106 Senate seats and 57 of 190 in the Chamber, well under a third in both houses. The Laureanistas (dubbed the *Alvaristas* following the death of Laureano Gómez) assumed an equivocal role. There was now some tendency among them to disparage the coalition idea itself and to align themselves tactically with the MRL and the ANAPO as "The Opposition," which then left the supporters of the National Front system with less than the critical two-thirds majorities in either house of the new Congress.

A curious feature of the 1966 congressional elections was the presentation by several minor parties, notably the Christian Social Democratic Party (*Partido Social Demócrata Cristiano*—PSDC) and the Colombian Communist party, as well as nonparty groups such as the Union of Colombian Workers (UTC) and an artists' organization, of separate slates in a few departments under the rubric of one or the other (or both) traditional parties. None won any seats. But the phenomenon demonstrated the broad tolerance of the bipartisan system for virtually any group willing to run under the Liberal or Conservative electoral label.

The last National Front election to date has been the contest for the presidency in May 1966 between Carlos Lleras Restrepo, the joint nominee of the *oficialista* Liberals and the Ospinista Conservatives, and José Jaramillo Giraldo, a Liberal nominated by the ANAPO. A bipartisan commission headed by former President Alberto Lleras Camargo was formed in late 1965 to back the candidacy of Lleras Restrepo and the National Front was now frequently referred to as the Front of National Transformation (*Frente de Transformación Nacional*—FTN). The MRL considered running López Michelsen once more for the presidency. However, in face of the setback the MRL had suffered in the March elections, López de-

28. Alzate died in November 1960; Laureano Gómez died in July 1965.

clined. The ANAPO and the MRL also failed to agree on a joint opposition candidate, while the Alvaristas declared their intention of supporting no candidate. The ANAPO therefore challenged Lleras on its own, although it apparently garnered some votes from adherents of the MRL and the Alvaristas. Jaramillo was a virtual political unknown (though he was a former senator and member of Rojas' ANAC) and he had campaigned for only about a month. But he garnered a significant protest vote of almost 30 per cent of the total. Even so, the bipartisan coalition had once more emerged intact from an electoral test.

TABLE 7

RESULTS OF PRESIDENTIAL VOTING, MAY 1966 [29]

	Votes	Percentage of Total
Carlos Lleras Restrepo	1,844,952	71.1
José Jaramillo Giraldo	734,674	28.3
Others	14,079	0.5
Total	2,593,705	99.9

The competition that formerly took place between parties in Colombia has thus been channeled into competition among factions which operate nominally under the umbrella of the two historic parties, even though as a rule they lead separate organizational lives. This factional rivalry has comprised the principal threat to the continued existence of the institutionalized coalition. For the latter assumes the "integral health" of the two parties to function effectively—there must be a recognizable majority in each party that will support the key features of the bipartisan pact. Ironically, the National Front has probably had the effect of fostering such divisions by eliminating, through the devices of parity and alternation, the potential penalty of the loss of power to the opposition party.

Furthermore, the schisms within both parties made difficult the enactment of the legislation which both Presidents Lleras and Valencia proposed to Congress. The forging of a program of action in the context of

29. *El Tiempo,* May 6, 1966. The figures are unofficial, with about 99 per cent of the vote tabulated. "Others" includes votes for other candidates, votes in blank, and invalid votes.

a two-party coalition is difficult enough in itself. When to that difficulty are added serious divisions within both cooperating parties, and a constant threat that the coalition's support in the electorate may dissolve in favor of groups opposed not only to men but to the system itself, the entire enterprise of attempting to carry out modernization on the basis of an interparty agreement is called seriously into question.

THE NATIONAL FRONT: MODERNIZATION

The first priorities of the National Front were political peace and the restoration of the constitutional order, taking precedence over any objectives of economic development or social reform. Hence, the accords between the party leaders were directed primarily at the political arena. Yet there were some who envisaged the National Front as more than a political truce, who saw it as a means to the larger end of uniting Colombians around certain goals of development. Above all, it early became clear that if the National Front was to endure for sixteen years, if it was to capture the popular imagination, and if it was to prevent another military regime, or a "solution" from the Left, it must evolve a program with economic and social content. The purpose of the National Front thus became not only "to achieve peace between the parties" and "to perfect democratic institutions" but also to "stimulate economic development and forge the structure of a modern society not divided by the tremendous inequalities which today characterize it, which offers to all its members remunerative employment, a decent standard of living, protection against risks, free access to education, and broad opportunities to rise to positions of leadership both in the sphere of private activity as well as in the field of public affairs." [30]

Such changes were hardly to be revolutionary. On the whole they were to be confined within limits that would not damage the fundamental interests of the most influential adherents of the two traditional parties. Moreover, the very nature of the National Front placed the responsibility for reform in the hands of leaders most of whom were themselves members of the Colombian elite. Moderate reforms were to be effected in order that more basic changes would not become necessary. Just as reform was likely to be of modest scope, economic growth rather than structural

30. *Programa del Frente Nacional, 1962* (Bogotá, Editorial ARGRA, 1962), p. 4.

change was to receive the emphasis as an engine of modernization. The first consideration was to enlarge the pie; to divide it more equitably was secondary.

The economic program of the National Front has encompassed three broad, interrelated aspects: recovery and stability, growth and diversification, and regional development.

A worsening economic situation, including a markedly unfavorable turn in Colombia's balance of payments brought on by declining coffee prices and liberal credit terms for imports, had contributed to the fall of Rojas Pinilla. An accelerating inflationary spiral had also set in during the last phase of the Rojas regime. The restoration of the country's economic health was therefore the first economic consideration of the successor governments of the junta and the National Front. An austerity program which restricted imports while attempting to hold the line on wages and prices permitted the repayment of some $300,000,000 in commercial debts by early 1959, in spite of low coffee prices. The rate of increase in the cost of living was also slowed significantly.

Yet mounting imports, expanded credit to promote economic development, and continued low export earnings soon weakened the peso and in November 1962 the government felt called upon to devalue it.

During 1963 the cost-of-living index climbed more rapidly than at any time in at least 25 years.[31] A scarcity of foreign exchange likewise continued to plague the country. Despite impressive gains toward economic stability under the first government of the National Front, by 1963 Colombia was once more in serious economic difficulties, difficulties which have unquestionably been a major factor in the recent poor electoral showings of National Front candidates and in the general malaise which seemed to have overtaken the country during the years of the Valencia administration.

The blueprint for the government's efforts to stimulate growth, the General Economic and Social Development Plan for 1961–70, was announced in December 1961. Colombia was the first Latin American country to present such a development program in accordance with Alliance for Progress goals, although it was actually a revised version of a four-year plan drawn up in 1960, prior to the advent of the Alliance. The plan called

31. See the issues of *Revista del Banco de la República*, which include data for obreros' cost of living in Bogotá as far back as 1938.

for a 5.6 per cent annual growth rate for the economy as a whole and a 2.5 per cent growth rate per capita. It hoped to augment the net per capita annual income of Colombians 62.5 per cent during the ten-year period. The plan envisaged 10 billion dollars of investment of all kinds, public and private, foreign and domestic; investments by the Colombian government alone were expected to treble over the decade.[32] In addition to Alliance and other bilateral funds, an international consortium, headed by the International Bank for Reconstruction and Development, was organized to mobilize external financial resources for Colombia's development.

The ten-year plan proved in many respects unrealistic. However, overall growth rates, though not measuring up to the goals set under the plan, have been moderately good: 4.9 per cent in 1961, 5 per cent in 1962, 3.3 per cent in 1963, 6 per cent in 1964, and an estimated 3.3 per cent in 1965.[33] As an integral part of economic growth the National Front governments have attempted to spur investment, exports, and the diversification of production by means of tax incentives and other measures. Meanwhile the share of the national budget allotted to public investment increased from about 25 per cent in 1958 to more than 40 per cent by the early 1960s.[34]

Finally the governments of the National Front have promoted regional development, largely through the device of semi-autonomous regional corporations. The Cauca Valley Corporation (cvc) has been injected with new life under the National Front. It has undertaken programs such as flood control, drainage, irrigation, reforestation, electrification, and agricultural extension. Several other regional corporations of lesser magnitude have also been created.

In all, the governments of Presidents Lleras and Valencia have done more to stimulate economic development than any prior administrations, and it seems fair to say that the Colombian elite has taken some important strides toward the mobilization of both domestic and foreign resources for the purposes of development. Yet very serious difficulties remain, nota-

32. *Plan General de Desarrollo;* see also Currie, *Ensayos sobre Planeación,* pp. 163–78, for a critique of the 10-year plan.

33. The rates are for gross domestic product. The 1961–64 figures were taken from the respective editions of *Cuentas Nacionales.* The 1965 figure is a preliminary estimate provided by Professor Albert Berry of Yale University.

34. See Inter-American Development Bank (IADB), *Institutional Reforms and Social Development Trends in Latin America* (Washington, D.C., 1963), pp. 119–22.

bly those of price stabilization, the balance of payments, productivity, and an over-dependence on the international coffee market. Furthermore, the rate of growth of the gross domestic product has not been significantly different than in the years preceding the National Front.

Social reform, in the sense of a more equitable distribution of economic resources and social opportunities, is of course not readily separable from economic development. As a matter of fact, the 1962 program of the National Front expressly looked to economic growth as one means by which more Colombians would come to have incomes sufficient to provide themselves with some of the social services otherwise performed by the state. The governments of the National Front have at the same time sought to "stimulate social change in a direct manner" [35] by revising the tax structure, improving health, educational and other services, financing public housing, fostering self-help through programs of community development, and carrying out an agrarian reform.

Tax reform is an area in which it is especially difficult to distinguish whether the objective is economic or social. Most tax reform under the National Front has had the primary aim either of stimulating private investment and of channeling it in directions desirable from the point of view of economic development, or of providing revenue which the government could utilize for public investment. Several of the reforms also had implications for the redistribution of income, however. For example, a law of December 1960 and its subsequent implementing decrees decreased the tax rates on personal incomes of less than 75,000 pesos per year (at the time worth roughly U.S. $10,000; today about $5,000) and increased those on larger incomes. The rate on the highest bracket was raised to 51 per cent, giving Colombia one of the steepest gradations of income tax rates in Latin America. In addition, a tax was levied for the first time on windfall profits from real estate operations.

The constitutional reform approved in the plebiscite of December 1957 provided that the national government was annually to invest no less than ten per cent of the general budget in public education. The program for education subsequently set forth in the ten-year development plan envisaged the construction of facilities for 22,000 classrooms in four years, although because of a shortage of funds and certain administrative difficulties this was later extended to six years. Since only an estimated 25 per cent of teachers in Colombian primary schools had had professional

35. See *Programa del Frente Nacional*, pp. 10–11.

teacher training, facilities were to be provided for the training of 9,500 teachers in the same period, as well as of 2,900 administrators. The training of some 11,000 teachers already on the job was also contemplated.[36]

The coalition government has devoted considerable attention to housing. In contrast to the 18,178 housing units it built during its first sixteen years of existence (1942–57), the Institute of Territorial Credit (*Instituto de Crédito Territorial*—ICT), Colombia's public-housing agency, was responsible for the construction of 15,502 units in the years 1958–60, 18,793 in 1961, and 31,898 in 1962.[37] The number of housing units to be erected by ICT during the life of the ten-year development plan was projected at 332,000. Although by the end of 1962 it was estimated that an urban housing deficit of almost 280,000 units remained, a review of progress in mid-1963 indicated that the rise in that deficit had been halted and a small beginning had been made toward actually reducing it.[38]

Significant progress has also been made in the fields of health, and municipal water supplies and sewage systems. Budgetary allocations for the Ministry of Health have risen significantly, and a start has been made toward the creation of 200 community health centers under the ten-year development plan. Under the plan, 405 villages and towns were to be supplied with either new or improved water and sewage facilities.

The National Front governments, and various private and semi-official agencies as well, have also put considerable effort into community development (*acción comunal*). Community development in Colombia has had two broad purposes or aspects.[39] The first has been to contribute to the

36. *Plan General de Desarrollo*, Part I, p. 233; *Programa del Frente Nacional*, p. 24; and *El Espectador*, Aug. 14, 1963, p. 10.

37. *Colombia en Cifras* (Bogotá, Librería Colombiana-Camacho Roldán, 1963), p. 422.

38. *El Tiempo*, Aug. 15, 1963, p. 9. See also Memorandum from Acting Director, AID, Bogotá, to Housing Advisor, May 1, 1963, entitled "Progress Report—Techo—March 31, 1963."

39. For the rationale of accíon comunal see Orlando Fals Borda, *Acción Comunal en una Vereda Colombiana*, Monografías Sociológicas No. 4 (Bogotá, Universidad Nacional, Departamento de Sociología, 1961); *Acción Comunal en Colombia* (Bogotá, CARE and Federación Nacional de Cafeteros de Colombia, 1962), pp. 2–3 and passim; and República de Colombia, Ministerio de Gobierno, División de Acción Comunal, Sección de Investigación y Planeamiento, *Informe Nacional sobre el Desarrollo de la Comunidad en Colombia Presentado a la Secretaría del Consejo Interamericano Económico y Social de la Unión Panamericana*, Mimeo. (Bogotá, 1963), pp. 7–11. Most of the following discussion of acción comunal derives from these sources and from E. Gordon Alderfer, "The People, Sí," *Américas, 13* (May 1961), 2–9, and *2 Años Después. Colombia Adelante* (Bogotá, USIA, 1963).

material process of development, through community self-help, by the
building of schools, clinics, feeder roads, recreational facilities, and sewage systems. The reasoning is that for economic development to have its
full effect it would be impossible to rely on the resources of government
alone, that without the mobilization of local resources development would
only increase the material gap between city and village, between rich and
poor, and that such lopsided development would end in its own frustration.

The second purpose was to alter the passivity of the Colombian campesino in the face of change, to create a sense of participation and involvement in his own betterment, and to promote forms of community cooperation which would help to mobilize him for that end. This would entail,
as an essential facet, the formation of civic committees which were both
representative and composed of community leaders infused with the spirit
of self-improvement. Marketing cooperatives, and other cooperative undertakings might also be involved. To succeed, acción comunal would
mean the modification, on the part both of the campesino and of the governmental or private agency which provided the initial stimulus, of the
deep-seated attitudes of a paternalistic political culture. It would also
require the renewal of communal life in places where the violence and
political hatreds of recent years had torn communities asunder. It was, in
fact, the desire to find fundamental solutions to the violence that provided
much of the initial impetus for the National Front's interest in community
development.

The ideal pattern for a true project of community development begins
with the assignment to a community by some outside agency of a *promotor*, sometimes accompanied by a team (an *equipo polivalente*) including typically a doctor, an agricultural technician, and a woman trained to
teach home economics. The promotor, or the team, then attempts to
determine which problem (for instance, the construction of a new school)
is of particular urgency and concern to the community and seeks to organize a committee of citizens to resolve the problem. The promotor also tries
to acquaint the people with the availability of certain kinds of assistance
from government agencies or private organizations or firms. If the initial
steps are successful, the citizens' committee will hopefully remain in being
to carry out still other community projects. The real test of success comes
when the outside agents who first moved the community to action with-

draw. The people are then left on their own to conduct elections to the citizens' committee and to make their own requests of government agencies and private organizations from which they may be entitled to receive loans, supplies, or technical assistance.

Fals Borda has adjudged the effects in one community: "No longer are those campesinos the submissive and ignorant ones who when the patrón passed took off their hats and greeted him with reverence or fear." [40] The statistics for schools, bridges, or aqueducts built, or for community centers established are in some areas of the country modestly impressive, and hundreds—even thousands—of community juntas have been formed throughout Colombia. The number of trained promotores is nevertheless small, and the campesinos' apathy deep-seated. Some of the organizations engaged in promoting acción comunal tend, moreover, to view it in a distinctly paternalistic light. Such an attitude derives in part from a half-conscious motivation to improve rural conditions without altering the real balance of social power in the countryside. Even in some communities where juntas exist and promotores have been assigned, the expectation lingers that community welfare depends upon the patrón rather than on the initiative of the community itself. [41] In still other cases, juntas have been created at the instance of politicians who, far from seeing such citizens' groups as challenges, have seen in them opportunities for the mobilization of support and the addition of a new façade to their own political machines. Juntas of communal action may be useful devices for requesting outside funds which can redound to the benefit of the politician able to claim responsibility for obtaining them. [42]

In sum, the existence of a junta, or even the presence of a promotor, does not ensure that deeply rooted attitudes and patterns of behavior have been eradicated. Acción comunal is apparently beginning to have a significant impact in certain communities. Its potential—for attitude

40. Fals Borda, Acción Comunal, p. 60.

41. Cf. A. Eugene Havens, "Critique of 'Proposal for an evaluation of Acción Comunal as an instrument of agricultural modernization and national economic development in Colombia,'" Mimeo. (1963[?]); and Holt, Colombia Today, p. 136.

42. According to one study, the workers of a Medellín textile factory felt left out of community development programs and inadequately represented on barrio committees for civic improvement. Centro de Investigaciones Sociales (CIS), Compañía Colombiana de Tejidos S.A. (Coltejer), Estudio sobre las Condiciones Sociales y Económicas de los Trabajadores de la Compañía y Posibilidades de Mejoramiento (Bogotá, CIS, 1962), pp. 178–84.

change, as well as for the material improvement of the conditions under which the Colombian campesino lives—may be great. But as yet, most Colombian communities have not experienced communal action in its true sense, and the evolution of a truly participant political culture in wide areas of rural Colombia would seem quite distant.

The agrarian reform enacted as Law 135 of 1961 and subsequently elaborated by various implementing decrees has been at once the most important and the most controversial undertaking of the National Front in the area of social reform and economic development. It is the touchstone of the coalition's reformist goals and of its ability to effect reform in the face of political opposition, some of it from within its own ranks. The stated aims of the reform were economic, as well as social, and included the augmenting of agricultural productivity by promoting more efficient land use and the conservation of natural resources. Nevertheless, it is social reform that in the text of Law 135 is put first among its objectives.[43]

The immediate motivation for the law's passage was neither economic nor social, however, but political. A number of the leaders of both parties in the coalition, but in particular Carlos Lleras Restrepo, at the time *jefe único* of the Liberal party, realized that for the National Front ever to attain real popular appeal it must offer a comprehensive, attractive program that would prove its interest in the Colombian masses. Moreover, it was hoped that the initiation of an agrarian reform would help to prevent an agrarian revolution, or a recrudesence of violence on the pre-1958 scale. The advent of the Castro Revolution in Cuba did much to stimulate this line of thinking. There were also political considerations of a more immediate, electoral kind. The MRL had won impressive support in the elections of March 1960, much of it in rural areas. This put heavy pressure on the oficialista Liberals, especially since they would be calling on Liberals to vote for a Conservative presidential candidate in 1962 according to the plan of alternación. At the same time, the Liberals could exert

43. The texts and a legalistic discussion of Law 135 and several of its supplementary decrees may be found in Alberto Aguilera Camacho, *Derecho Agrario Colombiano* (Bogotá, Ediciones Tercer Mundo, 1962). For the following discussion of Law 135 see also *Tierra: 10 Ensayos sobre la Reforma Agraria en Colombia* (Bogotá, Ediciones Tercer Mundo, 1961); Hirschman, *Journeys toward Progress,* chapter 2; and *Land Reform and Social Change.*

considerable leverage for the support of an agrarian law on the Ospinistas, who shared the government and who would need Liberal endorsement of their nominee as the joint candidate of the coalition.

Despite scattered outbreaks of violence and sporadic land invasions in some places, direct agitation or pressure by Colombia's campesinos for new agrarian legislation was largely absent. The campesino was (and is) poorly organized for concerted political action and he has had little voice in the councils of either the Conservative or the Liberal party. Nor does organized pressure group action from any other source seem to have played a major role in the passage of Law 135.

It is of considerable significance, however, that Lleras Restrepo, the chief architect of the law and the chief navigator of its passage through Congress, was working in a climate of public opinion favorably disposed to agrarian reform, at least in the abstract. Either during the course of the debate on Law 135 or in the years thereafter it is difficult to find anyone who has been opposed to agrarian reform in *principle*. In September 1960 the Colombian Church spoke officially of the necessity of an agrarian reform law. All political factions and parties, and all sectors of the press, gave at least lip service to the idea of an agrarian reform. Many landowners also supported the concept, especially as it might apply to the division of uncultivated land or the colonization of public lands.[44] The fact that large-scale Colombian agriculture was becoming increasingly commercialized, and that squatting had already effectively divided some of the large haciendas, made a law directed principally at the unproductive semifeudal large estate more attractive to some landowners than it would have been two or three decades earlier. The law also received support from certain economists and government officials who were not otherwise particularly interested in agrarian reform but who saw in it a device for increasing agricultural productivity and hence countering inflation and an adverse balance of payments.

As it emerged, Law 135 stressed the distribution of large landholdings to campesinos who lacked land or held only very small parcels. In any given area, publicly owned lands were to be divided first, followed if necessary by uncultivated privately owned and poorly cultivated private

44. Aaron Lipman, "Perception of the Colombian Agrarian Reform as a Value" (Typescript of paper presented at the annual meeting of the Rural Sociological Society, Los Angeles, Cal., Aug. 1963), pp. 8–9.

properties. Provision was made for the expropriation of effectively cultivated lands in special cases, such as those where the owner had subdivided his property and rented out individual lots without making any financial or managerial contribution of his own, where minifundio holdings were to be enlarged, or where "cultivation" meant extensive cattle grazing on fertile valley lands in regions where it was desirable to move campesinos from eroded mountain slopes. Private owners of cultivated or poorly cultivated properties were to be permitted to retain 100 hectares of arable land in case of expropriation.

Compensation for expropriated lands was similarly graded according to degree of land utilization. Thus owners of uncultivated lands were to be recompensed by 25-year, 2 per cent bonds; owners of inadequately cultivated lands and lands worked by sharecroppers and tenants, by 20 per cent cash up to certain limits, with the remainder in non-negotiable government securities repayable in eight equal installments carrying 4 per cent interest; and owners of adequately cultivated lands by 20 per cent cash with the remainder in five equal installments carrying 6 per cent interest.

The campesino who was provided with land under the agrarian reform was to pay for it, typically over a period of fifteen years on terms which were not particularly generous compared with agrarian reform programs in other countries.[45] Acquisition of title to such lands was made conditional upon performance for a certain period; nor was the purchaser to be free to resell or rent lands so acquired.

Law 135 gave attention to a second agrarian problem, the minifundio. Consolidation of excessively small holdings was to be undertaken and the subdivision of properties resulting in holdings of less than three hectares was made illegal. Still other provisions of the law dealt with credit, technical advice, irrigation, and other forms of assistance to the farmer which would be needed to make the new properties productive.

A very important feature of the law—one that Law 200 of 1936 did not contain—was the creation of the Colombian Institute of Agrarian Reform (*Instituto Colombiano de Reforma Agraria*—INCORA) to administer the law, with broad powers of implementation of the law's provisions. INCORA was to have a general manager appointed by the president, with a board

45. Joseph Thome in *Land Tenure Center Newsletter* (Madison, Wis., The University of Wisconsin), No. 17 (May–June 1964), pp. 6–7.

of directors composed of representatives of the relevant official and semi-
official government ministries and institutes, the Society of (Large) Farmers, the Association of Cattlemen, Catholic Action (to be appointed by
the archbishop primate), the rural workers, and the armed forces, plus two
members from both the Senate and the Chamber of Representatives. The
board was to be selected on a basis of political parity; the Congressional
members were also to represent the four major regions of the country.
INCORA was guaranteed by Law 135 100 million pesos annually in the
national budget, plus the proceeds from agrarian reform bonds.

As of April 1965 INCORA had authorized a number of cadastral surveys,
initiated 11 irrigation projects covering 300,000 hectares, consolidated
minifundios in a few areas, advanced credit totaling more than 40 million
pesos to more than 3,000 peasant families, and constructed almost 700
kilometers of feeder roads with another 1,100 planned or under construction. In line with Law 200 of 1936 it had also declared "the extinction of
private domain" with respect to almost 1,400,000 hectares of land which
had not been cultivated for 10 years. However, it had given titles to only
22,000 families, the great majority of whom were colonos, squatters who
already occupied but did not own their individual plots. *New* parcels
could be numbered in the hundreds, rather than in the thousands. Significantly, too, in view of INCORA's limited financial resources, the expense of
resettling families on new parcels was running about U.S. $2,000 each.[46]
Despite a certain initial dynamism in its application, the impact of Law
135 had so far been a modest one.

The gap between the law and its realization has been the consequence
of several factors. Lack of adequate information on such diverse matters
as soil conditions and land titles, and a shortage of competent administrative and technical personnel are among them. The Laureanistas and the
MRL, both at the time in the opposition, refused to participate in the public commission which drew up the law, then opposed its passage in Congress. The MRL and others on the Left have continued to assail the
government's handling of agrarian reform as too little and too slow. On
the Right, the INCORA's attempts to expropriate some cultivated lands have
been assailed as deviating from the law's intent. Likewise, 100 million

46. From a speech by Enrique Peñalosa, the director of INCORA, printed in *El
Tiempo,* March 24, 1965, p. 26. For the above data see this speech and Carlos Lleras
Restrepo in *El Tiempo,* April 19, 1965, p. 8.

pesos a year has proved a relatively small sum for a meaningful agrarian reform; given Colombia's fiscal difficulties not even that amount has always been available. Meanwhile landowners have made use of the cumbersome legal procedures required for the government to expropriate land, as well as direct pressure on the government, to delay or even avoid expropriation.

The controversy that has flared over agrarian reform indicates that this, more than any other National Front program, has touched a delicate nerve. The interests of at least certain elements among the elite are being directly attacked. But it is also clear that the steps are modest and gradual, and that Law 135 in itself is unlikely to reorder markedly the shape of social and political power. The fragility of the National Front and the strength of the opposition to Law 135, as well as the expense of any land reform which seeks to be "technical" and also to compensate rather liberally the expropriated landowners, place very real limits on the changes that can be effected.

Generally it can be said that the agrarian reform, like the rest of the coalition's program, attempts to advance the modernization of Colombia, to carry out those measures that would stimulate productivity, and to meet the most pressing social needs, while avoiding any very fundamental assault on the wellsprings of elite power.

LEADERSHIP UNDER THE NATIONAL FRONT

The first president under the National Front dispensation, Alberto Lleras Camargo, was its principal architect and in other ways was the ideal choice to make the system work. His previous one-year presidency had been marked by elections—elections that the Conservatives had won —in which the central government had scrupulously refused to intervene despite insistent pressures from fellow Liberals to do so. As Director-General of the Organization of American States from 1947–54, Lleras had been out of the country during the period of the most extreme political partisanship as well as at the time of the coup of June 13, 1953. Both his social background and his social philosophy marked him as a man in whom the elite could place its confidence in the existing crisis.[47] Lleras

47. See *Quién es Quién en Colombia*, 3rd ed., pp. 223–24; and Arthur P. Whitaker, *The United States and South America: The Northern Republics* (Cambridge, Mass., Harvard University Press, 1948), pp. 87–89, for data on Lleras.

was a dedicated constitutionalist and very much attuned to liberal values such as civil liberties and free elections. Yet in social and economic matters he was very much the moderate. Sometimes criticized by Conservatives for lacking "force," he was more often assailed from the Left for being a product of Colombia's "Athenian democracy" with its absence of concern for the masses and their needs.

If the National Front was the construction of a modernizing elite, Alberto Lleras Camargo was a true son of such an elite; if it was a product of moderation, fair play, and an evolving tendency to give the opposition its due, Lleras epitomized that spirit; if the National Front was the political device which could place Colombia once again in the ranks of those states of Latin America that inspired international confidence, Lleras enjoyed a high reputation abroad. Insofar as it depended on one man it would rest with him whether the National Front would prove a solution to the problems of violence and partisan intransigence, and whether "modernization from above" could succeed in Colombia.

As the near-perfect embodiment of its precepts, Alberto Lleras had been Mr. National Front. The man who succeeded him in August 1962 was likewise identified with the Front's creation and had for a time been its prospective first president. While sincerely committed to the ideal of the coalition, Valencia was very different from his predecessor. He had been born in the southwestern city of Popayán, the cradle of more than a dozen Colombian presidents and an area where the social distinctions and values of the traditional landed elite remained strongly embedded even in the mid-twentieth century. Valencia was given to flowery rhetoric, and his undisciplined oratory occasionally led him to commit unpolitic blunders. His appearance, which includes a black mustache, and hair worn just long enough to produce a slight wave in back, added to the impression of a somewhat anachronistic personal and political style. The net effect was to present an image which suggested, in contrast to Lleras, the stereotyped picture of the classic Colombian politician of the nineteenth century rather than the president of a modernizing nation skilled in the ways of administration and attentive to the undramatic facts of the balance of payments and the annual rate of economic growth.

Valencia was frequently accused of executive ineptitude. He delayed appointing an ambassador to the United States for almost a year following his inauguration; late in 1962 he felt forced to support a wage increase decreed by his Minister of Labor apparently without his own prior approval. For a time he seemed unable to contain pronouncements of his Minister of War, General Alberto Ruiz Novoa, that were critical of his government. Even Ruiz' eventual resignation from the Cabinet early in 1965 was brought about at the insistence of the army's high command, which felt that Ruiz' involvement in political controversy was damaging the military's unity and reputation.

From the start of his administration, and even before, critics representing almost every shade of political opinion censured Valencia for maladroitness, lack of firmness, and a fuzzily romantic approach to the problems of the country. Added to the inherent problems of the National Front system itself, and of the nation's economy and social order, was what almost all Colombians regarded as a weak president, one whom they had difficulty respecting.[48]

It is debatable, however, whether the prime responsibility for the faltering of the National Front after 1962 rested as much with President Valencia as with the system itself. To give Valencia his due, he at times surprised his countrymen with forthright action just when they were beginning to despair and when a coup seemed inevitable. His firm assertion of authority in the face of a rash of strikes in the summer of 1963 was one example. Moreover, there was a tendency in retrospect to depict the Lleras administration in more roseate tones than it perhaps merited. Thus it is the second government of the National Front that deserves most of the accolades for the really systematic reduction of violence below the level of 2–3,000 deaths a year which prevailed during the Lleras years. Lleras, too, came in for his share of criticism in 1961, as Valencia did subsequently, for failing to move resolutely when strikes threatened to paralyze the nation. Valencia was likewise a victim of economic dislocation arising from policies which both he and Lleras followed in an attempt to right the country's balance of payments difficulties. On Valencia fell the popular dissatisfaction over the resulting devaluation and inflation.

Most of all, the president was the captive of a system which favored accommodation over resolute action. Valencia's political skills were partly responsible for the temporary union of the major Conservative factions in

48. Good capsule characterizations of Valencia may be found in Pat M. Holt, "Constitutional Development in Colombia" (Paper prepared for delivery at the 1963 annual meeting of the American Political Science Association, New York, Sept. 1963), pp. 13–16, passim, and in Holt, *Colombia Today*, pp. 67–70.

1963. But in essence the problems of intraparty factionalism continued unabated, and to these were added an increasing tendency for pressure groups to become assertive in their demands on the executive. In January 1965 the two major labor confederations, initially with some support from representatives of business, threatened a general strike in the face of a new sales tax on non-necessity items. The strike was averted, partly by divisions in the ranks of the prospective strikers, partly by a capitulation by the government to some of their main demands. In recent years periodic consultations by the president with the combined representatives of the country's major pressure groups (the so-called "*fuerzas vivas*," literally the "live forces," which also include the parties), at "summit conferences" designed to reach mutual accommodations on some of the country's economic and social problems, have become virtually institutionalized. The government thus seems to have been forced into the position of not deciding on any major action without the agreement of the major pressure groups.

One cause of this situation has been the erosion of the popular base of the government coalition. In the plebiscite of December 1957, almost 4.4 million Colombians voted, an overwhelming majority of them in favor of the National Front reforms. With the exception of the 1962 congressional elections, until 1966 each subsequent election under the National Front— whether for president or Congress—was marked by a decline in the number of voters participating compared to the previous election. In the congressional elections of March 1964 the total vote dropped to 2,261,190, the lowest figure since the inauguration of the Front. Although the March 1966 elections evidenced some gain in the numbers voting, the totals still indicated an abstention rate of well over a half of those eligible. And this despite guarantees for the freedom of the actual electoral process unsurpassed in Colombian history.

The trend toward abstention has become a matter of considerable concern to the coalition partners, and a subject for lengthy analyses by political pundits. Abstention of course has one advantage for the Front—it at least means that many of those presumably dissatisfied with governmental performance, or with the operation of the bipartisan coalition, have not so far been willing to translate that disillusionment into a massive vote for those who would end or transform the system. Instead, there are increasing numbers of "the alienated non-involved." [49]

49. See Kenneth Johnson, "Political Radicalism in Colombia: Electoral Dynamics of 1962 and 1964," *Journal of Inter-American Studies* (Jan. 1965), pp. 15–26.

TABLE 8

PER CENT OF THOSE REGISTERED ACTUALLY VOTING IN ELECTIONS, 1946–1966 [50]

Election	No. of Voters	Eligible Voters [a]	% Voting of Those Eligible
May 1946 (presidential)	1,366,272	2,450,696	56
March 1947 (Chamber)	1,472,689	2,613,586	56
June 1949 (Chamber)	1,719,440	2,773,804	62
Nov. 1949 [b] (presidential)	1,140,646	2,856,339	40
Dec. 1957 (plebiscite)	4,397,090	6,080,342	72
March 1958 (Chamber)	3,693,939	5,365,191	69
May 1958 (presidential)	3,108,567	5,365,191	58
March 1960 (Chamber)	2,542,651	4,397,541	58
March 1962 (Chamber)	3,090,203	5,338,868	58
May 1962 (presidential)	2,634,840	5,404,765	49
March 1964 (Chamber)	2,261,190	6,135,628	37
March 1966 (Chamber)	2,843,450 [c]	7,126,980	40 (est.)
March 1966 (presidential)	2,593,705 [c]	7,126,980 [d]	36 (est.)

50. For all elections except those of 1966, see Registraduría del Estado Civil, *Organización y Estadísticas, 1964*, pp. 134–36. Some of the figures in this table may vary slightly from those in Table 7 since they are taken from different sources. For the two 1966 elections see *El Tiempo*, March 28 and May 6, 1966, respectively.

a. Neither prior registration nor possession of a cédula was required for the 1957 plebiscite. In the 1958 and 1960 elections eligible voters included those in possession of an identity document (cédula), plus those specially inscribed on the electoral rolls. In subsequent elections a cédula has been required, as was generally the case during the 1940s. However, the cedulazation process was then less advanced than it is today. Thus while the percentage of those eligible who voted during the 1940s is nearly on a par with the National Front years, the number of eligible voters was proportionately much smaller.

The high rate of abstention has meant that the government's claim to a solid popular base has become less and less credible. Given the lack of interparty competition, the leaders of the two traditional parties have found it difficult to base appeals to the electorate on the old partisan grounds. At the same time, they have been unable to replace such appeals by raising new social and economic issues. Prohibited by their own rules from having recourse to the old battle cries, and prevented by their elite-dominated party structures from generating dramatic new programs, the Liberal and Conservative parties have lost much of the reason for their existence. The result has been a political vacuum. The second government of the National Front was thus especially vulnerable to the demands of pressure groups and of factional groupings within both parties. For, besides the problems of consensus attainment inherent in the National Front, the government has lacked a real popular mandate which even a stronger president that Valencia would need to play effectively the role of modernizer.

During the first half of 1965 matters reached a crisis stage for President Valencia and the two-party coalition. In January there was a threatened general strike. The extraordinary session of Congress convoked in February did little to speed action on the president's proposals. A wave of kidnappings of prominent personalities, and the ensuing deaths of some, shook confidence in the government's ability to maintain the public security and led to the formation of self-defense groups in the better residential sections of some cities. A student strike produced enough disorder to serve as the pretext for the government's declaration of a modified state of siege in May. Then in June the peso soared to its highest rate yet in relation to the dollar, ranging from 17–20 to 1. Meanwhile the president's efforts to maintain neutrality among the Conservative factions led to the partial alienation of the Ospinistas, although they continued to cooperate in the government as did the Laureanistas and the Alzatistas. On some

b. The presidential election of November 1949 was noncompetitive. The figures for eligible voters are not available for the 1951 and 1953 congressional elections, which the Liberals also did not contest.

c. 1966 figures on the number of voters are slightly understated, since final returns were not available at the time of writing.

d. It is not clear whether additional citizens obtained cédulas between March and May 1966. The March figure is therefore also used for the May election; the difference would be very small in any case.

issues, however, the Laureanistas flirted with the ANAPO and MRL forces in Congress. Rumors persisted of a coup which would replace the president with a civil-military junta or with another Conservative presumably more capable of dealing with the national problems. The period of acute crisis passed, however, and President Valencia completed his term amid a new wave of general optimism over the future.

The accession of Lleras Restrepo to the presidency in August 1966 was to bring to the office a man of considerable administrative talents and knowledge of economics, with extensive experience in business. A relative of Lleras Camargo, although not particularly close to him politically, he was less the man "above parties" than his cousin. He had been either "single chief" or member of a committee of directors of the Liberal party on at least six separate occasions. Usually considered slightly left-of-center within the Liberal party, he was the principal architect of the agrarian reform law of 1961 and has been dubbed by Albert Hirschman a consummate "reformmonger." Lleras Restrepo as president would therefore possess many of the qualities President Valencia allegedly lacked. As a representative of the Liberal majority, and as a driving force for modernization within the National Front framework, he might even win back some Colombians from their present stance of electoral abstention. On the other hand, he is a product of the Colombian elite and he would of course be constrained by the constitutional framework and intrinsic political difficulties of the National Front arrangement.[51] His presidency would further test the viability of the system as such, as distinct from the particular man who had been chosen to make it work.

THE NATIONAL FRONT: CONSENSUS AND MODERNIZATION

The National Front was born because "The greatest enemy of a Conservative is not a Liberal (nor vice versa) but a dictator."[52] But it was an attempt to go beyond the transient coalitions of the past by institutionalizing for both of Colombia's historic parties an equal share in the direction of the state. Succinctly put, "Each party agreed not to try to win an election in return for a guarantee that it would not lose one."[53] Take away all

51. For data on Carlos Lleras Restrepo, see *Quién es Quién en Colombia*, 3rd ed., pp. 176–77.
52. Laureano Gómez in *El Frente Nacional*, p. 16.
53. Holt, *Colombia Today*, p. 47.

possibility of exclusive control of the government by one party, and with alternation take away even any partisan dispute over the presidency—all this for sixteen years—and you take away also the motives for political violence: "If there are many who kill or die for power, there will be few who kill or die to serve." [54] The intent was to effect consensus by putting into constitutional form the "rules of the game" respecting the opposition and the ways of political compromise which had never really evolved as part of the nation's political culture.

Underpinning the new political arrangement was the enlarging role of government in the nation's economic life. The Colombian state had become increasingly interventionist since the 1930s and the economy itself had grown both more productive and more complex. The control by one party over all access to government jobs and government favor, implying the simultaneous exclusion of the other one half of Colombians, was becoming less and less feasible. The National Front marked the recognition of such facts on the part of the Colombian elite. The old divisions were becoming less relevant in the face of a rapidly developing economy.[55]

Paradoxically, the most serious political problem facing the bipartisan experiment has not been one of conflict between the parties but that of factionalism within each. The practice of according proportional representation to intraparty factions in legislative bodies makes of each election essentially two parallel party primaries, deciding struggles for power or office internal to each party. The primary and the general election are thus one and the same. The altered pattern of factional representation within the Congress which sometimes results can prove disruptive to the intricate negotiations between the parties. This occurred pursuant to the congressional elections of 1960 in which the Laureanistas lost their majority within the Conservative party to the Alza-Ospinistas.

Moreover, the two-thirds requirement in Congress means that a combination of opposition factions of both parties, plus, on occasion, defections from oficialista ranks on particular issues, can at times seriously hamper legislative action. Since 1960 the government has on various occasions lacked a two-thirds majority. Since the Laureanistas have generally

54. Luis López de Mesa, "Exegisis de la Novísima Reforma Constitucional Colombiana," *Universidad de Antioquia*, No. 134 (July–Sept. 1958), p. 523.
55. See Hernández Rodríguez, *Alternación ante el Pueblo*, pp. '69, 75–76, and 83, for this point.

supported the Front itself, and the opposition has not usually been able to coalesce, the situation has not become critical. Nevertheless, some important bills, including the agrarian reform bill in 1960–61, have met rather effective resistance from the MRL, from the Laureanistas, and more recently from the ANAPO.

Neither of these difficulties is as crucial to the very existence of the coalition as is another. This is the danger that within one of the parties a faction opposed to the concept of the National Front might win a majority.[56] This would call into question not merely the particular composition of the government or the fate of its program, but the system itself. It would confront those in both parties who supported the Front with a choice: to continue governing with the majority of one party and the minority pro-Front faction of the other, based on the rationale that to operate the system it must rest on the political support of those who favor its continuation (the so-called "qualitative" approach), or to bend to the numerical opposition majority within a given party and attempt to work out a modus vivendi between it and its coalition partner (the "quantitative" solution). Presumably the latter might be at least conceivable since, though an opposition faction might oppose the Front, it would face the problem of how to coexist with the other party without precipitating either civil war or the intervention of the military.

There are other possibilities, even more drastic in their consequences for the Great Coalition. One would be its rejection by a majority of the electorate through defeat of pro-Front factions in both parties in a congressional election, or defeat of the Front's presidential nominee by a rival of his own party. Still another would be the victory of the presidential candidate of one party in a year in which the constitution prescribed that the presidency was to go to a member of the other. The logic of the López Michelsen candidacy in 1962 was precisely that his victory would constitute a new "plebiscite" which would force revision of the National Front agreement.[57]

Actual disruption of the National Front by such means seems unlikely in the immediate future. The above are nevertheless suggestive of some of the political pitfalls facing the Front and help to explain the inordinate

56. As a result of the 1966 elections the ANAPO came very close to becoming the leading Conservative faction.

57. See Hernández Rodríguez, *Alternación,* for a cogent presentation of that logic.

attention which goes into factional maneuvering on the part of those working for its success, often at the cost of delay in facing pressing national problems. Elections therefore tend to center on the issue of the continuation of the National Front. Even apart from factionalism among those supporting the Front itself, elections usually call forth from within each party a slate opposed to the National Front as an institution. The coalition is thus placed under the strain every two years of having to undergo what is in effect another plebiscite to determine whether the very system shall survive.

With the end of the second four-year presidential term of its scheduled sixteen-year duration and the inauguration of Lleras Restrepo the National Front had met the first test of any political arrangement—it had survived. And whether or not it completed its indicated life-span it would have several marks to its credit in helping to build political consensus and political stability in Colombia. It had succeeded to a noteworthy degree in dampening the spirit of intense political partisanship, at least between the two parties if not among their various factions. It had led to the evolution of mechanisms, both formal and informal, for arriving at understandings between the parties, including the selection of joint presidential nominees. The National Front had also witnessed the transfer of the presidency from one party to the other. If one included the accession of a Liberal in 1958 as a similar transfer, the National Front had already been responsible for three contiguous alternations—no small achievement in the context of Colombian, or Latin American, political history. The Great Coalition had likewise overseen the restoration of a large measure of civil and political liberty for Colombians. Although arrests of "subversives" occurred which at times seemed arbitrary and born of official hysteria, and although third parties could not present candidates for office under the system of strict parity, the contrast with the previous nine or ten years was striking. A resurgence of militarism had meanwhile been avoided—although the loyalty of the military to constitutionalism undoubtedly would continue to depend upon the ability of the politicians to maintain the political peace—and all attempts at a forcible comeback by Rojistas had been frustrated. Furthermore, the coalition had thus far retained at least the minimum necessary popular support and had fended off the anti-National Front forces, the victory of which within either party would create a political crisis of serious proportions. Finally, there was the probability that, even if the National Front did not complete its statutory life-span, a part of its original intent would be preserved in the form of a constitutionally acknowledged role in government for the party in opposition. That much was suggested by the wording of the plebiscitary reform of 1957 which in various of its clauses did not limit constitutional changes to the expected duration of the Front.[58]

The potential significance of the National Front is greater still. For from its beginning it has been far more than an ingenious attempt to secure political peace by means of an institutionalized coalition. It was also to serve as the instrumentality through which the Colombian elite hoped to modernize the country under its own auspices. One facet of this effort is an enhanced role for the state in accelerating economic development. The other entails government initiative in such fields as taxation, housing, education, health, community development, and agrarian reform, seeking thereby to provide some of the conditions necessary for economic development, to assuage the potential explosiveness of social inequities, and to secure a popular political base for the sectors of the traditional parties that are partners in the coalition government.

It may therefore be concluded that the Colombian elite, or rather a significant portion of it, has become a modernizing one with a view to moving the nation through a period of rapid economic growth and social change without further violence or another military dictatorship, and above all without social revolution. The ultimate *objective* is the preservation of the position of the elite; the *method* involves a greater consciousness than in the past of what survival of the Colombian ruling class may require in terms of controlled change. As former President Alberto Lleras candidly put it, the National Front was conceived, among other reasons, "in order that the national governing class might dedicate itself for sixteen years to realizing a gigantic effort of progress and justice, without tearing itself to pieces." [59] The ultimate political question is whether this will be sufficient. Failing the development of more effective institutional links between the elite and the masses, and the involvement of a broader segment of the population in both the decisions and rewards of development, the best intentions and the best leadership skills of a modernizing elite might well prove unequal to the tasks of change.

58. See ibid., esp. pp. 94–100.
59. Lleras Camargo, quoted in *Revista Javeriana*, Aug. 1961, p. (41).

PART IV

The Dynamics of Change

7

THE GOVERNMENT

THE ADMINISTRATIVE TRADITION AND THE WEAK STATE

If France is a nation with rival representative and administrative traditions of government whose primacy within the state has alternated periodically since the French Revolution; and if in Great Britain those two traditions have been successfully fused; in Colombia, as in Latin America generally, they persist in uneasy coexistence.[1] For Colombia has been, and remains, a product both of the Spanish Empire and of a revolutionary epoch which gave birth to republics of liberal individualism. In Colombia the republic has never really eliminated the centralizing paternalism of the imperial administrative state. Nor have the two successfully merged. Instead, many of the forms and attitudes which characterized the empire have survived to infuse and often dominate the representative state which presumably had superseded it during the second decade of the nineteenth century.

Colombia has had ten constitutions in the years since 1811. The present one has been in force since 1886, despite some major amendments, including two codifications in 1936 and 1945.[2] All of these constitutions have been republican, based in theory on popular sovereignty; all have provided for a separation of powers between executive, legislative, and judicial branches of government; all have protected civil and political liberties in some substantial measure.

1. See the chapters by Nicholas Wahl and Harry Eckstein in Samuel Beer and Adam Ulam, eds., *Patterns of Government* (2nd ed. New York, Random House, 1962).
2. Gibson, *Constitutions,* contains English translations of all the Colombian constitutions and codifications up through 1945. For a Spanish version of the current text which includes the amendments of the National Front period see Escuela Superior de Administración Pública (ESAP), *Organización Constitucional del Estado Colombiano* (Bogotá, Editorial Bremen, 1962).

Two facets of this representative side of Colombia's political tradition are worth particular notice. The first is that the Colombian Congress has generally been stronger and more resistant to executive encroachment than the national legislatures of most other Latin American states (with the especially notable exception of Chile). The distinction is admittedly highly relative and subject to striking lapses. Yet the reaction of a Liberal Congress to the programs of President López in the years 1937–38; the struggles between president and Congress in the years 1946–49; and the lethargic response of Congress to the initiatives of the executive under the National Front make it quite clear that the legislature has often not been a rubber-stamp. Contrary to experience elsewhere in Latin America, such phenomena as the state of siege, the forced adjournment of Congress, and dictators acting by decree and without congressional sanction have been rare in Colombia, especially in the twentieth century. The years 1949–58 have constituted the major recent exception. But even President Gómez found that he was unable fully to control a Congress made up exclusively of members of his own party, while Rojas' own legislative creature—the ANAC—at times objected to the exercise of his fiat.

A second Colombian distinction is the relatively greater respect for civil and political liberties compared to most other Latin American countries. This can be seen in the free and vocal press that has been one of the country's cherished traditions. To be sure, that tradition has been abridged on occasion, notably under the state of siege in the years after 1949, although even then not completely for very much of the time. But in keeping with the norms of the country's "Athenian democracy" systematic censorship or suppression has been rare. Today, when Colombia's ruling elite is in the greatest potential danger of its history, newspapers which openly call for violent revolution have generally been free to publish. The chief limitation on a fully free press in Colombia is that it is largely in the hands of those who control other forms of power. Difficulties in obtaining financing and advertising usually have kept newspapers not representing the views of some faction of the elite to weekly or irregular publication schedules or to short-lived existences.

In fine, dictatorships have been few and there is a significant measure of reality to the representative side of Colombian political tradition, even though it has existed within the context of a politics of limited participation.

Nevertheless, the heritage of strong, paternalistic, centralized power has been paramount. To begin with, the Colombian constitution accords to the president very great authority, considerably more, certainly, than that held by the chief executive in the United States. The Colombian president has the power of the item veto. He also has a free hand in naming and removing Cabinet ministers, ambassadors, governors of the departments, and most other executive officers, without the necessity of congressional approval.

In addition, Article 121 asserts that "In case of foreign war or internal disturbance the President may, with the signatures of all the Ministers, declare the public order disturbed and all or part of the Republic to be in a state of siege." Under the provisions of this article the president may suspend any laws that he regards as incompatible with the state of siege, and he may issue those decrees which he deems necessary under the circumstances. As set forth in the Constitution of 1886 these powers were to have their limits, including a constraint against repeal of extant statutes and the requirement of ministerial countersignatures. But since *suspension* of any law was not forbidden, and the ministers could be named and replaced at will, such caveats were of minor import. It was upon Article 121, in fact, that the post-1949 regimes founded the legality of many of their actions.

There is one constitutional limitation on presidential power that does not apply in some other presidential systems—a prohibition against the chief executive's immediate reelection. Generally speaking, however, the power accorded the president by the Colombian constitution is formidable.

Nor has Congress been reluctant to delegate considerable additional authority to the president. Legislation that leaves broad leeway to detailed elaboration by means of executive decree is common and constitutional provision is made for Congress' granting extraordinary powers to the president for rule-making purposes (Art. 76). Thus in 1963 Congress granted the president special powers to issue decrees in the fields of fiscal and judicial reform, both highly important areas which impinge on many vital interests. As Pat M. Holt has commented, "What all this amounted to, in effect, was that the Congress was asked (and seemed willing) to give the President power to do something for which Congress itself was not willing to take the responsibility. This is not a very happy commentary on the growth of representative government of limited powers." [3] This is not to say that the Colombian Congress has become docile; it assuredly has not,

3. Holt, "Constitutional Development in Colombia," pp. 15–16.

as its initial recalcitrance over Law 135 of 1961 testifies. However, it is more effective at obstruction than at positive action. For the most part, its power to enact legislation is a power to formalize what has been decided elsewhere. Its utility is largely confined to its acting as a sounding board for opinion in the country and as an instrument to glean benefits for various local interests.

The *relative* impotence of Congress is reflected in popular image, which portrays it as dilatory, negative, and prone to "immobilism." Its members' own view of it is best demonstrated by the very high rate of absenteeism and the readiness with which some major political leaders yield their seats to *suplentes* (alternates). It is not only the strength of the president that accounts for this, but the weakness of the congressmen's ties with the constituents they presumably represent. A seat in Congress is looked on primarily as an honor or a perquisite rather than as a post from which to serve the public (or which must be so used if reelection is to be achieved). One critic has called the Colombian Congress "a tribune for oratorical debates, a kind of proscenium for the rhetorical jousts of gentlemen but not for the study of laws and measures contributing to economic and social progress." [4] Colombians find it something to be marveled at that individuals in the United States can write or call or wire their representatives in Congress to demand action on a bill, to lodge a complaint against an administrative official, or to request some similar action. Without such grassroots support—and pressure—the Colombian Congress is all the more subject to the blandishments of the executive.

The Colombian judiciary likewise bears strong traces of the administrative tradition. The system of law is that of the codified Roman law, and juries of one's peers play little role in its application. An important place is granted to administrative law, with a Council of State as the supreme appeal body in that area. The Supreme Court does have the final decision in cases where legislative acts have been vetoed by the president as being unconstitutional and his veto has been overridden by absolute majorities of both houses of Congress, or when the question of the constitutionality of a law or decree issued under the government's emergency or decree powers is brought before it by a citizen or is referred to it by Congress.[5] Such provisions, along with Colombia's legalistic traditions, do constitute

---

4. Gutiérrez, *La No-Violencia*, p. 54.

5. The Council of State has jurisdiction in cases involving the constitutionality of ordinary executive decrees.

something of a restraint and the courts have on occasion modified the clear intent of a law through their interpretation of it.[6] But the members of the Council of State and of the Supreme Court have generally not been appointed for life, with the majority, in pre-National Front days, normally corresponding to the partisan coloring of the administration. The judiciary was neither able nor willing to pose an effective barrier to the deterioration of legal guarantees of civil and political liberties during the 1950s.

This situation is not entirely the counterpart of executive strength. It stems in equal measure from the judiciary's involvement in the play of partisan politics, of "connections," and of favoritism toward those highest on the social scale. There has also been a serious overloading of court dockets. Such circumstances have led to considerable cynicism on the part of Colombians toward their system of justice. For a variety of reasons, while the writing, codifying, and citing of law plays a central role for Colombians, it is often the law of the ideal, or of distant authority. Its norms tend to be only weakly internalized, while the organs which interpret and apply the law fail to elicit the kind of public support that would be necessary in any showdown with the executive.

The dominant role of the Colombian executive is further enhanced by a unitary, centralized administration. Municipal councils are elective, as are departmental assemblies. But governors are appointed by the president, and mayors in turn by the governors. The powers of the departmental assemblies are primarily administrative rather than legislative (the assemblies are termed administrative corporations by the constitution), and the governors have the right of absolute veto over their actions (Art. 194). The fiscal powers of the departments and municipios are limited. Even supposedly semi-autonomous agencies such as the special credit institutions and the Social Security Institute, which have been established over the last several decades to cope with various aspects of a modern economy and society, are substantially subject to presidential authority.

It is ultimately on the president and the central government that all the organs of administration throughout the country depend. The administrative tradition inherited from the colony is thereby largely maintained. Local government, which Tocqueville considered a bulwark of democracy in North America, is correspondingly weak.[7] As it is, the government

6. Hernández Rodríguez, *Alternación ante el Pueblo,* p. 107.

7. Alexis de Tocqueville, *Democracy in America,* ed. Henry Steele Commager, World's Classics Edition (London, Oxford University Press, 1953), chapter 5. Gabriel

of the Colombian municipio is responsible in the first instance to the governor who appoints its mayor, rather than to the community. Popular participation in the political process is to that extent frustrated and the distance between government and the people is widened. The ancient Spanish tradition of the municipality lingers mainly as a memory.

Above all, constitutional provisions and institutional behavior are supplemented by a set of attitudes among Colombians that induces them to look for decisions to their social or legal superiors. There is a marked tendency to expect largesse from the government, from one's patrón, or from some other individual or entity representing power and authority. Authority is expected to be paternally interested in the welfare of those over whom it exercises jurisdiction and its acts are supposed not to be arbitrary. But there is little conception of common action for a common goal, scant tendency to exercise local initiative, and little feeling of political self-confidence.[8] As the study of one Colombian community put it: "Both colonos and workers of all categories . . . suffer feelings of inferiority and inadequacy with regard to political activities and decisions, in the face of the intellectual capacity and the economic power of the higher ranking employees . . . the hacienda owners, and the paternalistic political leaders . . . and in the face of the . . . power of the high officials and organs of the State."[9] Contributions by way of taxes, military service, or obligatory labor on municipal projects have produced few visible benefits in return, especially for the campesino. As a rule he rarely considers making reciprocal demands.[10] For the most part Colombians are not true participants but subjects, much as their ancestors were under the Spanish monarchy.

Almond and Sidney Verba have attempted to give the concept a comparative empirical referent in *The Civic Culture* (Princeton, N.J., Princeton University Press, 1963); see e.g. pp. 188–89.

8. A subject political culture is defined by Almond and Verba as one where there is a high frequency of passive orientations to the "output" or administrative side of the political system. It is distinguished from a parochial political culture, where a high proportion of persons attach little or no meaning to the actions of government, and from a participant political culture, where individuals feel they are not merely subject to political authority but are able and willing to participate in or otherwise influence the decision-making process. See Almond and Verba, *The Civic Culture*, pp. 17 ff.

9. Centro de Investigaciones Sociales (CIS), *Estudio sobre las Condiciones del Desarrollo de la Región de Tibú (Catatumbo), Cúcuta* (Bogotá, CIS, 1960), p. 233.

10. Cf. Pearse and Rivera, *La Tenencia de la Tierra*, p. 129.

The republican legitimation of Colombian political institutions therefore clashes with the reality of the country's administrative tradition of government, and with a structure of social power and a set of attitudes toward political life which in important respects limit or make ineffective popular participation in government.

Centralized government, with authority concentrated in the executive branch and founded on a subject political culture, does not necessarily imply a strong state. On several grounds the Colombian state may be considered a weak one.

One mark of the strong state is its ability to expect or enforce compliance with its laws. Yet smuggling (of coffee, cattle, arms) over Colombia's long land and sea frontiers is a persistent problem; tax evasion is routine; and Colombians readily acknowledge that they carry forward the colonial tradition of *"se obedece, pero no se cumple"* (one obeys, but does not comply) with respect to the law.

The violence of the past fifteen years—still not entirely eradicated—has been both evidence and a partial cause of the government's inability to assert its authority over all Colombians. From 1949 until 1958 certain areas of rural Colombia were in virtual rebellion. Even after the political peace of the National Front, bandit gangs terrorized parts of the countryside and received aid, coerced or willing, from residents. Other districts, including the bailiwicks of some former guerrilla leaders, have remained almost immune to outside authority.[11] In the cities, beginning about the time of the bogotazo, crimes of robbery and burglary markedly increased. Citizens of the upper and middle classes, regarding public protection as inadequate, began to pay mobile watchmen's patrols for the nighttime protection of their homes.[12] In late 1964 and into 1965 there was a wave of kidnappings of prominent persons for the ransom they would bring. A major consequence of these several forms of violence has been an undermining of public confidence in organs of authority such as the police, the courts, and political and governmental leaders.[13] That the government has felt it necessary to resort repeatedly to the state of siege and to extraordi-

11. See below, chapter 13, for a more thorough treatment of rural violence and the so-called independent republics.

12. Lipman, *El Empresario Industrial,* p. 68.

13. Cf. Aaron Lipman and A. Eugene Havens, "The Colombian Violencia: An Ex Post Facto Experiment," Mimeo. (Madison, Wis., University of Wisconsin Land Tenure Center, 1965); and see below, chapter 13.

nary powers since the mid-1940s reveals how weak the inherent authority of the state actually has become.

The Colombian government also fails to provide adequately a number of those services usually considered incumbent on the modern state. This is notably true with respect to education, where the public school system has failed to keep pace with the demand. In the city of Bogotá, for example, the number of private schools increased from 856 in 1951 to 2,277 in 1960, without a corresponding rise in the number of public institutions.[14] Where programs of public works or social welfare have existed, individual and regional interests have tended to dilute them, or their execution, to the point that truly national programs become difficult to carry out. In the first two days of the 1963 regular session of Congress, for example, 47 of the 49 bills introduced dealt with assistance to specific regions or localities rather than with broad national concerns.[15] The budget, too, becomes a vehicle for interests which are not those of development. Much of this is inevitable, even desirable, in a political process which aspires to be democratic. But insofar as it overwhelms and *determines* policy in a nation that is attempting to evolve coherent programs of development, it poses serious problems.

The instruments for the execution of economic and social policy have also been weak and uncoordinated in Colombia. True, since 1934 and even before a number of agricultural and industrial credit institutions have been established through government action (for example, the Institute of Municipal Development, the Institute of Industrial Development, and the Agrarian Credit Bank), a steel mill was erected under government auspices at Paz del Río in the department of Boyacá, a government oil corporation was created, the Cauca Valley Corporation was launched, and an institute was formed to administer the social security laws. Through such activities the state has become deeply involved in the economic and social arenas. The Colombian state is therefore a good deal stronger today than it was at the start of López' revolution on the march. It has been gradually assuming some of the functions formerly carried out by private individuals or by the Church, and it has been taking on new tasks previously not performed at all. Nevertheless the economic and social programs of

14. Lipman, *El Empresario Industrial*, p. 68.

15. Pedro Tascón Martínez, "Los Proyectos Electoreros," *El Colombiano* (Medellín), July 26, 1963, p. 3.

the government still fail in large part to reach the campesino. Lacking, too, has been any real order of priorities, and any systematic consideration of how the nation's resources can best be applied to its overall and rapid development. A further obstacle to the effective implementation of national policy is a dearth of personnel trained to carry out the administrative and technical tasks of modernization.

Yet another manifestation of the weak state, which at the same time has the effect of strengthening the presidency, is the deferment to the chief executive of problems that arise at all levels throughout the society. It is true that in all presidential systems this is so to a degree. But in Colombia the president is called upon to mediate an unusually broad range of disputes—student strikes, bank clerks' strikes, sugar workers' strikes, and departmental political questions—and frequently at an early stage in their development.[16] The other organs of government very often prove inadequate to the case, as do more informal processes. This in turn forces the president to devote his personal attention (or that of his ministers), and to stake his own prestige, on the resolution of such matters.

Lastly, many Colombians, because of poor communications, illiteracy, their economic condition, or their social attitudes, have little awareness of national issues, and little interest in a common national welfare. Their lives and their political consciousness—to the degree that they possess the latter at all—center on the *patria chica* (little fatherland). The state is remote. It may make demands on the campesino, but it does not inspire his deep loyalty. The Colombian state therefore cannot count on evoking broad understanding or popular support for its policies. The majority of Colombians have thus far not come to identify their own well-being with that of the nation and with their own responsibility for the nation's welfare. Yet this is essential if the administrative state is to be made truly representative and the weak state ultimately to be made strong.

THE SPOILS SYSTEM

One feature of a weak state, its lack of neutrality, has been evidenced in Colombia by the prevalence of the spoils system, especially in the years before establishment of the National Front. The rule of one party has fre-

16. For this phenomenon in Peru see James Payne, *Labor and Politics in Peru* (New Haven, Conn., Yale University Press, 1965). He terms it *"political bargaining."*

quently meant the almost total exclusion of members of the other from government. The parties have treated government as an objective to be seized and, once won, as a bastion in which to intrench themselves like armies of occupation, subsisting on the bureaucratic booty of battle. The phenomenon has not been confined, of course, to Colombia, but its virulence there and its impact on the political system have been augmented by several factors and have particular relevance for Colombian political behavior.

For Colombians posts in the bureaucracy entail a certain social standing. Even a clerkship is at least a white-collar occupation. This attitude is to be anticipated in a society where manual labor and commercial enterprise have traditionally been scorned. For some, such as those from upper-class backgrounds who have lost out economically, or for members of the old middle class, a government post may be one of the few personally acceptable means of livelihood. For others, a government job may be a channel of upward social mobility, a leap from the status of obrero to that of empleado. This produces a situation similar to that noted by Lipset in American trade unions, where the attractiveness and social prestige of union offices give their holders a large stake in retaining their positions.[17] Beneath the skin of every Colombian, it is said, breathes a public employee.

Government, and those in government, are likely to be regarded as sources of personal favors or benefits rather than as vehicles of service to a generalized public.[18] This is consonant with a political culture which has small regard for the "anonymous other," or for common efforts pursued for common objectives, but instead stresses the ties of kinship and the patria chica. Colombian administration is reputed not to be particularly corrupt in the more flagrant sense of large-scale bribery. But nepotism, "connections" (*palancas*), petty bribery, and similar means of acquiring private influence and advantage are widespread. In addition, the importance of the executive branch of government means that the key points of

17. Lipset, *Political Man*, pp. 402–04.

18. The Reichel-Dolmatoffs note of the community of Aritama, " 'Employment' especially connotes any position carrying prestige but almost or wholly devoid of personal responsibility (i.e., a sinecure) and is highly desirable, in fact is regarded as a privilege. Even members of the political administration, schoolteachers, or truck-drivers do not 'work'—and indeed do not feel obligated to maintain a continuous effort." Reichel-Dolmatoff, *The People of Aritama*, p. 259.

access in the political process are not in the legislature, but in the government departments where contracts are let, licenses approved, rulings enforced, and settlements in labor disputes arbitrated. It is therefore usually more important to have influence in the administration than to be able to exert political pressure on a chairman of a congressional committee or to sway popular opinion through a public relations campaign. In short, it is highly desirable to be a part of the "army of occupation" that has captured the executive branch. In the face of a bureaucracy which is not neutral, political victory for his party or group may become crucial for the individual who depends on it or who seeks to manipulate it for his own ends.

All this might have less significance if it were true, as Tocqueville remarked about the United States, that in neither party was any great number of private interests affected by success or defeat.[19] The opposite, however, has been Colombia's situation. There the government is the greatest industry, the greatest employer, the greatest educator, the greatest spender, and the greatest, if not the only, dispenser of glory: "owing to the weakness of our autonomous or independent institutions, many people mistakenly think that here there is no possible glory, if it is not . . . political glory, as if the true glory . . . could not be attained outside of the public posts which so dazzle and blind us. In such a society, the conduct of the government is decisive on the conduct of the members." [20] In more developed societies, a greater diversity of centers of economic and social power, and the relative availability of opportunities for profit and employment apart from governmental favor, mean that in matters affecting their daily lives and their economic survival most men are not vitally dependent on who controls the government.

Not so with many Colombians. Thus the expenditures of the Colombian government comprise a larger percentage of the national income than that of the United States government, despite the latter's huge outlays for defense and foreign aid.[21] A 1962 survey of employment patterns in three Bogotá districts found that 13 per cent of the employed worked in "government services." A study of a community in a rural area reported that

19. Tocqueville, p. 58.

20. Gonzalo Canal Ramírez and Jaime Posada, *La Crisis Moral Colombiana* (Bogotá, Editorial Antares, 1955), pp. 112–13.

21. Alberto Galindo, "La Estructura Económica del País," in *La Nación ante la Universidad*, p. 81. Cf. also Molina, *Laureano Gómez*, p. 123; he refers to the budget as "the umbilical cord of Colombian history."

between a fourth and a third of the families of the town had at least one member in a paid official post.[22] In the relative absence of nongovernmental channels of social mobility the competition for recruitment to political positions becomes a substitute.

Colombia's centralized and unitary form of government has meant that the party which captured the national administration was able to dictate the appointments of such officials as mayors, police chiefs, district judges, and even teachers in the public school system. It is also the national administration that is largely responsible for public works and many services in a country where difficult terrain and the paucity of local tax resources make these particularly important to many local interests.

> To lose power . . . meant that the mayor of the town would turn into a dangerous enemy, that the official of the branch of the Agrarian Bank would refuse the loan, that the new teacher would look with disfavor on one's child attending school, that the official of the Department of Health would first attend his fellow partisan of the other party because he was "of the same ones" and that it was necessary to remain at a prudent distance from the local police.[23]

For all the above reasons, the stakes riding on control of the central government tend to be high in Colombia. The result is that "Politics presides over everything: love and hate, peace and war, good fortune and misfortune, health and happiness, poverty and riches, in a word, good and evil." [24]

Many Colombians have ascribed to the spoils system a major role in the bitter antagonisms between the country's traditional parties. Thus the Pact of Sitges declared that it was necessary to "suppress the concept that the political victor has a right to the spoils of the vanquished and to transform the public administration from top to bottom, replacing all the employees with a new set of favorites. The tragedy of each transfer of power

22. Antequera Stand, *Ocupación y Desocupación,* p. 45; and Pearse and Rivera, p. 129. Colombian public employees (national, state, and municipal) numbered 183,000 in 1963, exclusive of employees of the semi-autonomous agencies and the military; *El Tiempo,* Aug. 5, 1963, p. 32, citing figures of the National Statistical Department (DANE).

23. *Semana,* Oct. 28–Nov. 3, 1958, p. 12.

24. Cuéllar Vargas, *13 Años de Violencia,* p. 76.

in Colombia has been precisely [that] . . . the current employees promote violence in order to defend their posts and aspiring employees promote it in order to acquire them." [25] It does seem probable that the contest over public posts has contributed to the intensity of Colombian political struggles, but its responsibility for la violencia should not be overemphasized. Other nations have had spoils systems without Colombia's civil strife.

A second consequence of the spoils system is that it increases the dependence of the lower party ranks on the parties' leaderships, since places in the bureaucracy, as well as appointments to such positions as judge, teacher, and municipal official, depend on party loyalty. Whiteford notes, for example, in his study of Popayán, that many of those who work for one of the political parties are members of the lower class who seek through such political ties to attain posts with the government that will entail for them advancement on the social scale.[26] The spoils system accordingly acts as a deterrent to the non-elite sectors of Colombian society finding their own independent channels of political expression.

Finally, the tenacity of a system that ties bureaucratic appointments to the color of one's political affiliation is a drag on the process of modernization. There are few enough trained persons to perform technical and administrative tasks; lack of adequate personnel is in fact one of the key bottlenecks in Colombia's programs of economic development and agrarian reform. A system of spoils adds to the difficulty by leading to wholesale dismissals with each change of administration, and by inducing the misallocation of a scarce resource. It may likewise discourage those with development skills from accepting positions in the public service because of the questionable tenure of such jobs or the expectation of political interference in their performance. Such persons are already less susceptible than others to the attractions of government employment since their talents are in demand in the private sector, usually at higher salaries.

The spoils system thus has implications for public order and the party system, for continued elite control of Colombian society, and for the efficacy of the state as an agent of modernization. In its Colombian guise it is a prime illustration of the effects of combining a strong executive and a unitary central government with a state that in many essentials may be termed weak. Although the National Front has sought to mitigate the

25. *Por qué y cómo se Forjó*, p. 35.
26. Whiteford, *Two Cities*, p. 123.

effects of such a system, it has done so more by dividing the spoils equally than by attacking the roots of the problem.

THE ELECTORAL SYSTEM

For any nation that purports to have representative government, the process by which officials are chosen to legislate and to govern largely determines to what degree it meets that claim. Colombia, a republic for a century and a half, has a long representative tradition. Yet the country's administrative tradition is much older and far stronger. It might be expected therefore that the latter would permeate the former, not only with respect to the relationships among the various organs of government, but also in the way in which both the president and the Congress are elected to office. An examination of the functioning of Colombia's electoral system once again makes clear that the realities of the pattern of social power and ingrained cultural attitudes have produced effects which in many ways are more closely coincident with an administrative than with a representative tradition.

In the light of Colombia's political traditions and social structure, which stress authority and rule by an elite, one might expect to discover restrictions on political participation in the constitution and in the election laws on the assumption that "The time-honored method of regulating admission to political power has been the prescription . . . of legal requirements for voting and office-holding." [27] Most modern constitutions have of course eliminated such barriers as a part of the evolution from regimes of limited participation to a politics of mass participation. Perhaps surprisingly, this has also in the main been true of Colombia.

The Colombian constitution does contain provisions requiring that the president and senators shall have previously held certain specified high governmental offices, or shall have been university professors for at least five years, or shall have practiced a profession which requires a university degree.[28] But equivalent qualifications in practice characterize incumbents of similar posts in many democracties (the majority of congressmen in the United States are lawyers, for instance) and it would be unlikely in any

27. Avery Leiserson, *Parties and Politics* (New York, Alfred A. Knopf, 1958), p. 94.
28. Articles 94 and 115. Between 1886 and 1945 there had instead been an annual income qualification of 2000 pesos for these two offices. Under the constitutions extant from 1853–86 there were no property or income restrictions for office. Prior to 1853 there were generally property qualifications of some kind.

event for a Colombian to reach high office without such attainments. Consequently, these are hardly significant limitations in themselves, however indicative they may be of the realities of recruitment patterns for the upper ranks of officialdom.

In regard to voting, women, it is true, were not granted the right to vote until 1954. Similarly, except for the years 1853–61, it was not until 1936 that both literacy and property qualifications for voting in elections for president and the Chamber of Representatives were struck from the constitution. Again with the exception of the years 1853–61, voting was indirect for the office of president until 1910, and for senators until 1945.

For most of its history, then, the Colombian constitution has placed stringent restrictions on voting, especially for a nation where literacy and property qualifications were formidable barriers. Yet by 1936 most of these had been eliminated; in any case all male citizens had been entitled to vote for municipal councillors and deputies to the departmental assemblies since the nineteenth century. Today any Colombian citizen may vote who is twenty-one years old, who has not lost his political rights by judgment of a court, and who has obtained a cédula. Legal restrictions on electoral participation are therefore no longer a significant means of regulating the admission to political power in Colombia. They have never really been the principal means.

At various stages of Colombian history presidents have been chosen by Congress, by constituent assemblies, by special electoral colleges, and by direct popular vote. With the exception of the several "elections" of General Rojas Pinilla by the ANAC, the latter system has prevailed since 1910, with a plurality sufficient to elect. Pursuant to a law of 1929 the Chamber of Representatives (as well as departmental assemblies and municipal councils and, since 1945, the Senate) have been chosen by a system of proportional representation known as the electoral quotient. This replaced the "incomplete vote" method of proportional representation by which, in a given electoral jurisdiction (e.g. a department or a municipio), the party obtaining the most votes was accorded two thirds of the seats. The party winning the second largest proportion of votes obtained the remaining one third.[29]

Under the current system (as well as the old) representation in the Sen-

29. The "incomplete vote" had prevailed since Legislative Act (constitutional amendment) No. 3 of 1910. Phanor James Eder, *Colombia* (London, T. Fisher Unwin, 1913), Appendix J, reprints its text.

ate and the Chamber is allotted by departments according to population. The only difference in the constituencies of the two houses is that the proportion of Senate seats to population is slightly less than half that of the Chamber. Elections for senators and representatives and for departmental assemblymen are at large within each department; those of municipal councillors, within each municipio. There is no requirement that a candidate be a resident of the department in which he seeks election; in fact it is by no means unusual for a prominent individual to run for several offices in various departments at the same time in order to attract votes to the party list, though he may have no intention of serving in all, or even in any of them. The contingency of multiple officeholding is provided for by listing on the ballot alternates (suplentes) equal to the number of candidates. A suplente takes the place of a legislator whenever the latter signifies that he does not wish to occupy his seat, although the legislator can choose at any time to resume his place.[30]

Since 1929 the electoral quotient has been used in any election where more than two seats are at stake. It works as follows: The total votes for senator or representative in a department (Cundinamarca, for example) are first divided by the number of seats at issue, in order to determine the quotient. The quotient is then divided into the vote for the lists of the several parties or, under the National Front, the factions of each of the two historic parties. Omitting for the moment any remainder, the dividend constitutes in each case the number of seats won by that party. The seat(s) remaining after such a division goes to the party(ies) with the largest residual(s) that does not meet the quotient. Thus if there were 11 Senate seats at stake in Cundinamarca and 500,000 votes for senator, the quotient would be 45,455 (500,000 divided by 11). If the Liberals had received 300,000 votes and the Conservatives 200,000 in the pre-National Front years, the Liberals would be awarded 6 Senate seats on the basis of the quotient and the Conservatives 4. With one seat still unaccounted for, the Liberal residual of 30,000 (left after dividing 300,000 by the quotient) would be greater than the Conservative residual of 20,000, thus giving the Liberals the additional Senate seat. As the system functioned before 1958 minor parties could win seats in the same way, by receiving votes equiva-

30. Suplentes are not personal; they take the place of a *principal* according to their place on the list. The exception to election to multiple offices is that, according to Article 1 of the constitution, no one may be elected to more than one seat in the National Congress at the same time (though he may be elected both to Congress and to various departmental or municipal legislative seats).

lent to the quotient or greater than the residuals of the major parties in a given department or municipio. Since 1958, of course, third parties as such have been excluded from the contest.

The candidates themselves win election according to their rank order on their respective party lists. In the illustration just cited the first seven on the Liberal list would win seats, as well as the first four on the Conservative list. Lists are made up by the party (or factional) leaderships. There is thus no opportunity for the voter to select individual candidates, as there was under the system of the "incomplete vote." He may choose only a list, although, if he wishes, he may choose different party lists for different offices.

Voting is not compulsory in Colombia, and voter registration centers on the possession of a cédula. However, the number of one's cédula bears no necessary relationship to one's residence within a given municipio. Although this may present no problem in small communities with only one polling place, in cities the voter must determine from a posted list the location of the polls where his particular cédula number will be accepted. Ballots in Colombia are provided not by the state, but by the parties, according to certain standard legal requirements. If the voter has not obtained a ballot beforehand, there are party workers at the polls to provide him with one.

Holt, believing that "The electoral process can itself shape the kinds of political institutions that participate in the election and that result from it," [31] makes two principal criticisms of the Colombian electoral system. The first is that proportional representation and the use of suplentes tend to remove elected officials from the people they are supposed to represent. There is no way to pick and choose among candidates; candidates may not even be resident of the department or municipio in which they are running; the successful candidate may never serve, being replaced by his suplente; at-large elections for whole departments dilute accountability; and proportional representation places undue power in the hands of the party leaders through their control of the candidate lists. The result, Holt feels, is that it becomes practically impossible for the Colombian Congress to act as a bridge between the individual citizen and the remote and powerful central government.

Holt's second criticism is of the registration process, which often forces

31. Holt, *Colombia Today*, p. 66. Much of this discussion of electoral machinery is based on the excellent treatment in Holt, pp. 60–66.

voters in cities and the larger towns to vote outside their neighborhoods, thus making it more difficult for some individuals to exercise their franchise. It might be added that the printing and distribution of the ballot by the parties leaves room for chicanery by reducing the role of the potentially more neutral state in the electoral process.

Such criticisms of the Colombian electoral system from the standpoint of representativeness have much validity, although one may question whether proportional representation might not provide a greater sense of security for political minorities than would single-member districts during the years of transition to competitive politics following the eventual end of parity and alternation. A single-member district system might also check the rise of third parties after 1974, even though the admission of new political blood through such channels might be desirable. Nonetheless, it is not the nature of election mechanics that has determined the essence of the political process any more than it has been legal restrictions on voting and officeholding. It has been instead the more informal devices, and the general conditions of Colombian society, which have placed the Colombian electoral system more in the administrative than in the representative tradition of government, and which have helped to preserve control of the state in elite hands.

The most obvious of these devices and conditions have been fraud and various forms of intimidation, which marked virtually all Colombian elections prior to the era of the National Front. The election of 1946 was, probably, one of the few exceptions. This is not to say that the outcomes of most elections were necessarily *decided* by such means. Much took place on the local level that was not sanctioned by national political leaders and did not amount to nationwide adulteration of the vote. In many instances the "in" party would undoubtedly have won even a wholly free election.

Fraud might take place in the registration stage, where electoral boards controlled by the incumbent party sometimes arbitrarily excluded members of the opposition from the electoral rolls. It might involve "voting the cemetery," simple ballot-box stuffing, or commands by army officers that their troops vote in a certain way. Finally, fraud might take the form of falsifying the count of the ballots. In this century the decade of the 1920s was particularly rife with charges of fraud made by the Liberals against the Conservative administrations of that period.

During the 1930s the Liberals, especially under President López, tried to reform some of the electoral practices for which they had earlier criticized their opponents. This apparently sincere attempt to combat fraud was largely unavailing because of the inability to eradicate its practice on the part of the Liberal caciques. Ironically, there is a considerable body of opinion, stemming from a variety of political quarters, that López' own reelection in 1942 was marked by extensive voting irregularities.[32] The Conservatives continued to charge, right up through the 1949 elections—which the Liberals won although they were conducted under a Conservative government—that thousands of false cédulas had been issued during the foregoing Liberal regimes and that over the years Conservatives in considerable numbers had been refused the vital document.[33] While electoral practices undoubtedly improved somewhat in the period 1930–46, it would hardly be correct to say that the era of Liberal rule was substantially free of fraud.

An alternative method has been electoral intimidation. Its techniques have included laws permitting incarceration on petty pretexts—designed for use in rural areas immediately prior to election day—and, above all, physical coercion. The latter might entail forcible exclusion from the polls by armed bands of one of the parties; the creation of a state of disorder in a particular locality so that elections could not be held there; or the intimidation of the adherents of one of the parties so that they dared not vote. Customarily the party in power was responsible, often with the connivance of the authorities. Conservatives accused the Liberals of such practices during the 1930s; Liberals accused the Conservatives of the same after the latter came to power in 1946. Sometimes admitting by inference that they had been responsible for such incidents, the Conservatives justified them as a response to prior Liberal fraud.

One of the results of the adulteration of the electoral process through violence and fraud is that it tends to make that process meaningless, by depriving those who might desire a change of the opportunity to effect it

---

32. See *La Oposición y el Gobierno, Del 9 de Abril de 1948 al 9 de Abril de 1950* (Bogotá, Imprenta Nacional, 1950), pp. 40–41; Osorio, *Gaitán,* p. 171; and Nieto Rojas, *La Batalla contra el Comunismo,* p. 32.

33. Cf. Azula Barrera, *De la Revolución,* pp. 190–91 and 256–57; Bedoya, *De Desterrado a Presidente,* pp. 230–31. For charges of Conservative fraud in the years after 1949 see Germán Arciniegas, "La Dictadura en Colombia," *Cuadernos Americanos* (Mexico), 49 (Jan.–Feb. 1950), 8–9.

by democratic means. Yet even when a Colombian has had an opportunity to vote more or less freely for his Conservative or Liberal choice, the political realities have often been such that he has been unwilling or unable to oppose the "powers-that-be" or to use his vote to promote his own advance on the economic or social scale. In other words, even simon-pure elections could do no more than remove the most obvious barriers to the operation of genuine electoral democracy in Colombia. As Antonio García has said, "The electoral reform of López centered the problem of political democracy on the identification of the person by means of a cédula, not on training for citizenship, nor on the political responsibility of the parties and their representatives, nor on the elimination of the social factors which have converted the people into a crowd without capacity to exercise consciously any sovereignty, any liberty, any mandate." [34]

The level of development of Colombia's economy, the structure of Colombian society, and the experiences of Colombian political history have together deprived many Colombians of both the desire and the ability to participate effectively or independently in the electoral process. Sunk in poverty and illiteracy, many Colombians are too apathetic or unaware even to vote. Prior to the era of the National Front, voter turnout seldom reached forty per cent of those eligible.[35] Ben G. Burnett found, in a comparative study of voting in Colombia's then fifteen departments, that absence from the polls was correlated with illiteracy, which stood, and still stands, at almost forty per cent.[36] Other Colombians, while they may vote (or even engage in violence on behalf of their party) do so at the command or instigation of the more powerful. To vote the way one's patrón votes is usual. To be called upon to vote for the party of one's hereditary allegiance is also common, with real choice excluded by the pulls and pressures which sustain those allegiances and by the fact that the party's candidates represent elite interests which the average voter has little hope of challenging.[37] "The Colombian, in general, doesn't have sufficient education, economic independence, or time to defend himself

34. A. García, *Gaitán*, p. 214.
35. See Registraduría del Estado Civil, *Organización y Estadísticas, 1964*, pp. 134–36; and Burnett, "The Recent Colombian Party System," p. 24.
36. Burnett, pp. 139–41.
37. See below, chapter 8, for an extended analysis of these points.

. . . from the forms of coercion which are exerted by economic and political powers actively interested in the [composition] of the future Government." [38] Finally, apart from ignorance, apathy, and subtle forms of economic and social pressure, there are the ingrained attitudes of a subject political culture, attitudes which lead to resignation about the influence a citizen can exert, unless it is through palancas or the ties of compadrazgo.

In the actual formality of voting the light of Colombian electoral democracy has occasionally shone. On the level of conscious, effective political choice based on a certain minimum of social independence, on a welling-up of political desires from below which go unheeded by party leaders only at the risk of their positions, and on a certain awareness of where one's most obvious interests seemingly lie, Colombia's democracy has in the past fallen far short of the norm that many of its friends have pronounced it as long since having attained.

Are elections, then, a meaningless farce serving no purpose? Not at all. What legitimacy does attach to the government of Colombia is a republican legitimacy, one of whose central tenets is popular choice of the nation's rulers. Elections, together with the Congress, are the principal concessions of the administrative state to the representative tradition which destroyed the monarchy, if not its spirit, in the second decade of the nineteenth century. A second purpose of elections is the opportunity for those who control the system to demonstrate an apparent rapport with the people. Thus it is a particular phenomenon of election campaigns that the politicians, on the whole representative of elite interests or themselves members of the elite, come before the lower classes by way of speeches or fiestas to attempt to prove that they are their faithful interpreters.[39] It is a function of elections in all democratic systems to serve as this kind of bridge between the politician and the voter; it may be particularly important for the maintenance of a system such as the Colombian, where the distance between the two is normally great and alternative channels of communication are weak. A final function of elections is, indeed,

38. Lleras Camargo, *Sus Mejores Páginas*, p. 20.
39. Cf. Moisés Castillo, "Desarrollo y Organización Política en Buenaventura," in *Estructura y Organización Social* (Bogotá, Universidad Nacional, Facultad de Sociología, 1961).

choice, choice at least of candidates and parties on the part of the elite among its own members, who have as a rule controlled both major parties as well as the outcome of elections.

THE NATIONAL FRONT AND THE STATE

The National Front, in part by the very nature of its machinery, as well as by conscious effort, has lessened the power of the executive. Alternation means that a president must give way to a successor from the opposite party. Parity significantly restricts his former freedom to appoint and dismiss officials. The provision that Congress shall set the rules for a civil service is designed to limit further his control of the bureaucracy. The requirement of a two-thirds congressional vote for the passage of legislation hinders the president's ability to impose his will on a majority of that body. The very concept of a government of joint responsibility requires a constant process of negotiation and bargaining between the president and the parties and their various factions. Finally, a constitutional amendment approved by Congress in 1960 modified the emergency powers accorded the president by Article 121. It was put through primarily at the insistence of the Liberals, who still feared the advent of a Conservative president after their experiences of the previous decade and a half. The amendment stipulates that the president must convene Congress in the same decree that he proclaims a state of siege. If he fails to do so, Congress shall convene itself. Congress is to remain in session throughout the period of a state of siege and it may submit any presidential decree issued during that time to the Supreme Court for a decision as to its constitutionality.[40]

Yet, at the same time that the parties, in the interests of interparty consensus, have hedged around the powers of the president and his ability to use the office for partisan purposes, they have weakened the presidency as an agent of modernization. In other developing countries the tendency has been to devolve more authority on the executive in order to further social reform and rapid economic development, frequently at the expense of some of the niceties of democratic politics. In Colombia immobilism has been institutionalized for a period of sixteen years.[41] President Alberto

40. ESAP, *Organización Constitucional*, p. 172, contains the text of the amendment.
41. Cf. the interview with Alfonso López Michelsen published in *El Espectador*, July 21, 1963, p. 5A.

Lleras Camargo lamented during the first National Front administration that the government had been left "with the representation of everyone and without the power to influence anyone." [42] To the necessity of the president's working with Congress and his own party has been added the need to win the cooperation of a substantial segment of the other traditional party as well. One saving factor has been that what the two-thirds rule took away from the president, the resort to extraordinary powers has partially restored.

The National Front has been able to do little to strengthen the Congress, either as a constructive counterpoise to the executive or as a pillar of a strong state with close ties to the people. Numerous proposals have been made for strengthening Congress' internal organization and for providing it with improved staffing. Penalties have at times been invoked against members of the Chamber of Representatives absent from either plenary or committee sessions, while the officers of the Chamber have addressed plaintive pleas to the directorates of the two political parties "with the purpose of soliciting your decisive collaboration in our struggle to organize the body over which we preside, eliminating particularly the parliamentary absenteeism which has been increasing in a shameful way and which threatens to paralyze legislative business." [43] Congress has done little to divest itself of its reputation for dilatoriness and sterility, however.

The achievements of the National Front have been largely the consequence of executive initiative, with only the reluctant approval of Congress, as in the case of agrarian reform, or under the aegis of the president's extraordinary or state-of-siege powers. Moreover, there remains the possibility that the two-thirds rule will prove a temptation for a future government seeking swift action to countenance the rule's unconstitutional circumvention. Insofar as relations between the president and the Congress are concerned, the National Front has not altered the fundamentals of Colombia's administrative state, even while it has enhanced Congress' powers of obstruction.

The plebiscitary reform of 1957 sought also to strengthen the judiciary, to protect it from executive encroachment and the play of partisan politics. It provided for the application of parity to both the Supreme Court

42. *New York Times,* July 4, 1960, p. 2, quoted in Martz, *Colombia,* p. 329.
43. *El Tiempo,* Aug. 28, 1963, p. 18.

of Justice and the Council of State and declared that their members were to remain in office during good conduct and until they reached retirement age. Vacancies were to be filled by cooptation. Although the implementation of these provisions has been challenged on various legal grounds, they have seemingly become accepted practice.

Some attention has been paid to reform of the lower courts and of legal procedures in an effort to ameliorate the system of justice as it applies directly to the citizen. In September 1963 Congress authorized the government to carry out such reforms by decree. One of the principal lines of attack was to be the expedition of court business. In late 1963 the Minister of Justice estimated that there were 500,000 cases pending, with the backlog growing by 40,000 cases per year (for a population of 16 million). Since most kinds of criminal cases can be dismissed if they are not heard within a specified time, twice as many cases were dying on the judicial calendar as were being dealt with. Needless to say, the stimulus to crime and to mistrust of the country's system of justice was great. The hope was to decentralize the system by stationing judges with wide powers in each municipality in order to settle as many cases as possible at that level without the need to take them by stages all the way to Bogotá.[44]

Colombia's judicial system has been so enmeshed in politics and in red tape in the past, and the attitudes toward it have been so skeptical, that the fulfillment of effective reform will not be easy. In the long run, improvements which will bring the operation of the judiciary into closer line with popular needs for an expeditious system of justice may be more important than permanent tenure for members of the Supreme Court. Whether the former can be accomplished, and whether Colombian justice can be at least partially rid of its class and partisan biases, remain to be seen.

The governments of the National Front have similarly concerned themselves with the decentralization of administration, including the devolution of greater fiscal autonomy upon the departments, and especially the municipios. The 1962 Program of the National Front mentions such prob-

44. For a summary of the reforms in their early stages see Richard Eder, "Colombia Seeks to Speed Justice," *New York Times*, Oct. 17, 1963, p. 36. For the problem of judicial reform during the Lleras administration see *Realizaciones del Primer Gobierno del Frente Nacional* (Bogotá, Escuela Superior de Administración Pública, 1963), pp. 20 ff.

lems at several points. The practical progress has not been great, however. Moreover, the desire to strengthen the internal structure of the state, to bring governmental action into closer line with varied local and regional circumstances and into closer touch with the people, clashes to some extent with other goals of modernization. The experience of INCORA, which by Law 135 was given discretional authority to decentralize its functions, is illustrative. Most of the regional committees seldom met, and were accorded only powers of recommendation to an already overburdened central office. Some delegation of authority to project directors has indeed occurred. But in general, in INCORA's case at least, effective reform and a decentralization of functions appear to be largely incompatible.[45]

Acción comunal constitutes the main endeavor to modify the attitudinal basis of Colombia's administrative tradition. It is much too early to measure its success, but the experience of its initial years and the magnitude of the task suggest that its impact will neither be uniform nor immediate.

The National Front governments have meanwhile tried to improve the economic planning and advisory mechanisms of the state. An Office of Planning created in 1951 had become virtually dormant. Therefore in 1958 a National Council on Economic Policy and Planning was established, composed of four full-time and several ex officio members, along with an Administrative Department of Planning and Technical Services. These bodies were given considerable responsibility for conducting research and making recommendations relating both to short-term economic stability and long-range development. In 1963 the council was reorganized to eliminate the full-time members and replace them by a council of Cabinet ministers and other officials. The aim was to coordinate more effectively the activities of the planning mechanisms with the operations of the various government departments.

During the Lleras administration the Department of Planning had considerable esprit de corps and seemed to have the ear of the president. For a time a man in whom President Valencia had particular personal confidence (Diego Calle, later Finance Minister) headed the office. The United States government has also tried to bolster the department's role by insisting that the programs presented to it under the Alliance for Progress be channeled through the planning office. From the beginning, though, there have been serious problems of coordination between the

45. Cf. Charles Anderson, in *Land Reform and Social Change*, p. 10.

Planning Department and the ministries and other agencies of government. Politically, the department ranks in strength and prestige below the executive offices that administer economic policy, and its plans have often tended to be a bit abstract and removed from the realities of practical economic problems. That there is such an office, which for the first time is taken seriously by the president (as well as by the United States government), nevertheless seems significant. The very fact that Colombia has undertaken through the new planning institutions to engage in long-range economic programming is noteworthy.[46]

The creation of INCORA and of several regional development corporations, expanded health and housing programs, and the army's civic-military action [47] are examples of the government's attempts to span the gulf between government and the people, between national purposes and local needs. Yet "there is still a tremendous and potentially fatal gap" between legislative provision and its implementation.[48] The agrarian law is a case in point, where enforcement confronts political resistance as well as technical and administrative difficulties. The continuing sporadic violence is another illustration of the distance between governmental intentions and reality.

Nor is there much indication that the masses of Colombians have come to identify their own goals with those of the nation. The National Front has by and large failed to evoke the mystique which might make this possible.

One of the main goals of the creators of the National Front was to put an end to the spoils system, which they regarded as a prime motive for political violence. Of fourteen articles in the plebiscitary reform of December 1957—several of them procedural—four dealt wholly or in major part with the question.

Parity was to be the principal device. Not only seats in elective bodies, but officials and employees at all levels of the public service, were to be distributed equally between the parties as a part of the coalition agree-

46. See José Consuegra, *Apuntes de Economía Política* (Bogotá, Ediciones Tercer Mundo, 1964), for an account of recent planning efforts in Colombia. Actually, the so-called Currie Plan of 1949 was something of a precursor to more recent efforts. Cf. Currie, *Ensayos sobre Planeación*, pp. 164–66.

47. See below, pp. 302–03, concerning the army's program of civic-military action.

48. *Prospects for Political Stability in Colombia with Special Reference to Land Reform* (Madison, Wis., University of Wisconsin Land Tenure Center, 1962), p. 8.

ment. Here reform was confronted with a preponderance of posts held by Conservative appointees of recent administrations. However, an expansion in the number of government employees after 1958 obviated the necessity of wholesale dismissals; some aver that the new employees were added solely to make the advent of parity as painless as possible. Another difficulty has been that in some Colombian communities almost all residents belong to one party; hence parity sometimes has been hard to effect at the local level for the very practical reason that there was literally no one to fill one half of the available positions. There have been other problems as well, which by their nature cannot be permanently resolved. One is that true parity requires not merely a quantitative but also a qualitative distribution of posts, which obviously leaves it open to many subjective and variable considerations. Equally troublesome has been the need to adjust the distribution of posts within as well as between the parties, giving representation more or less according to current strength to those factions of each party that support the National Front.

The executive at each level of government (the president, governor, or mayor) is responsible for realizing parity within his administrative jurisdiction. Usually he, or the official most directly concerned, does so in consultation with the respective national, departmental, or municipal party directorates, or those of the appropriate factions. Changes made in one or two posts, if they involve any shift in the party or factional designations of the incumbents, may require further readjustments in the form of a chain reaction. Unresolved disputes are referred to a higher level. Well into the second four-year government of the National Front there was evidence that the ideal of parity in all the various branches of the administration had not been fully attained. Thus the following telegram appeared in *El Espectador* of Bogotá on July 22, 1963:

The Liberal Directorate of Socorro [department of Santander] requests the National Liberal Directorate and [Liberal] Congressmen to intervene directly with the Minister of Communications and the Minister of Justice to the end of the fulfillment of parity in this city where in the circuit jail there are nineteen Liberal [employees] to thirty-two Conservatives and in the telegraph office eighteen Conservatives to five Liberals.[49]

49. *El Espectador*, July 22, 1963, p. 5.

Still, only two days prior to the publication of this complaint, President Valencia felt that he could "declare with the deepest satisfaction that, upon completing my first year in office, parity has been almost totally achieved, for in order that it be absolute as I promised in my inaugural address all that is required are some appointments that will be made within the next two weeks." [50] Quite obviously, it would be almost impossible to fulfill any system of parity absolutely, in all respects and at all levels of government. Yet in spite of some continuing difficulties in its application, the mechanics of parity have worked more smoothly than most dared to hope at the time of its inception.

Parity has probably been in part responsible for bringing about a reduction in partisan rancors, although it is still much too soon to say whether it has also helped to lay the basis for a political culture of compromise among at least the leaders and cadres of the two traditional parties. Parity may prove to be a useful and necessary interim stage in the permanent institutionalization of neutrality in the Colombian public service, which could take the form of continued proportional representation of the parties in the bureaucracy after 1974. The sixteen-year duration of parity could also furnish the time required for the gradual introduction of a merit criterion for employees of government.

The establishment of just such a career service was to be another step toward the creation of a neutral state. Proposals for the establishment of a civil service for Colombia had been made at least as early as 1915, and some legislation had been passed in an effort to create one.[51] Nevertheless, by 1958 there were still practically no tenure positions in the public administration with advancement based on performance and seniority. The Declaration of Sitges had affirmed that the formation of a career service was "most urgent," and the constitutional amendments approved in December 1957 contained several provisions designed to serve as the basis for its establishment. The president and other officials of the executive branch were constrained to exercise their powers of appointment and removal "within the norms which Congress lays down to establish and regulate the conditions of access to the public service, [the conditions]

50. Ibid., July 21, 1963, p. 10A.
51. *Convención Nacional del Partido Republicano* (Bogotá, 1915), pp. 165–85; and Fernando Plata Uricoechea, *El Régimen Constitucional en Colombia y en los Estados Unidos* (Bogotá, Editorial Cromos, 1943), p. 99.

of promotion by merit and seniority, and [the conditions] of retirement, resignation, or dismissal." Employees under the civil service were to be prohibited from participation in partisan politics. A separate article specifically forbade the intrusion of political considerations into their hiring, promotion, or removal.

Congress has passed the enabling legislation creating a career administrative service for Colombia. A School of Public Administration has since been opened in Bogotá under government auspices, with the assistance of foreign advisors and foreign foundation support. Nevertheless, the number who fall under the civil service is still much closer to one per cent than to one hundred, or even ten, per cent of government employees.

Colombia has a long way to go toward the establishment of the neutral, rationalized bureaucracy that is generally held to be an essential of the truly modern state. Parity, while it may reduce the partisan causes of violence, cannot solve the problem of the weak state. Mario Laserna has pointed out that such a device does not eliminate the spoils system so much as it equalizes the shares among the contestants and that it may even help to institutionalize the evil.[52] Perhaps the best that can be expected of parity is that it may provide the *opportunity* for other seeds to be planted. As yet the first shoots, in the form of an administrative service based on merit, are barely above ground.

Nonetheless, something of a new concept of public service has taken hold, especially at the professional level, in the years since the inauguration of the coalition experiment. There is now a nucleus of young Colombians dedicated to their country's development over and above partisan considerations, often accepting positions with the government at the sacrifice of more lucrative opportunities in private employment. They are engineers, economists, agronomists, the new technocrats. They currently staff such agencies as the Department of Planning of the National Planning Council. They are not themselves products of the new career service. But they bring to government service a new spirit. Many have been educated abroad or have taken special courses outside the country, often in the United States.[53] They work within the framework of a political sys-

52. Laserna, *Estado Fuerte*, pp. 85–86.

53. Cf. e.g. Corporación Autónoma Regional de los Valles del Magdalena y del Sinú (CVM), *Informe* (Bogotá, Editorial Antares, 1962), p. 12, where it is pointed out that the average age of all regular Colombian technical employees of CVM was 29 and that all had had some training abroad.

tem which, while necessarily attentive to the political requirements of parity, can at least admit to executive and bureaucratic positions persons of both major political affiliations. Meanwhile the idea, at least, of a civil service has become accepted, and with it has come a recognition of the need to educate for administrative and technical tasks.

The full-fledged development of a civil service may have to wait on a factor which Rafael Núñez noted eighty years ago: "The motives for disturbing the peace will be less and less powerful as the official system ceases to monopolize the opportunities of work." [54] As economic development proceeds it is probable that the functions of government will expand considerably. Yet as opportunities for profits grow in industries which depend more on governmental *policy* than on licensing favors, as additional fields of employment open, as articulate new groups press their claims on the political system, and as demands for an efficient bureaucracy to meet the requirements of a modern society become more pronounced, it is likely that the spoils of office will become of less central concern to Colombians.

Efforts at electoral reform prior to the era of the National Front had rather limited success. Laws assuring minority representation in the Congress, in effect from 1910 to 1929, rested on the political assumption that the Liberals would remain the minority. The electoral quotient subsequently enacted did not prevent the political hegemonies of the 1930s, '40s, and '50s. The cédula did not wipe out fraudulent voting practices. Even the end of literacy and property qualifications for the vote could not bring the electoral participation of adult males to the fifty per cent mark. Other realities, social and political, were too strong.

The principal electoral innovation of the National Front was, of course, the elimination of competition between the parties for a period of sixteen years. The hope was that beginning in 1974 competitive elections could once more be held, without the danger of violence. The electoral quotient, with its virtues and its faults, was retained for the period of the coalition agreement, but it was now to apply among the factions of the two major parties rather than between the parties themselves. The government has bent its efforts to step up the registration of voters and ensure the purity of the suffrage. Emphasis has been placed on *cedulación*. The National

---

54. Rafael Núñez, as quoted in Francisco García Calderón, *Latin America: Its Rise and Progress,* trans. Bernard Miall (New York, Scribner's, 1917), p. 211.

Registrar reported that by December 31, 1962, 86.57 per cent of all adults over 21 were in possession of a cédula, which by a law of 1961 had been made a requirement for most civil acts as well as for voting.[55] There were also attempts in the elections of 1962 to set up polling places at which voters could register in advance so they could vote in their own neighborhoods rather than at the possibly distant sites corresponding to their cédula numbers.

By the close of 1962 there were still almost a million eligible Colombians, the great majority of them women, who lacked cédulas. The provision of convenient registration places had produced mainly confusion. For the elections of March 1962 some sixty per cent of the election officials, chosen by lot from cédula lists, failed to put in an appearance at the polling places to which they had been assigned. Charges of fraud have been made from time to time in various localities by members of one faction against those of another of the same party, or against the electoral machinery generally, and isolated incidents of violence have accompanied several of the elections under the National Front. Yet these are minor blemishes. The percentage of Colombians registered to vote is impressive; and the judgment of most observers is that violence and fraud have played a minimal role in elections since 1957.[56] Continuing weaknesses in the electoral process derive from apathy and alienation, as evidenced by the high rates of abstention under the National Front, and from the nature of a social system which denies to many true personal and political independence.

There have been no competitive elections among the parties since 1949. It is therefore hard to say what role fraud and overt electoral coercion would again play if the two principal parties were to abandon their current coalition. However, the influx of rural dwellers to the cities, where electoral manipulation is more difficult, and the progress made under the military and coalition governments in cedulazation and other reforms, will probably permanently modify Colombia's ancient electoral practices.

The growth of an electorate characterized by awareness, interest, and independence from subtle pressures is another matter. To bring the level of participation to even a consistent fifty per cent of Colombian adults

55. Registraduría del Estado Civil, *Organización y Estadísticas, 1962*, pp. 217 and 261.

56. For problems relating to registration and fraud in the 1962 elections, see ibid., pp. 229 and 234; and Holt, *Colombia Today*, pp. 60–66.

will be a major effort. Rather than on laws, and devices such as cedulazation, it will depend primarily on changes in social patterns, and on
changes in attitudes toward authority and toward the role of women in
society, especially in rural areas. Improvements in both the level and
meaningfulness of participation will also depend on a transformation of
the parties into organizations which more adequately reflect the desires
of the middle and lower classes.

In sum, there is evidence that the National Front, by its very existence
as well as by its specific efforts, has done much to eliminate the grosser
abuses of Colombia's traditional electoral system. The prospects seem
good that at least some of this will carry over into the post-National Front
period. On the other hand, it may be some years before Colombia will
attain the kind and degree of electoral participation generally considered
to be a fundamental trait of the modern state.

Colombia today faces the need for a strong executive coupled with a
strong state in order to achieve modernization. At the same time, if political stability is to accompany change—indeed if modernization itself is to
be attained fully—the state must be made more representative or participative. There is some truth to the charge that the National Front has
not faced this dilemma squarely. The Great Coalition has attempted to
repair the abuses of the old order by means of gimmicks such as parity,
while failing to elicit the kind of popular allegiance or consent necessary
to carry forward the process of creating a modern state. These charges
are not wholly just. Such measures as electoral reform, the initiation of a
civil service, the establishment of INCORA, and the promotion of acción
comunal, go beyond the ephemeral to build for the future.

No regime could hope to create a truly participative society in a few
years. Yet the fundamental question remains: whether a modernizing elite
such as the Colombian can obtain its objectives of development without
involving, in some form, the participation of broader sectors of the society.
The administrative tradition in itself will no longer do. Just as inadequate
is a representative tradition which limits itself to the more formal dimensions of voter participation and which ignores the need for a strong government. What is required is a fusion which permits effective action,
which recognizes that traditional political attitudes toward authority will
not change rapidly, but which also seeks to involve the previously excluded majority in both the elaboration and the execution of societal goals.

8

THE TRADITIONAL
PARTIES (I)

PARTY ORGANIZATION

By almost any standard the two "historic collectivities," the Conservative and Liberal parties, have been focal points of Colombian political life for at least a century. Despite persistent factionalism, the occasional appearance of third parties, and long periods of one-party hegemony, the two parties have survived and have put down exceedingly deep roots. Most Colombians—even those who have known and cared nothing of doctrines and programs—evidence a profound psychic attachment to one or the other. The civil wars of the nineteenth century, as well as the more recent violencia, have been fought very largely in the names of the parties.

"Above all else, [parties] vary according to the structure of domination within the community . . . it is impossible to say anything about the structure of parties without discussing the structural forms of social domination *per se*." [1] Max Weber's dictum is as true of Colombia as of the societies with which he was more familiar. It is thus not surprising to find the social domination of an upper class paralleled in Colombia's two major parties, both in their formal constitutions, and more especially in the realities of internal party life. The parties also bear a not wholly accidental resemblance to the Colombian state in their patterns of strong central authority linked with rather weak organizations, only sporadically effective discipline, and a low level of popular participation in decision-

1. Max Weber in H. H. Gerth and C. Wright Mills, trans. and ed., *From Max Weber: Essays in Sociology* (New York, Oxford University Press, 1946), p. 195.

making. Both state and parties are marked as products of the same society and political culture.

The heart of Colombian party life has traditionally been the patrón-client relationship whose typical embodiment has been that between hacendado and campesino. At the service of the hacendado, and acting as mobilizer and manipulator of the rural vote, has been the *gamonal,* usually himself a government official, an overseer, a local merchant or a landowner.[2] Given such a system, rooted in the pattern of social power, the necessity for any formal party organization was for long minimal. As long as the electorate remained small, control of a district by a powerful individual, or by a few persons connected through kinship ties, was readily effected. In more recent decades the patrón or his agents have supplied the necessary leadership to the campesinos at election time. Meanwhile the hacendado has used his power over the vote, as well as his connections with the upper class, to occupy directive posts, or otherwise to wield his influence, at the departmental or national levels of his party.

As a general rule, those dependent on a patrón look to him for political guidance. They know that to vote against his wishes would be to "lose credit" with him. Some patrones make it a point to hire only those of their own party so that their employees will be more amenable to their political direction. But it is doubtful that most campesinos even conceive of voting in a manner distinct from that of their patrón, or of those local political leaders who in turn owe their positions to him. On election day the function of party officials is to shepherd electors to the polls, to hand them the party ballot, and to ensure that the voters actually cast their ballots for the proper list.

Election campaigns, particularly in rural areas, are therefore attempts to "animate the masses" and to reinforce assured loyalties, rather than to

2. Fals Borda defines gamonales as "petty political leaders whose position in society permitted them to exert influence upon rural voters. . . . The machine organized by these leaders was designed to perpetuate them and the higher-ranking caudillos in power. They saw that their friends, employees, and followers went to the polls and voted 'right,' paid for the liquor consumed as a reward, and acted as protectors of the constituents." Fals Borda, *Peasant Society,* p. 241. A similar pejorative term is *manzanillo,* also a mobilizer and manipulator of the vote but in whom the powers of protection or coercion are less pronounced and those of the unscrupulous politician using demagoguery as a principal weapon are accentuated. Cf. Gutiérrez, *La No-Violencia,* pp. 14–15.

convince.[3] Political allegiance is not rendered on the basis of the perceived interests of economic groups or classes, but on grounds of personal, family, regional, or dependent attachment. The patrón-client relationship, by which a politician can "deliver" a set number of votes for his party, and which carries over the pattern of social and economic domination into politics, is central to the operation of both of Colombia's traditional political parties.

The beginnings of more formal party organization are obscure. There are very occasional reports of the meetings of party conventions during at least the latter two decades of the nineteenth century, and apparently directorates operated sporadically for both parties.[4] By the 1920s both Liberals and Conservatives had evolved somewhat more elaborate organizations. Such a development was no doubt prompted by the gradual increase in the number of eligible voters as the rate of literacy grew, and by the beginnings of rapid urbanization and rural unrest which presented a need for better organization of those uprooted or disoriented from old relationships. For the Liberals a more systematic party structure was their best hope of rebuilding their fortunes, given their eschewal of the path of civil revolt in the years following the War of the Thousand Days. The role of the gamonal was by no means erased as a consequence. The old pattern of patrón-client relations was merely supplemented or overlaid by a series of party assemblies and directorates from the national down through the departmental and municipal levels.

According to its statutes, each party has biennial national conventions. Attending each are the respective party's members of Congress, its national directorate, the presidents and vice-presidents (Conservative) of the departmental and territorial directorates, former presidents of the Republic who are members of the party, and delegates from the departments

3. Cf. CIS, *Estudios sobre . . . Sonsón*, esp. pp. 214 and 222, for depiction of a campaign in a municipio of Antioquia.
4. A Conservative convention took place in 1879 but it is not clear whether it was the first; a central committee of the party also seems to have been established about the same time. Cf. *Los Programas Conservadores* (Bogotá, Directorio Nacional Conservador, 1952), pp. 12 and 14. A Liberal convention was held in 1892, but it is also unclear whether that was the first: cf. Eduardo Rodríguez Piñeres, *Diez Años de Política Liberal, 1892–1902* (Bogotá, Librería Colombiana, 1945), pp. 7–14. See also Burnett, "The Recent Colombian Party System," for the development of Colombian party organization.

and territories elected by the party assemblies at those levels (Liberal), or by the party's departmental deputies or municipal councillors (Conservative). The Conservatives also include certain former Cabinet ministers and governors and special women's delegates. Both Conservatives and Liberals in the past added representatives of workers and youth organizations, but there is no such provision in new statutes adopted by the Liberals in 1963 or by the Conservatives in 1964. The national conventions of both parties select the party directorates (in the Liberal case either one director or a plural directorate of three, plus a central political commission of eight members), and nominate their party's candidate for president every four years. There are parallel assemblies or conventions at the departmental level and, in the Liberal case, at the municipal level as well. According to the Liberal party's statutes these assemblies choose their respective directorates. In the Conservative statutes, there is no express provision for the choice of departmental directorates; municipal directorates are to be chosen by the departmental directorates. The Liberal assemblies in addition have the right to select the party's candidates for elective office within their jurisdictions.[5]

Since at least 1922 the statutes of the Liberal party have provided for the election of the members of the municipal assemblies of the party by the direct vote of all Liberals of the municipality.[6] These local assemblies are to select delegates to departmental assemblies, which in their turn choose a major part of the delegates to the national convention. The pre-1964 Conservative statutes stipulated that three popularly elected delegates, selected according to criteria laid down by the respective departmental directorates, would be sent by each department to the national convention. The 1964 statutes substitute election of those delegates by Conservative legislators. In sum, both parties are in part formally structured on a decentralized basis. The Liberal party, in particular, adds a substantial measure of popular participation.

Whatever the formal provisions of the statutes of both parties, reality often is something quite different. Party elections and conventions fre-

5. Most of the material on the parties' statutes has been taken, for the Conservatives, from *Estatutos del Partido Conservador,* Draft proposals (Bogotá, 1964); and, for the Liberals, from *Estatutos del Partido Liberal, 1963* (Bogotá, Directorio del Partido Liberal, 1963). The pre-1964 Conservative statutes may be found in Guillermo Salamanca, *Los Partidos en Colombia* (Bogotá, Editorial 'El Voto Nacional,' 1961), Appendix D.

6. *Los Partidos en Colombia* (Bogotá, 1922), pp. 452–68.

quently are not held as scheduled. Nullification of such elections when they go against the wishes of the national party leadership is by no means unknown. Even when held as prescribed in the statutes and their results respected, elections have reflected primarily the will of the gamonales. An official of the Liberal party affirmed in 1963 that his party's "plebiscites" had not fulfilled their purported objective. And a Conservative who had helped draw up his party's statutes more than a decade before acknowledged in 1961 that they had been little applied in practice.[7]

Real control of both parties rests with the party directorates, which tend to be self-perpetuating. Rather than popular choice, the actual process at the municipal level permits the selection of the directorate by local or even departmental magnates. Departmental and local assemblies often meet but irregularly and there are frequent lapses in the continuity of the directorates. Vacancies are often filled by appointment by the superior directorate. The national directorates of the parties have, and use, substantial authority to intervene in organizational matters at the regional and local levels. National conventions are in practice dominated by the incumbent party leadership, which is guaranteed representation without the need to be elected as delegates.

At least nominal attempts have been made to broaden the base of the parties by explicitly inviting to the conventions representatives of workers, students, women, and other groups. The need to do so is indicative of the unrepresentativeness of the regular party structure and of the channels for the selection of convention delegates. Yet the effect of such devices in democratizing the parties has been minimal. For example, in March 1959 the organizing commission for the Liberal party convention issued regulations providing for fifteen delegates representing workers and campesinos (who together comprise the great majority of nominal Liberals) out of hundreds of delegates. Of these, ten were to be chosen by "the existing federations," which in practice meant the leaders of key unions who themselves were eager for political office on the Liberal ticket. The five others were to be chosen by the Liberal directorate of the federal district of Bogotá.[8]

Similarly, the parties' candidates for public office are in actuality chosen

7. Interview with Liberal party official (Bogotá, Aug. 1963); and Salamanca, *Los Partidos*, pp. 321–25. For an example of such practices see "Normas sobre Elecciones Internas del Liberalismo," in *El Espectador*, Dec. 23, 1959.

8. *El País* (Cali), March 13, 1959.

by party leaders. Little popular participation in the process is evident, whatever party statutes may stipulate. The system of the electoral quotient and the party list places selection almost necessarily in a few hands. It provides an excellent way for party leaders to protect themselves, since there are always "safe" departments where those at the top of the ticket are certain to be elected. If the party is in office, the choice of candidates may be dictated or strongly influenced by official intervention.[9] In short, decisions respecting the composition of electoral lists are seldom the product of the deliberations of party assemblies or of any other form of intraparty democracy.

The financing of the parties—the amounts and sources of party funds, and the relationship between contributions and subsequent favors rendered—is a matter in which only the bare outlines are apparent. Each party organ is supposed to have a treasurer, and there are rather elaborate provisions in both parties' statutes concerning the management of the party treasury. Funds are raised through voluntary contributions, by means of fiestas and similar public functions (the 100- and 1,000-peso-a-plate dinner has come to Colombia) and, under the new Liberal statutes, through dues. Both parties oblige party members holding public office to contribute to the party coffers. Official funds have undoubtedly gone to the same end in times past. Income from sources such as these probably serves to sustain the national, regional, and local headquarters of the parties, plus travel, correspondence, and other housekeeping expenses of the party organizations. Headquarters of the parties, even at the national level, are scarcely elaborate, and the expenditures are fairly small. The bulk of campaign funds comes from the candidates themselves, and from their friends and relatives. Most of this appears to be on a personal and individual basis rather than in the form of contributions by groups or firms who hope thereby to influence public policy. In any case, control over party financing rests largely with the notables who dominate other aspects of party life.

The press, too, serves as an instrument of party direction by the elite. Almost in its entirety it is partisan, and newspaper publishing and journalism serve as vehicles for political careers. *El Tiempo,* a Bogotá Liberal daily and the newspaper with the country's largest circulation, is owned by Eduardo Santos and was an important factor in his rise to the presi-

9. Cf. *La Política Oficial*, passim, for President López' efforts to combat this tendency during his first administration.

dency. It is currently the principal spokesman for the *oficialista* wing of the Liberal party and the most consistent supporter of the National Front. At the beginning of the Santos administration Alfonso López founded *El Liberal* (1938–51) to wage his campaign for reelection in 1942. Laureano Gómez established *El Siglo* in 1936. *El Colombiano* of Medellín and *La República* of Bogotá speak for the Ospinista faction of the Conservative party. Most other newspapers are similarly affiliated to one or another political group. Newspapers therefore act as the virtually official voices of the party chieftains; in fact the pre-1964 Conservative party statutes granted the party press explicit representation at national party conventions. "Always, the capital newspapers [plus *El Colombiano* of Medellín] have been looked upon as the official voices of party heads, even of factional chiefs. It is no exaggeration to say that the provincial adherents of the parties scan the great capital dailies chiefly to keep abreast of the party's grand strategy as it emanates from Bogotá." [10]

The coming of the airplane to overleap Colombia's formidable topographical barriers has accentuated the leading role of the press of the capital, or the "great press" as its political detractors derisively refer to it, by making it more readily available nationwide. In recent years radio has come to supplement the newspaper, with particular stations or programs often owned or sponsored by the same individuals or groups who control the daily press. The mass media therefore serve as organs of party control and indoctrination from the top down. Journalism becomes a preferred route into politics, as well as virtually a prerequisite for political advancement and for the effectuation of political leadership on the national scene.

Over the years both parties have sought to mobilize greater mass support, and to solidify their influence among particular groups, through the development of affiliated organizations. As early as 1922 the Liberal convention pledged the party to the foundation of Liberal night schools, Liberal publishing houses, and Liberal lawyers' committees to defend fellow partisans from harassment by the Conservative authorities. [11] Both parties have promoted women's, youth, and student affiliates and barrio

10. Fluharty, *Dance of the Millions*, p. 264. See *Cultura y Economía*, pp. 65–104, for a description and history of Colombia's principal newspapers. Since they are so highly partisan, they have at times of acute political tension been subject not only to censorship but to violence. Examples are the sacking of *El Tiempo* and *El Espectador* in September 1952, and of *El Siglo* during the bogotazo.

11. *Los Partidos en Colombia*, p. 431.

improvement committees. The Association of Liberal Veterans, composed of veterans of the nineteenth-century civil wars, formed in 1930 to protect the new Liberal regime of President Olaya from a possible Conservative coup. Dissolved and later reconstituted, the association took upon itself the promotion of the interests of the party and of Liberal veterans with claims to jobs and pensions. At one time it reportedly had centers in all municipalities of the country.[12] For many years the Liberal party and the Confederation of Colombian Workers (CTC) were closely although not formally linked, with Liberal politicians active in CTC affairs and CTC officials appearing on Liberal electoral lists. From time to time intellectuals of both parties have formed their separate circles or organizations for the discussion of national problems. The Economic Society of Friends of the Nation (*Sociedad Económica de los Amigos del País*) is a current Liberal group and the Center of Colombian Studies (*Centro de Estudios Colombianos*) its Conservative counterpart.

There has been, then, something of a tendency for persons of differing political views to align themselves in functional groups along a partisan divide. Of the two traditional parties, the Liberals have gone farthest in their efforts to promote such organizations. But on the whole such affiliates have been short-lived or have kept up only sporadic existences. While the Colombian parties show traces of being "parties of integration," in the sense used by Sigmund Neumann,[13] they remain for the most part rudimentary in this aspect of their development. Most of the affiliated organizations have been dominated by small coteries or have been rather readily manipulated by politicians. In general they have not provided a meaningful voice in party leadership for their members.

Colombia's Conservative and Liberal parties have, on paper, much of the framework of modern parties. The apparatus of assemblies and directorates at the local, regional, and national levels, presidential nomination by convention, mass affiliates, fund-raising machinery, and a party press—all are there. Colombia's traditional parties are therefore something more

12. *Convención Nacional de Veteranos Liberales* (Bogotá, Imprenta Nacional, 1938), passim.

13. The party of integration demands an influence over the individual's life that extends "from the cradle to the grave." Ideally it means that the party member participates in professional or work associations, credit unions, and similar organizations and activities which are specifically affiliated to his party. Cf. Sigmund Neumann, ed., *Modern Political Parties* (Chicago, University of Chicago Press, 1956), pp. 404–05.

than mere parliamentary alignments of notables. Yet it remains true that in the functioning of their internal machinery, in their methods of financing, in the role of their press, and in their control of mass organizations they essentially reflect the patrón-client nexus which has been the core of traditional Colombian party politics.

THE "HEREDITARY HATREDS"

Such patterns of intraparty relationships, while having profound implications for political change in Colombia, are not in themselves unique. Parties elsewhere have been organized in roughly similar manner, and have been characterized by like relationships between leaders and followers. The distinguishing mark of Colombia's party system is that, as one of her political patriarchs phrased it, the parties seem less political organizations than "hereditary hatreds." [14] These "determinisms which date from far in the past" [15] help to account for the remarkable stability of the parties, even in the face of rapid social change. Other Latin American nations reveal traces of such hereditary antagonisms in the historic attachments of given regions or families to particular parties. But it is in Colombia that traditional political sentiments and loyalties go deepest, have persisted longest, and have had the greatest portents for the polity.

The Colombian is very early socialized into enmity toward one and loyalty to the other historic party. "Among the most remote childhood memories of a Colombian are . . . those of political parties similar to two races which live side by side but hate each other eternally." [16] Most Colombians, when asked about their loyalty to one or the other party, give answers closely related to family and inheritance: because my father was a Liberal (or Conservative); because of blood, race, or tradition; because I was born a Liberal; or because of ancestral hatred for the adversary. [17] Sometimes there is a relationship, proximate or remote, to some "martyr of the cause" to whom homage is paid in the home "like a god of the hearth in primitive

14. Miguel Antonio Caro; cited in Puentes, *Historia del Partido Liberal,* 1st ed., p. 6.

15. Misión "Economía y Humanismo," *Estudio sobre . . . Colombia,* p. 110.

16. Hernández Rodríguez, *Alternación ante el Pueblo,* p. 168.

17. See the study of Abel J. Avila G., "Valores e Ideologías Políticas en Lata (Bolívar)," in *Estructura y Organización Social,* pp. 82–84.

societies." [18] One Colombian has described the following incident in his own socialization into partisanship:

> When they assassinated Uribe Uribe [General Rafael Uribe Uribe, a Liberal hero killed in Bogotá in 1914], I was a child of nine, but I recall that when in my distant home in the Department of Boyacá my mother read me, with a barely audible voice tremulous through her tears, the stories of the dastardly crime which the newspapers of the day carried, I cried with her, chilled by the fearful drama. As for my father, his eyes still cloud with tears . . . when he speaks to me of the . . . heroic times of his adored Liberal Party. [19]

The absolutistic view of the world fostered by Colombian political culture, with all controversy tending to be conducted in quasi-religious, highly moralistic terms, provides an environment in which flourish the "systems of hate." The prominence of the church-state issue throughout Colombian history has undoubtedly heightened such tendencies. The prestige accorded to intellectuals and to polemical discourse may encourage this bent, even when the mass of party adherents have not the sophistication to view party differences in ideological terms. Moreover, as Wahl notes of France, an administrative political culture is probably conducive to irresponsibility in political parties and hence to ideologism in politics. [20] Also strengthening the absolutistic view of politics in Colombia may be the virulence of a spoils system in which "for the Conservatives of Sasaima there is no hospital." [21] When one's livelihood and one's honor (in a society where honor is highly valued) turn on victory or defeat, politics may well take on highly emotional and even violent connotations. The press, which sometimes seems able to channel at will the deep rivers of partisan sentiment that flow through the Colombian political landscape, is prone to print one-sided or exaggerated accounts of violence and other political events. Insofar as the parties are parties of integration they intensify the pattern of divisiveness by encompassing social realms other than the nar-

18. Eduardo Santa, *Nos Duele Colombia* (Bogotá, Ediciones Tercer Mundo, 1962), p. 37.

19. Puentes, *Historia del Partido Liberal,* 1st ed., preface.

20. Nicholas Wahl, "The French Political System," in Beer and Ulam, eds., *Patterns of Government,* p. 353 and passim.

21. Guillermo Salamanca, *La República Liberal* (2 vols. Bogotá, 1937), 2, 152.

rowly political. At the same time, the weakness of the party organizations may induce their leaders to continued reliance on appeals to sentiment, tradition, and vengeance.

Yet most of these attributes pertain as well to Latin American societies other than the Colombian. In the absence of at least some of them the evolution of a pattern of hereditary hatreds might not be possible; alone they are not a sufficient explanation for its development. It is particularly difficult to account for the strength of partisan attachments among the campesinos. For it is especially notable of Colombia's Conservative and Liberal parties that intense feelings of attachment to one or the other are not confined to the elites or the ideologues. They extend to the villages and farms of rural Colombia. Partisan loyalties seem, in fact, to have their greatest tenacity in the countryside, where both the propensity and the capacity to view politics in ideological terms is presumably weakest.

Orlando Fals Borda has depicted the processes at work in his *Peasant Society in the Colombian Andes* and in his *El Hombre y la Tierra en Boyacá*. He traces the origins of partisanship among the campesinos to the feudal-like authority which the landowner or patrón traditionally held over his tenants and agricultural workers. This permitted him to enlist them on behalf of himself and his party in the days of the nineteenth-century civil wars. Whichever side the patrón took in politics, whether in battle or at the ballot box, those dependent on him perforce also took. The division of the Indian *resguardos* (reservations) similarly crystallized partisan identifications among the rural masses. Forced to become an individualist and "left alone in an unknown world which contemporaries called 'democratic'," the Indian sought a means of survival in dependence on a cacique or gamonal of one or the other political party.[22]

The frequency of civil wars and the party struggles they represented—characteristics less true of most other Latin American nations—cemented the cohesion of particular communities around one of the political contenders. As Pearse and Rivera note in their study of Tenza, the oldest people still recall the ferocity and persecution of the civil wars of sixty and more years ago.[23] "Open warfare caused each locality . . . to strengthen its internal political bond as a means of survival in civil conflicts. In this man-

22. See Fals Borda, *Peasant Society*, p. 244, and, for the general point, chapter 15; see also Fals Borda, *El Hombre y la Tierra*, p. 191.
23. Pearse and Rivera, *La Tenencia de la Tierra*, pp. 127–29.

ner politics became . . . as important as life itself—it was identified with [the] struggle for existence." The spilling of blood created a desire for vengeance "and preparedness for retaliation [became] a *sine qua non* for family survival. Hereditary political cohesion [was], therefore, indispensable." [24]

Many Colombian communities emerged from the civil wars of the second half of the nineteenth century politically homogenized. Studies of Tenza, in Boyacá, where there are today 1,336 Conservative families and only 27 Liberal; of the municipio of Sonsón, Antioquia; and of Saucío, Cundinamarca, illustrate the pattern.[25] Political uniformity is by no means universally the case, even in smaller localities, and is much less true of larger urban centers. But its incidence is frequent. Using data from the March 1962 elections and surveying three of the most important Colombian departments—Antioquia, Santander, and Valle—it becomes clear that 32 per cent of the municipios in those departments had electoral margins for one or the other party of at least 10 to 1. An additional 28 per cent showed margins of at least 3 to 1. Thus more than half of the municipios in those departments are preponderantly composed of either Liberals or Conservatives, while almost a third are homogeneous to the virtual exclusion of the adherents of one of the parties.[26] If hamlets and villages incorporated within municipios (which often embrace several populated places) were taken into account, and for which figures are unavailable, the percentages of single-party communities would certainly be increased. As it is, votes like 5,683 (Conservatives) to 11 (Liberals) for the municipio of Cocorná, Antioquia, and 4,244 (Liberals) to 88 (Conservatives) for Corinto, Cauca, are by no means uncommon.

To voice sympathies for the minority party, or even to wear its colors (red for Liberal; blue for Conservative), may be to risk, as the gentlest

24. Fals Borda, *Peasant Society*, pp. 241–42 and 210. Cf. also Almond and Verba, *The Civic Culture*, pp. 132–43 and 297, concerning norms which bar the entry of opposing political views into primary groups, notably in Italy. The hypothesis is that political conflict is so intense that the primary group can be protected from it only by exclusion.

25. Pearse and Rivera, p. 127; CIS, *Estudios sobre . . . Sonsón*, p. 220; and Fals Borda, *Peasant Society*, passim.

26. The author's calculations based on data in Registraduría del Estado Civil, *Organización y Estadísticas, 1962*. The three departments are located in different parts of the country; a perusal of the 1962 election returns from other departments indicates that they roughly follow the pattern of the departments selected.

sanction, social ostracism. A shout of "Long live the Liberal (or Conservative) party" on a street or in a cafe peopled by adherents of the opposite party is likely to provoke instant physical challenge. To change one's party loyalty (unless one moves to another community where he is unknown) is to be considered an apostate and a traitor.

The communal aspects of any substantially traditional political system —aspects which pervade the "community" of the elite as well as of the village—sharply limit the freedom to alter one's political allegiances. For, as Lucian Pye has noted, any change in political identification requires corresponding changes in one's closest social and personal relationships.[27] Yet in Colombia the matter goes further. Not only do political loyalties tend to persist. The political culture and various structural features of the political system, as well as the heritage of civil war and "the circle of revenge," have produced a climate of violence and of hatred for the adversary which has profoundly affected the course of Colombian politics. The system of mutually exclusive loyalties fostered by the patrón-client cast of politics is reinforced by the intense politicization to which Colombians are exposed. Political rivals are seen as "total" enemies and the political culture becomes badly fragmented. This situation has contributed to political violence, which in the years since 1947 has taken a greater toll than during any similar period in the country's history.

Intolerance has had as its corollary the lack of a "moderate middle" and the absence of a "swing" vote. For if everyone is subjected from his early years to a process of political socialization which impresses on him for life the "Mark of Cain" of one or the other party, there is virtually no one left to convince by an appeal on the basis of issues or candidates. There is also less of a need for elaborate party organizations since appeals to traditional sentiments are a principal means of mobilizing one's partisans. Instead of the two political rivals trying to adapt themselves to the winning over of the uncommitted voter or of the weak supporters of the opposing party, the two "hereditary hatreds" have faced each other across an unbridgeable chasm.

A further and most significant consequence of this intense partisan

27. Lucian W. Pye, *Politics, Personality, and Nation Building* (New Haven, Conn., Yale University Press, 1962), pp. 16–17. The campesino fears "excommunication" from his party, and indeed from his community, if he deviates from the political norm. Cf. CIS, *Estudios sobre . . . Sonsón*, p. 214.

cleavage is the exclusion of the masses from any real voice at the centers of decision-making. Their identification with the names Conservative and Liberal have militated against the development of a consciousness of mutual interests of any other kind. Up to the present in many rural areas the national, regional, or local political leader is able to utter those words or give those orders which will trigger the traditional loyalties and hatreds of the peasant and galvanize him into action on behalf of one of the contending groups within the elite. The rural masses do, in a sense then, participate in politics, but only as fodder for the cannon or the ballot box.[28]

The vertical, patrón-client structures of the parties are thus reinforced by the intensity of partisan feelings. Together these two features of the traditional party system have worked to preclude the emergence of a modern party politics in Colombia.

VARIATIONS ON THE TWO-PARTY SYSTEM

There are two attributes of the Colombian party system that on their face belie the rigid pattern of bipolar opposition thus far outlined. One is persistent factionalism; the other, the alliances that have from time to time been constructed between the parties. Both are integral to the functioning of the system.

Factionalism has characterized the Colombian parties since their inception a century or so ago. The advent of the National Front has, if anything, accentuated it by temporarily diminishing the pull to unity resulting from bipartisan competition. The deeper causes of the long-continued factional splintering within the parties stem from several sources: the nature of the administrative state, which leads to lack of party discipline on the part of legislators who have had to bear little responsibility for government action; the minimum of popular control over political leadership, which has permitted it to perform irresponsibly; the cult of personalismo; and the importance of personal followings and loyalties, as distinct from group interests and socioeconomic issues, in the internal politics of the parties.

Factional feuds have most often been a response to personal rivalries or the tactical considerations of ambitious politicians, although at times they arise from genuine clashes of interest and doctrine as well.[29] Factions fre-

28. The phrase is that of Osorio in *Gaitán*, p. 79.
29. Lilo Linke attributes persistent factionalism in Colombia to clashes of genera-

quently differ, too, on the advisable degree of cooperation with the other party. At any given moment there are usually at least two opposed tendencies, if not always recognizable factions, within each party—one relatively intransigent, the other more inclined to accept cooperation with the opposition. Often the more instransigent wing is able to put the moderates in the difficult position of being considered somewhat less than loyal by those in their own party who believe that the "truth" cannot be compromised.

Factionalism has had at least three significant consequences for Colombian politics, aside from the obvious one of weakening the ability of the majority to govern and vitiating the minority's power to oppose. In the first place, factions have frequently served as the functional equivalents of an opposition party. Often the party out of power has been hampered in its access to the polls, or it has lost power because of a profound breach in its own ranks, or, on occasion, as a result of defeat in civil war. Under the circumstances the dominant party has tended to divide. "There not being anyone to offer legal opposition to the Liberals, whether in parliament or even in the press, they had to divide, by the force of things, to argue concerning the public interest, making opposition to themselves." [30] Schisms have likewise occurred in the "out" party. However, an examination of Colombian political history shows that intraparty differences which have been carried to the point of a de facto rupture have been more characteristic of the "ins" than of the opposition.

Secondly, on every occasion that power has alternated between the parties, with the single exception of the accession of the Liberals in 1861 through successful armed revolt, a change in the party in command has been directly attributable to a split in the dominant party. In a two-party system such as that of the United States swings from lengthy dominance by one party to prolonged control by the other usually depend on "critical" elections, such as those of 1896 and 1932, when whole groups of a party's supporters move semi-permanently into the opposite camp. [31] In Colombia

---

tions. Cf. Lilo Linke, *Andean Adventure: A Social and Political Study of Colombia, Ecuador, and Bolivia* (London, Hutchinson, 1945), p. 146. That there is some substance to this is shown by the current Liberal division; the MRL tends to include a relatively high proportion of younger members of the party.

30. José M. Samper, *Los Partidos en Colombia* (Bogotá, 1873), p. 82.

31. Cf. V. O. Key, Jr., "A Theory of Critical Elections," *Journal of Politics, 17*, 3–18.

the governing party, when unified, has practically always been able to control the outcome of elections. Besides, there are few who would voluntarily shift their voting allegiance from one election to the next. Hence, power changes hands primarily as a result of a split in the leadership of the ruling party, which leads to large-scale defections or to the party's running two presidential candidates. This has the consequence of "paralyzing the instruments of power, whose electoral efficacy is invincible," [32] and permitting the victory of the opposition candidate. It is thus as a result of factionalism, and not of a switch in the opinions of the mass of the voters, that alternation has customarily taken place in Colombia.

A third trait of Colombian factionalism is that it has frequently led to the formation of third parties, or to virtually independent groupings, without permanent disruption of the two-party order of things. The curious thing about such splits is not only that they have been short-lived, but that their members have continued to consider themselves as ultimately loyal to that body of tradition, sentiment, and ideology which has grown up around each historic party.[33] Examples are Rafael Núñez' Nationalist party of the 1880s, the Republican party in the years after 1910, and the post-1950 Conservative division. Even the current MRL has as its eventual aim that of rejoining the main body of the Liberal party (hopefully after the party's conversion to the image of the MRL).

The situation is similar to that of nineteenth-century England where factions such as the Peelites and Liberal Unionists came to operate as virtual third parties, subsequently to re-merge with one or the other traditional party. The chief distinction between the Colombian and English cases is that in England such splits usually served as stepping stones for the dissident faction to enter the *opposite* party. In Colombia party ties have usually proved strong enough so that the dissidents have rejoined their *original* party. In one sense, then, Colombian party factions have acted as safety valves, allowing for disagreement without destroying the two-party system. By the same token, the continued gravitational pull of the original party has helped to produce a rigidity which makes lasting change in the party system more difficult to achieve.

At the opposite pole from internal party schisms have been those occa-

32. Azula Barrera, *De la Revolución*, p. 135.
33. This point is brought out particularly well in Rodríguez Piñeres, *Diez Años de Política Liberal*, passim.

sions on which the two traditional parties have muted the partisan struggle itself by forming regimes of coalition or national unity. Seemingly paradoxical in a party system such as the Colombian, coalitions are made possible—sometimes virtually mandatory—by the fact that the leaderships of the Liberal and Conservative parties share membership in a fairly small and exclusive upper class. Their common interests are at times recognized to override any immediate stakes in the continuance of partisan strife. Moreover, there is a degree of tolerance among the party leaders, a certain amount of camaraderie at social gatherings, where political opponents may joke together much in the manner of professional Republicans and Democrats in the United States.[34] Indeed, the rank-and-file are more likely to be intense about party allegiances and less prone to compromise with the sworn enemy than are the party leaders. The former more often live in isolated, politically homogeneous communities where scant contact with the opposition makes them feel more different than they actually are.[35] At any rate, the party leaderships have been able at certain critical moments to join temporarily in order to prevent political fanaticism from tearing the polity apart altogether and destroying the elite itself along with it.

Coalitions between the party leaderships, or between factions of both, have played an important role in Colombian political history. They have sometimes acted as transitional regimes for the transfer of power. Thus after a Liberal, Enrique Olaya Herrera, had been elected president in 1930, he formed a regime of National Concentration, including in his administration a number of Conservatives. By this action he allayed the fears of Conservatives at the advent of their opponents to office and enabled the peaceful transfer to take place. Similarly, a Conservative politician admonished his party against any immediate attempt to regain power in the late 1930s "because the necessary stage of ministerial collaboration has not been gone through, and while this requisite is not fulfilled the transition would be too abrupt for the Liberal Party to tolerate." [36]

Coalitions have also at times provided a respite from civil strife. By putting partisanship temporarily aside, such arrangements have allowed

34. Cf. Holt, *Colombia Today*, p. 47.

35. Cf. on this point Myron Weiner, *Party Politics in India* (Princeton, N.J., Princeton University Press, 1957), p. 263.

36. Augusto Ramírez Moreno, *Una Política Triunfante* (Bogotá, Librería Voluntad, 1941), p. 9.

the nation to recover from its wounds and to enjoy periods of material progress. The Nationalist party founded by Núñez in the 1880s to serve as a vehicle for a program of "regeneration" was an attempt to bypass the old political divisions in the interests of stability and progress after years of the ravaging effects of extreme federalism. Similarly in 1902, General Benjamín Herrera, a Liberal, made peace with the government aboard the United States warship "Wisconsin," breaking his sword on the ship's armament and declaring that it was time to place "the fatherland above the parties." [37] There followed Liberal participation in a series of Conservative governments, the founding of the short-lived hybrid Republican party, and the era of the forty-five year peace.

A further function of coalitions has been to unite the upper class to counter a possible threat to its position from the lower rungs of the social order. The power struggle within the elite has not been permitted to create a vacuum into which the lower or middle groups might rush. If the violence of the Colombian parties' mutual antagonism precludes calling their rivalry simply "an elaborate sham of the two front benches," as the old Tory-Whig conflict in Britain was once described, it is still true that the elite groups who control both parties have remained essentially united on "their determination to keep in existence the same type of society, a type of society from which they both [have] benefited." [38]

Evidence of the interplay between party strife on the one hand, and the formation of alliances between the leaderships of the two parties on the other, comes out strongly in an analysis of the period between 1946 and 1950, when the acuteness of interparty clashes alarmed cooler heads in both parties. They formed the National Union to stay the excesses of extreme partisanship. The latest and most ambitious attempt at coalition is of course the National Front. It, like the National Union earlier, comprises among its objectives all three historic functions of Colombian coalition governments.

Just as Colombia's partisan division along dualist lines has masked what is in many ways a pluralist reality, it has also obscured a certain bedrock political unity of the Colombian elite. While often seeming to disrupt the workings of a straightforward two-party politics, both factionalism and

37. It is not without significance, of course, that Colombians have tended to consider country and party mutually exclusive in this sense.
38. Sigmund Neumann, "Toward a Theory of Political Parties," *World Politics, 6,* 551, quoting Hilaire Belloc and Cecil Chesterton.

the tendency to form coalitions at critical periods have been highly functional to what otherwise might long ago have become an impossibly rigid system.

THE TRADITIONAL PARTY SYSTEM—STABILITY AND CHANGE

Despite the vicissitudes of factionalism and the intrusion of coalitions, Colombia's Conservative-Liberal dichotomy has had a remarkable continuity. Leslie Lipson has set forth the characteristics of two-party systems as follows, based on his studies of British and Commonwealth politics: "(1) Not more than two parties at any given time have a genuine chance to gain power. (2) One of these is able to win the requisite majority and stay in office without help from a third party. (3) Over a number of decades two parties alternate in power." As Lipson goes on to show, this definition does not require that at all times a political system is literally characterized by only two parties. It allows for relatively long ascendance by one party, the disappearance of one party and the emergence of another in its place, and brief periods of three significant parties. Presumably the definition does not exclude fraud or violence as techniques of the party struggle, since he dates British parties from the eighteenth century when corruption and "rotten boroughs" were notorious. The important thing is that the above conditions constitute the norm "from which any departure is only temporary and to which the system always returns." The Colombian party system has so far met this test.[39]

By another criterion, that both parties should hover around the fifty per cent mark in voter allegiance, the Colombian is also decidedly a two-party system. Because of the influence which the incumbent government has customarily exercised over the ballot box, it is difficult to discern with any exactness the percentages of the electorate loyal to the parties at a given time. It may be that the Conservatives held a "permanent" majority during the nineteenth century, taking into account the Church's influence in rural areas.[40] Since at least the 1930s indications are that, with a widened and more urbanized vote, the majority has been Liberal. Since the initia-

39. Lipson, "The Two-Party System in British Politics," pp. 338–39. Colombia also fits the criteria for two-party systems set forth in Avery Leiserson, *Parties and Politics*, pp. 167–68.

40. Even some Liberals admitted the Conservative majority during the latter half of the nineteenth century. Cf. Indalecio Liévano Aguirre, *Rafael Núñez* (Bogotá, Compañía Grancolombiana de Ediciones, 1959 [?]), p. 126.

tion of the National Front, under bipartisan electoral machinery, the Liberals have generally won between 55 and 60 per cent of the vote. In the 1964 and 1966 congressional elections the Liberals won just over fifty per cent of the vote cast. This probably signified that abstention was heaviest among Liberals rather than any real shift in partisan choice.

By various standards, then, Colombia's has been a two-party system. Yet its performance has been radically different from the classic two-party systems of the Anglo-Saxon world. The internal structure of the Colombian parties, the nature and depth of the antagonism between them, and the peculiarities of factionalism and interparty coalitions produce a series of effects which distinguish the Colombian party system from those of the United States and the British Commonwealth.

Colombia's system of parties is a mirror of the hierarchical social pattern. The parties have served largely as instruments of control from above rather than as the means of effective political expression for broad strata of the population. They have been inhibitors rather than promoters of democracy. It is true that both parties cut vertically through all social layers of the population, making them in terms of their followings genuinely "polyclass." But diversity of membership does not necessarily entail wider participation in the political process, especially when such membership is primarily based on hereditary loyalties. Not the breadth of the membership but the number having some voice in party decisions is the more relevant consideration.

The party contest in Colombia at bottom represents a struggle among rival segments of the elite which are able to involve in it, for the reasons elaborated, their respective followings or clienteles. Since most Colombians have been forever marked, as a matter of family tradition or community cohesion, with the brand Conservative or Liberal, segments of each social class are channeled by an imposing system of dikes into the two partisan bands. It is this as much as anything else that has prevented the emergence of a class- or policy-based politics in Colombia.

The Colombian parties have played a singular role with respect to one particular responsibility which commonly falls to democratic parties, especially those in a two-party system—the accommodation or aggregation of a multiplicity of interests. Colombia's two major parties each contains among its members landowners, merchants, intellectuals, campesinos, workers. Yet instead of the parties acting as vehicles of compromise among these groups, the parties for the most part serve to manipulate the majority on behalf of the more powerful members. Both the vertical organization of the parties and the "hereditary hatreds" ensure that members of each interest group or social class are arrayed politically against others of the same group.

The wide variety of groups, interests, and ideological tendencies represented among each party's adherents are not aggregated in the usual sense. It is true that the gamonal, in keeping with the norms of reciprocity of the patrón relationship, ideally seeks to maximize the interests of his followers or clients by securing for them government jobs or by obtaining public works for the region. It is also true that party leaders at the departmental or national seats of government have traditionally made themselves available to delegations of campesinos or to private individuals who have cared to present to them their petitions for redress in particular matters. But means such as these, characteristic of patrón-client relationships, do not in themselves involve, except very loosely, the same kind of bargaining and negotiation among *group* interests that are characteristic of broad-based parties elsewhere. Indeed the factionalism of the parties is testimony to the difficulties of accommodating interests which are in large part those of personal and communal rivalry.

Missing from the Colombian political scene is a moderate middle which both parties try to win and toward which both tend. The absence of a substantial number of voters who will switch their support from one party to the other puts a severe strain on the system. Alternation of the parties in power can be achieved only by a split in one of them. Competition between alternatives is not in itself an adequate condition for the existence of a democratic party system. There must also be "rules of the game" and some willingness on the part of the electorate to be flexible in its political choices in order that competition will be both peaceful and meaningful. The parties in a two-party system are therefore not necessarily realistic, pragmatic, and moderate, nor does such a system invariably presuppose a willingness to compromise. A two-party system, if it is composed of two irreconcilable blocs, may actually exacerbate violence rather than act as its sublimation.[41]

Colombia's parties have accordingly failed to perform effectively an-

41. Cf. V. O. Key, Jr., *Politics, Parties, and Pressure Groups* (4th ed., New York, Crowell, 1958), pp. 12 and 224.

other of their presumed democratic functions: that of managing the peaceful succession to authority. The victory of one party over the other has seldom been attained under conditions which the loser felt it could accept. The presidential succession has frequently been challenged by violence or subversion. The classic Latin American obstacle to stable government—the difficulty of accepting the victory or the potential victory of the opposition—has in Colombia been accentuated by the traditional hatreds between the parties.

Thus several features of the Colombian party system contrast sharply with two-party systems in other parts of the world. They suggest that "the political effects of the two-party system or of the multi-party system are essentially variable . . . it is futile to expect from the one . . . effects necessarily beneficial for political life, and to predict of the other . . . that it will necessarily lead to confusion and deterioration." [42] The number of parties may be much less important than the relationship between them, or the way in which they relate to other parts of the social and political systems.

Colombia's parties have constituted one of the aspects of its political system most resistant to change. Nonetheless, the traditional party system is in serious straits, as so many of the nation's intellectuals have pointed out. Past crises centered on which party was to rule the state; today the system itself is on trial.

Evidence of the crisis is plain enough. The bogotazo, and the recent years of prolonged guerrilla warfare—both of which have gone far beyond the traditional dimensions of violence in the Colombian political system—are indications that the parties have not been responding effectively to the demands of sectors of the population newly awakened to political consciousness. Gaitán's meteoric rise, and the overt intervention of the military in politics in 1953 after half a century of its absence, were further symptoms of the parties' inadequacies. The recent rise of *gremio* politics, in which economic associations, labor unions, and similar organizations make claims directly on the government or take independent action on their own behalf, is yet a further mark of the slowness with which the parties have reacted to new social and political forces. Most recently, wholesale electoral abstention has signalled a growing alienation.

Colombia's traditional parties are in difficulties because the services to

42. G.-E. Lavau, *Partis Politiques et Realités Sociales,* Cahiers de la Fondation Nationale des Sciences Politiques, 38 (Paris, Libraire Armand Colin, 1953), p. 49.

which her citizens aspire can no longer be dispensed on the basis of individual favors obtained through the operation of a patrón-client system of politics. It is no longer enough to deal in terms of family, clientele, or patria chica. Colombian politics is becoming nationalized. Groups and classes distinguished by economic interests and seeking resolution of their claims on the state through government *policy*, rather than through the allotment to them of more jobs and contracts, are coming to play an increasingly vocal role in the political arena. Yet the parties have not yet learned to become effective intermediaries between such groups and the government by channeling their claims through the party machinery and into party demands and programs.

The elite-ruled parties have failed to evolve effective means for the admission of potential counter-elites to a share in their direction, or to establish genuine grass-roots organizations and a degree of internal democracy. The parties' chieftains are essentially those of yesterday, or their close relatives: Alvaro Gómez Hurtado, Mariano Ospina Pérez, and Guillermo León Valencia for the Conservatives; Carlos Lleras Restrepo, Alberto Lleras Camargo, and Alfonso López Michelsen among Liberals. Meanwhile, a new generation has reached maturity, and groups previously taken for granted or represented in party circles by their patrons among the elite are finding the old obstacles on the path of political advance and participation more intolerable.

The ancient appeals based on hereditary enmities are also becoming less of a guarantee of unquestioning support, especially in the cities. It is not so much that the old loyalties have as yet been abandoned, but that the supporters of the traditional parties are beginning to demand that their allegiance be rewarded with something more tangible, and of a different order, than revenge against their fellow workers or campesinos. The National Front has made the situation more acute by making less plausible the traditional ties which have linked the elite groups of the parties to their respective mass followings. There are, in fact, some incipient signs and portents that the old party politics is evolving in new directions, and even that the traditional party sentiments may be eroding.

Little is known of the effects of migration on partisan loyalties. But logically, movement from one's community and immersion in the more anonymous context of urban life affords at least the possibility of change. The fact that almost all the cities of Colombia tend to vote Liberal suggests that such changes have taken place, although this may in part represent selective migration from the countryside as a result of the differential effects of rural violence on Liberals.

Just as important, urban dwellers are more prone to political awareness, and less susceptible to the. influence of the *gamonal*. Whiteford found in his study of Popayán that the lower class was quite politically conscious. He reports that during the heightened political tensions of the 1949–50 period, when speeches were being given or the proceedings of Congress were being broadcast, the radios of the lower-class section of the city were turned almost exclusively to these programs.

Those exposed to an urban environment are more inclined to see politics in terms of social groups or classes, less in terms of the rivalries of kinship or community, even when traditional political loyalties remain strong. It is especially interesting to note that the fanatical Liberal loyalties of the majority of the lower-class residents of Popayán (loyalties which for the most part probably originated in the villages from which many of them had emigrated) had been turned into a vehicle of expression for class grievances. The lower-class *Popayanés* seemed to obtain an emotional release by hearing these grievances aired and their redress promised. Association with the Liberal party gave members of the lower class the feeling that their problems were of national concern. It also gave them a certain sense of solidarity over and against the propertied interests—in Popayán largely identified with the Conservatives. Under the umbrella of support for their party it permitted them to take a position of legitimate opposition to the upper class. This was true even though the class basis of party affiliation was clouded by the fact that many of the Liberal leaders were also of the upper class.[43]

Another small ripple of change, perhaps indicative of a coming groundswell, is evident among intellectuals. Persons identified with various parties and factions have cooperated in founding *Ediciones Tercer Mundo*, which publishes books by individuals of almost every political persuasion. A similar departure was *Contrapunto*, a weekly founded in early 1965 expressly to present a spectrum of viewpoints. It regularly contained columns by authorized spokesmen of most major political groups.

Still another sign is that the parties have in some measure adapted their programs and policies to the new circumstances. As early as the 1930s the

43. Whiteford, *Two Cities*, pp. 116 and 134.

Liberals felt it advisable to enact into law extensive provisions for the protection of labor. Under the National Front both parties have supported the passage of Law 135 of 1961. The election campaigns of both parties, as well as their official programs and the speeches and writings of their leaders, increasingly speak out on social and economic issues in recognition of the fact that the traditional appeals may not be an entirely reliable base of support for the future. At the same time, the failure of many to vote in recent elections under the National Front is a mark of the modest success of such attempts thus far.

In recent years the Liberal party in particular has taken some significant steps to strengthen ties with the mass of its membership, to tighten its organization, and to improve party unity. The new party statutes, drawn up by Carlos Lleras Restrepo, then director of the party, and adopted in 1963, embody the proposals for a modernized Liberal party.[44] A significant innovation is that the membership is to be divided into active members and simple adherents. The former are required to pay dues in return for a party *carnet* authorizing them to participate in the internal elections of the party and making them eligible for directive posts and to be candidates for public office under party auspices.

Considerable attention is devoted in the new statutes to the organization of affiliates and to the nature of their relationship to the party. Thus Article 5:

> There may be affiliated to the party feminine, masculine, or mixed associations, of political, cultural, or social action, or whose objective is to group together the Liberals of particular economic, professional, or work organizations, or which have as their aim the establishment of a closer cooperation among the various economic and social sectors which coexist in the party, whose foundation may be promoted by the party leadership or which Liberals may form spontaneously.

Affiliation to the party itself may take place through these organizations, and at least ninety per cent of the affiliate's members must be inscribed party members at the time that its formal association with the party takes place. However, it is explicitly provided, notably in a party resolution issued subsequently to the statutes, that the aims of such organizations need

44. The following discussion is based primarily on *Estatutos del Partido Liberal, 1963.*

not be exclusively political but may include the promotion of communal action and the improvement of the standard of living and of education of the middle and popular classes.[45]

Express provisions are made in the statutes for regular reports of the actions of Liberal representatives in legislative bodies, and even in the committees of Congress, to the appropriate party organs; for secret vote in the party caucus as to who is to represent the party as officers of the Congress and on congressional committees; and for the disciplining of those legislators who fail to comply with caucus decisions. In an attempt to reduce factionalism and provide a place in the party organization for all Liberal "tendencies," the electoral quotient is to be applied in internal party elections. Women are to be assured a place in the party hierarchy by the allotment of a minimum number of positions on municipal and regional directorates of the party (the national directorate is not mentioned in this connection). In presenting the statutes for the party's consideration, Lleras Restrepo noted that the principal task of Liberals was to carry the whole party, and with it the country, toward the Left, without at the same time making of the party an instrument of class warfare.

Inscription of membership was begun almost immediately, but there has been some criticism that rather than putting party membership on a new basis it was often the gamonal or the manzanillo who was buying up the carnets for distribution. As a newly-formed affiliate, the League of Liberal Youth (*Liga de la Juventud Liberal*) seems to be particularly active and has formed branches in several cities.[46] A beginning has therefore been made; powerful social and political forces suggest its urgency; and the reforms have behind them, in Lleras Restrepo, a man who has become the president of Colombia. But a modern party is not built in a day or a year and the supplanting of the patterns of influence and the techniques of mobilization of the party faithful that have so far prevailed will take fundamental reorganization. The recommendations of a National Assembly of Liberal Directors in March 1964 reflected concern with both the abstention prevalent in the elections of that month and with the need for greater speed in the rejuvenation of the party. The assembly and its several special committees issued proposals "to stimulate the organization of

45. *El Tiempo*, Aug. 23, 1963, pp. 1 and 22.
46. See Liga de la Juventud Liberal, *Insurgencia Nacional* (Bogotá, 1963).

the campesinos, the workers, artisans, and the members of the economic middle class"; to improve the party's campaign techniques and the diffusion of its message, including the creation of "committees of ideological agitation"; and to establish permanent party functionaries at all levels of the party organization.[47]

The Conservatives, too, have recognized the need to reorder their party's structure: "In the . . . years of the political truce a renovated Conservative Party must be built, with a modern organization, with concrete programs which present adequate solutions for the problems of our time." [48] There is evidence of an attempted revitalization of Conservative youth activities, and new statutes were adopted in 1964 which incorporated changes comparable in some ways to the 1963 Liberal document. The new by-laws include a distinction between militants (with carnet) and affiliates; create secretariats for youth, women, workers, and cooperatives and communal action; and establish an Institute of Political Diffusion to propagate the party's philosophy.[49]

Yet the modernization of traditional, elite-run parties like the Colombian is far easier to set forth in party documents than to put into execution. In spite of changes and adaptation, the imprint of the past is still firmly affixed on the behavior of the parties and the electorate. Curiously enough, the very nature of the traditional parties, while raising formidable barriers to their modernization, provides them with at least some assets for its accomplishment. It may be that the time-honored loyalties which they evoke will be a stabilizing influence during the period when they are adjusting their structures and their appeals along new lines. This seems to have occurred, for example, among the lower class of Popayán. It is also possible that the existing polyclass composition of the parties will enable them to become effective aggregators of a multiplicity of interests more readily than might otherwise be the case.

Again, much depends on whether the parties' leadership reacts to the exigencies of the mid-twentieth century with sufficient speed and thoroughness. Neither party has yet become a forum where new voices, non-

47. *El Tiempo*, April 25, 1964.
48. Directorio Nacional Conservador, *Plataforma de Acción Política y Social, 1957* (Bogotá[?], 1957), p. 38.
49. *Estatutos del Partido Conservador*.

elite voices, may find expression. The governing group has been afraid to abandon its reliance on old techniques and battle cries to strike out in new directions. The dilemma has been posed by Alberto Lleras Camargo:

> For this generation there are two roads, two alternatives . . . Is it going to continue to cultivate the same following that it inherited? If so, it is obvious that it has to proceed with the same tools and the same fertilizers that served to grow the excellent crops of heroic fidelity to the old principles and the old motives of battle and resign itself to those crops diminishing each day in quantity and quality. Or will it formulate a policy for current facts and problems and resolve to risk the contingencies of a redistribution of forces, which will then no longer be determined by lineage and village, nor by Liberal and Conservative families . . . but by the new intellectual, economic, and social interests of today's people.[50]

50. Lleras Camargo, *Sus Mejores Páginas,* pp. 33–34.

9

THE TRADITIONAL
PARTIES (II)

THE QUESTION OF POLITICAL DUALISM

The organization and functioning of Colombia's traditional parties, plus the historically derived sentiments that have attached to them, explain a great deal about Colombian politics, including the likely directions of political change. Yet we have so far scarcely touched on the bases of the split *between* the parties, a split which in its origins and its leadership has been primarily a division within the elite itself. Why not simply one party, as the political expression of upper-class rule? or several, as the expression of·the factionalism that in any case has existed? In short, what have been the foundations of Colombia's political dualism?

At first glance it is tempting to dismiss such questions with the answer that the terms Conservative and Liberal are meaningless designations, that the parties merely represent chance combinations of notables and their retinues which through years of political combat have become frozen into opposing "systems of hate." In this interpretation the parties trace their origins, as well as their continuity, exclusively to rivalries of families, cliques, and "cults of personality," reinforced by the process of intense political socialization which most Colombians undergo.

A related characterization of Colombian parties is that they are "rival bands of brigands fighting over literal loot." [1] Politics in this light is little more than a contest of "ins" versus "outs," based on the desire of those who have no share in the current spoils of office to throw out those who do and themselves partake at the public trough.

1. Cf. Fluharty, *Dance of the Millions*, pp. 23 and 227–33, for this view.

There is little doubt that this does describe the incentives for participation in political life on the part of many Colombians. The role of the spoils system, as depicted earlier, suggests as much. It is obvious, too, from our discussion of parties to this point, that their internal functioning is highly dependent on the connections of patrons and their clienteles. These things are crucial to Colombian party politics. But the fact that cliques (or parties) are based on personal relations does not necessarily mean that there is no divergence on values and policy objectives.[2] Nor does it discount the possibility of support of one or another party by high and relatively stable proportions of the voters of particular social groups or regions. There have been and continue to be differences in the philosophies which the Colombian parties bring to national politics, differences in the policies they have advocated, differences in their social bases. It is for such distinctions that we still need to account, particularly since they seem to be undergoing significant transformations.

IDEOLOGY AND THE PARTIES

Many observers have considered Colombian parties to be ideological parties par excellence. The classic expression of this comes from Francisco García Calderón: "In Colombia exalted convictions are the motives of political enmities; men abandon fortune and family, as in the great religious periods of history, to hasten to the defence of a principle. These *hidalgos* waste the country and fall nobly, with the Semitic ardor of Spanish Crusades . . . Obedient to the logic of Jacobinism, Colombia perishes, but the truth is saved."[3] Rafael Núñez, who certainly did not deny that other factors played their part in politics, felt that party unity could not be forged by meetings of the party machine or by common interest in spoils or material domination, since these were ultimately corrupting and fragile. "Only the attraction of ideas can reunite men, when, by the very nature of things, the attraction of material benefits is weakened or disappears."[4] Indeed, it is difficult to read the programs of the Colombian parties, or the speeches or writings of their leaders and adherents, and not get a sense of rather profound difference of philosophy and approach.

2. Cf. Pye, *Politics, Personality, and Nation Building*, pp. 18–19.
3. García Calderón, *Latin America*, p. 202.
4. Núñez, *Los Mejores Artículos*, pp. 46–48 and 85–94.

The Conservative has showed a marked preference for a social and political order in which tradition and religion play paramount roles. His ideology has strong Hispanic and Catholic overtones. He believes that the Church should be protected and assisted by the state and work in consonance with it as an associate pillar of society. He therefore looks with beneficence at clerical involvement in secular affairs, and askance at the activities of non-Catholic religions in the country. In the realm of social policy Catholic principles should ideally infuse public action. A 1957 manifesto of the Conservative Committee of Economic and Social Action declared: "the key to the prevailing social unrest can be found in the contradiction which exists between the sad situation of the Colombian community and the formidable thought of Conservatism in social and economic matters, which is wise and just, based as it is on the truth of Catholic philosophy." [5] In keeping with this general orientation, the family, rather than the individual, occupies the central position in the social order, and attitudes toward the role of women in society are conservative ones. As mentor of the moral order, the Church's role in education—public as well as private—is to be a key one, and to preserve that role has been a central tenet of Colombian Conservatism. Innovation, in this order of things, will often be looked on by the Conservative as the product of pernicious doctrines imported from abroad, and as an assault not merely on this or that institutional arrangement but as a challenge to the very moral foundations of society.

Order and hierarchy are other key words in the lexicon of the Colombian Conservative. His emphasis is on a strong central authority, a strong executive arm, and on firm measures in dealing with popular disturbances or threats to the status quo. He is also likely to stress the claims of discipline and hierarchy: hence the lament of Laureano Gómez that "the indis-

5. Directorio Nacional Conservador, *Plataforma, 1957,* p. 37. The discussion of Conservative philosophy that follows is based substantially on this programmatic statement, on *Los Programas Conservadores,* on the Conservative press, on the writings of various Conservative leaders, and on conversations with individual Conservatives, both leaders and followers. The subsequent discussion of Liberal philosophy and its difference from that of the Conservatives is based as well on interviews, the Liberal press, and the writings of Liberal leaders, especially Alejandro López, *Idearium Liberal* (Paris, Ediciones La Antorcha, 1931), and López Michelsen, *Cuestiones Colombianas,* passim. See also Burnett, "The Recent Colombian Party System," pp. 149–59, and, for the parties' approach to economic questions, Ospina Vásquez, *Industria y Protección,* passim.

pensable bonds of hierarchy are broken. Authority is disregarded." [6] In politics the attention paid to such values carries with it an implied scorn for majorities of "the one-half plus one," and there has run through Conservative thinking a persistent strand which favors a Senate with employers, workers, universities, the Church, and other groups and entities represented on a corporate basis rather than as part of a mass electorate.

In economic and social policy the Conservatives blend a somewhat modified nineteenth-century liberalism with elements from the papal encyclicals. The Conservative has traditionally looked on property as a natural right and he has been reluctant to accept state intervention which might modify that right (although he has not usually objected to state protection of established rights). In recent years, however, he has accepted "intervention" for the purpose of enabling the regime of free competition to function more smoothly and to promote economic development. He has even come tacitly to accept the doctrine, actually implicit in Catholic social thought, that property has a social function.

The attitude the Conservative assumes toward social policy is generally paternalistic. Benevolence and charity on the part of the state or the employer is the preferred route to social betterment and is seen as a Christian obligation. Thus the party's Platform of Social and Economic Action of 1957 proposed that the government grant reductions in taxes for those employers who gave voluntary gifts and bonuses to their workers. But the *right* of the worker or the campesino to claims against the employer, and particularly his organization into bodies which will promote the class struggle, are viewed with suspicion. There is an inclination to look upon most strikes as subversive and to regard as the desired norm a unionism which will not challenge the existing order of things or raise the specter of class warfare.

Most Conservatives at least nominally back some type of agrarian reform, and the majority in the party supported Law 135 of 1961. More emphasis is placed on progressive taxes on uncultivated land, however, than on parcelization, and more on producers' cooperatives than on agricultural unionism. The Conservative's is an outlook which sees in rural Colombia, in the earth, the root of real virtue and social health. It is in line with this

6. El Presbítero Jerónimo (pen-name of Gómez), quoted in *El Espectador*, Aug. 19, 1963, p. 1.

conception that the Conservatives think of themselves as "the party of the campesinos."

In contrast to Hispanic traditionalism and the teachings of the Catholic Church, the classic stance of the Colombian Liberal has taken as its inspiration the tenets of nineteenth-century liberalism. The individual guided by reason, rather than the family or the community bound by the wisdom of tradition, has for him constituted the core element of the social order. At times carrying his opposition to the point of "free-thinking" and attacks on the Catholic religion as such, he has in general remained a Catholic personally while he has inveighed against the Church's influence in what he has regarded as secular affairs. His main political concern during the nineteenth century often seemed to be to rid Colombian public life of that pervasive influence, whether in politics, in education, in the registration of births and deaths, in the ownership of land, or in the realms of ideas and popular custom. He was an early advocate of the expulsion of the Jesuit order from the country and for a time was able to carry out this intent. It was also the Liberals who confiscated Church lands in 1861. Liberal regimes have taken the lead in the promotion of secular and popular education in Colombia.[7] Today, many of the old Church issues are dead or dormant, but the Liberal remains in his heart a proponent of the separation of Church and state and of the reduction of the Church's role in education. He also favors toleration of other religions. In all, the rationalist and secularist trends of the modern world have been more congenial to the Liberal than has Hispanic-oriented traditionalism. In principle he has regarded change as desirable, and adaptation to it a necessity of life (at least so long as this does not entail any fundamental displacement of rule by an elite).

Rather than order and hierarchy, the Colombian Liberal stresses liberty and popular rule. Despite the fact that individual Liberal presidents, once in power, may have been on occasion as eager as any Conservative president to exert the authority of the executive, the Liberals as a party have emphasized the decentralization of political and administrative authority. During the nineteenth century their extreme federalism pushed the nation to the brink of dissolution. In spite of the fact that Liberals often have

7. Cf. Fals Borda, *Educación en Colombia*, passim.

been as wary as any Conservative of rule by the masses, it has been the Liberals who have usually taken the lead in extending the suffrage and upholding freedom of speech, the press, and the academy. In the Liberal creed, rights have come before duties, and the popular will (at least as that will is interpreted by its spokesmen among the Liberal elite) before the claims of hierarchical authority.

Liberals began their journey in Colombian history as the advocates of a fairly extreme version of laissez faire. Their aim in the economic field was the abolition of those taxes, restrictions, and privileges held over from colonial days which threatened the operation of a free economy. Slavery, the Indian resguardo, and a variety of taxes, tariffs, and state monopolies fell under the Liberal axe in the middle of the last century. The Liberal continued for long to give his backing to free trade (as did, in fact, the Conservative most of the time, if in a less dogmatic way). However, the Colombian Liberal party has gradually come to accept as necessary and desirable a greater role for the state in economic life. It was the Liberals who engineered the inclusion of a clause in the constitutional codification of 1936 granting such powers to the government. Meanwhile the Liberals, who earlier took the position that property was a natural right, have come to view it as having a social function. Under President Alfonso López they wrote that, too, into the constitution.

Major labor legislation, as well as the initiative for such agrarian reform laws as those of 1936 and 1961, have come primarily from the Liberal party. Such legislation points up a basic difference in the Liberals' approach to social policy: they are less inclined to paternalism and readier than the average Conservative to recognize or confer rights. They have been more prone to look to legislation and government action, and to rely on its efficacy to solve social ills. Moreover, it is not on the papal encyclicals that the Liberal has based his social philosophy but on the thought and experience of a modernized liberalism.

Today, important elements within the Liberal party are trying to prove that it is Colombia's party of the democratic Left and are bending their efforts to see that it assumes that role, in its program as well as in its organization.

"In order for the Liberal party to be a party of the Left, it has to cease to be the old party which concentrates the whole of its action in the defense of the institutions of representative democracy and of political rights.

If either were in danger, we would act to preserve them. But while they are not, a party of the Left cannot waste its time and its opportunities dedicating itself to their defense. Its guideline is the social ascent of the masses, the [economic] development of the nation, [and] its independence from all foreign powers." [8] Whereas the Conservative party portrays itself as the party of the campesinos, the Liberal party stakes its claim to be "the party of the people."

These are no more than tendencies, of course: contrasts in temperament, orientation, and attitude as much as they are differences in specific policy proposals. "More than a doctrine, our parties always constituted an attitude and a sentiment of Colombians toward life." [9] At times the doctrines have been vague and points of divergence not clearly discernible. Occasionally a certain unity of view has prevailed, especially during those periods when the party leaders' membership in a common elite has been reflected in coalition. Philosophical differences have not necessarily precluded collaboration. The matter of distinctions has been further complicated by the doctrinal evolution within both the Liberal and Conservative parties. The Conservatives, whose ideology derives in considerable part from mercantilist and corporatist sources, have become over the century or more of their existence the chief partisan defender of free enterprise in Colombia. The Liberals, once ardent supporters of laissez faire and the property rights of the individual, have modified their position (perhaps more in theory than in practice). They now propound a role for government in the economy and uphold the ultimate social function of property, the reversal resembling that which took place in the Democratic party of the United States between the days of Jefferson and those of F. D. Roosevelt.

Still another factor making it difficult to draw sharp characterizations of Colombia's two historic parties is that each within itself runs a wide ideological gamut. The Conservative party has harbored points of view ranging from aristocratic republicanism to Christian socialism and quasi-Falangism; and Liberals vary from defenders of the tenets of classic nineteenth-century liberalism to "New Dealers" and a few quasi-Marxists.

8. Liga de la Juventud Liberal, *Insurgencia Nacional*, p. 5.

9. Alfonso López Michelsen, *Colombia en la Hora Cero* (2 vols. Bogotá, Ediciones Tercer Mundo, 1963), *1*, 20.

Given such diversity it is not surprising that at times members of a wing of one party have been closer to a faction of the other than to some of their fellow partisans on the issues of the day.

Yet differences there are and have been, differences which sometimes appear to be more those of tone and approach than of actual behavior, but which stand out in the realm of policy as well if one compares the administration of Alfonso López, for instance, with that of Laureano Gómez. The distinctions spring from contrasting views of the nature of man. To the Conservative, man is by nature both a social being, and an imperfect being disposed to use his will and intelligence badly unless admonished and restrained by tradition and authority. To the Liberal, man is fundamentally good, corrupted by a society which limits his freedom.[10] The Conservative has thus tended to uphold a doctrine of Catholic-oriented traditionalism, as modified by its operation within the formal structure of a constitutional democracy and a liberal economy. He is a cross between a European-style traditionalist and a capitalistic-oriented conservative of the United States. The Liberal, on the other hand, has been rooted essentially in the ideas of classical liberalism, tempered by the requirements of gaining and holding power in a social and political environment which in many ways is illiberal. In the twentieth century he has recognized the imperatives of economic development and social change. The Liberal philosophy is therefore a mixture of nineteenth-century liberalism and modern conceptions of the welfare state operating in the context of a society ruled by an upper class to which the leading Liberals themselves belong.

Ideologies give reasoned frameworks to otherwise imperfectly articulated interests, desires, and views of life. More than that, in Colombia party ideologies have become the "exalted convictions" of which García Calderón spoke, with attendant implications for political peace. The Colombian experience has borne out Leiserson's dictum that "The more that differences between parties are assumed to be ideological, the more discussion of these differences occurs in a context of struggle between ultimate moral ends." [11] It follows that it would be a mistake to discount the role of ideology in the formation and subsequent development of the

10. Cf. Laserna, *Estado Fuerte*, p. 58.
11. Leiserson, *Parties and Politics*, p. 260.

partisan breach within the Colombian elite. But it would also be an error to ascribe too much to principle, even when it has become functionally autonomous in Leiserson's sense. Even that most evidently ideological matter of them all, the religious question, has to a large extent been concerned with power and property. In the early nineteenth century the Church was the owner of large tracts of land, controlled education, and played a direct role in politics and government. What was in appearance an ideological question was in considerable measure a contest over the degree of influence and material wealth which the clergy was to hold in Colombian society.

Colombian political battles have often been fought in the name of opposed ideologies and views of life. This very fact has been a prime contributor to the intensity with which the game of politics has been played. Yet it is misleading to see Colombia's partisan divisions as exclusively or even primarily ideological, even when they are articulated as such. Parties in Colombia as elsewhere have served material as well as ideal ends.

THE SOCIAL BASES OF THE PARTIES

In attempting to examine the social bases of the Liberal and Conservative parties we are faced at once by the virtual nonexistence in Colombia of the opinion surveys which have formed the empirical basis of such studies as *The American Voter*.[12] The use of aggregate data, which matches voting returns from particular geographic or administrative areas with census information on the social composition of their population, is likewise made difficult in Colombia because of the nature of both the census and the electoral statistics. One must recognize, too, that voting has often been less than wholly free, particularly in rural areas. Even when technically free, the campesino may well vote according to the dictates of his patrón. To complicate matters further, one of the parties has occasionally abstained altogether from the polls. There are two kinds of statistical data that can be of some use, however, in analyzing the social roots of the Colombian parties, especially if one places his heaviest reliance on the "clean" elections under the bipartisan National Front. One is a regional comparison; the other a differentiation along rural-urban lines.

12. Angus Campbell et al., *The American Voter* (New York, Wiley, 1960).

Breakdowns of party voting by departments are largely unavailable for the last century and the first two decades of this. Yet from data beginning with the presidential election of 1918 we can obtain a fairly good picture of the regional bases of party strength in recent decades.[13]

It thus appears that the departments of Nariño and Huila in southwestern Colombia, plus Antioquia, have been the most staunchly Conservative over time, although the Conservative margin in Huila is now quite narrow. The department of Caldas was traditionally Conservative. But the Liberals surpassed the combined vote for the two Conservative candidates there in the 1930 election, even though the national government was in Conservative hands, and the Liberals have been victorious in several other elections since. Of late the margin of victory for either party has usually been small and Caldas may best be described as politically balanced.

On the other side politically, the Atlantic coast department of Atlántico and the sparsely populated Pacific coast department of Chocó have not voted Conservative in any election since at least 1918. Cundinamarca, containing the national capital, Bogotá; Tolima, in central Colombia; and the Atlantic coast departments of Bolívar and Magdalena have all usually remained Liberal, at least subsequent to the election of 1930, and generally by margins of from one and a half to two and a half to one. Since its creation in 1954 the department of Córdoba on the Atlantic coast has also voted Liberal by rather substantial margins. The territories (*intendencias* and *comisarías*) generally vote Liberal as well. Valle and Cauca have returned Liberal pluralities in most elections, but generally by smaller percentages. The relative closeness of the elections in these two departments places them among the more politically competitive in the nation. The department of Meta, formed in 1960 in the eastern plains, is also quite evenly balanced politically, though leaning Liberal.

The three departments whose voting records raise the most perplexing

13. The assessments of party strength by departments are taken, for the elections of 1918 and 1922, from *Colección Jorge Eliécer Gaitán*, pp. 149–50 and 167–70; for elections subsequent to that date through 1960 from the annual *Memorias* of the successive Ministers of Government to the Congress and from Burnett, pp. 81–111 (who relies mainly on the *Memorias*); and for the 1962 and 1964 elections from Registraduría del Estado Civil, *Organización y Estadísticas*, for the respective years. It appears from other evidence that the continuity in the regional distribution of party strength with earlier periods has been great.

problems for generalization are Boyacá, Santander, and Norte de Santander, contiguous departments along the Venezuelan border in eastern Colombia. Prior to 1946 the three were either *strongly* Liberal or *strongly* Conservative, depending on which party held national power at the time —at any rate during the period for which we have data. In the elections since 1958 Norte de Santander and Boyacá have both remained heavily Conservative while Santander has shown a fairly even distribution of party strength with a slight Liberal edge.

Examining the facts more closely we find that in general those departments with important commercial and industrial activities, and the newer, sparsely populated departments without long-established quasi-feudal social structures, tend to be Liberal politically. By the same token those departments which have been most isolated from the mainstream of Colombian industry, mining, and commerce, and most attached to the ancient modes of agriculture, have on the whole been Conservative.[14]

There are two groups of departments which constitute seeming exceptions to these generalizations. One is made up of the departments of Antioquia and Caldas, the latter populated by Antioquians during the nineteenth century. The Antioqueños have in recent decades become the country's bankers and entrepreneurs, and should presumably be Liberal. However, their involvement in industrial pursuits is in the main a twentieth-century development. It would seem that their Conservatism is related to their attachment to the Church and, possibly, a carry-over from their nineteenth-century isolation and regional opposition to the then relatively more commercialized, "industrialized," and Liberal Colombian east. The rise of a fairly substantial peasant middle class among the Antioqueños and *Caldenses* which in many ways is highly traditional, may have reinforced the region's Conservative proclivities. At the same time, recent gains by the Liberals in both departments, and the tendency for Antioquia to become the center of a moderate Conservatism, quick to reject the extremists in the party when their actions have threatened to damage the stability necessary for economic growth, indicate that the advance of commerce and industry there is having its impact on politics. Hence, these exceptions are in some ways more ostensible than real.

14. Burnett, pp. 81–111 passim, speculates on the causes of the regional distribution of party strength. The report of the Misión "Economía y Humanismo" *Estudio sobre . . . Colombia,* is a good source for sociological data on the departments.

The other group of departments which is, or was, an apparent exception to our rule concerning Conservative and Liberal areas comprises Boyacá, Santander, and Norte de Santander. Their earlier very wide fluctuations in party strength *followed* but did not *cause* alternations of the parties on the national scene. This suggests, above all, fraud and voter coercion perpetrated by the governing party. Such a contention is supported by the fact that, pursuant to the triumph of the "outs" in 1930, these departments were the centers of the political violence which took place at that time. Again, it was in Boyacá that elections had to be most frequently curtailed because of the violence that accompanied them immediately following the victory of the opposition Conservatives in 1946.[15] Such exaggerated electoral shifts have taken place elsewhere, especially in municipal elections, and suggest similar causes. But it is in the above three departments that party voting varied in the past so directly according to the party in power as to defy explanation on other grounds in a partisan context such as the Colombian.[16] More recently, in elections held under bipartisan rule, the socially and economically more traditionalist departments of Norte de Santander and Boyacá have shown themselves to be the most staunchly Conservative in the nation. The more industrialized Santander has voted Liberal by a small margin, even while its traditionalist rural areas vote strongly Conservative. In the end, then, these departments, too, conform to our earlier generalizations.

Analysis of urban-rural differences in the vote and of voting patterns within departments confirms the tendency already noted for Conservative strength to coincide with the socially and economically traditionalist areas of the country; the Liberal, with the more commercialized, industrialized, and less traditional sections.

Thus if one takes the eleven Colombian municipios which tallied at least 25,000 votes in the March 1962 elections, one finds that the overall Liberal margin of 295,567 in those communities more than accounts for the nationwide Liberal majority of 281,239. Furthermore, *every* city with a vote amounting to 25,000 or more returned a Liberal majority; all, with

15. See *Memoria del Ministro de Gobierno . . . de 1946*, pp. viii, xix, xxxii, and 55–56.

16. It is hard to say why these departments more than others should have been particularly subject to electoral fraud and coercion. I have come across no piece of evidence to suggest why this should be so.

TABLE 9

PARTY VOTING IN CITIES CASTING MORE THAN 25,000 VOTES,
MARCH 1962 SENATORIAL ELECTION [17]

City (and Department)	Conservative	Liberal	Liberal Plurality
Armenia (Caldas)	8,307	19,937	11,630
Barranquilla (Atlántico)	14,967	46,182	31,215
Bogotá (Cundinamarca)	76,292	199,270	122,978
Bucaramanga (Santander)	9,370	31,007	21,637
Cali (Valle del Cauca)	30,156	66,205	36,049
Cúcuta (Norte de Santander)	5,889	20,574	14,685
Ibagué (Tolima)	7,996	22,089	14,093
Manizales (Caldas)	19,583	20,292	709
Medellín (Antioquia)	42,956	51,192	8,236
Palmira (Valle del Cauca)	6,488	18,804	12,316
Pereira (Caldas)	12,900	34,919	22,019
Totals	234,904	530,471	295,567

the exception of Medellín and Manizales, the capitals respectively of
Antioquia and Caldas, did so by margins of better than two to one.[18] In
those communities where the vote totalled between 10–25,000, Liberal
municipios still predominated overwhelmingly, but by the lesser ratio of
16 municipios to 4. In fact, of the 24 Colombian municipios casting at
least 12,000 votes in the election, only Pasto, the capital of Conservative
Nariño, gave a majority of its votes to the Conservative lists. Among
municipios with 5,000–10,000 votes cast the proportions were 37 with

17. The figures were adapted by the author from Registraduría Nacional del Estado
Civil, *Organización y Estadísticas, 1962*. The vote for Senators was used. The data
and their interpretation should be viewed with caution for at least three reasons: 1)
The source presents the vote by muncipio, an administrative unit which may include
an urban center plus scattered smaller hamlets. The distinction between urban and
rural communities thus cannot always be assumed by size alone; 2) There is obviously
no way to tell from the statistics precisely who in urban or rural areas is voting Conservative or Liberal; 3) The distinctions made between traditionalist and nontradi-
tionalist areas in what follows are the author's own judgments or are inferred from
size of place; the concept itself is of course unknown to the data. Nevertheless, both
the data and the interpretation conform with what else is known of the social bases
of Colombian politics and they lead quite consistently in the same direction. They are
therefore believed to paint an accurate picture.

18. In the wake of massive Liberal abstention in the elections for the Chamber of
Representatives in March 1964 both Medellín and Manizales went Conservative.
Registraduría del Estado Civil, *Organización y Estadísticas, 1964*.

Liberal majorities to 32 with Conservative majorities. Below this size the trend reverses itself to give the Conservatives an edge.

Within individual departments one finds some striking divisions between traditionalist Conservative districts and Liberal ones. The two relatively new and burgeoning cities of southern Caldas, Pereira and Armenia (the latter now in the department of Quindío),[19] yielded a combined Liberal majority of 33,619 in a department in which the Liberal vote exceeded the Conservative by a mere 4,476. Calarcá, in the same region, produced a 6,192 Liberal plurality, while La Dorada, a port on the Magdalena River, added another 6,418 in a vote in which the Conservatives received only 330 votes to the Liberals' 6,748. In these four communities, three located in an area which has seen recent rapid growth and the fourth a commercial hub for river traffic, the Liberals garnered almost half of the votes they won in Caldas (70,572 out of 148,544). The Conservatives, on the other hand, won only 24,313 in these communities of the 143,568 they won in the department. The Conservative vote, virtually half of the departmental total, was concentrated in rural areas and more traditionalist municipios, although the Conservatives split almost equally with the Liberals the vote of Manizales, the capital of Caldas.

The pattern was repeated, to take one further example, in Santander, where the industrializing city of Bucaramanga and the oil city of Barrancabermeja gave the Liberals a combined margin of 30,778 votes in a department where they surmounted the Conservative total by only 13,335. When one takes into account the Liberal showing in places like the Magdalena River port of Puerto Wilches (a 4,689 plurality of 6,435 ballots cast), the contrasting Conservative strength in traditionalist rural Santander becomes apparent.

In summary, it can be said that nationwide Liberal strength resides above all in the cities and that, broadly speaking, the larger the city the more likely it is to be Liberal. There are exceptions. Thus in traditionalist regions some cities—Medellín, Manizales, and Pasto, for example—may be more Conservative than their size might foretell. Yet among the some-

19. The Quindío is a mountainous, coffee-growing region embracing southern Caldas primarily but including contiguous parts of the departments of Tolima and Valle. It was settled largely through southward Antioquian migration in the latter part of the nineteenth century. Much of it was constituted as a department in January 1966.

what smaller municipios of the 5,000–10,000 vote range, where the number of Conservative-leaning communities almost equals the number of Liberal, one frequently finds that those which vote Liberal are river ports (such as La Dorada and Puerto Wilches); or industrial towns (such as Sogamoso, Boyacá, the site of Colombia's steel mill); or suburbs of Bogotá (for example, Fusagasugá); or "frontier" towns (such as Florencia, in the intendancy of Caquetá). Within departments—even those generally considered to be traditionalist—there are often areas with nontraditional characteristics which have a tendency to vote Liberal and may at times give the Liberals a department-wide edge.

Whether the comparison is based on the vote of entire departments, on urban-rural differences, or on other ecological factors, the results are generally consistent. The Conservatives' greatest strength is in those areas where traditionalist or subsistence agricultural patterns are strongest, or where something of a peasant middle class has developed. Areas of industry, mining, and trade, as well as newly developed areas, are likely to be Liberal. Accordingly, in addition to ideological differences which have given meaning to Colombia's partisan split, the political support of the two parties comes from different segments of the society. The division has not so much involved class distinctions as it has urban-rural ones or, more broadly, the nature of relationships to traditional Colombian society.

THE "COLONY" VERSUS THE "REPUBLIC"

The foregoing discussion has sought to make apparent that Colombian parties have had deeper roots than either personalism or the arbitrary alliances of clans, cliques, or regions could give them. Yet the characterization of Colombian parties as ideological is a considerable oversimplification. A purely class-based analysis is also fallacious in a political system where members of the elite have controlled both major parties and where voting patterns as a rule do not follow class lines. Thus large landowners and campesinos in the same region are usually to be found in the same party. The typical explanation of traditional Latin American Conservative-Liberal divisions which places the trilogy of large landowners, high clergy, and army officers with the Conservatives, and merchants and professional men with the Liberals is likewise inadequate. It contains a sub-

stantial measure of truth, but it runs afoul of the fact that, in Colombia
at least, significant numbers of large landowners have been Liberals and
many merchants and intellectuals have been Conservatives.

A different explanation is therefore called for, one which encompasses
what is valid in each of the others.

In essence, those groups, regions, and families that in the years of its
formation coalesced in the Conservative party were defending the social
and economic status quo as it had emerged, relatively unscathed, from the
colonial period. They were the privileged landowners and slaveowners;
the families of the most nearly unimpeachable abolengo; contractors and
merchants who profited from certain state monopolies; residents of regions
largely untouched by the unsettling effects of commerce and industry and
most isolated or feudal-like; and the clergy, whose doctrines, property,
and status were threatened by the proponents of liberalism.

For their part, the Liberals wanted to sweep away these residues of
privilege passed on from the "incomplete revolution" of the Wars of
Independence. They were the importers and exporters not tied to state
monopolies; tobacco growers and others involved in commercial-crop
agriculture who wanted to be free to sell as they willed, without state
participation in the profits; army officers whose recent land grants were
limited either in their extent because the Church held so much of the good
land, or in their development because slavery and the Indian reservations
restricted the availability of cheap labor; French-influenced intellectuals
enamored of liberal and utopian socialist ideas; and artisans and small
property holders who wished to do away with privilege. Their common
cry was "Down with monopolies, slavery, privileges." [20]

The "champions of tradition" thus faced the "soldiers of liberty." Economic in an important degree, the dichotomy was more accurately one of
vested interests of all kinds, opposing new ones seeking to establish themselves through the application of nineteenth-century liberal principles as
they understood them. This should not be taken to imply that most Liberals wished to undermine elite domination of Colombian society. The
struggle was, after all, primarily within the elite itself, with others serving
as Liberal or Conservative camp followers. The Liberals did not seek to

20. José Ramón Lanao Loaiza, *Mirando las Izquierdas* (Manizales, 1935), p. 36. Cf.
Nieto Arteta, *Economía y Cultura,* for a generally similar interpretation which stresses
economics. Cf. also Samper, *Los Partidos en Colombia,* pp. 5–22.

destroy the *patterns* of social and economic power, such as the system of large estates, but rather to partake of their benefits.

Philosophically, the struggle was between those who held to ideas inherited from a colonial system based on hierarchical authority, a quasi-feudal social structure, and a prominent social role for the Catholic Church; and those affected by the ideas of free-thinking, free trade, and liberal democracy. Both sides accepted republican institutions as a substitute for monarchy. But independence had stopped short of eliminating some of the inherited economic, social, and intellectual bonds which, in the Liberal view, held back their country, and themselves along with it. In the eyes of Conservatives, the Liberals were ignoring the "real" Colombia based on reverence for Hispanic tradition and Catholic Christianity and were trying to substitute for it an "abstract country" which took its cue from foreign ideas inapplicable to the new nation.[21]

The stage was set for both ideological and armed disputes. On one side were those who upheld the values of the old order, plus the interests which those values defined and rationalized. On the other were those who wished to bring on the new and so give greater scope to the interests which they sought to advance.

Of course, the circumstances and principles which preside at the birth of parties do not necessarily sustain their continued existence. And change, once instituted, brings with it its own vested interests in the new status quo. The Liberals, having enacted the reforms of the 1850s and 1860s, which abolished slavery, temporarily diminished the power of the Church, and eased various restrictions on free commerce, moved forward as a party, despite deep-seated internal schisms, partly on the basis of upholding what had been won. For some this was land, for others an end to state controls, and for still others a greater degree of local autonomy. Throughout, there remained the danger that the Conservatives, and with them the Church, would rise to reclaim their position in the state. The attraction of those policies and principles which had led the Liberals as a party to their years of political domination, and their adherents to an era of affluence, remained strong. The Conservatives, too, continued to heed the clarion calls of the early political battles. Both parties were confirmed in their loyalties and antagonisms by the civil wars fought between

21. See e.g. José Galat Noumer, "Origen y Causas de la Crisis," in *La Nación ante la Universidad*, pp. 57–66.

them off and on during much of the latter half of the nineteenth century and by the highly moralistic terms in which those antagonisms were couched.

When the issues that had informed their origins became at times dormant, the parties took on quite clearly the aspect of "rival bands of brigands." Yet an investigation of the social bases of contemporary Colombian politics shows that much of the same alignment of groups, issues, and philosophies which marked the birth, childhood, and adolescence of the parties has continued. Amid almost perennial factionalism and occasional coalitions the two groups of partisans have preserved much of their original character for more than a century.

Personal rivalries, as well as a desire to capture power either for its own sake or for the immediate rewards in material gain and prestige which it might bring, have clearly comprised much of the substance of Colombian politics. But in the absence of some such concept as the "colony" versus the "republic" it becomes difficult to give meaning to the origins and continuity of group and regional allegiances, to the differences in the policies effected by the two parties when in power, or to the obvious seriousness with which Colombians have taken ideological distinctions.

WHY TWO PARTIES?

Yet, even if we know something of the nature of the parties, and the grounds of difference between them, why should their number be two?

Maurice Duverger has said that "the two-party system seems to correspond to the nature of things, that is to say political choice usually takes the form of a choice between two alternatives." Thus it is possible that under republican governments the need in a legislature or electorate in the end to reduce each issue to two alternatives produces an initial bias toward a dualism of parties.[22] Nevertheless, the very numerous instances of one-party and multi-party systems are evidence that such a tendency to duality, if it exists, frequently becomes a plurality in practice, or resolves itself into a single party.

22. Maurice Duverger, *Political Parties*, trans. Barbara and Robert North (New York, Wiley, 1954), p. 215. Cf. Fabiola Aguirre de Jaramillo, "Por Qué en Colombia Son Dos los Partidos Políticos," *Cuadernos Americanos* (Mexico), *44* (March–April 1949), 28.

Similarly, it may be that the need to elect the president, in a nation where he is the primary focus of political authority, has been important in producing alliances for the purpose and hence a two-party system. This is Pendleton Herring's explanation for two parties in the United States.[23] And Carlos Holguín Holguín, in a perceptive article on Colombia's party system, has declared that "For my part, I have believed that . . . the presidential regime . . . has imposed among us the two-party system, and has impeded . . . the foundation of other parties." [24] Historically, it appears that the adherence of various groups and factions in 1848 to the single candidacy of General Hilario López was a key factor in their formal coalescence into the Liberal party. Yet, again, a student of comparative politics must note that there are many presidential governments which obviously have not led to the growth of two-party systems, or whose two-party systems have with time become multi-party. The contemporary examples in Latin America alone are legion.

Mario Laserna has suggested that a weak state is an important cause of the tenacity of Colombia's two-party system. Since the principal guarantee for an individual—in a society in which he cannot rely on the protection of a strong and neutral government (or on other kinds of associations)—is the political party, and the strength of the party depends on numbers, it makes little sense to begin a third party.[25] Once more, however, there are numerous weak states which lack two-party systems.

Another view looking toward the nature of political institutions as a cause of political dualism is that plurality elections will tend to produce two parties while proportional representation will result in a multi-party system.[26] Prior to 1905 plurality elections for legislative bodies were the rule in Colombia. From 1905 to 1930 the law guaranteed minority representation in legislative bodies by granting an automatic one third of the seats to the leading minority party in a given department or electoral district, while at the same time allotting two thirds to the majority. Accordingly, a third party had to defeat one of the two major parties in a particular district to achieve representation. For our purposes, this con-

---

23. Pendleton Herring, *The Politics of Democracy* (New York, W. W. Norton, 1940), p. 124.

24. Carlos Holguín Holguín, "Los Partidos Políticos," *Universidad Nacional de Colombia,* 2nd epoch, No. 17, 1953.

25. Laserna, *Estado Fuerte,* p. 98.

26. Duverger, passim; and E. E. Schattschneider, *Party Government* (New York, Farrar and Rinehart, 1942).

stituted plurality voting more nearly than proportional representation. Moreover, since 1910 the Colombian president has been elected by plurality vote.

This prevalence of the plurality system throughout much of Colombian history might lead one to the conclusion that it had been a primary factor in the maintenance of a two-party system.[27] Yet during the period after 1930 when full proportional representation was in operation for legislative elections no genuine third party garnered more than a handful of seats in Congress (although the Communists on occasion gained control of the municipal councils in several small towns). The vote for third parties in nationwide elections seldom surpassed the miniscule figure of three per cent of the total. Most of these elections were held in years when there was no presidential election and so were presumably not unduly subject to the pull of the plurality vote for president. As Burnett concludes, "Perhaps the most interesting aspect of Colombia's proportional representation system is that third parties have not fared any better than they did under earlier electoral practice." [28]

On the contrary, proportional representation may have helped to a degree to reinforce the two-party system by allowing dissident factions to gain representation according to their strength in the electorate while still not forcing them from the party. Retaining the original party label, or some version of it, they have usually been reabsorbed into officialist ranks after one or two elections. Since 1958 this kind of factionalism has been rampant. It is possible that important third parties would have emerged after 1958 but for the constitutional prohibition on their running candidates under the National Front agreement. But this must remain in doubt. Faced with possible defeat at the hands of the opposite party, there might rather have been greater pressure on the factions within each party to bury their differences.

It may be feasible to attribute to the plurality vote some secondary influence in molding Colombia's two-party system. Yet in general it is

27. As early as 1915 the electoral commission of the Republican party proposed a change from the "incomplete vote" to a form of proportional representation that would permit the representation of all minority parties according to their proportion of the vote. The party evidently felt the existing system hurt their electoral chances. The party's eventual failure may be partial proof of this estimate. Cf. *Convención Nacional del Partido Republicano,* p. 273.

28. Burnett, "The Recent Colombian Party System," p. 114.

probably correct to affirm with Holguín that "among us, the regime of proportional representation of the parties and the electoral quotient, did not foment, as might be believed, the division of the parties. It has only served to determine the strength of dissidences within a given party." [29] Furthermore, there is about as much evidence to show that parties determine the electoral system as vice versa.[30]

In reality, the long-standing division of Colombian society into two blocs of interests and views of life which we have called the "colony" and the "republic," appears to be foremost among the causes of Colombia's political dualism. Once having set out on their separate paths, the parties became subject to what V.O. Key called "the persistence of initial forms." [31] Barring the appearance of some major new factor on the political scene which was not manageable within the existing framework, the original forms tended to sustain themselves. The intense politization to which Colombians have been subjected, the importance of the spoils of office, and the crucible of civil violence have strengthened that tendency.

Further reinforcing the dual pattern has been the circumstance that the major issues of Colombian politics—religion, the centralist-federalist controversy, and certain issues of social and economic policy—all have evoked roughly the same political cleavage, at least until very recently. Those who were on one side on the religious question were, with some exceptions, on the same side with regard to the others, and vice versa. This had the simultaneous effect of limiting the parties to two and forging them into "irreconcilable blocs." [32]

The weakness of non-elite groups has also helped to prevent political divisions from proliferating. With the campesinos, the middle sectors, and the urban lower class lacking significant independent power, Colombian politics has the more readily kept to its two original partisan channels.

The approximate balance of strength among Colombia's several regions has probably also had a hand in limiting the number of parties. Any polit-

29. Holguín, p. 44.
30. Lipson, "The Two-Party System in British Politics," p. 350; cf. also Lavau, *Partis Politiques*, for a searching critique of explanations of two-party systems which stress the electoral system rather than social factors.
31. Key, *Politics, Parties, and Pressure Groups*, pp. 227–28.
32. Cf. Herbert J. Spiro, *Government by Constitution* (New York, Random House, 1959), p. 379.

ical party which based itself solely on one section of the country would find itself a perpetual minority, unable to win national power. Therefore Colombia's parties have in part constituted alliances among regional oligarchies. Political dualism has been in this sense a simplification of the actual regional plurality.[33] However, this should not obscure the fact that party loyalties have cut across regional boundaries and that it has been in considerable measure the geographical concentration of various interests which has given political regionalism its reality.

It may be that the requirements imposed by the attempt to acquire access to government—in a political system where decisions that may seriously harm or benefit various groups or regions are made at the national level and in the executive branch—as well as the electoral system, have contributed to limiting the number of Colombian parties to two. But the persistence of the two-party system has derived primarily from the nature of Colombian society and in particular from the bifurcation of interests and ideology among the politically articulate, as confirmed by loyalties accrued during a series of historic crisis situations. The nature of this dualism suggests that two-party systems do not necessarily arise only in homogeneous, pragmatic political cultures such as those of the United States and Great Britain; a society divided into two irreconcilable blocs may serve as well.

CHANGE AND POLITICAL DUALISM

Today, despite the momentary lull in competitive party politics and acute partisanship under the National Front, the reflections of earlier bitter struggles between the political spokesmen of traditionalism and liberalism permeate Colombian political life and help largely to explain the contemporary voting patterns of a two-party politics. It is nonetheless clear that the second half of the twentieth century is bringing changes which will certainly have profound consequences for the traditional parties. New issues and new interests have arisen, calling into question the ancient social foundations of the parties—and their ideological orientations. Even the survival of the two-party system itself is in doubt.

As the religious issue has become muted, and as the centralist-federalist

33. Azula Barrera, *De la Revolución*, p. 12, suggests this function of Colombian parties.

controversy has become consigned to the limbo of history, the old ideological frontiers between the two elite-ruled parties have begun to blur, as Alfonso López noted many years ago.[34] In part these have been superseded by such modern socioeconomic issues as agrarian reform and state intervention in the economy. Indeed for a time, under the prodding of Alfonso López and later and briefly under the urgings of Gaitán, it seemed as though the old grounds of dispute between the parties would merely be replaced by new ones more relevant to the concerns of Colombians of the twentieth century. However, when the elites of both political persuasions realized the potential for class warfare that this trend contained, they began to see a common interest in economic development and in a controlled social reform which would obviate any basic change in their own status. They recognized that the old party disputes were lesive of their mutual stakes in a modernizing society. The National Front, which has both forged the requisite political peace through bipartisan institutional arrangements and elaborated a united approach to social and economic problems, is the most noteworthy manifestation of this recognition. Differences between the parties have not been erased thereby. The Liberal party, for example, still tends on the whole to back agrarian reform more vigorously than the Conservative. But the gap has been narrowed and the points of similarity emphasized.

Accompanying this development, the lines of factional division within the parties, which once focused largely on personal rivalries, on disputes over political tactics, or on the old ideological questions, have shown at least some signs of coming to revolve around twentieth-century economic and social issues. This is particularly evident among Liberals. Thus the split between oficialistas and the MRL in part follows new lines. Factionalism within the Conservative party has to date been almost completely a matter of personalistic squabbles, notably between the followers of former Presidents Gómez and Ospina, although among young Conservatives there are social Christian strains appearing which indicate that this may be changing.

Several possibilities remain open regarding the future evolution of the Colombian party system. One is the eventual union in a single party of the elites of the traditional parties, with the National Front the initial phase in such a development. An opposition party would then presumably

34. Cf. the 1945 speech by López reprinted in *Semana*, No. 677, pp. 27–28.

arise composed of both Conservative and Liberal reformists, based on common class interests and a common outlook on social and economic matters. Or, as Colombia urbanizes, the "mass" of the Conservative party might fade away to a rural rump and the new party of the lower and middle classes would essentially derive from former Liberal sources. In any event, the current "vertical" political division, its foundation a split within the Colombian elite, would shift to a "horizontal" one between classes, much as happened in Great Britain with the rise of the Labor party.

An alternative possibility would see the Conservative party evolving in the direction of a Christian Democratic party and the Liberal party in the direction of a Social Democratic or Aprista-type party (perhaps without the Marxist overtones some of these parties have had elsewhere). Still another would envision a splintering of the traditional two parties into at least four, with the historic lines of division being crosscut but not entirely superseded by socioeconomic or class issues. The result would be a Conservative party, a Social Christian party, a Liberal party, and a Socialist party (and probably others as well), after the fashion of the Chilean party system. A final possibility would entail the retention by both parties of their current polyclass nature while adapting their programs and appeals to the mandates of change. This is much the course that they have so far sought to pursue.

Perhaps the best that we can do, during this rather artificial period for party politics, is to recognize these major possibilities and to note that there is enough evidence in Colombian party history, and in the implications of current and recent changes, to make any one of them conceivable. Two concluding points must be added. One is the historic tenacity of the two traditional parties and their proven adaptability. The other is that the changes which they must in the future confront and somehow incorporate go far beyond, and are of a different character, than any they have so far been called upon to face.

The bases of the old politics are eroding, but the parties have not quite dared to face the new circumstances squarely. It may be that once the National Front comes to an end the competitive two-party system will never regain the hold it once had. Freed of the constraints of parity, there will probably be new pressures for dissident factions to reunite. Yet it seems likely that the emergence of politically articulate groups outside the elite will entail no less than an increasing incidence of minor parties, ad hoc parties, and factional splinters operating as third parties.

Whatever shape the Colombian party system eventually takes, it seems inexorable that it will assume many of the dimensions of a politics of social class. As a result, the classic intra-elite cleavage between traditionalists and liberals will either fade away or, more likely, merge in not wholly predictable ways with the alignments of a new age.

THE OPPOSITION

THE OPPOSITION AS COUNTER-ELITES

To the analysis of the Conservative and Liberal parties as instruments of elite rule must be added another dimension of Colombian political life— the movements and parties that have come forward to challenge the existing order. In their own proposals for change, such organized counter-elites represent responses to modernization alternative to that of the elite's preferred tutelary reform. On their potential strength, as well as on the viability of the traditional parties, depends the future of political change in Colombia.

There were traces of organized opposition to elite rule during the nineteenth century and as early as the colonial period. A *"comuneros"* revolt of 1781 had such overtones, although it was primarily a protest against certain royal taxes. The so-called Democratic Societies of artisans of the middle of the last century were another example, but they were more in the nature of pressure groups than a political movement. They in fact gave their support to the Liberal party during its formative years. Today's Left makes much of such precedents, and on a number of grounds they have important places in Colombia's historical development. Though radical in many ways for their time, they challenged the prevailing pattern of elite rule only tangentially.

Only since the third decade of this century has organized opposition begun to challenge the traditional power structure. Some groups have acted as political movements within or on the fringes of the traditional parties; others have formally constituted themselves as third parties contesting for political office, or seeking to do so; still others have taken the form of political action groups which instead stress "direct action" and political agitation.

The principal political and ideological challenge to the rule of the Colombian elite has come from the Left. It has had two main strands, the reformist and the revolutionary. The first has sought merely to gain a *share* in power for new groups and the enactment of policies in their behalf. The revolutionaries call for the *total* overthrow of the old order. The reformists as a rule have stayed within the rubric of the Liberal party. Those who advocate a more drastic upheaval, whether by violent or peaceful means, have generally founded new parties or resorted to direct action.

Another potentially important source of opposition has come from what it seems more accurate to call the non-Left than either the Left or the Right. While drawing much of their ideological sustenance and support from basically traditionalist sources, its adherents have advocated reform in the patterns of economic and political domination. They are, in a certain sense, traditionalist reformers. The two principal manifestations of this type of opposition have been authoritarian populism and Christian Democracy, which nonetheless differ from each other in significant ways.

The most notable thing about counter-elite groups in Colombia has been neither their variety nor their influence, but their failures. We have already examined Gaitanismo, a movement of the reformist Left long since defunct, in its historical context. By looking at the other parties and movements which have developed in recent decades as the political expression of counter-elites we may help to account for the durability of elite control. At the same time, the rising pressure of social forces, heretofore only imperfectly accommodated by the traditional parties, may in the future be more effectively harnessed by the counter-elites to move the nation onto untried paths.

THE MOVIMIENTO REVOLUCIONARIO LIBERAL (MRL)[1]

The current primary embodiment of reformism of the Left is the Movimiento Revolucionario Liberal (MRL), originally the Movimiento de Recuperación Liberal, whose principal wing is led by Alfonso López

1. The principal sources for the following analysis of the MRL have been the MRL press, particularly *La Calle* and *Izquierda;* the daily press; the writings and speeches of López, including *Consideraciones sobre la Reforma Constitucional por medios de la cual se establece la alternación forzosa de los partidos en la presidencia de la República* (1958); *Conceptos Fundamentales del M.R.L. No. 3,* Discurso de Alfonso

Michelsen.[2] The MRL originated among a group of Liberal intellectuals and professional men who had founded the weekly newspaper, *La Calle*, in 1958. Its members held their first convention in February 1960. For most practical purposes the MRL has operated as a separate political party, with its own organization, program, press, and lists of candidates, and its leaders have sometimes referred to it as such. However, it has retained Liberal in its name, and has run as a competing Liberal faction in elections under the National Front. The leadership of the MRL has, in fact, proclaimed as its objective the remaking of the Liberal party from within. Its members have continued to consider themselves to be the "authentic" Liberals, the fulltime Liberals (*liberales de tiempo completo*): "Therefore I listen with horror to youthful audacities that one must cease being Liberal in order to be a better revolutionary or that we must omit the designation 'Liberal' from our Movement, in order to detach ourselves once and for all from our roots."[3]

As it developed from an abstract plane of intellectual nonconformity into a genuine political movement, the original *La Calle* group began to pick up supporters and allies who were dissatisfied with the leadership of the Liberal party, or with the operation of the National Front. Some of these were Liberal politicians, notably a group in the department of Antioquia who had personal disagreements with the party's leadership. Others were Liberals who saw a chance to further their political ambitions in a new movement. Still others simply could not abide "transaction" with the traditional Conservative enemy. There was little interest among them in social reform.

A different kind of political support accrued to the movement from those more concerned with modifying or challenging the rule of Colombia's incumbent elite. Some had been associated with a small dissident Liberal group which had supported Rojas Pinilla. Others were less inter-

---

López Michelsen ante la Convención de Ibagué, Noviembre de 1962. (Bogotá[?], 1962), and *Colombia en la Hora Cero;* and interviews with López, Bogotá, Aug. 21, 1963, and with Indalecio Liévano Aguirre, another MRL leader, Bogotá, Aug. 16, 1963.

2. This may be a good place to warn the reader of the rather free use made in party titles and for rhetorical purposes of the term revolutionary, in Colombia as well as in Latin America generally. "Revolutionary" in such connections may or may not signify revolution in the sense we have used the term; in the case of the MRL it does not. Similar problems arise in regard to such terms as "socialist."

3. López Michelsen, *Conceptos,* p. 6.

ested in remaking or capturing the Liberal party than in sponsoring a National Democratic Front composed of "progressive" members of all parties to effect a fundamental transformation of Colombian society. Some, though by no means all of them—men like the former rector of the National University, Gerardo Molina—were Marxists or had been rather consistent followers of the Communist line.

Finally, the Colombian Communist party allied itself tacitly to the MRL, although in contrast to the other groups it did not form an integral part of the movement. Rather, the PCC gave its electoral and propagandistic backing to the MRL. A few PCC members were included on MRL electoral lists, the MRL and the PCC sometimes held joint rallies, and the Communists attempted to influence the programmatic stance of the movement.

El Tiempo, arch enemy of the MRL, portrayed the resulting combination as a "heterogeneous group—in which capitalists with a desire for political advancement march arm and arm with revolutionaries of doubtful antecedents." [4] Holding it together was a common disaffection from the National Front, plus an attachment to the most readily available vehicle for the expression of that opposition—the still politically potent name of López.

Prior to 1958 López Michelsen had primarily lived the life of an intellectual. Reared as a member of an upper-class family and himself a member of the exclusive Bogotá Country Club, López was at the same time the author of a novel, *Los Elegidos* (The Chosen Few), which depicted Colombia's upper class as oriented toward foreign standards and concerns and as a narrow group which needed new blood. Urbane, cultured, intelligent, and articulate, López nevertheless remains somehow the dilettante, not really the political organizer, not quite at home on the political hustings and with the masses, not quite possessed of the aura of charisma. In North American terms, he may be too much the egghead, and too much of an aristocrat to boot, to lead a movement which, in order to attain ultimate success, must mobilize the middle and lower reaches of Colombian society. To Julio César Turbay, a political enemy, "He has the qualities suitable for a member of a planning council, but he lacks those indispensable for leading a mass movement." [5]

4. *El Tiempo,* Jan. 26, 1962, p. 4.
5. Interview with Turbay conducted by Elvira Méndez and reported in *Nuevo Boyacá,* July 1963, p. 21. Turbay has been a principal figure among oficialista Liberals.

During most of the first eight years of the National Front the MRL has been its leading critic. The MRL has accepted parity in administrative posts as a factor for the promotion of peace between the parties. However, it regards parity in legislative bodies and in the Cabinet as paralyzing governmental action and advocates proportional representation in both. Although López at first defended the constitutional reform that barred third parties from office as necessary to ensure strict parity in all offices between the major parties, the MRL soon began to attack this provision vociferously as antidemocratic and as restricting the chance for new forces to find an outlet. The MRL has also strongly criticized what it has regarded as repressive acts of the government toward various strikes and demonstrations.

It is alternation, however, that has been the movement's principal political target. In the MRL view, alternation inhibits the rise of new leaders and the expression of demands from emergent groups for a period of sixteen years during which Colombia is undergoing rapid social and economic change. An end to alternation, and to parity in legislative bodies and in the Cabinet, would presumably prepare the way for the majority Liberal party, and the new blood within it which the MRL claims to represent, to carry forward without Conservative obstruction a program of economic development and social reform more consonant with the needs of the country than current National Front policies. It is in this sense that López has spoken of Colombia's problem as being essentially political. "It is the question of how the camel of social reform and social revolution can pass through the needle of a Constitution [which institutionalizes] parity, alternation, and the two-thirds vote." [6]

In the social and economic realm, the MRL declared its immediate objective to be government action to ensure health, education, and housing for all Colombians, beginning with urban centers. Hence the designation by which the original MRL platform was sometimes known, the *Plan de* SET, for the Spanish words *salud* (health), *educación*, and *techo* (roof, housing). Also supported was "a true agrarian reform," with emphasis on taxation as the means to induce both more productive land use and the parcelization of the latifundios. Subsequent MRL pronouncements have criticized Law 135 of 1961 as ineffective and inadequate, while nevertheless praising the establishment of INCORA as the institutional means to

6. López Michelsen, *Colombia en la Hora Cero, 1,* 90–91.

carry out the inoperative land use provisions of Law 200 of 1936. In labor relations the Plan included demands for abolishing the prohibition on strikes in the public services, for the legalization of strikes of solidarity (with other workers involved in labor disputes), and for the prohibition of dual unionism in order to attain "unity of the working class." [7] There were proposals for higher taxation, especially on luxury consumer goods. This was seen as a means of obtaining increased revenue for social and economic programs without diminishing incentives to invest in necessary production by further use of the relatively high but poorly enforced graduated income tax. Finally, the Plan de SET called for greater government initiative in the planning of Colombia's economic development. The role of the state in a developing nation must be to force sacrifices in consumption in the interest of development. As López later put it: "we believe that the development of Colombia can only be accomplished with a strong State, a strong party, . . . and with the support in the streets of the whole of the population." [8]

In the international field the MRL has advocated a more independent and nationalistic policy. It has stressed Colombia's affinity to the "third world" of the emerging nations, and has supported closer trade relations with the Sino-Soviet bloc as a means of decreasing Colombia's economic dependence on the United States. Its leader has declared that foreign investments should be limited to those which would assist in the country's development and which do not compete with national industry: "Colombia has to stop being a mother to foreigners and a mother-in-law to Colombians." [9] On the other hand, the nationalization of the petroleum or other industries has not had a place in official MRL doctrine, despite its advocacy by some on the Colombian political Left, and the MRL leadership has specifically rejected the proposal that Colombia withdraw from the Organization of American States. Although López and other MRL leaders have been skeptical of the Alliance for Progress, doubting its adequacy and the firmness of the United States commitment, in general they accept the idea, at least, as good, and favorable references to specific accomplishments or programs of the Alliance appear in López' speeches.

7. This provision was added to the Plan at the convention, probably at the insistence of the MRL's Communist allies.

8. López Michelsen in *Izquierda*, July 26, 1963, p. 7.

9. Alfonso López Michelsen, "Influencia del Capital Extranjero en la Economía Colombiana," *Revista Bolívar*, 51 (March–Apr.–May 1959), 494–95.

While statements of sympathy for the Cuban Revolution—often without the qualifications that López usually gave his own—were frequently forthcoming from MRL spokesmen, the emphasis was on the right of Cuba to carry out its experiment and the practical lessons Colombia might learn from both its successes and its errors. Imitation was not suggested, in fact was expressly rejected, notably by López: "we have never considered the adoption of the program of the Cuban Revolution as a substitute for our Plan SET." [10]

In the four congressional elections held since its founding the MRL has won 21.5 per cent (1960), 36 per cent (1962), 33 per cent (1964), and 25 per cent (1966) of the Liberal vote. In the presidential election of 1962 its candidate received 24 per cent of the votes cast for all candidates, although constitutionally he could not have assumed office if he had won. For what groups has the MRL program had an appeal? An examination of data from the 1962 elections, when the MRL reached its peak to date and when abstention less obscured the "natural" distribution of the vote than in 1964 and 1966, points to the surprising conclusion that the Movimiento Revolucionario Liberal has been much stronger in smaller cities and towns and in rural areas than in the large cities. Thus while nationwide the MRL was obtaining 36 per cent of the Liberal vote in March 1962, in those seven cities which cast 35,000 or more votes the MRL won only 23 per cent. The contrast is even more striking when the large-city vote for the MRL is compared to the MRL vote in the rest of those particular departments in which the larger cities are located, as Table 10 illustrates.

The only exception to the general picture is Barranquilla, Atlántico, where the city vote for the MRL was higher than in the rest of the department. It should be noted, however, that Atlántico is the smallest in geographical extent of all of Colombia's departments and is dominated by the city of Barranquilla; the distinction between city and hinterland is therefore less relevant there than elsewhere. In any case, these 1962 patterns are generally duplicated, if somewhat less decisively, by returns from the 1960 and 1964 congressional elections.[11]

At the same time, there is no consistent trend differentiating the vote in

10. López Michelsen, *Conceptos,* p. 9.

11. See República de Colombia, Registrador Nacional del Estado Civil, *El Sufragio y la Identificación Ciudadana en Colombia—1959 a 1961* (2 vols. Bogotá, Imprenta Nacional, 1962), and Registraduría del Estado Civil, *Organización y Estadísticas, 1964.* The breakdown for 1966 was not available at the time of writing.

TABLE 10

ECOLOGICAL DISTRIBUTION OF THE MRL VOTE IN SELECTED DEPARTMENTS, MARCH 1962 SENATORIAL ELECTION[12]

Department	MRL vote in largest city or cities of department	MRL % of Liberal vote in largest city (ies)	MRL vote in remainder of same dept.	MRL % of Liberal vote in remainder of same dept.	Difference between MRL % of Liberal vote in remainder of dept. and largest city (ies) of same dept.
Antioquia	11,404 (Medellín)	22	52,070	47	+25
Atlántico	7,113 (Barranquilla)	16	2,677	9	− 7
Caldas	11,715 (Pereira and Manizales)	21	37,434	40	+19
Cundinamarca	39,636 (Bogotá)	19	34,742	28	+ 9
Santander	14,253 (Bucaramanga)	46	52,974	63	+17
Valle	22,150 (Cali)	34	64,478	58	+24

12. Data taken from Registraduría del Estado Civil, *Organización y Estadísticas, 1962.*

medium-sized cities from that in smaller municipios. The distinction between the MRL and the oficialista Liberal vote is less clearly urban-rural
than in the Liberal-Conservative case. Instead it reflects a dichotomy between the metropoli of Colombia on the one hand and the rural areas
plus the smaller provincial cities on the other. Several possible explanations, not necessarily mutually exclusive, may account for this. First of all,
the distribution of the MRL vote may represent the discontent and malaise
of those parts of Colombia where relative stagnation contrasts with the
rapidly growing and modernizing large urban centers. The gap between
cities like Bogotá, Medellín, and Cali and the rest of the country with
respect to wages, educational opportunities, available public services, and
various other amenities of modern living is almost certainly increasing
rather than diminishing and this circumstance may be reflected in the
vote.[13] A second possibility, and one stressed by López Michelsen himself
in election post-mortems, is that the old appeals to political passions upon
which the MRL—as the embodiment of Liberal "authenticity" and the foe
of alternation—has unquestionably relied to generate much of its mass
support, are particularly irrelevant in the cities. There problems of health,
education, housing, jobs, and public services interest the citizen, and it is
to these concerns that the MRL has failed to address itself adequately.
Still another cause for the pattern of electoral support for the MRL may
be that the middle sectors, which are numerous only in the larger cities,
have been wary of the radical guise in which the MRL has sometimes
appeared. The MRL's associations with the Communist party may have
hurt it among those groups.

From the beginning of its short life the MRL has been subject to severe
internal stresses stemming from inherent organizational problems, from
differences over program and tactics, and from clashes of personality and
political ambition. Once it expanded beyond the original *La Calle* group,
the MRL became more of a coalition than a unitary movement. Besides
this fundamental organizational weakness, there was disagreement between those whose objectives were first of all political and internal to the
Liberal party, and those whose goal was to develop a broad appeal to
the masses of all parties in the interest of sweeping reform or even social
revolution. Serious rifts early appeared over such matters as cooperation

13. Cf. Gutiérrez, *Rebeldía Colombiana*, pp. 125–26.

with the Communists, the MRL's attitude toward Castro's Cuba, and the advisability of participation in the Cabinet of the National Front. Some resented López Michelsen's personal domination of the movement, questioning the effectiveness of his leadership and characterizing him as opportunist and "transactionary."

The consequence has been an internal hemorrhaging beside which even the factionalism of the traditional parties pales. For the first two or three years the patchwork held together. Thereafter the MRL began to divide. Some, denouncing Communist influence in the MRL, or finding their political aspirations now satisfied within the main body of the party, returned to oficialista ranks. By late 1962 and early 1963 various splinter groups began to peel off from the left wing of the movement.

The principal among these has been the so-called *Línea Dura* (Hard Line) of the MRL (also called the National Committee of Revolutionary Action of the MRL) founded formally on May 8, 1963. It was led by Alvaro Uribe, like López a member of the Colombian elite and one of the original *La Calle* group. The new group proclaimed itself to be the true MRL and succeeded in capturing control of *La Calle;* thereupon López' group, henceforth often referred to as the *Línea Blanda* (Soft Line) of the MRL, founded its own rival paper, *Izquierda*. There were many grounds for the division. Unquestionably Uribe saw himself as a more effective and charismatic leader than López. The Línea Dura objected to what it regarded as López' tendency to look with favor on MRL participation in the government and to compromise with the oficialistas. The Línea Dura in fact rejected the remaking of the Liberal party as an MRL goal and opted instead for the formation of a *Bloque Nacionalista* (Nationalist Bloc) which would seek support from all parties and groups for the formation of a new popular-based party. The program of the group was more radical than that being expounded by López. It included the nationalization of the petroleum industry by stages, as well as the nationalization of the Bank of the Republic and otherwise closer state control over credit and private banking. It claimed that it preferred the peaceful path to power if so permitted by the existing power structure. Yet its leadership refused to rule out revolution and asserted the need to prepare the Colombian masses for such an eventuality.

Running its own candidates for the first time in March 1964 the Línea Dura garnered some 89,000 votes, or roughly 8 per cent of the Liberal total, compared to the Línea Blanda's 276,000 and 25 per cent. Thereafter Uribe changed his political tack to denounce the Communists whom he at first tried to court. He increasingly talked of a revolutionary nationalism, patterned after that of Nasser and Sukarno and assisted to power by the Colombian army. Partly as a result of this shift, the Línea Dura suffered defections and by early 1966 had virtually disappeared. Uribe turned his energies to the Popular Nationalist Movement (*Movimiento Nacionalista Popular*—MNP) founded in late 1964.[14]

The second important faction to break away from the main body of the MRL was its former youth movement, the MRL Youth (*Juventudes del MRL*—JMRL). This break signalled an impatience with the MRL's reformist orientation. The JMRL supported a radical agrarian reform, and advocated the formation of a Front of National Liberation, electoral abstention, and the possible use of violence to accomplish its aims. It was outspoken in its support of Castro and the Armed Forces of National Liberation, the Venezuelan terrorist group. It generally followed a pro-Peking line in international affairs. Though numerically small, the JMRL temporarily wielded important influence in the Colombian student movement. However, the JMRL, too, has tended with time to fade out of existence.[15]

These are the main groups that have split away from the original MRL. There are others, some remaining as semi-autonomous groups, others operating as factions and cliques within the main body of the MRL. Their existences are often fleeting and their precise relationship to the MRL difficult to determine. Their importance is that, along with the Línea Dura and the Juventudes del MRL, they divert into internecine warfare many of the energies that might otherwise go to building a politically effective counter-elite.

Meanwhile, the MRL's alliance with the Communists has worn thin. After a long period of hesitation, during which López sometimes spoke at Communist-organized rallies under portraits of Lenin and Castro, and

14. Sources concerning the Línea Dura include *La Calle;* Alvaro Uribe, *El Nacionalismo, Motor de Nuestro Tiempo* (Bogotá, Colección "Sol Naciente," No. 1, 1964); and an interview with Uribe (Bogotá, Aug. 29, 1963).

15. For the JMRL see in particular Juventudes del M.R.L., *Plataforma Política* (Bogotá, Ediciones "Voces Libres," 1961[?]); its newspaper, *Vanguardia del MRL;* and Allen Young, "Revolutionary Parties in Contemporary Colombia" (Stanford, Cal., Stanford University, Institute of Hispanic American and Luso-Brazilian Studies, 1963).

at other times appeared to disavow Communist support, the leader of the MRL pronounced the movement as firmly opposed to undue links with the Communists. In a speech to the MRL convention of November 1962 he affirmed the movement's continued acceptance of Communist votes, but pronounced it an error to have permitted the PCC to use the shadow of the MRL to indoctrinate the masses and ruled out further joint manifestations. Henceforth Communist candidates were not to appear on MRL lists, nor would the MRL surrender its autonomy by joining in a Popular Front of all leftist groups as some were advocating.[16] The Communists have in turn accused López of betraying the masses. Nevertheless, some measure of accommodation remained and the Communists continued to support MRL electoral lists in some places.

When one looks at some of the alliances López has made, and at the virulence of some of the pronouncements of MRL spokesmen, one is tempted to conclude that here is a movement seeking social revolution. And there is a degree of truth in such an estimate. The MRL has called itself Revolutionary. Communists have infiltrated the MRL organization in some localities. The left wing of the movement has from the beginning advocated some version of a Popular Front with revolutionary groups. Finally, statements have frequently appeared in the MRL press that parrot the Communist line on such matters as Cuba. Yet a closer look modifies this picture considerably. As Tad Szulc has said, López is "a wealthy intellectual who talks of a social revolution but hopes for modera-tion."[17]

The campaign appeals of the MRL, and the support it has received from the electorate, continue to hark back in substantial measure to the traditional appeals of Liberal hegemony. Organizationally, the MRL re-sembles the traditional parties more than a revolutionary group. Further-more the MRL program shows a hesitant approach to change. Its tax and agrarian reform proposals are on the whole moderate. On the international plane, its leaders show a reluctance to advocate a full-scale neutralism, or to suggest Colombia's withdrawal from the Alliance for Progress. The themes that persist instead call for a moderate nationalism: an insistence

16. López Michelsen, *Conceptos*, pp. 5–7.
17. Tad Szulc, "Colombia Faces Political Crisis," *New York Times*, March 26, 1961, p. 31.

that Colombia be master of its own fate and halt the "progressive deco-lombianization" of the national economy and national values; and a demand that the state assume a greater role in economic development, essentially through the stimulation of private enterprise. Although there is an emphasis on the admission of new groups to a voice in the political leadership of the country, it is clear that the MRL is extending a welcoming hand above all to the younger generation and the middle sectors, rather than to the "popular" classes.

Although it was apparently against his father's wishes that he launched his opposition to the National Front, there is indeed considerable evidence in what López Michelsen has said and written that he considers himself the continuer of his father's political works. The important difference—besides those accounted for by circumstance and the intervention of 30 years of turbulent political history—is that the MRL seems more thoroughly committed than was the revolución en marcha to achieving a genuine share for other social groups of the power the elite now holds almost exclusively.

The leadership of the movement (as well as of the Línea Dura and the JMRL) has been made up primarily of politically non-conformist sons of the elite, and of middle-class intellectuals and professional men. Alvaro Uribe, one of the founders of the MRL and leader of the Línea Dura, has been quite explicit about it: "The motor of change lies in an intermediary social group, composed of people who have had access to a certain amount of education, professional people, intellectuals, technicians, employees, specialized workers, almost all of the students, people, I repeat, who in the main, live at the service of the dominant class, relatively well paid . . . but who nevertheless don't have an opportunity . . . for influence in the country or the community." [18]

The prospects of the MRL are clouded by its factionalism, the weakness of its organization, the tactical and programmatic equivocations of its leadership, and López' own personality, which some regard as lacking in those qualities of the politician that his father possessed in their quintessence. For the immediate future there is the further problem that arguments against alternation may at the moment seem academic to Liberals who again saw one of their own assume the presidency in August 1966.

18. Uribe, *El Nacionalismo*, p. 22.

Nevertheless, the movement has exerted a strong pull within the Liberal party, even among some who adhere to the official party leadership, because of its posture as the organization of "authentic" Liberals and because of its reformist program. It is doubtful that in the foreseeable future the MRL could capture control of the Liberal party. At the same time, if it were to gain in strength, the official Liberals might be forced into meeting it halfway in order to avoid weakening the party permanently. Apart from a few individuals on its left wing, the MRL is not a revolutionary movement to depose the elite altogether; rather, it is an attempt to break the elite's *monopoly* on social, political, and economic power. This is why compromise between it and the traditional elite groups of the Liberal party could eventually serve their mutual interests. Meanwhile some of the factions that have left the main MRL ranks, such as the Línea Dura, remain in essence committed to reform, while others like the Juventudes del MRL have moved into the revolutionary Left, to whose other components we now turn.

THE REVOLUTIONARY LEFT

In the wake of World War I an intellectual effervescence, the first small rumblings of worker unrest, and the example of the Bolshevik Revolution produced the beginnings of modern Socialism and Communism in Colombia. A short-lived party calling itself Socialist, though moderate and reformist in orientation, was formed in 1919 and succeeded in winning a scattering of elective posts in the next two or three years. A self-styled *Grupo Comunista* also came into being about 1924 in Bogotá. Similar small circles, composed mainly of intellectuals, were founded in other cities. Various of these groups, with some support from workers, coalesced in December 1926 to found the Revolutionary Socialist party (*Partido Socialista Revolucionario*—PSR), which in 1928 was admitted to membership in the Third International. Despite such affiliation, the PSR was a conglomerate of Liberals who looked upon it as a vehicle for opposing the Conservatives then in power, of those who looked to direct action and coups d'etat as the means to effect a real revolution, and of a few who sought to build a revolutionary movement along Leninist lines. The party virtually dissolved in 1930 with the defection of many of its members to the victorious Liberal party; still others helped to create the Communist party of Colombia (pcc) in July of the same year.[19]

Following the collapse of the psr a few who continued to think of themselves as Socialists associated themselves with Gaitán's unir; after the latter's eclipse, they constituted a small group called *Vanguardia Socialista*. Then in 1943 Antonio García and other left-wing intellectuals founded the League of Political Action (*Liga de Acción Política*—lap). The League issued a manifesto proclaiming the "crisis of the traditional order" and calling for steps to preserve Colombian democracy and sovereignty. Specifically, it advocated such measures as agrarian reform, nationalization of basic resources and industries, and closer economic ties with other Latin American nations. But although the lap included persons who are still prominent in Colombian political circles, it soon disintegrated, most of its members entering the Liberal party and a few joining the Communists.

By 1950 García had undertaken to organize a Colombian Socialist Movement, which some three years later became the Colombian Popular Socialist party (*Partido Popular Socialista Colombiano*—ppsc), "nationalist, popular, democratic, socialist, autonomous." The ppsc claimed to represent a "new socialism," the only revolutionary substitute for communism, different both from Marxism and from utopian socialism, as well as from European democratic socialism with its exclusive concern for reform by parliamentary means. At the same time the ppsc maintained ties with other Socialist parties in both Europe and Latin America and put greater emphasis in its programmatic statements on political democracy than on any form of violent revolution. This "new socialism" declared itself to represent a third position, a synthesis, both domestically and internationally, of the antitheses capitalism and communism. Claim-

19. For the early history of Socialism in Colombia see Robert J. Alexander, *Communism in Latin America* (New Brunswick, N.J., Rutgers University Press, 1957), pp. 243–46; and Comité Central del Partido Comunista de Colombia, *Treinta Años del Partido Comunista de Colombia* (Bogotá, Ediciones Paz y Socialismo, 1960), pp. 10–22. The remainder of the following analysis of the political career of Socialism in Colombia is based primarily on Liga de Acción Política, *Manifiesto al País: la Izquierda ante el Presente y el Porvenir de Colombia* (Bogotá, Ediciones Políticas "El Común," 1943[?]); A. García, *Gaitán*, passim; Luis Emiro Valencia, *El Nuevo Socialismo y Antonio García* (Bogotá, 1955), *Estatutos y Doctrina Política del Movimiento Socialista Colombiano* (Bogotá, unpublished, undated); and *El Socialismo Colombiano y el Plebiscito* (Bogotá, 1957).

ing ideological affinity to Gaitán, its program was similar to that of the LAP.

The PPSC supported the regime of General Rojas Pinilla from first to last in the hope that he would deal a fatal blow to the oligarchy, and García at one point became one of Rojas' economic advisers. The party was consequently discredited after the tenth of May, 1957. It set about in difficult circumstances to try to recoup its image as a party of the Left. To the PPSC the National Front was nothing more than the newest machination of the Colombian oligarchy. It naturally attacked the parity system under which third parties were excluded from political office. Ultimately, a number of its leaders were attracted to what they regarded as Cuba's nationalist revolution. Appealing mainly to youth, they were soon organizing movements with revolutionary aspirations in several Colombian cities. In the process the PPSC itself disintegrated. Colombian Socialism as a political movement never really recovered from its alliance with the Government of the Armed Forces. Its search for the means by which to carry out the socialist and nationalist revolution led its leadership to place its hopes alternatively in the democratic process, in the military, and in a revolutionary activism which eschewed the old party forms. Never strong in any case, and repeating the experience of the PSR, Colombian Socialism again lost the struggle for survival.

The Colombian Communist party has met with somewhat greater success.[20] Its three and a half decades of continuous existence make it the longest-lived third party in Colombian history, though it has never attained even the temporary significance of the Nationalist party of the late nineteenth century or of the Republican party in the decade after 1910.

The PCC's first years were marked by ineffectiveness and by sectarian isolation from the main currents of Colombian politics. However, in the era of the Popular Front elsewhere, the party gave its backing to President López and his revolution on the march and joined forces with Lib-

20. The best available sources concerning the PCC are Alexander, pp. 243–53; Comité Central, *Treinta Años;* the party's publications, esp. its newspaper, *Voz Proletaria* (formerly *Voz de la Democracia*), its ideological review, *Documentos Políticos,* and such documents as *Documentos del Octavo Congreso del Partido Comunista de Colombia* (Bogotá, Editorial Diario Jurídico, 1958). During the years 1944–47 the PCC was known as the Social Democratic party *(Partido Social Democrático*—PSD).

erals and others to found the Colombian Confederation of Workers (CTC) in 1936. Later the Communists were to take themselves to task for having too unqualifiedly supported López to the neglect of the independent spirit and organization of their own party. The party continued to support López during his second term, in part as a bulwark against the threatened reaction led by Laureano Gómez. It also looked with favor on López' relatively pro-labor stance, and in 1944 the Minister of Labor reciprocated for the government by personally conveying his greetings to the Second National Congress of the PCC. In March 1945 the PCC reached its greatest electoral strength to date when it polled some 27,000 votes in the legislative elections, elected four members to the Chamber, and won eight seats in departmental assemblies.[21]

In the presidential elections of the following year the Communists supported the official Liberal candidate, Gabriel Turbay, rather than Gaitán, whom they disdained as "fascist." Although the PCC shifted to support of the Gaitanista Liberals following the election, it could not completely live down its initial opposition to the popular hero, a move which had displeased many members of the party. Furthermore, the party was deeply divided at this time over the issue of "revisionism."[22] The result was that its candidates obtained only 15,000 votes in the elections of 1947. The party lost its representation in Congress and retained only one departmental assembly seat, in addition to membership in scattered municipal councils.[23] The attitude of the Conservative governments was also influential in the continued decline of the Communist party. Measures were taken to cripple the CTC, in which the Communists had important strength, and the PCC suffered the official repression to which Liberals also were subject. Finally, under the military regime, the party was declared to be illegal, a status which ended in December 1957 when most of the

21. *Memoria del Ministro de Gobierno . . . de 1945,* pp. 62 and 94.

22. A faction led by Augusto Durán, the former secretary-general of the party, broke away in 1947 to form the Communist Workers' Party (*Partido Comunista Obrero*) but did not survive. The Communists reunited in 1950 but shortly divided again. The *Duranistas* are still a fairly important minority among organized labor on the Atlantic coast and in Bogotá. They publish a monthly newspaper, *Palabra del Pueblo.* However, they are otherwise unimportant and have no formal organization. They are considered traitors by the PCC.

23. *Memoria del Ministro de Gobierno . . . de 1947,* p. 185. The 15,000 votes were for deputies to departmental assemblies. The total Communist vote for seats in the Chamber of Representatives was less than 12,000 and for Senate seats about 6,400.

laws and decrees of the Rojas government were rescinded by the plebiscite.[24]

The Communists supported the "positive" aspects of the 1957 plebiscite, as well as the election of Lleras in 1958, as steps toward the restoration of constitutional order. At the same time, they have been highly critical of the "negative" features of the National Front such as its oligarchic nature, the exclusion of third parties, alternation, and the dependence of Colombia on the leader of the "imperialist" camp, the United States.

The PCC achieved the election of a few of its members to office in 1958 by running them on Communist-front slates which had Liberal designations. In 1966 they again ran some "Liberal" slates of their own. Some Communists have gained office through inclusion on lists of the MRL: under current constitutional provisions such tactics are their only means of getting elected, although the party is legal in other respects.[25] Because of such artificial electoral conditions, it is impossible to determine the Communists' present voting strength. It seems highly probable that, were it free to do so, the party would be able to improve on its 1945 peak performance, although not strikingly so.

Communist influence in Colombia has not been confined to the electoral field. From the foundation of the CTC the Communists have often been numerous among its leadership, both at the national level and in its constituent unions and departmental federations. At various periods up to 1950 the Communists virtually controlled the CTC or one wing of that badly divided organization. In 1950 they withdrew from the CTC, which at that point was dominated by the Liberals. Coupled with official disfavor and repression and the simultaneous rise of the Union of Colombian Workers (UTC), the split caused Communist influence in labor to decline markedly. When the CTC revived after 1957, the Communists regained much lost ground at the local union and departmental federation level.

24. The plebiscite in effect invalidated legislation passed by the ANAC. The PCC was thus automatically made legal once again even though the same plebiscite approved the parity arrangement whereby third parties would be excluded from all offices, legislative and appointive.

25. It might be wondered why Communists are not more strictly excluded from running under the Liberal label. However, the concern in preventing third parties was not fear of Communism, but a desire to achieve exact parity. There was also a reaction against the tendency of previous regimes to label many Liberals indiscriminately as Communists.

However, they have not been able to seize control nationally, and in December 1960, the CTC expelled six of its affiliates for being Communist-dominated. These included the Federation of Workers of the Valle (*Federación de Trabajadores del Valle*—FEDETAV) and five industrial unions in the Bogotá area. Subsequently, the Communists have attempted to form their own national labor confederation as a rival to the CTC and the UTC. A fair estimate at the present time would probably place 10 to 15 per cent of Colombian organized labor in unions substantially controlled by Communists.[26]

The PCC has garnered some strength among campesinos, notably in a few largely mountainous districts in southwestern Cundinamarca and in southern and eastern Tolima. For some three decades the Communists have exercised effective jurisdiction over a district near the town of Viotá, about forty miles southwest of Bogotá. It is sometimes referred to, not wholly facetiously, as the Republic of Tequendama, since it allegedly has its own system of justice, its own militia, and its own tax-collection procedures. It originated in the late 1920s or early 1930s when tenants employed on several large coffee estates in the area occupied portions of the estates as their own. They eventually purchased the land from the owners and in some cases continued to work on the latters' remaining lands as well. The movement was led from an early point by Communists who organized *ligas de campesinos* (peasant leagues) and "self-defense" organizations. Though not composed exclusively of Communist party members, these organizations were controlled by the party. Despite one or two abortive attempts at invasion, the area has remained inviolate from the actions of the authorities, perhaps because it never became a center of violence, even during the years of guerrilla struggle. The terrain would make it difficult to dislodge the occupants, and in any case a modus vivendi seems to have been reached with the large landowners of the region. The enclave has served as a haven for Communist cadres and as a center where clandestine activities of the party could be carried on during periods of repression. Other areas under Communist control exist in the same general area, on both sides of the eastern cordillera, although none of them quite approach the durability or the degree of self-containment of the Viotá area. Among them are the Sumapaz region, southeast

26. See below, pp. 330–41, for further details on the Communist role in organized labor.

of Viotá, and the Marquetalia region, on the border between the departments of Tolima and Huila. Other rural areas of Communist influence are
to be found in areas of recent colonization in the department of Meta and
the intendancy of Caquetá. Altogether they number perhaps half a dozen.

Although notable for the fact of their existence, their importance should
not be exaggerated. The total number of campesinos in such areas is at
most a few thousand and there is little evidence of their willingness to risk
their own local gains in an attempt to carry out a nationwide agrarian
revolution.[27]

The Communists have had some success in enlisting support among
youth and intellectuals. Affiliated to the party is the Union of Colombian
Communist Youth (*Unión de la Juventud Comunista de Colombia*—
UJCC). The Communists held a virtually controlling position in the now
defunct National Union of Colombian Students (*Unión Nacional de Estudiantes Colombianos*—UNEC) and were influential in its predecessor, the
Federation of Colombian Students (*Federación de Estudiantes Colombianos*—FEC). They apparently play an important role in the new National
Federation of University Students (*Federación Universitaria Nacional*—
FUN).[28] Communist influence is also significant among both the student
body and the faculty of the Universidad Libre in Bogotá, although
charges that the university is Communist-dominated are exaggerated.
(The University is in any case much smaller than the Universidad Nacional and only one among several in the city of Bogotá.) The Communists have organized various front groups among intellectuals, including
societies of friendship with the Soviet Union, Communist China, and
Cuba, as well as "peace" committees. But these have been limited in
membership, sporadic in their functioning, and largely ineffective.

The PCC has claimed to be the party of the proletariat and has gained
some influence among members of that class. There has also been a significant complement of campesinos among the party's membership and on
the party's central committee. However, during the 1940s the party de-

27. See E. J. Hobsbawm, "The Anatomy of Violence," *New Society* (London), April
11, 1963, pp. 16–18; Eugene K. Culhane, "Red Pocket in Colombia," *America, 102*
(Mar. 12, 1960), 701–04; and *Special Warfare Handbook*, pp. 429–31. Where Communists in such areas have taken to guerrilla activity it has generally—though not always—been in "self-defense" against government attempts to assert its own authority.

28. For further details on the Communist influence among students, see below,
pp. 341–51.

feated a move to purge its leadership of non-manual workers, and the all-important national executive committee and secretariat have been dominated by intellectuals and men of lower middle-class origin. According to one of its former officials, "It was obsessed with being a working-class party, but it was basically a party of intellectuals." [29]

The long-range goal of the Colombian Communists is the revolutionary reconstruction of Colombian society. Its immediate goal is the creation of a "Great Patriotic and Democratic Front . . . based on the loyal collaboration of the forces of the Left, on unity of action of the working class and on the alliance of the workers and peasants" [30] and centered around a "minimum program" which includes full democratic liberties, stepped up agrarian reform, the independent industrial development of the country, and an independent foreign policy. The Colombian ruling class is declared of course to be an enemy. But the most invidious attacks are reserved for "yankee imperialism," with the PCC going to considerable lengths to prove itself the staunch defender of Colombian national sovereignty.

Throughout most of its existence the PCC has favored the peaceful route to power:

> It is necessary to struggle firmly against the opportunism of the Left, particularly dangerous in the period in which the conditions for a revolutionary situation are ripening. The opportunism of the Left, or extremism, characterizes itself by disdain toward legal activities, . . . in its negation of the primordial importance of the political work of the working class, and, naturally, in the adventurist thesis which proposes armed guerrilla struggle as the only and immediate form of struggle. [31]

In line with this posture, the PCC has given its loyalty to the Communist party of the Soviet Union in its dispute with the Chinese. The contest between the two orientations first caused a split within the ranks of the UJCC. At the Fifth Plenum of the Central Committee of the UJCC held in February 1964, a strong pro-Chinese faction was expelled from the organ-

29. Gutiérrez, *Rebeldía Colombiana*, pp. 36–37.

30. Gilberto Vieira White, secretary-general of the PCC, in *Voz de la Democracia*, Aug. 29, 1963, p. 3.

31. Quoted in Young, p. 12.

ization, whereupon it constituted a new group, the *Juventud Comunista Colombiana* (as distinguished from the *Unión de la Juventud Comunista de Colombia*).[32] Early in June 1965, a pro-Peking group split from the party proper, accusing the PCC leadership of betraying the revolution. This new entity—known as the Communist party of Colombia-Marxist-Leninist—gave explicit support to a guerrilla group calling itself the Army of National Liberation (*Ejército de Liberación Nacional*—ELN). Perhaps propelled by this competition, at the tenth party congress held in January 1966 the PCC supported the action of those guerrilla groups with a genuine mass base (at the same time denouncing petit-bourgeois ultrarevolutionaries) as "the patriotic response" to the growing role of the United States in assisting the government's anti-guerrilla campaign.

The PCC has its own publishing facilities and issues a weekly newspaper, *Voz Proletaria* (formerly *Voz de la Democracia*), and an ideological review, *Documentos Políticos*. The best current guess as to party membership is about 10,000, plus sympathizers and collaborators, although some estimates place the number considerably higher. This is more than double the membership at the time of the fall of the Rojas dictatorship, and the party is today probably stronger and better organized than at any time since its founding. It is still very far from being a major force in Colombian political life, however, and its growth rate has apparently levelled off following a post-1957 spurt. If one compares the memberships of the hemisphere's Communist parties to the populations of the several countries, the Colombian party is proportionately one of the smaller in Latin America. The PCC was the eighth largest in Latin America in 1963, although the country was fourth in population.[33] Therefore, while Communist influence among organized labor, in a few rural districts, among students and intellectuals, and in some of the splinters of the MRL is by no means negligible, the PCC's political power is on the whole rather meager. Its leadership seems to have become bureaucratized and unimaginative. There is no real possibility of a Communist-led revolution in the foreseeable future and there is no immediate prospect that the PCC will be able

32. Cf. *Actualidades* (Newssheet for youth and students published by the *Instituto de Asuntos Internacionales de la Juventud*), *4* (March 23, 1964), 3–4, for these internal struggles.

33. For 1963 figures on the comparative sizes of Latin American Communist parties see Rollie Poppino, *International Communism in Latin America: A History of the Movement 1917–1963* (New York, The Free Press of Glencoe, 1964), p. 231.

to attain the degree of strength that the Communists have mustered at times in recent years in such Latin American countries as Brazil, Chile, and Venezuela.

Revolutionary sentiments have found expression in organizations other than the Socialist movement and the Communist party. Some of these have aimed at uniting the "progressive" forces of all parties in a mass anti-party or "above the parties" movement against the oligarchs as the preferred road to social revolution. Others have scorned all pretense at employing democratic procedures in favor of direct revolutionary action.

The ephemeral National Popular Union (*Unión Popular Nacional*— UPN), which was organized by some Liberals of the far Left and some maverick Communists in 1959, is representative of the former type. Rather closely resembling the Communists' call for a National Democratic Front of "workers, peasants, petit bourgeoisie, progressive intellectuals, and the national, anti-imperialist elements of the bourgeoisie," the UPN was looked at askance by the PCC because the party did not control it. Most of its members eventually entered the ranks of the MRL and came to comprise that movement's left wing.[34]

The United Front of Revolutionary Action (*Frente Unido de Acción Revolucionaria*—FUAR), in contrast, relied primarily on organized insurrection to revolutionize Colombian society.[35] The FUAR was a lineal descendant of the revolutionary National Popular Gaitanista Movement (*Movimiento Nacional Popular Gaitanista*—MNPG), organized by Gloria Gaitán de Valencia, daughter of the late Jorge Eliécer Gaitán, and her husband, Luis Emiro Valencia, a former leader of the PPSC, shortly after their return from a trip to Cuba early in 1960. The MNPG was in turn the heir of the National Liberal Gaitanista Movement (*Movimiento Nacional Liberal Gaitanista*—MNLG), a reformist group headed by Gloria Gaitán.

The FUAR itself was the outcome of a First Conference of Revolutionary Forces convoked in early 1962 at Luis Valencia's invitation. Attending

34. *El Tiempo,* Jan. 23, 1962, p. 12.
35. Concerning the FUAR see Fred Goff, "Colombia: The Pre-Revolutionary Stage" (Stanford, Cal., Stanford University, Institute of Hispanic American and Luso-Brazilian Studies, 1963); Young, pp. 13–17; the issues of *Gaitán* and *Batalla del Pueblo,* the newspapers of the movement and its predecessors; and the interview with Gloria Gaitán de Valencia published in *Síntesis, 1* (May 1964), 201–07.

were delegates of the MNPG and several regional revolutionary movements, most of which were offshoots of the PPSC. Representatives of the Juventudes del MRL attended, but the JMRL did not merge with the new organization as did the other groups. Within a few months of this conference the FUAR had branches in half a dozen Colombian cities.

The program of the FUAR was in a number of ways reminiscent of the old PPSC—"revolutionary socialism: popular, democratic, national"—with generous additions of opposition to United States "imperialism" and support for Castro's Cuba. More specifically, its program envisaged a radical agrarian reform; the nationalization of natural resources and other fundamental sectors of the economy; national economic planning; and solidarity with other "movements of national liberation." Tactically, the FUAR stressed "belligerent" electoral abstention and the necessity for armed struggle, notably that of guerrillas, as the route to power, although it did not discount the role that unity of the working class "at the base" could play in the coming revolution. FUAR was for a brief time the principal *Fidelista* organization in Colombia, and there is some evidence that it received not only moral support and guidance but also financial assistance from the Cuban government.[36]

Despite such backing, and in spite of its promising beginnings, the FUAR's success has been less than conspicuous. Valencia and his wife have severed their connections with the movement, allegedly because it had been thoroughly penetrated by police spies, and because it was failing to reach the masses. The FUAR survived their departure but was harassed by the government for suspected complicity in acts of terrorism and has since dwindled to almost nothing.

Another movement of the direct action variety is the Peasant-Student-Worker Movement (*Movimiento Obrero Estudiantil Campesino*—MOEC). An outgrowth in January 1959 of a student and youth protest against an increase in bus fares in the city of Bogotá, it appears to be loosely organized and to be primarily engaged in isolated attempts to form guerrilla bands and to carry out sporadic acts of urban terrorism. Although some of its members were apparently once associated with the UJCC, the Communist party has denounced the group as extremist and anarchic. Its ideological orientation is confused. However, a few of its leaders have evi-

36. See Goff, pp. 15–16n.

dently received training in Cuba, and it regards itself as Fidelista. Its numbers are probably in the hundreds, composed mainly of youth of middle-sector origin.[37]

The Revolutionary Armed Forces of Colombia (*Fuerzas Armadas Revolucionarias de Colombia*—FARC) was organized in 1966 to coordinate the guerrilla activities of groups operating in southwestern Colombia and those of the Army of National Liberation (ELN), which in late 1963 began operations in the mountains of eastern Colombia. An amalgam of Communists, former members of the MRL youth organization, and others, some of its members, too, appear to have received training in Cuba. While the FARC is so far limited in its numbers and radius of action, the government has taken it seriously enough to launch a full-fledged military campaign against it.

In mid-1965 still another revolutionary movement, the People's United Front (*Frente Unido del Pueblo*—FUP), was launched with Father Camilo Torres as its principal leader. Of upper-class lineage, Father Torres was a priest and a sociologist, and had been chaplain at the National University. His outspokenness in advocating revolutionary solutions for prevailing social inequities, and his efforts to found a political movement, finally caused the archbishop of Bogotá to deprive him of all priestly functions. He received some initial support from the Christian Democrats, but they began to fall away as the FUP came under the increasing influence of the extreme Left. Finally, late in 1965 Father Torres joined the ELN guerrilla forces. Early the following year he was shot down, gun in hand, during an ambush of an army patrol in the mountains of northeastern Colombia. A potentially charismatic leader with considerable appeal to students and youth, Father Torres' political career was cut short in his mid-thirties.

The object of such movements has been to destroy or drastically alter the pattern of elite domination of Colombian society from a position outside and in opposition to the two traditional parties and the National Front, and essentially by means of violence. The membership of all of them has been small, in some cases infinitesimal. Their political impact has been small as well, although their agitational potential cannot be entirely discounted in what is a fundamentally unstable social and political situation. None of them can compare even with the limited strength

37. See *Semana*, No. 644, pp. 13–15, and No. 647, p. 20; and *El Tiempo*, July 19, 1963, pp. 1 and 17.

and influence of the Communist party. So far, there has not appeared on the revolutionary Left a force which gives any indication of being able to overturn the basic patterns of power in the Colombian polity.

THE NON-LEFTIST OPPOSITION

Threats to the Colombian elite have arisen from sources other than the Left, whether reformist or revolutionary. Such groups share with the Left a predisposition toward change; they differ from it in their closer ties to Colombia's traditionalist heritage. They have in common among themselves their claim to constitute a "third force" between or "above" both capitalism and communism.

One strand of this opposition from the non-Left is the populistic authoritarianism represented originally by the Third Force of General Gustavo Rojas Pinilla and today by the *Alianza Nacional Popular* (ANAPO). The deposed dictator returned to Colombia from exile in October 1958, partly in a quixotic effort to vindicate himself before the country. He may also have hoped that his erstwhile supporters and elements of the military would rise on his behalf. Instead, he was tried by the Senate on grounds of malfeasance in office and of having brought indignity on the presidency. Charges centered on his alleged use of his high office to acquire cattle ranches and to smooth the way for illegal imports for his friends. Early in 1959 he was sentenced to the perpetual loss of all political rights, including the right to vote and to hold office, the denial of all honors as a retired member of the military, and the deprivation of the pensions due him as a former military officer and president.[38]

Following Rojas' release from custody in late 1960 he and some former associates and members of his family organized the ANAPO, which declared its opposition to the National Front and the "oligarchs" and sought to "revive" the bond between the people and the armed forces. Rojas was allowed to enter the 1962 presidential race, despite the loss of his political rights, although the votes he won were declared null. In any case he ran poorly, receiving only 54,562 votes out of 2,634,840 cast. Meanwhile, in the elections of the previous March the ANAPO had captured 2 senatorial seats and 6 seats in the Chamber of Representatives, as well as 12 depart-

38. The best source for the trial is *Rojas Pinilla ante el Senado*. Rojas' political rights were restored in late 1966.

mental assembly seats, thus establishing itself as a respectable though distinctly poor third among Conservative factions.[39]

By the time of the 1964 elections the situation had changed in the ANAPO's favor in at least three respects. The first and least important was a decision of the Supreme Court which absolved Rojas of criminal charges stemming from his actions while president. (His trial before the Senate had been a civil action only.) An aura of respectability was thus restored to the General. Secondly, the rise in the cost of living which followed devaluation was causing disaffection with the National Front. The point was accentuated by Rojas' campaigning on behalf of ANAPO candidates. During the course of a speech he would hold up a cake of *panela* (a kind of brown sugar basic to the popular diet) and remind his audience of the difference in its price now and when he was in power. Finally, events within the Conservative party had greatly improved the ANAPO's strategic position. With the temporary union of the two major wings of the party in March 1963 the ANAPO remained the only significant Conservative opposition to the government.

The result was striking gains for ANAPO candidates in the March 1964 elections. They won almost 27 per cent of the Conservative vote, as well as 1.4 per cent of the Liberal vote (almost 14 per cent of the national total), increasing their seats in the Chamber from 6 to 27.[40] Following upon the congressional elections of 1966 the ANAPO became the leading voice of opposition to the National Front and in the May presidential election put up its own candidate (a Liberal, and thus legally eligible). He garnered nearly 30 per cent of the vote—a good showing considering his late start in the race, his relative personal obscurity, and the failure of other opposition groups to unite behind him.

Rojas has not pinned all his hopes on electoral means, however. In

39. Registraduría del Estado Civil, *Organización y Estadísticas, 1962*. The ANAPO's proportion of the total vote was nonetheless under 4 per cent and of the Conservative vote about 8 per cent.

40. Registraduría del Estado Civil, *Organización y Estadísticas, 1964*. 26 of the ANAPO seats were Conservative, 1 Liberal. During 1965 the ANAPO leadership made additional efforts to establish itself as a movement within both parties by appointing "chiefs of debate" under both party rubrics. The intention was to prepare for the possibility of an ANAPO presidential candidate under the Liberal label in 1966, while at the same time vindicating ANAPO as a movement above the parties. See *Alianza Nacional Popular*, the movement's newspaper, for the week of June 4, 1965.

August 1963 he was arrested and detained for more than a month for allegedly having plotted a coup, or disturbances which would lead the army to carry out a coup. Following the March 1964 elections, even while he boasted of the coming presidential victory of an ANAPO candidate, he suggested that his followers might prevail upon him to take power forcibly before that time: "the people cannot wait two years for a change. . . . I have been holding them back and will continue to do so as long as I can, but if it proves impossible I shall have to put myself at their head." [41] Meanwhile Rojistas were implicated on several occasions during the early '60s in acts of terrorism or in demonstrations which became small riots.

Precisely the kinds of changes which the ANAPO hopes to carry out if it should achieve power are a matter of some conjecture. It has described itself as "a Christian and nationalist movement which seeks the union of the Liberal and Conservative populace with the aim of attaining power in order to put it at the service of the people." [42] Presumably its policies would be patterned somewhat after Rojas' previous rule. Its spokesmen call for a "revolution" which gives to all Colombians opportunity, land, credit, peace, medical assistance, and lower prices, but detailed proposals are generally lacking. The emphasis instead is on a "revolution" "against the swindlers, against the empresarios of hate, against the corrupt politicians, against the sordid bosses, against the traitorous intellectuals, against the pharisees of democracy, against the exporters of capital to Swiss and North American banks, against the real promoters of violence." [43] Punishment of "the guilty," of the persecutors of Rojas Pinilla, and the elimination of plutocracy and privilege are constant themes. The appeal is above all to the lower middle and working classes; election data suggest that it has had an effect. At least, the ANAPO's support has come disproportionately from the large cities.[44] Nevertheless, the preferred "revolution" is not, properly speaking, to be one of class against class, but rather a revolution of the outcasts against the privileged, resulting in popular and national unity.

41. Richard Eder, "Coup in Colombia Hinted by Rojas," *New York Times,* March 22, 1964, p. 7.

42. María Eugenia Rojas de Moreno, Rojas' daughter, in *Alianza Nacional Popular,* June 4–11, 1965.

43. Ibid., Aug. 22–29, 1963.

44. Contrast this to MRL strength outside the large cities.

The odds are long against the ANAPO's attaining its objectives. Rojas himself is 66 and not very well. There is little evidence that the ANAPO is solidly organized; to generate support it seems to depend mainly on the enthusiasm aroused by the traditional *gira* (speaking tour) and on Rojas' modest amount of charisma. At bottom the Rojista strategy seems to depend on creating enough popular disaffection and unrest to induce the military to step in. Yet current indications are that the top ranks of the military are anti-Rojas and that even if a coup were to occur it would be unlikely to be in Rojas' name. The ANAPO's main significance is as a focus of protest against the National Front and its possible effect on the coalition should the ANAPO in the future win a plurality of Conservative congressional seats.

A somewhat similar movement, the National Democratic Movement (*Movimiento Democrático Nacional*—MDN), is of more recent origin. Its chief intellectual architect is Alberto Zalamea, the editor of *La Nueva Prensa*, a weekly political and news magazine which stresses the necessity of "a great alliance of wills" against the oligarchy and the "imperialists" in order to give the country "an authentic national conscience." *La Nueva Prensa* claims to sponsor a "third position" which is the only alternative between oligarchic rule and communism in Colombia. "The National Revolution is today a myth. But only myths move peoples. Throughout the length and breadth of the land nationalist groups are being formed. Groups that wish to include the majority of Colombians. Groups which believe in the possibility of a Revolution which is not necessarily one based on class. A Revolution which puts aside the false dichotomy between Left and Right by which the governing elite sustains itself." [45]

To achieve their ends, Zalamea and his associates looked longingly to the military and during 1963 began to give fulsome praise to the Minister of War, Major General Alberto Ruiz Novoa, as a man who saw the need for a nationalistic "revolution." The Church, too, was given its due as one of Colombia's traditional institutions which could help to lead the country to a better and genuinely nationalistic future. In early 1965 Zalamea was a key figure in the founding of the MDN, which was to support Ruiz Novoa, by then out of the Cabinet, as a Liberal candidate for the presidency in 1966. For a time the ANAPO, the Línea Dura of the MRL, the Christian

45. *La Nueva Prensa*, Aug. 28, 1963. *La Nueva Prensa* appeared for a brief period during 1963 in daily newspaper form.

Democrats, and others looked with varying degrees of favor on the new movement.

The ideology of the MDN was, like the ANAPO's, somewhat vague. Ruiz stressed the necessity for a "national goal" and the formation of a "modernizing coalition" "above the parties." He proposed a social and economic program based on Christian principles of social justice and including an end to monopolies, a minimum wage for all Colombians, the elimination of illiteracy, the liberalization of credit to small farmers and small businessmen, and an agrarian reform based on "the limitation of holdings." [46] The MDN's limited appeal seems to be mainly to the middle class, both urban and rural, and especially to those of the middle sectors who may hope for change but who at the same time may fear the Communist ties of some of the leftist groups.

For the MDN the objective was to gather about it enough of the opponents of the National Front, as well as the abstainers in the 1964 elections, to place its man in the presidency in 1966. However, the movement subsequently split into two factions headed respectively by Zalamea and Ruiz, with the former oriented somewhat more to a Nasseristic approach to modernization than the latter. When Ruiz failed to gain the support of any major opposition group for his candidacy (though the ANAPO momentarily considered doing so), he bowed out of the race for president. Not to be discounted is the outside chance of military support for a nonelectoral venture, yet it seems unlikely. For Ruiz, since his retirement from the army and from the Cabinet early in 1965, appears to have little support among active officers.

A different type of opposition from the non-Left is that of Christian Democracy, represented in Colombia primarily by the Christian Social Democratic party (PSDC), founded in August 1959.[47] Christian Democracy has been a much-used term in Colombia. The Conservative party claims

46. Alberto Ruiz Novoa, *El Gran Desafío* (Bogotá, Ediciones Tercer Mundo, 1965), pp. 139–40. This book is a collection of speeches by Ruiz Novoa. Concerning the MDN see also *La Nueva Prensa*, No. 132 (1965).

47. The following discussion of the PSDC is based on its own publications, including the newspaper *Nuevo Orden* (Cali) and the pamphlet, *Partido Social Demócrata Cristiano* (Bogotá, Ediciones Caribe, 1961[?]); on Francisco de Paula Jaramillo, *La Democracia Cristiana: Una Nueva Perspectiva para Colombia* (Bogotá, Ediciones Caribe, 1962); on DECE (formerly *Boletín Informativo Demócrata Cristiano*), published in Santiago, Chile (formerly in New York); and on interviews with Jaramillo and Alvaro Rivera Concha, both leaders of the PSDC, Bogotá, Aug. 30, 1963.

in its program to be following the social precepts of the papal encyclicals, and various Conservative factions have from time to time sought to preempt the Christian Democratic designation. Its main import for Conservatives has been to urge upon the elite a greater paternalistic concern for the less fortunate. The PSDC on the other hand seeks to modify the pattern of elite rule. For the PSDC Christian Democracy "is an authentic third position in face of the false dilemma 'capitalism or communism' with which both materialisms have wanted to confront the world." It sees itself as "A vanguard political force which considers the artificial classification between 'Left' and 'Right' to have been superseded and also does not accept classification as a force of the 'Center.' . . . Its proposals of audacious social advance logically extend farther than those of the Communists." [48]

It is difficult to assess the party's strength among the electorate. In March 1966 a PSDC slate (listed under the Conservative rubric) won several thousand votes in Bogotá, but the party's membership figures are unavailable, although they likely approximate 3 to 4,000.

Despite its small numbers, the party has made considerable organizational progress. It has established branches in the major departmental capitals; has formed youth, women's and labor affiliates; has opened party centers in Bogotá and in other cities; and has set up a series of training courses for its cadres in such subjects as press and propaganda, and oratory. It or its sympathizers publish several newspapers and periodicals, most on a monthly or irregular basis, and it has created its own publishing house, *Ediciones Caribe*.

The party claims to have ties to a number of unions in Antioquia, and to scattered unions elsewhere, although its leaders assert that they merely want to educate labor to Social Christian precepts rather than to involve it in partisan politics. The PSDC has a few sympathizers in the UTC, but PSDC leaders state that while they would like to convert the UTC leadership to their ideology they have no intention of trying to take over that labor confederation. Instead, they are hoping to increase the number of Colombian unions linked to the Latin American Confederation of Christian Union Members (*Confederación Latinoamericana de Sindicalistas Cristianos*—CLASC).

The strength of the PSDC lies, in the main, with students, intellectuals,

48. *Partido Social Demócrata Cristiano*, p. 3.

and professional people. The PSDC leadership is composed of middle-class elements and sons of the elite: its program and pronouncements are above all directed at middle-sector interests. Its youth organization, the *Juventud Revolucionaria Demócrata Cristiana,* appears to be the most active among its affiliates. Regionally, the PSDC is seemingly strongest in Antioquia and in the Bogotá area. The Church, meanwhile, has neither condemned the party nor given its support. A few clerics are associated with it, and there is a belief on the part of some that the Jesuits had a hand in bringing it into being. There is no organic link between the Church and the party, however, and priests play no conspicuous role in its activities. The PSDC makes it a point to declare itself to be non-clerical, non-confessional, and open to members of all faiths who support its program.

In its program the PSDC calls for a new, "communitarian" concept of property, by which all those employed in a firm share in both its profits and its management. Private property is to be protected by the state, which is at the same time to take steps to place it within the reach of everyone. The state should "have full power to guarantee the just distribution of wealth, being able to undertake expropriation, for example, of property inveterately left idle, even without indemnization." [49] The state is also to maintain "strict control" over such services as banking, insurance, and transport, and "to control effectively" the exploitation of natural resources. Turning to agrarian reform the PSDC platform advocates the provision of cultivable land to campesino families willing and able to work it, but the stress is on provision of credit, access roads, education, and similar services and amenities.

A distinctive feature of the PSDC platform is its interest in strengthening the family and both private and public morality. Toward these ends the party proposes family subsidies and the promotion of cultural and sporting centers. It sees in cooperatives, communal action, and heightened fiscal and administrative powers for the municipios a way to bring the individual into a more fruitful relationship to society at large. Surprisingly perhaps, rather little is said on the subject of the Church and religion. Religious freedom is expressly defended, and the Church is admonished to refrain from interference in purely temporal or administrative matters. At the same time, the state is "to support all those initiatives [of the

49. Ibid., p. 13.

Church] which benefit the community" [50] and the Church's role in education is to be assured.

The National Front, in the PSDC view, has evolved into an undemocratic monolith. Chief among the party's specific proposals for change in the system is of course the need to put an end to the exclusion of third parties from political participation. The PSDC is particularly critical of what it considers the government's lack of attention to social problems. In international affairs, the party puts strong emphasis on cooperation—economic, political, cultural—among the Latin American nations. It advocates an independent, but not a neutralist, foreign policy.

The PSDC is a strong proponent of democracy, although there are occasional hints from its spokesmen that if peaceful change is made impossible violence will be resorted to. Although the party is barred from elective office until 1974, its leaders express some hope that the system can be revised before then by a "popular plebiscite." Its supporters have generally voted in blank, rather than abstained, in National Front elections. In 1966, however, the party ran its own lists in a few localities.

The PSDC likes to think of itself as revolutionary, not in its methods, but in the nature and degree of change which it advocates, and there are probably a few genuine revolutionaries among the Christian Democrats, especially in its youth movement. For the most part, though, it is reformist. Its stipulations on property go little beyond profit-sharing and an increased state control over economic development. Its agrarian reform proposals are rather vague. The emphasis is on the humanization of economic and social life based on Catholic principles, not on the wholesale overturn of the existing order.

The Christian Social Democratic party is today a miniscule factor in the Colombian political arena and it seems likely to remain so for at least the duration of the National Front. Yet the strength of the Church and of Catholic loyalties in Colombia; the fact that the country's largest labor confederation, the UTC, is already oriented toward Catholic social doctrine; and numerous signs of self-examination and of a searching for new paths among some younger Conservatives argue that Christian Democracy has a future before it in Colombia. This could take one of two paths, or both simultaneously: the expansion of the PSDC into a political factor of major importance; or the increasing adoption of Christian Democratic

50. Ibid., p. 12.

programs by the Conservatives. The depth of traditional political sentiments in Colombia suggests that the latter is the more likely. However,
the Chilean experience, where Conservatives and the Christian Democrats differed too deeply on socioeconomic issues to continue in a single
party, could be repeated in Colombia. Meanwhile, the PSDC has the advantage of youth, great initial enthusiasm, and links to other and powerful
Christian Democratic parties in Europe and elsewhere in Latin America.
Various kinds of guidance and training are therefore available to it which
should measurably assist its development. Its real test can only come,
however, when it has the opportunity to compete for votes among the
Colombian electorate.

Those Colombians whose political response to change is that of Christian Democracy have in common with the advocates of a populistic authoritarianism their reliance on traditional institutions and values to help
effect that change, their rejection of the class struggle as the axis of political combat, their scorn for the traditional party system, and the essentially reformist nature of the changes they seek. They differ from them in
the methods they would employ to effect those transformations, although
under current conditions there may be some inclination among Christian
Democrats for a solution involving a strongman. There are contrasts, too,
in the nature of their respective appeals—the PSDC relying more on reason
and the religious sense; the ANAPO and the MDN, on demagoguery and
the image of the caudillo. Their support also tends to be elicited from
different sectors of society—that of the PSDC from intellectuals, students,
and professional men; that of the ANAPO (though not its leadership) from
the urban lower and lower middle classes; that of the MDN falling somewhere in between. Among them only the ANAPO has so far had any real
measure of success. Yet the earlier rise of Perón in Argentina and Vargas
in Brazil and the achievements of Christian Democracy in Chile suggest
the real possibility of such a "third force" ultimately filling the void left
by the failures of Colombia's traditional parties.

THE FAILURES OF OPPOSITION

The various parties and movements of the non-Left share with the Left
their mutual opposition to the domination of Colombian society and politics by the reigning elite. A thread of nationalism—both in the sense of

national independence and that of national development—further binds together the diverse counter-elite groups. The distinction between the Left and the non-Left opposition in Colombia is therefore hardly a sharp one. It is tenable mainly in the degree that the former has its roots in liberal, the latter in traditionalist, Colombia.

So far, while the Left has generally been stronger, both have been relatively weak. Even as signs of popular inconformity with the governments of the National Front have increased, the result has been apathy and abstention. The vote for factions opposed to elite rule—for the MRL and its splinter groups and for the ANAPO—have never as yet extended to as much as a third of the total ballots cast and never to more than about ten per cent of the eligible electorate. Furthermore some of those votes have reflected the ancient party hatreds as much as the expression of mass grievances.

The central problem of counter-elite opposition groups has not been suppression. True, counter-elite parties and political movements have from time to time been subjected to considerable harassment by the government. Yet only from about 1949 to 1957 have they been suppressed more or less systematically, and only during the years 1954–57, when the Communist party was outlawed, has an opposition group actually been made illegal. Indeed, in a sense, the non-Left opposition was in power during the Rojas years and some elements of the Left, notably the PPSC, far from being suppressed, attached themselves to the regime. There is of course the current anomaly that, while third parties may organize, publish, and agitate, they are not free to run candidates for office. But the flexibility of the National Front, which allows virtually anyone who so desires to lay claim to either the Liberal or Conservative label, draws a bit of the sting from such restrictions. On the other hand, discrimination in employment is practiced against known members of groups such as the MRL, while advertising is evidently often denied the opposition press. The opposition also obviously faces great difficulties in its campaigns of proselytism, especially in rural areas where traditional modes of politics persist most strongly.

Compared to the situation of opposition groups in many Latin American countries over the years, that of Colombia's has been a favored one. Nothing in the modern history of Colombia can compare to the lengthy dictatorships of Juan Vicente Gómez (1909–35) or Marcos Pérez Jiménez

(1948–58) in Venezuela or the long periods of illegality suffered by the APRA in Peru. One might argue that, on the contrary, the relative benignity with which the Colombian opposition has been treated has been its undoing. It may be that only a certain optimum of real adversity can produce the toughness of spirit, the disciplined political organization, and the degree of unity required for the growth of a strong party aimed at undermining the existing order.

A more tangible source of the general weakness of the opposition in Colombia has been its sectarianism, the isolation and bickering among themselves of the various groups and grouplets that make it up. Some look to the ways of democracy to attain their ends, some to a mass-based "popular unity," some to terrorism and guerrilla warfare, and still others to a military coup. There are reformist Liberals, Socialists, Communists, Christian Democrats, populists, Fidelistas, nationalists, each group putting forth its own solutions to the country's problems, and each spending much of its time and energy excoriating the others. In addition to clashes over tactics and doctrine, clashes of personality seem endemic. There have been various attempts at unity among the parties and movements of opposition, notably the persistent Communist pleas for a broad "democratic" front. But each group has wanted to have unity on its own terms, to keep its autonomy of action, and to retain the leadership of the resulting coalition.

Such splintering and factionalism in part obey causes similar to those that have rent the traditional parties. It may also be relevant that in their great majority the leaders of the opposition parties are intellectuals. The importance they attach to words compared to pragmatic concerns merely accentuates what is already a feature of the political culture. Consequently, disputatiousness regarding ideas and theories is carried to an extreme.

The intellectualism of the opposition leaders, and their elite or at least upper middle-class origins, may also be responsible for the failure of most of them to strike much of a response among the masses. Only Gaitán succeeded in doing so and he was in class origin and physical appearance closer to those same masses than most others who today or in the past have sought to lead them. Moreover, coupled with intellectualism and elitism has been a lack of attention to the prosaic minutiae of organization. Only the Communist party has done much to overcome this weakness, although the PSDC seems to have made a fairly good beginning. As the fate of the Gaitanistas after April 9, 1948, so well demonstrates, even powerfully felt needs can dissipate and have little lasting effect if they lack organization. Some elements of the Colombian opposition have looked to the army to substitute for their own lack of organizational strength. This is a dangerous gambit, however, since it makes a party dependent on a force it cannot really control.

The Colombian Left and non-Left alike have lacked caudillos with popular appeal. Neither López Michelsen nor Rojas Pinilla really meets the requirements, whatever their other assets of leadership. Only Gaitán has done so among the leaders of counter-elite groups and his premature death makes it impossible to know the end result of his attempt to combine the roles of popular caudillo and leader of the Liberal party. How important this lack of a charismatic leader has been is of course conjectural. For some observers it is the paramount reason for the past and present failures of movements seeking change in Colombia. To hope to succeed in an assault on a well-intrenched elite, it may be necessary to have the leadership of a popular caudillo who can evoke loyalty on a basis which transcends traditional allegiances and yet in its *personalismo* is itself highly traditional.

Colombian opposition groups have had still other difficulties of their own creation. One has been the tendency of some among them, especially the PCC but also the Fidelistas, to look to foreign solutions to problems of change, and to political tactics which have not always been applicable to Colombian conditions. Another has been an inclination to oscillate between *entreguismo* ("sell-out-ism") and anarchic or quixotic direct action. The history of the Communist party, which is the oldest of the Colombian opposition groups, has been replete with such shifts—at one moment all-out support of the government in power (e.g. that of Alfonso López); at another (as for a brief time during the Rojas years) reliance primarily on guerrilla action. The PCC has matured somewhat in this regard in recent years, hewing to a middle line of building its organization for the long-term. But the opposition as a whole has tended to be composed on the one hand of those who would rather readily yield to the temptations of office were the opportunity offered, and those who follow the call of the *golpe* or mass insurrection. The result has been a debility of organization and a dissipation of energies.

A partial explanation for the failure of opposition groups in Colombia thus lies in their failures of leadership, organization, tactics, and unity. The profounder causes, less subject to the idiosyncrasies of individual political movements, are to be found in the broader social and political context in which such groups have had to function in Colombia.

Changes have occurred here as elsewhere, however. Opposition groups are more numerous, and over all probably stronger and more vocal, than at any previous time with the possible exception of the heyday of Gaitanismo. Significantly, the spectrum of counter-elite opposition has been broadened to include groups whose roots are in some measure in traditionalist Colombia. Most important, the signs of alienation from the existing order are more evident than before. The proliferation and variety of opposition groups is one indication. Another is the progressive abstention which has occurred in elections under the National Front. Still another is the gradual rise in the anti-system protest vote, whether represented by the MRL or the ANAPO. Professor Whiteford, who has spent considerable time in the city of Popayán at various periods beginning in 1947, reports that in 1963 he "found considerably more tension, frustration, and expressed antagonism toward the status quo than I ever encountered before." [51] Certainly the only period to compare with the early '60s in this regard would be the late 1940s.

Indications are that in the coming years—or certainly when the restrictions of the National Front come to an end—new opportunities will open for the opposition of both the Left and the non-Left. Their ultimate success will depend partly on their own ability to develop coherence, organization, and leadership, as well as on their capacity to adapt their programs and tactics to real Colombian conditions. The fate of the various alternatives to "reform from above" will likewise depend on the way in which the Colombian elite and the institutions of the traditional order themselves meet the problems of change.

51. *Land Reform and Social Change*, p. 17.

TRADITIONAL
INSTITUTIONS

THE MILITARY

Two of the central institutions of traditional Latin American society have been the armed forces (among which the army has usually played the paramount role, both militarily and politically) and the Roman Catholic Church. Ostensibly their functions have little to do with politics except, in the former case, to guarantee the survival of the state, and in the latter to give it a moral sanction. In reality, in most Latin American nations the respective impacts of the military and the Church on the political system have had much wider ramifications. Both the army and the Church have taken part in the struggle for power and have helped to make and unmake presidents. They have usually put their weight behind the maintenance of the fabric of elite control. The extent to which both the armed forces and the Catholic Church are adopting modernizing attitudes and roles is therefore of very great significance for the Latin American countries' evolving responses to change. The importance of these two traditional institutions to contemporary Latin American politics is further enhanced by the fact that both possess qualities enabling them to play a unifying and consensual role in nations often characterized by deep internal rifts, whether these have been inherited from the past or cut by more recent currents of change.

The historic role of the Colombian military in politics, while important, has actually been a lesser one than in the great majority of Latin American countries. Recent figures show that Colombia ranks 15th among the

20 Latin American countries in the percentage of its population between 15 and 64 years of age who are in the ranks of the military, and 17th in military expenditures relative to its gross national product. And this is in spite of a quite recent regime dominated by the military, as well as serious internal violence to combat.[1]

Colombia has had its share of men on horseback, especially during the nineteenth century. But many of them have been armed civilians rather than professional soldiers, and most have acted in the name of one of the two historic parties rather than as leaders of a military institution. Regimes dominated by the military have been in power a bare dozen years throughout Colombian history. On only four occasions—1830, 1854, 1900, and 1953—has the army overthrown a constitutionally chosen president. In one of these instances, that of 1900, the coup merely deposed a decrepit president in the midst of civil war and replaced him with the vice-president. In this sense, despite the turbulence of much of the country's history, there is considerable truth in the affirmation of one Colombian that "The pen and the word have been, among us, weapons more decisive than the sword." [2]

This situation has not been fortuitous. It has followed at least a semi-conscious policy on the part of the Colombian upper class to keep the military in its place and to prevent any challenge from that quarter to the rule of a civilian elite. This attitude was probably reinforced in the early years of the republic by the circumstance that much of the army which liberated Colombia was composed of troops from the Venezuelan part of what was then known as Gran Colombia and was therefore opposed in its attempts to dominate the government by the civilians of Nueva Granada (the present-day Colombia).[3] At any rate, the Colombian Constitution of 1832 was unique among early Latin American constitutions in providing that Congress, rather than the chief executive, should exercise ultimate control over the armed forces. That constitution gave to Congress the

1. Russett et al., *World Handbook*, pp. 77–80. The budgetary share of the Ministry of War dropped from almost 20 per cent under Rojas to 13.2 per cent in 1961; cf. *Special Warfare Handbook*, p. 528.

2. Azula Barrera, *De la Revolución*, p. 70. For an historical treatment of the role of the Colombian army see Tomás Rueda Vargas, *El Ejército Nacional* (Bogotá, Editorial Antena, 1944).

3. Cf. J. León Helguera, "The Changing Role of the Military in Colombia," *Journal of Inter-American Studies* (July 1961), p. 351.

power to fix annually the size of the military establishment, required its concurrence in the appointment of officers above the rank of lieutenant colonel, and stipulated that the War Minister be a civilian.[4] Some of these provisions were modified in later years, but Colombian constitutions have in general been more restrictive than most in Latin America concerning the independent authority of the military. In fact, the Constitution of 1863 permitted the formation of state militias, and the Liberals virtually eliminated the national army in the following years, substituting for it a national guard. Although the latter became in its own right an instrument of Liberal administrations, the professional military organization remained weak during much of the nineteenth century. While Latin American constitutions are sometimes honored more in the breach than in the observance, they nonetheless indicate the intentions of those who draw them up. In Colombia the intention has usually been to curb the power of the military.

In the years after 1909, following the termination of the War of the Thousand Days and the abortive dictatorship of General Rafael Reyes, the intervention of the military in Colombian politics was minimal, although its potential role was seldom absent from the minds of politicians.[5] True, some of the old caudillos of the civil wars remained active in politics during the next two or three decades. Both presidential candidates in 1922 were veterans of the party wars. Under the Conservative regimes of the 1920s soldiers were sometimes "voted" by their officers, or otherwise used to influence the outcome of elections, in continuation of practices engaged in by both parties during the nineteenth century.[6] The army, too, helped to "maintain public order," as in 1919 when troops killed several workers demonstrating in Bogotá, and in 1928 when the army shot down the banana workers in an incident which Gaitán made a cause célèbre.

Yet the army in this period was essentially an instrument, not a directing force. Despite the fact that a majority of its officers were Conservative, the army did not act to prevent the accession of the Liberals in 1930, al-

4. Cf. John J. Johnson, *The Military and Society in Latin America* (Stanford, Cal., Stanford University Press, 1964), pp. 56–57.

5. The professionalization of the army began during the Reyes administration (1904–09). Military reforms were introduced, a cadet school was founded, and a Chilean mission was brought to assist with training.

6. Cf. e.g. *Los Partidos en Colombia,* p. 15 and passim.

though there were some officers who might have done so had the Conservative president called upon them.[7] Nor did the army try to capitalize on a brief undeclared war with Peru in 1932–33 to enhance its political position. In fact, during these early years of the thirties Colombia was one of only three Latin American countries to retain a civilian-controlled government.[8] Nevertheless, the Liberals were a bit uneasy about the army and its domination by Conservative officers, and there was some evidence that at one point in 1936 some Conservatives tried to stir elements of the army to action on their behalf.[9]

The Liberals accordingly took several steps to prevent the possible use of the military against them. In 1930, with the support of a Conservative-dominated Congress, they put through a law prohibiting members of the army on active duty from voting and from belonging to political parties. In the constitutional codification of 1945 this was extended to include all members of the armed forces and the national police.[10] During President López' first administration his Minister of War instituted a series of transfers of distrusted officers and promotions of younger ones, thus tightening the loyalty of the army to the administration. The president took the lead in attempting to instill in the army the sense of a new mission, that of helping to develop the country's thinly-populated plains and jungle regions. The Liberal administration also nationalized the departmental police forces and tried to build the police into something of a Liberal-oriented counterweight to the army.[11]

For a time these measures served their purpose. However, López' apparent scorn for the traditional role and importance of the army (he once referred to the army as a group of parasites),[12] the political interference in transfers and promotions, and the favoritism shown the police aroused resentment. When to these factors were added in the early 1940s the exam-

7. Rueda Vargas, p. 258; and Osorio, *Gaitán*, p. 133.

8. The others were Uruguay and Costa Rica. Cf. Edwin Lieuwen, *Arms and Politics in Latin America*, rev. ed. (New York, Frederick A. Praeger, 1961), p. 61.

9. Eduardo Santos, *Una Política Liberal*, pp. 20–22.

10. See Eustorgio Sarría, *La Democracia y el Poder Militar* (Bogotá, Editorial Iqueima, 1959), chapter 1, for a study of the constitutional and legal position of the military.

11. For this latter point see Monseñor Germán Guzmán, Orlando Fals Borda, and Eduardo Umaña Luna, *La Violencia en Colombia*, (2 vols. Bogotá, Ediciones Tercer Mundo, 1963–64), 2, 357 ff.

12. Osorio, p. 229.

ple of the Argentine army's coup against a civilian regime, the Conservative agitation against López, and the apparent moral and political disintegration of the second López administration, the stage was set for a military uprising in July 1944, centered in the city of Pasto in southwestern Colombia. Although sympathy for the revolt was fairly widespread in the army, most of the military in the end remained loyal and the coup collapsed.[13] The rapid resumption of authority by the government, and the court martial of those implicated, pushed the army once again into the background. There it might well have remained but for the inability of the parties to preserve political tranquility, and their failure to channel effectively the forces of change.

Some of Gaitán's supporters later lamented that the Pasto coup was a "leap into space" without concrete political goals or organized civilian backing; that it discredited and demoralized the army at a time when it might have begun to assume a social revolutionary role. Others have speculated that if the army had accepted Gómez' proposition to form a governing junta on April 9, 1948, the bloodbath of the next years might have been avoided.[14] The performance of the regime of General Rojas Pinilla after 1953 argues against both propositions, that is, either that the army could at the time have become an effective vehicle for social revolution, or that its rule would have assured political peace.

Following the bogotazo the army found itself more and more involved in attempts to maintain public order. With the sharpening of partisan bitterness after 1946 it came to be looked on by the Liberals as the only guarantor of elections in some areas. Liberals frequently called on the Ospina administration to institute military rule in localities, or even in whole departments, that were threatened by political violence. On the other hand, the government began to make greater use of the army to assist the police in preserving order, which usually involved fighting Liberal guerrillas. President Ospina called on the army to close Congress in November 1949 under the state of siege proclaimed at that time. In an

13. Helguera, p. 351, attributes part of the responsibility for the attempted coup to the buildup of the army during the short war with Peru a decade earlier and during World War II. See also *El Gobierno, el Ejército, y las Medidas del Estado de Sitio* (Bogotá, Imprenta Nacional, 1944) concerning military involvement in the episode.

14. Cf. Osorio, p. 281, and A. García, *Gaitán*, pp. 308–09, for the former view; cf. Andrade, *La Internacional Negra*, p. 87, for the latter.

attempt to ensure the army's loyalty, Ospina began to favor the promotion of officers from Conservative families. Some care was also taken to assure the partisan loyalty of those recruited into the ranks.[15] Moreover, beginning at the time of the bogotazo the Ministry of War came customarily to be given to a general, thus taking it out of the civilian hands in which it had lately rested with the exception of a period in 1944.

By the time Laureano Gómez assumed the presidency in 1950 some in the army were becoming restless in their new role as instruments of partisan political warfare. Edwin Lieuwen points up two additional, international influences which were acting on the Colombian army in the early fifties. One was the participation of a Colombian battalion in the Korean conflict, which perhaps stimulated the army's nationalism and its sense of mission. The other was United States military aid, which strengthened the army. "United States military aid must certainly be considered as one contributing factor that helped to tip the balance, bringing the Colombian army back into politics after a half-century of civilian rule." [16] Naturally the army increasingly came to feel that it was the only force with the strength, the will, and the sense of the national interest to surmount the division of the country into two.

> En Colombia, que es la tierra
> de las cosas singulares,
> dan la paz los militares,
> y los civiles dan guerra.[17]
> (In Colombia, which is the land
> of strange things,
> the soldiers bring peace,
> and the civilians make war.)

What brought the army back into command in the political arena, a place it had held only exceptionally in Colombian history, was the failure of the country's civilian political leadership to perform the most elementary of its functions, that of preserving the peace among Colombians.

15. Cf. Guzmán et al., *1*, 263–64.
16. Lieuwen, *Arms and Politics*, p. 231.
17. Quoted in Gregorio Sánchez Gómez, *Sociología Política Colombiana* (Cali, Sánchez Gómez Hnos., 194?), p. 44.

The years 1953–58 proved a chastening experience for the military. Many of its members, discovering that "The military profession is poor schooling for learning the difficult art of government," [18] were uncomfortable in their newly assumed role. In the years immediately following the "days of May" the leaders of the traditional parties did their best to treat gingerly the wounded military pride, while simultaneously urging on the armed forces the necessity and the honorability of an apolitical posture. Typical was the address of President-elect Alberto Lleras Camargo to a military gathering in May 1958:

The Armed Forces must not deliberate in politics, because they have been created for all the nation, because the entire nation, without exceptions of group or party or color or religious beliefs . . . have given them arms, have given them the physical power . . . to defend their common interest, have given them special rights, have freed them from many rules that govern civil life, have granted them the privilege that they be judged on their military conduct, and all this with one single condition: that of not falling with all their weight and their force upon innocent citizens. [19]

Lieuwen, writing in 1959, classified Colombia as a country in which the military was once again essentially out of politics, although he added that the situation remained somewhat unstable. [20] Yet the legacy of the Government of the Armed Forces and, above all, the continuing crisis of the Colombian polity, coupled with rapid societal change, have meant that the Colombian military has continued to assume a political role, even out of power, which it had long since virtually lost.

In the first place, problems of public order, for which the armed forces have always had a major responsibility, can be expected to recur. In rural areas the army has had increasing success in its battle against la violencia, but this sore on the body politic has not been altogether healed. In urban areas it is the army and the national police (one of the armed forces) which are called upon to contain outbreaks of social conflict. The army in effect governed the city of Barrancabermeja for several weeks in mid-1963 when a petroleum workers' strike resulted in damage to the

18. Eduardo Santos, "Latin American Realities," *Foreign Affairs* (June 1956), p. 256.
19. Quoted in Martz, *Colombia*, p. 319.
20. Lieuwen, pp. 168–69.

installations of the nationalized company, ECOPETROL, and threatened to lead to further disturbances. The armed forces are not necessarily mere *instruments* of government in such instances. They are also among the more insistent of those calling upon the government to take a strong stand against the possible disruption of public order. Indeed it was General Alberto Ruiz Novoa, the Minister of War, rather than the Ministers of Interior or Justice, who signed the decree invoking Article 28 of the constitution in August 1963 that permitted the army to make detentions during the petroleum workers' strike. The armed forces and their representatives in government circles feel that they have a vested interest in public order and in the army's institutional integrity. They mean to act to preserve them, or to force the politicians to do so according to the military's own lights.

Nor is this all. The army, or at least General Ruiz, its chief spokesman in the period of the early 1960s, has interpreted the role of the military more broadly to be that of a unifying force as well as the upholder of public order. Harking back to the original spirit of the 13th of June, 1953, there is some tendency for the military to see itself as a disinterested promoter of national development, above the madding crowd of squabbling politicians. Thus the General has on several occasions charged that pressure groups within Colombia's ruling class are impeding the country's progress and development.[21] In short, the armed forces have been both a prop and a prod to the National Front.

Furthermore, the armed forces as an institution have become an important factor in the actual promotion or retardation of social and political change itself. The military is, first of all, the possessor of skills and facilities which are in short supply in most modernizing nations. This is less crucial a factor than in those developing nations where the structure and techniques of a modern economy and society are relatively weaker than they are in Colombia, but it is nonetheless important. The Colombian army has recognized the contribution it can make to development, General Ruiz declaring that "the vast potential of the military's human resources and its technical and professional know-how must be used productively."[22] By raising the literacy levels of their recruits, many of whom are illiterate or semiliterate campesinos; in implanting in its person-

21. Cf. Ruiz Novoa, *El Gran Desafío,* pp. 94–95.
22. *New York Times,* May 24, 1964, p. 33.

nel some of the technical skills of a modern society, from truck-driving to engineering; and in augmenting the national economic infrastructure through such activities as road-building and airport construction; the armed forces have become a catalyst of at least certain kinds of change.

Long sensitive about its task of quelling disturbances with bullet and bayonet, the military is trying to create a new image by combatting the causes of the violence and social disorders it has been called upon in the past to meet exclusively with force. One major evidence of this new perspective has been the program of *acción cívica-militar* (civic-military action). Something of the sort was begun on a local scale in the eastern plains during the early 1950s. Since about 1960, with advice and some assistance from the United States military mission in Colombia, it has developed into a program of increasing significance. The idea is to employ the army's men, equipment, and skills in projects of social and economic development, especially in those areas currently or in the recent past affected by la violencia. Acción cívica-militar has two main aspects. One comprises short three or four day visits of military teams to selected localities to dispense medical and dental services, distribute gifts of food and other items, and to provide technical advice and services of various kinds. The longer-run projects entail the construction of roads, schools, and health clinics. The objectives of the program are several. One is to assist in the development of remote or backward areas, using available men and equipment. Another is to make the beneficiaries aware of the government's interest in their welfare in the hope they will reject the blandishments of Communists and Fidelistas. Probably most important as far as the army is concerned is to restore the confidence of the citizenry, and especially of the campesinos, in the armed forces (and in the government generally), a confidence weakened during the years of violence. The hope is to deprive the existing bandits or guerrillas of the current or future cooperation of the rural population.

The effects of civic-military action are difficult to judge. The army expresses optimism and feels the results have justified the energies expended. And there are independent indications that in given instances the program has been well-received by the campesinos after some initial suspicion. It is probably also true, however, that scattered localities and not the countryside taken as a whole have been measurably touched by the program. There does seem to have been some change in the campesinos' attitude toward the army, but this may be as much the consequence of the fact that the army is no longer killing campesinos as of civic-military action. The effect on the army itself is equally hard to evaluate. Enthusiasm for it has not been universal throughout the ranks. Yet it seems certain that a new spirit of national development and service has permeated important segments of the officer corps. Whether in the long run such functions as civic-military action will prove wholly compatible with the soldier's sense of high mission and "glory" is at the moment an imponderable.[23]

A final sense in which the military has become involved with change is more obviously political, namely, its alignment or potential alignment with particular opposition parties or movements advocating their own solutions for Colombia's modernization.

Alternations in the social composition of the officer corps have been leading in this direction. The military increasingly serves as an avenue for the rise of ambitious members of the middle sectors to positions of power and influence. A substantial but undetermined percentage of officers in the Colombian armed forces still come from elite or upper middle-class families. But many now derive from families owning small farms and, although 70 per cent have rural backgrounds,[24] many officers today also come from the urban middle sectors. Rojas himself is of rural middle-class stock and his regime in part reflected inconformity with the game of politics as played by the elite.

Another factor has been exposure to foreign military contacts, especially those with the military of the United States and of other Latin American nations. Conceptions of a modern military organization in a modern nation, as well as the ideological and political cross-currents playing upon the armed forces in other Latin American countries, are becoming part of the lexicon of Colombian officers. Their view of their relationship to the rest of society is being altered as a result. In the words of one of them, "without doubt it is on the hinge of this spiritually renovated Army that turns the fate of Colombia." [25] Among civilians there are

23. See Major General Alberto Ruiz Novoa, *La Acción Cívica en los Movimientos Insurrecionales* (Bogotá, Imprenta de las Fuerzas Militares, 1963); and "El Nuevo Ejército," in *La Nueva Prensa*, Oct. 23, 1962, pp. 35 ff., for discussions of civic-military action in Colombia.

24. Johnson, *Military and Society*, pp. 105 and 107.

25. Colonel Alvaro Valencia Tovar, quoted in *La Nueva Prensa*, June 22, 1963.

those—even some who were happy to see Rojas' downfall—who look back on the military regime with nostalgia. They flirt with the idea of a reentry into politics by the military for the simple reason that they see no other way to break the power of the traditional elite or to provide the essential strong hand to carry the country through its phase of industrial "take-off."

Among those who today look in some measure to the army are the MDN, Alvaro Uribe of the Línea Dura, and of course General Rojas Pinilla, who has claimed that, despite the hostility of the army's high command, "from major down, almost all of the officers are with me." [26] There is little sign that the officer corps as a whole has been won over to any given ideology or movement. However, the general philosophy and spirit of the non-Left opposition does seem to have influenced some officers, and the years 1964–65 brought a greater civilian uneasiness concerning the political designs of the military than at any time since the first months of the administration of Alberto Lleras. The hope placed by some of the counter-elite groups in the army is expressed by Uribe: "No one is under the illusion that the armed forces are going to make the revolution by themselves. But the army, or a part of it, confronting a crystallized public opinion, a combatant people clear in its purpose—whose formation is the task of the revolutionary leaders—can change from being militaristic with a sense of caste and nothing more, to nationalistic with a sense of the fatherland, with a sense of the people." [27]

There would be a real risk that, even if the military identified with such goals at first, it might well prove more interested, once in power, in increased pay and more rapid promotion than in economic development or social reform. In any case, it would be controlling, and quite possibly not controllable. Given such circumstances, it might neglect or even hamper fulfillment of the tasks prescribed by its ideological mentors. Moreover, the army and change are in some respects incompatible. The necessarily hierarchical structure and authoritarian spirit of the military establishment could well inhibit the army's identification with "disruptive" forces. The increasing professionalization of the armed forces may instill a desire to remain apart from politics altogether. The employment of the armed forces as a brake on the more violent manifestations of the class struggle—

26. Quoted by Eder in "Coup in Colombia," *New York Times*, March 22, 1964, p. 7.
27. Uribe, *El Nacionalismo*, p. 13.

and the tendency of the military to see itself in such a role—further limits their potential association with change.[28]

Yet the stir among the military of new ideologies and political movements; the changes taking place in the composition and training of the officer corps; the army's dedication to the program of civic-military action; and the military's new view of itself as a unifier and stabilizer all mark the emergence for Colombia's armed forces of a new political role. For the present they have given their support to a government of an elite committed to defensive modernization. In the future their attitudes seem likely to develop in a somewhat more nationalistic and reformist direction. At the least, it is doubtful that any Colombian government in the years ahead can fail to take account of the power or the political purposes of the military. Should the party struggle once again get out of hand, should civilian bickering appear to paralyze the nation's development, or if there should loom the danger of real social revolution and a threat to the military's prerogatives, full-scale military intervention would be a virtual certainty. Despite superficial appearances that it is "out of politics," the military, by its action or inaction, will play an important role in determining the course of Colombia's political approach to modernization.

THE CHURCH

If the political role of the Colombian armed forces has been less striking than that of most Latin American military establishments, at least until recently, the role of that other ostensibly non-political pillar of traditional Colombian society—the Roman Catholic Church—has been more pronounced than elsewhere. What Mecham said thirty years ago, in his monumental study of church-state relationships throughout Latin America, that "the Catholic Church has been more tenacious in its hold upon national and civil life in Colombia than in any other Latin-American country," is probably still the case.[29] Colombia has a ratio of one priest per

28. Thus in February 1963 army troops were used to protect trucks transporting cement from a struck plant at Santa Barbara in the department of Antioquia to the industrial center of Medellín. The result was a clash between soldiers and workers in which several workers were killed.

29. J. Lloyd Mecham, *Church and State in Latin America* (Chapel Hill, N.C., University of North Carolina Press, 1934), p. 141. See Mecham, chapter 5, for an outline of the historical role of the Church in Colombia. He includes the text of the Concordat of 1887.

3,650 Catholics, a proportion of clergy exceeded in South America only by Chile, Ecuador, and the Guianas. The observance of the formal acts of religion also seems to be higher than in most other Latin American countries.[30]

The Church in Colombia emerged from the Wars of Independence somewhat weakened by its loss of the protection of the Spanish Crown, by the uncertainties of republican life, and by the spirit of liberalism which informed the movement for independence. It nevertheless retained an extremely powerful position, including the ownership of large tracts of land and a virtual monopoly over education. Prelates occupied important administrative positions in the early years of the republic and the clergy constituted from one quarter to one third of the early republican congresses.[31] Liberal governments during the years 1850–80 greatly reduced the Church's dominant position. Indeed for a time the situation was almost one of state control of the Church. During this period ecclesiastical property was confiscated, with the exception of actual Church buildings and residences of the clergy; religious orders were abolished; cemeteries were secularized; marriage was declared to be an obligatory civil ceremony; and the government exercised a so-called "inspection of cults." The Church's hold over education was loosened. The Jesuits were expelled from the country (then readmitted during a brief Conservative interregnum, expelled again by the Liberals, and finally, under the Conservatives, invited to return once more).

At the instance of President Rafael Núñez the Church was restored to its privileged position in the Constitution of 1886 and by the concordat concluded with the Holy See in 1887. The Church did not regain its former lands, though it was granted a small state subsidy in lieu of their recovery and was accorded the right to acquire other lands in the future. It was once again given wide jurisdiction over education, marriage, and its own internal affairs, and it was assured the special protection of the state. At the same time, other religions were to be tolerated (which was on the whole interpreted to mean they could engage only in private worship) and the Church was nominally disestablished. The president of Colombia was to have a voice in nominations for vacant bishoprics and archbishoprics.

30. *Special Warfare Handbook*, pp. 182–83.
31. Carey Shaw, Jr., "Church and State in Colombia, as Observed by American Diplomats, 1834–1906," *Hispanic American Historical Review*, 21 (Nov. 1941), 579.

The constitutional codification of 1936 and a revision of the concordat in 1942 introduced some modifications, but neither fundamentally altered church-state relations. Essentially, the Colombian Church has held onto the position it regained in the 1880s, although new groups and forces are competing for a share in such fields as education which the Church once preempted.

Why the Church has retained such a powerful hold in Colombia is a question that admits only of a speculative answer. Mecham notes that prelates and royal officials often engaged in struggles for control in the colony of Nueva Granada and that the former generally proved victorious. This suggests that the Church may have been stronger and more firmly woven into the social and political fabric in the future Colombia than elsewhere in the New World. However, the comparative evidence for such a proposition is not at hand. The Church's success in the years after 1886 may be related to the rise of the Antioqueños, who have been simultaneously among the leading modernizers and among the most Church-oriented of Colombians. Modernization and support for the position of the Church to this degree coincided, rather than conflicted. The political dominance of the Conservatives after about 1886 and until 1930 is probably also relevant, guaranteeing the Church's reacquired position at a time when its privileges were being substantially modified elsewhere in Latin America. Whatever the cause, the role of the Church has been at least as important, and the issue of its status at least as sharply drawn, as in almost any other country of the hemisphere.

One concomitant of the struggle during the nineteenth century over the appropriate role for the Church in Colombian society was the intimate involvement of the Church in partisan politics. It would be too much to say that the Conservative party was nothing more than the political vehicle of the Church. Yet the Church did very closely identify the defense and aggrandizement of its interests and doctrines with the Conservative party. The connection outlasted the Liberals' tacit acceptance in 1910 of the church-state relationship embodied in the Constitution of 1886. The Church continued to exercise strong and direct influence in the selection of Conservative candidates for the presidency. It was in fact the failure of the archbishop of Bogotá, Ismael Perdomo, to perform this role effectively prior to the election of 1930 that led to Conservative division and Liberal victory in that year. The archbishop had answered a letter from the Conservatives in Congress certifying that all candidates under consideration were good Catholics and would receive Church support. When the party divided over two candidates, he first threw the support of the Church to one and then, hoping to heal the division and head off a Liberal victory, to the other. Even then he seemed to vacillate. The result was an appearance of indecision on the part of the Church and the defeat of the two Conservatives by the single Liberal in the race.[32] The clergy also continued to preach from the pulpit and admonish from the confessional that a vote for the Liberal party was sinful.[33] An attempt by a prominent Liberal leader to defend his party from the charge in a pamphlet entitled "On why Colombian political Liberalism is not a sin" was made prohibited reading for Catholics and was subsequently placed on the Index by the Vatican.[34]

Such attitudes intensified after certain reductions in Church influence, notably in education, were written into the constitutional reforms of 1936.

Remaining unresolved, in spite of the Papacy's agreement to certain modifications of the 1887 concordat, was the underlying issue of whether Colombia was to be officially Catholic and the Church the bulwark of the social order. By the late 1940s this issue had once again become a facet of the struggle between Conservatives and Liberals. Since the Church regarded the Liberal party, or at least very important elements of it, as anti-Church and as virtually Communist, it could but oppose that party by all means at hand. This animosity was heightened by the Bogotá riots of 1948, when the burning of churches and convents and, in a few cases, the killing of priests revealed a latent hostility against the Church among the urban masses. This was the Spain of 1936 all over again in the view of many of the clergy.[35]

Whiteford notes that in Popayán during this period the clergy threat-

32. See Salamanca, *La República Liberal, 1,* for an account of this episode and relevant documents. Salamanca is a Conservative opposed to Church involvement in politics.

33. Cf. e.g. *Los Partidos en Colombia,* p. 16 and passim.

34. Salamanca, *Los Partidos,* p. 197.

35. See Guzmán et al., *2,* 369, for a list of some of the attacks on the Church, both on its edifices and on its personnel, at the time of the bogotazo. See also Nieto Rojas, *La Batalla contra el Comunismo,* esp. chapters 5, 6, 10, 11 and Appendix for a relevant discussion and documents. The Conservative party officially accepted the 1942 revision of the concordat in 1949; see *Los Programas Conservadores,* p. 81.

ened lower-class Liberals again and again with excommunication if they voted for their party.[36] Prior to the 1949 elections several bishops issued pastorals which in effect prohibited the faithful from voting for Liberal candidates who might "wish to implant civil marriage, divorce, and co-education, which would open the doors to immorality and Communism." [37] The Church had found the advent of a Conservative regime in 1946 congenial to its purposes. The government acted to discourage Protestant missionary activity, which had begun to assume alarming proportions in the eyes of the Church (although a recent estimate places their Colombian numbers at only 46,000 [38]), and it looked with benevolence on the UTC, newly formed with clerical advice and assistance. With the accession of President Gómez in 1950 the Church's role in public education was extended and the clergy initially gave Gómez their enthusiastic support.

In the years of intermittent civil strife that began in the late forties a number of clerics, especially at the level of the parish priest, condoned Conservative attacks on Liberals. Some encouraged or even led those attacks. Since Liberals were identified by many priests as "heretics" and "enemies of the Church," such involvement was not surprising. In some communities parish priests denied the sacraments to Liberals and Liberals were refused burial in the local cemetery. The matter was complicated by the fact that in some localities it was Protestantism rather than Liberalism that was the target. Because most Protestants were also Liberals (though the reverse was of course not the case), the line between religious persecution and political violence became at times difficult to draw.[39]

For the most part the higher ranks of the Church hierarchy did not encourage or direct attacks on either Liberals or Protestants, although their chastisement of those who did seldom went beyond verbal admonition. The real difficulty lay with the position of the parish priest. He often felt threatened by anticlerical Liberalism and by the appearance of Protestant missionaries, who were often not reluctant to depict the priest and the Church as reactionary and corrupt and to engage in what could only be regarded in a Catholic community as inflammatory proselytizing. Occa-

36. Whiteford, *Two Cities*, p. 116.
37. Quoted in Martz, *Colombia*, p. 84.
38. Ibid., p. 140.
39. See ibid., pp. 139–43, for a balanced treatment of the alleged "persecution of Protestants" during this period.

sional attacks on the clergy by Liberals at the time of the bogotazo and
later added a further, frightening aspect in some areas to the situation of
the parish priest.[40]

If the Church has frequently concerned itself with the sometimes violent contest between Colombia's two traditional parties, it has in turn been
used by them to serve ends of partisan advantage. In the nineteenth century the Liberals played on fears of the economic and social power of the
Jesuits. Although since 1910 the Liberals as a whole have felt that the rak-
ing up of the coals of religious controversy could only harm their party,
most Liberals, given the choice, would still favor a lessening of Church influence in spheres of Colombian life they regard as secular. Some elements
of the Conservative party have meanwhile continued to make use of the
religious issue for political purposes. One foreign Catholic observer commented some years ago that, "We find a situation in which the Conservative party has taken unto itself more or less the defense of . . . the Catholic
religion. And has done it primarily, not for the interests of the Catholic
Church, or the propagation of the faith, but for the preservation of the
Conservative party . . . And they find themselves very, very frequently in
the position of holding to an idea . . . which is completely out of harmony
with the expression of the Church itself." [41]

It may be surmised that it was to the interest of the Conservatives to
keep the issue alive as one means by which they could hold onto the mass
of their own partisans against the appeals to economic and social betterment which the Liberals have seemed better able to make. Perhaps the
outstanding instance concerned the 1942 revision of the concordat negotiated by a Liberal administration. Laureano Gómez attacked it as an
attempt to destroy the Catholic faith, although the archbishop of Bogotá
publicly supported the agreement. By his tactics Gómez, dubbed "more
Catholic than the Pope," eventually alienated a portion of the Church
hierarchy, who in turn supported Gómez' factional rivals within the Conservative party when his time of crisis came in 1953.[42]

Whether as partisan itself, or instrument of partisanship, the Church's

40. Cf. Guzmán et al., 2, 369.

41. Richard Pattee, "Our Catholic State in Latin America," pp. 5–6, quoted in
Burnett, "The Recent Colombian Party System," p. 62 (Burnett's translation).

42. For the dispute between Gómez and the Church see *Laureano Gómez y la
Jerarquía Eclesiástica;* and Arciniegas, *State of Latin America*, p. 163. The Church
itself was deeply split in the controversy.

involvement in politics tended to nullify its potential role as pacifier in the years when Colombia cried out for someone to save the nation from the mounting wave of political violence. The Church was quite frequently identified, through word or deed, with acts of violence on the Conservative side. These "left their stain on the only spiritual and political power that might have been able to disarm the government and the parties. In place of religious and human reasons, the Church preferred 'political reason.' " [43]

In addiiton to its role as political partisan, the Church in Colombia has historically been a principal support of the traditional social system and of traditional values. The defense of its own institutional interests, the nature of its doctrines and internal organization, and its relationships to its flock have all led in that direction. The social origins of the members of the clergy have worked to the same end. Throughout most of Colombian history it was customary for at least one son of aristocratic families to enter the clergy. Although this is much less true today, a recent study shows that clerical vocations come preponderantly from the upper class and from the upper and middle reaches of the middle sectors. In the higher ranks of the Church hierarchy the proportions are greater still. Further confirming this attachment to the traditional order have been the rural origins of the majority of Colombian priests, even though a higher percentage of them derive from urban areas than is true of the population as a whole. [44]

The Church's power in Colombian society rests in part on such ties of the Colombian clergy to the elite. The Church's former position as a large landowner worked in a similar direction. The Church maintains an educational system of its own and in practice is accorded substantial control over the content of public education. Texts are subject to its approval; all schools must give Catholic religious instruction; and in some communities priests serve as educational inspectors. A majority of the country's secondary schools are owned and operated by the Church. [45] The Church and lay organizations affiliated with it are very active in the support and maintenance of charitable activities such as hospitals, soup kitchens, and orphanages. Many of these activities receive government support, especially in

43. A. García, *Gaitán*, p. 335.

44. See Pérez Ramírez, *El Problema Sacerdotal*, esp. chapters 6 and 7, concerning the social composition of the Colombian clergy.

45. Cf. *Anuario de la Iglesia Católica en Colombia, 1961* (Bogotá, Centro de Investigaciones Sociales, 1961), p. 961.

the form of food, clothing, and other supplies. Church officials are customarily appointed to important government commissions, whether they be to study agrarian reform or to bring an end to the violence. Clergymen take part in most public ceremonies. Church influence is also exercised through organizations such as the UTC which are primarily secular in nature but receive advice and other assistance from the Church or one of its religious orders. The Church maintains a periodical press, including a weekly semi-official newspaper, *El Catolicismo;* a radio network; as well as other organs of publicity and dissemination.

The influence of the Church is felt in still other ways which are tied more directly to its religious function. The confessional, the pulpit, the potential threat of excommunication are powerful controls. This is especially true among the campesinos, for many of whom the Church is one of the few sources of solace and beauty in a life of poverty and drudgery. The Church is the earthly representative of a Deity who in the eyes of the campesino controls life, health, and the bountifulness of his fields. The very nature of the Church—or at least the way in which the campesino looks at God and at the Church—reinforces attitudes of fatalism and passivity which are at the same time a quite natural reflection of the campesinos' position in society. In the small communities of rural Colombia the priest is often (although not always) held in considerable respect as an individual. Not only is he the representative of the Church and ultimately of God, but he is likely to be the man with the most education and one of the few who can act as a kind of mediator between the community and the outside world. His advice, on matters personal or political, is quite likely to be sought and heeded.[46] The impact of the Church on the lives of Colombians extends through the lay societies organized to perform such functions as maintaining the altar and organizing the celebration of religious holidays. Finally, the Church is the institution which par excellence embodies the traditional values of Colombian society and with which is identified the essence of being Colombian. It is practically the only institution which unites all classes, and in its strictly religious dimension transcends all parties.[47] It is the most generalized channel of communication

46. For the role of the Church in the life of the Colombian campesino see Fals Borda, *Peasant Society,* chapter 14; Pearse and Rivera, *La Tenencia de la Tierra,* esp. pp. 107–08; CIS, *Estudios sobre . . . Sonsón;* and Universidad Nacional, *Factores Sociales,* esp. p. 80.

47. Fals Borda, *Educación en Colombia,* p. 8.

in many of the country's small towns and rural districts,[48] and even in a sense for the country as a whole.

The Church has been and remains an axial institution of Colombian society. It has been a major bulwark of the traditional Colombian political system and of elite rule. It has engaged in the struggle for power between Colombia's two historic parties in an effort to defend what it has regarded as its institutional prerogatives. The contemporary Church still fulfills these traditional roles, but it does so in a substantially modified way. Instead of symbiotic alignment with the Conservative cause, the Church has come to act the political mediator and pacifier; instead of an unalterable status quo, it has come to advocate a limited measure of social reform.

From the very inception of the recent era of violence there were voices in the Church seeking to mollify the political tempers of Colombians. On the eve of the 1949 elections the archbishop of Bogotá and primate of Colombia called for a halt to the violence, urging mutual respect among men of all parties and ordering the clergy not to give their support to either of the contenders: "We order all priests under our jurisdiction . . . to abstain totally from furthering, encouraging, or supporting, directly or indirectly, all activities designed to obtain by means of violence or deception the accomplishment of determined political aims." [49] Similarly, in mid-1952 the Church cooperated in an abortive "Crusade for Peace" sponsored by the government of Acting President Roberto Urdaneta Arbeláez.[50] Individual priests often stood out in heroes' roles in their attempts to curtail political violence in their parishes. The account of Father Fidel Blandón Berrío in *Lo Que el Cielo No Perdona*, relating his experiences in western Antioquia in the early 1950s, describes one noteworthy instance.[51] Another priest tells of the following incident:

It was approximately eleven o'clock at night . . . when a loud shout brought me to the window of the parish house. . . . I saw a group of some fifty people shouting "vivas" to the Conservative party and the Catholic religion . . . when I heard them shout "Long live the Catholic faith," I called out at the top of my voice from the window: "Listen to

48. Cf. CIS, *Estudios sobre . . . Sonsón*, p. 45.
49. Quoted in Arciniegas, *State of Latin America*, pp. 167–68.
50. See Martz, pp. 83 and 143.
51. Blandón Berrío, *Lo Que el Cielo no Perdona*.

me, all you men and citizens of Rionegro: as a priest I forbid you to
shout 'Long live the Catholic faith,' for the Catholic religion does not
sanction violence." [52]

Such attitudes reflected genuine concern on the part of some higher
Church authorities and individual members of the clergy for the doctrines
of their faith and the welfare of their flocks. In part, such stands likewise
acknowledged that violence and chaos, once unleashed, may take unwonted directions and pose a danger to an institution like the Church.

With attempts by a military regime and then by a two-party coalition to
put "country above parties," the period since 1953 has witnessed a pronounced effort, particularly on the part of the higher clergy, to act the
peacemaker. Bishops and priests have frequently been members of "committees of pacification" in the countryside. The attitude of the Church has
without doubt had an important influence in tempering partisan spirits,
thereby assisting in the political experiment of the National Front. With
any possible Liberal danger to the Church blunted by the requirements of
political coalition, and with the basic social order clearly in need of shor-
ing up, the Church has felt it both possible and necessary to shelve its role
as partisan to concentrate on that of political neutral and pacifier. Rather,
the two roles now coincide, since the chief opponents of the Church are
also enemies of the National Front. To support the latter and to promote
its goal of political peace thus constitutes one and the same endeavor.

The needs of the Church and the government have been reciprocal.
Those who took the lead in the formation of the new bipartisanship acted
quickly to eliminate the clerical issue as a ground of discord and to confirm the Church as a foundation-stone of the coalition. In the pact of
March 20, 1957, it was agreed that the norms set forth in the existing constitution and in the revised concordat were those which should govern
church-state relations in Colombia. The constitutional reform approved
by plebiscite in December 1957 subsequently contained in its preamble
the explicit acknowledgment that one of the bases of national unity was
the recognition by both parties "that the Catholic, Apostolic and Roman
Religion is that of the Nation, and that as such, the public powers will
protect it and will see that it is respected as an essential element of the
social order." In the Program of the National Front drawn up in 1962 the

52. Quoted in Arciniegas, *State of Latin America,* p. 182.

Church's activities in the social and educational fields were expressly accorded "the sympathy and protection of the State." [53] As a matter of fact, the National Front has represented a political gain for the Church in at least two ways. One is that the Colombian constitution once again declares the Catholic religion to be that of the nation and grants it special protection, a status which had at least nominally been denied it by Alfonso López' constitutional codification of 1936. The second is that not just the Conservative party, but Liberals as well, have affixed their seals to documents affirming the position of the Church in Colombian society. No longer is the Church forced to be partisan, at least as between the two traditional parties, in defense of its interests. In recent political campaigns it has not been unusual to have Church dignitaries sitting on the same platform with leaders of the Liberal party.

Nevertheless, at the local level, there has been some continued involvement of priests in the factional struggles of Conservatives and in opposition to candidates of the MRL, which some clerics regard as Communist. Whether the deep passions aroused in the past by the religious issue ever reassert themselves will depend on the future course of partisan political competition and the nature of any future assault on the structure of social and political power in Colombia. The Communists and others on the Left have shied away from frontal attacks on the Church, recognizing its strength and influence. Yet the Church is one of the chief supports of an order of things which any truly radical movement must seek ultimately to destroy. It would necessarily once again become embroiled in partisan politics—albeit with new dimensions and with different contestants—should there arise a serious challenge to the existing social and political system.

The attitude of the Colombian Church toward social change has undergone significant alteration as well. A few of the clergy, though generally not those occupying positions of leadership in the Church, have developed a distinctly reformist and anti-elite orientation. More important for the moment is fresh thinking about social action, more in line with the Colombian elite's paternalistic reform, among the Church hierarchy, as well as among others in the Church such as the Jesuits.

Undoubtedly the new outlook represents the adaptation of a basically

53. *Programa del Frente Nacional,* p. 17.

conservative institution to conditions challenging its survival. Moreover, within the last few years, and especially since the reign of Pope John XXIII, stimulus has come from the Vatican to move in new directions. Both churchmen and lay observers cite this factor more frequently than any other in accounting for the incipient signs of a new spirit in the Colombian Church. Another reason for such changes, though of lesser importance at present, may be a gradual transformation in the class origins of those entering religious vocations. The Catholic clergy, like the army, has always provided a certain security, and even a degree of social mobility, for sons of poor and middle-class families. If, as is impressionistically the case, fewer sons of the upper class are now entering the priesthood, that fact could account partially for shifts in attitudes within the Church.

The most striking and quite possibly the most significant aspect of the Church's evolving orientation toward social problems is its position on agrarian reform. Although individual clerics have sometimes questioned specific applications of Law 135 of 1961, the Church has placed itself squarely behind it; in fact representatives of the Church formed part of the committee which structured the law. The Church has made it clear that it regards the concentration of landownership in a few hands as one of the keys to the country's social ills and that in its view the more equitable division of the land is an urgent matter. *El Campesino,* the weekly publication of *Acción Cultural Popular,* a Church-affiliated organization which directs its appeal particularly to the Colombian rural dweller, carries considerable material on the activities of the Colombian Institute of Agrarian Reform (INCORA). Other Church organizations have conducted seminars and promoted research on the subject, and some of the clergy have taken on the task of attempting to convince landowners of the need for change in regions where resistance to the reform is particularly stubborn.

The Church has sought to extend modernization, and at the same time its own influence, in rural areas through the radiophonic schools of Acción Cultural Popular. Formally founded in 1949 under the leadership of Father José Joaquín Salcedo, Acción Cultural Popular publishes *El Campesino,* which in 1963 claimed a circulation of more than 100,000.[54] It likewise conducts extension courses, and distributes textbooks and other educational materials. Its central activity, however, has been the radiophonic

54. *El Campesino,* June 30, 1963.

schools known as Radio Sutatenza. This is a network which now extends throughout most of Colombia and broadcasts educational, religious, and cultural programs which are in turn coordinated with classes conducted by teaching assistants in the various communities. Radio Sutatenza distributes small radio sets on which only its frequency can be picked up. Assisted by the Colombian government and UNESCO, its efforts have been centered on the teaching of the tools of literacy and improved techniques of agriculture and home care to the campesinos. It claimed to have made literate 154,000 persons in the years 1954–60 and to have educated some 210,000 persons in better rural living during the same period.[55] In 1962 891 Colombian municipios were reported to have functioning classes based on the radio programs, with 215,309 matriculated and 29,537 made literate during the year.[56] Claims probably exceed real achievements, however, which are in any case difficult to measure.

Again in the countryside, the Church has given its support to, and priests have participated in, community action projects. In some areas, including Sumapaz, where campesino radicalism has been strong, it has engaged in a kind of religiocivic action, sometimes in conjunction with the army and comparable in its own way to the latter's acción cívica-militar.[57]

The Church is also coming to recognize the desirability of focusing more of its attention than heretofore on the social problems of urban centers. Charitable programs such as the *Minuto de Dios,* designed to create model barrios on the basis of community labor, has been one approach. A more extensive, if more indirect attempt to confront urban problems has been the support and encouragement given the UTC by the Church, and especially by the Jesuits. The result has been the orientation of the largest Colombian labor confederation to Catholic social doctrine and to some extent to Catholic political purposes.

Other indications of changed attitudes within the Colombian Church and among devout laymen include the establishment of two social science research centers in Bogotá (one, the *Centro de Investigaciones Sociales,* is the Latin American center of the Church's International Office of Social Research; another, the *Centro de Investigación y Acción Social,* is a Jesuit

55. Concerning Radio Sutatenza, see *Anuario de la Iglesia, 1961,* pp. 1125–51; and Camilo Torres and Berta Corredor, *Las Escuelas Radiofónicos de Sutatenza—Colombia* (Bogotá, Centro de Investigaciones Sociales, 1961).

56. *Anuario de la Iglesia, 1962,* p. 377.

57. Cf. Guzmán et al., 2, 435–36.

entity); the formation of a Catholic employers' organization with social objectives, the Social Orientation of Colombian Employers (*Orientación Social de Dirigentes de Empresas*—osdec); the Church's support for the objectives of the Alliance for Progress; and the encouragement given by a few clerics to the formation of the Christian Social Democratic Party (psdc).

There is impressive evidence that the Colombian Church is no longer content to defend the status quo. At the same time the Church has hardly become an advocate of a sweeping social transformation. Church officials have from time to time spoken out against certain strikes which in their view have been unjustified or have tended to disrupt social order.[58] Politicians of the National Front, even Liberal politicians, continue to look to the Church as "an effective brake against the indiscriminate mania of civic protests, aggressive strikes and every kind of violent pressure on the authorities."[59] There are priests who are dubious about any change which might affect their positions of local power and who label the agents of change "Communists" or "Masons," although most parish priests have tended to support the agrarian reform. Indeed, by participating in the local agrarian reform committees, they may actually enhance their own prestige; they also seem to feel that the activities of Radio Sutatenza strengthen their position and therefore look upon them with favor. In some cases they are more skeptical of communal action since it creates a new focus of local authority. Moreover, the Church's influence in education continues to be largely a conservative one which has probably served to hold back the modernization of the country's educational system. Attitudes of fatalism, Church-sanctioned and inculcated in the poor over centuries, also cannot be rapidly overcome.

Finally, most of the programs of social action supported by the Church are decidedly paternalistic and quite limited in the reforms they seek to promote. What is proposed is change within the established order, and with the voluntary compliance of those who dominate Colombian society.

Insofar as the Church is successful in simultaneously promoting change and confining it within prescribed limits it serves as a legitimizer of defensive modernization. Fals Borda notes, for example, how in the commu-

58. See e.g. the statement issued in the name of the Church hierarchy by a Bishops' Committee on Social Matters, published in *El Espectador,* Aug. 29, 1963.

59. Editorial in ibid., a Bogotá Liberal daily, Aug. 31, 1963.

nity of Saucío a school-building campaign was made acceptable in the eyes of the populace, and the work of outsiders seeking to initiate a program of communal action was eased, by the blessing and public support which the local priest gave to the project.[60] This is also the case on a national scale. It seems certain that Law 135 of 1961 could not have been passed in the face of Church opposition, or perhaps even Church neutrality. The Church's support for the program is one of the reasons why virtually everyone in Colombia feels he must pronounce himself for it in principle, even though he may oppose it in practice. Yet while the Church's promotion of modernization has taken place within the framework of the prevailing social and political system and has in fact acted to stabilize that system, there is some danger for the Church, as for any established institution seeking limited change, that expectations may be aroused (for instance, through the radiophonic schools or the promise of agrarian reform) without providing for their effective satisfaction.[61]

One of the Church's most pressing problems arises from its own internal life. This is the scarcity of priests, and the relatively low level of training and even moral behavior of some, especially in the more remote rural areas, where some parishes are visited only occasionally by a priest. Part of the shortage is met by the infusion of European clergy: altogether perhaps half of the Colombian clergy is of foreign origin, although most foreigners are concentrated in the religious orders and not in the secular clergy. This is a potentially dangerous situation in view of gradually rising currents of nationalistic feeling; religious orders staffed largely by aliens are attempting to increase the number of Colombian vocations in recognition of that fact. Meanwhile a deficiency in the number and the quality of the clergy, despite the Church's impressive strength on many scores, is a factor which cannot be ignored in assessing its future in Colombia.

Given the increasing urbanization of Colombian society, the rationalism and secularism which accompany modernization, and the rise of competing groups and ideologies, it seems doubtful that the Church can maintain indefinitely its accustomed privileged position. Yet it may be that, at least for the short run, the social and political role of the Colombian Church will rather take on a new guise than diminish in importance. The sagacity with which it has adapted itself to the conditions of political coalition and

60. Orlando Fals Borda, *Facts and Theory*, p. 29.
61. Cf. C. Torres and Corredor, *Las Escuelas*, pp. 53–54.

paternalistic reform as epitomized by the National Front—indeed the extent of its role in the very creation and sustenance of this approach to consensus and change—should not be underestimated. If the National Front, or some other political embodiment of Colombia's modernizing elite, succeeds in leading the country through the next two or three decades of rapid development, and especially if a political movement should develop which effectively promotes the application of Catholic doctrine to contemporary problems, the Church may be assured a place of permanent political influence in Colombia.

In many respects the institutional goals of the Church, as those of the Colombian military, remain as they have been. It is the environment in which these traditional institutions must operate, and their perception of that environment, that have been altered. Both the Church and the army have moved away from their respective earlier roles of close partisan identification and apoliticality and have taken active parts in the promotion of bipartisan political order and stability. Both have shifted somewhat from outright defense of the status quo to the support of moderate elite-directed change. The magnitude of their political roles has not diminished—as far as the army is concerned it has actually increased. Rather, the relationship of the Church and the army to the social and political systems has undergone modification. At present both are aligned with the National Front and with the latter's objectives of consensus and modernization under the aegis of the elite. Yet there are signs, particularly in the army but also in the Church, that this may not always be the case, and that both the institutional goals and ideological predispositions of their leaderships may in the future lead them to avoid any overcommitment to the cause of the Colombian upper class.[62]

Of course, few institutions, and certainly neither the Colombian Church nor the Colombian military, are monolithic in opinion or action. The armed forces are comprised of four services, many commands, many ranks, men from different social levels and political backgrounds. The Church, for its part, includes a number of semi-autonomous religious orders, while

62. There are indications, for example, that some Colombian landowners blame the Church for its role in agrarian reform; interview with Father Miguel Angel González, a Jesuit associated with the Centro de Investigación y Acción Social, Bogotá, Aug. 22, 1963.

the problems and concerns of the parish priest are not the same as those of an archbishop. Within each institution there is a range of views regarding the social and political order. Despite the Church's long association with the Conservative party, for example, there are a number of priests whose family origins and present inclinations align them with the Liberals. Some churchmen supported the Rojas regime actively at the start; others preferred continued allegiance to Gómez. Some military officers early gave their full allegiance to the National Front; others conspired against it; still others now seek to infuse it with a greater dynamism. In the future we can expect continuing differences within both the Church and the military over the political strategies they are to pursue. Obviously, the outcome will be an important determinant of the success of Colombia's efforts at government by a modernizing elite.

12

INTEREST

ASSOCIATIONS

INTEREST GROUPS AND THE POLITICAL SYSTEM

If Tocqueville is right that in an egalitarian society associations stand in lieu of powerful private individuals, the reverse tends to be true of a quasi-feudal society.[1] The principle of hierarchy, rather than that of free association, has permeated Colombian political culture and most social relationships. In traditional Colombian society interests were articulated by the powerful few on behalf of their regions, their families, or their clienteles by means of personal, particularized relationships with those in authority. The number of interests that could not thus be dealt with and that were not subsumed by those of kinship or locale were few. There was in such a context both little need and little possibility for the growth of specialized associations organized on an occupational or economic basis.

With the increasing diversification of the economic and social structures, and with the sheer growth in the numbers of the politically aware, the traditional patterns for the expression of interests proved inadequate. Moreover, the substantial increase in state intervention in Colombian economic life during the 1930s and 1940s, including the proliferation of credit and regulatory agencies, led to the creation of economic associations for the protection and promotion of the mutual interests of those affected by state policy. Concurrently the governments of Alfonso López were fostering the growth of the labor movement. This in turn aroused labor's competitors in the political marketplace to organize themselves.

Many of the older, more informal means of urging demands upon gov-

1. Tocqueville, *Democracy in America*, pp. 376 ff.

ernment of course linger. It is even probable that these continue to be cumulatively more important than organized, associational interests. Personal, family, and client relationships still carry much of the burden of channeling claims to government. Even where an interest group has been constituted to perform such a function the personal connections of its president with officials of the government, or their common membership in a social club, may be the determinant of whether the views of the group receive due consideration. Nonetheless, it is certainly true that a wide array of interest associations has come to *complement* the traditional modes for the articulation of interests, and that many of them are listened to *qua* organized interest groups, regardless of the personal connections of their officers with bureaucrats or party politicians. Their advent and multiplication clearly have added a new dimension to Colombian politics and must affect any assessment of Colombia's current and future approach to change.

A very few organizations which could be classed as associational interest groups—groups expressly formed to advance the interests of their members—date from the latter two or three decades of the nineteenth century. The *Sociedad de Agricultores,* founded in 1871, was one; another was the Society of Engineers (*Sociedad de Ingenieros*), formed in 1887. Still others, including some labor unions, were founded during the early decades of this century. But most of them were transient, were sporadic in operation, and had scant political impact. The formation of the Colombian Federation of Coffee Growers (*Federación de Cafeteros de Colombia*) in 1927 presaged a new era of group organization. However, it was the mid-1930s, with the organization of the Confederation of Colombian Workers (CTC) and of the short-lived but powerful and highly political Employers' National Economic Association (*Asociación Patronal Económica Nacional*—APEN), that saw the pronounced growth in the numbers and influence of interest associations in Colombia.

The ensuing thirty years have witnessed their expansion into many areas of Colombian life. In 1963 a Permanent Committee of Productive Associations included some thirty associations or federations of bankers, insurance companies, manufacturers, construction companies, pharmaceutical manufacturers and distributors, hotel owners, cotton growers, coffee growers, merchants, and farmers.[2] Many had branches in various depart-

2. *El Espectador,* Aug. 30, 1963, p. 13.

ments and municipalities. Not included in the list of members were still other "production" associations—sugar growers, rice growers, cattlemen, transport entrepreneurs—nor the many labor and professional associations; groups such as Catholic Action and veterans' organizations; and the thousands of municipal or district improvement committees distributed throughout the country which often have as one of their objectives the extraction of favors from city or departmental governments.

The three politically most powerful of Colombian interest groups are probably the Federation of Coffee Growers, the National Association of Manufacturers (*Asociación Nacional de Industriales*—ANDI), and the National Federation of Merchants (*Federación Nacional de Comerciantes* —FENALCO).

The oldest of these, the Coffee Growers Federation, is likewise the most highly organized. In addition to a national committee and a congress which ordinarily meets every two years, there are municipal and departmental committees of the Federation in every place in the country where significant amounts of coffee are raised. The central offices of the Federation are in Bogotá and house a substantial administrative and technical staff headed by a general manager. The broad objective of the Federation is the defense of the interests of those who grow and sell coffee. More specifically, it concerns itself with the stabilization of coffee prices, both in the internal and the international markets; with the rationalization of production; with the expansion of coffee markets abroad; and with the improvement in the standard of living of the coffee grower.

The ANDI, twenty years after its founding in 1944, had branch offices in nine cities and had affiliated to it 540 enterprises employing 150,000 workers.[3] The ANDI has become Colombia's leading organizational advocate of free enterprise. In its own words, it seeks

to represent and defend the industrial interests of Colombia, fostering the development of existing industries and preparing the way for the creation of new ones and in general for the industrialization of the country; to present before the public powers and the country the needs and aspirations of industry and to defend said aspirations and necessities, in collaboration with the state; to advocate a policy of

3. La Asociación Nacional de Industriales de Colombia, *ANDI—Industria* (Bogotá, 1963), p. 3.

social justice based on realities, for the improvement of the standard
of living of Colombians; to exercise the right of petition before the
legislative and executive powers; to stimulate the production of raw
materials within the country; to work, finally, for the solidarity of the
interests of the group.[4]

In addition, the ANDI provides its members with a number of services including statistical data, research studies, and advice concerning general
economic conditions as well as the problems of specific industries. It also
maintains a department to study and counsel on labor-management
relations.

FENALCO was established in 1945, but its roots go back to 1937 and
the organization of a Bogotá Committee of Commerce. The Bogotá Committee subsequently convoked three national congresses of commerce, the
last of which, held in 1944, proposed the formation of a national organization. FENALCO is composed of merchants and businessmen. Its objectives include "just and equitable" tax policies, strict government control
of contraband, and an attempt to assure that "commerce occupies its due
place in the community."[5] FENALCO is separate from the Chambers of
Commerce; these exist in most sizable Colombian communities but have
no national organization of their own. The Chambers are primarily, although not exclusively, concerned with the defense or promotion of the
interests of their respective communities and are semi-official in nature.

In the techniques they employ and in the functions they perform in the
political system Colombian interest groups in many ways resemble those
of more modernized nations. There are some important differences, however.

Access to government is much more often sought and obtained through
the executive arm than tends to be the case in the United States, for example, and is more formally institutionalized. Lobbyists do exist; representa-
tions are made to congressional committees; threats of electoral retaliation
are not unknown; and some groups conduct fairly extensive public relations campaigns. Yet the focus of attention for most pressure groups is

4. Ibid.; see also *ANDI, Carta Mensual de la Asociación Nacional de Industriales*
for the philosophy and policies of the ANDI.

5. Ivan Serna Vélez, "Origen, Desarrollo y Futuro de FENALCO," *Universitas,*
No. 14 (1958), pp. 148–49.

normally on the actions of the executive branch of government. The central position of the presidency and the bureaucracy in the governmental process, plus the traditions of the administrative state, help to assure that this will be the case.

Furthermore, the government has found it desirable, even necessary, to link more closely to it many of the *gremios*,[6] which often outdistance the relevant agencies of government in technical expertise and administrative capacity. Some interest associations have by law been granted official consultative status with particular ministries or government agencies and some of the professional associations have acted as regulatory instruments for their professions. A government agency such as INCORA has on its board of directors official representatives of groups like the Sociedad de Agricultores, the Association of Cattlemen, rural workers, and Catholic Action. In most cases such representatives are chosen by the President of the Republic from a list submitted by the association in question. All associations must comply with certain legal stipulations in order to function lawfully; all must obtain the approval of the appropriate government office. Some interest associations have indeed been organized at the instance of government in order to provide greater stability to a given sector of the economy or to enable individual firms or landowners to carry out concerted action in their own and in the national interest. Some are partially subsidized by government. Delegations from the relevant ministries usually attend national conferences of the major associations as observers, and conferences are often formally opened by a Minister. Most interest groups expect the cooperation of government (and vice versa) on such matters as improvement of credit facilities, agricultural extension, and industrial training programs. President Valencia several times called meetings of representatives of the so-called *fuerzas vivas* to make recommendations concerning national policy. The proposals of a commission of the fuerzas vivas for the enactment of certain economic and social measures were in fact used as a basis for a series of bills submitted by the government to an extraordinary session of Congress called in early 1965.

The organization which most nearly resembles a semi-official organ of government is the *Federación de Cafeteros*. The Federation was founded

6. Literally meaning guild, the term gremio is used in Colombia to denote any group organized to defend its economic interests, particularly trade and professional associations.

as a private association of those interested in furthering the interests of the coffee industry. Nevertheless, subsequent laws and subsequent actions on the part of the Federation have resulted in a very close relationship with government. Of the eleven members of the national committee of the Federation five are the Ministers of Foreign Relations, Finance, Development, and Agriculture, and the government-appointed manager of the Agrarian Credit Bank. The Superintendent of Banking supervises the financial transactions of the Federation, which include the collection of what is in effect a tax on each bag of coffee exported. The manager of the Federation, who is appointed by the President of the Republic from a list of three names submitted by the Coffee Congress, in turn acts as Colombia's representative in international negotiations seeking to stabilize the price of coffee in world markets. By law all coffee exported from Colombia must meet standards set by the Federation, and coffee may be exported only by the Federation or by a private firm it licenses to do so. The Federation regulates the price to be paid the coffee grower for his crop. Funds of the Federation are even used to make loans to departmental and municipal governments. Such interlocking relationships have been stimulated largely by the great importance of coffee to the Colombian economy and the need to take concerted, officially backed action to promote the interests of Colombian coffee growers and traders in the face of world production and marketing conditions.[7]

Although the extent of the Coffee Federation's ties to government is atypical, the fact of institutionalized collaboration is not. There are at least two factors conducive to the formalization of interest group bonds with government, beyond the mere fact of the importance of the executive. One is that in a developing economy, as well as one which is unusually subject to the vagaries of world markets, it is to the interest of private groups to welcome government assistance and of government to have private associations engage in programs which it would be difficult for government to duplicate with its own personnel and facilities. Too, the government seems reluctant to countenance full autonomy on the part of powerful organizations. Still the impression should not be left that Colombian interest

7. See Holt, *Colombia Today*, chapter 6, for a good description of the activities of the Coffee Federation. For an analysis of the legal position of the Federation and its relationship to the government see Eustorgio Sarría, "Naturaleza jurídico-administrativo de la Federación Nacional de Cafeteros," *La Nueva Economía*, 1 (June 1961), 321–47. See also the organization's publication *Revista Cafetera de Colombia*.

groups are mere creatures of government. Colombian interest groups act *on* government as well as with it to promote their particular interests as against those of other, competing groups.

Compared to the United States, then, a relatively high degree of interest group activity takes place within the institutionalized context of consultative status and other such formalized relationships between government and private associations. There is also a propensity for the particularized, more informal patterns of interest articulation characteristic of traditional Colombian politics to persist even within the framework of modern organizations. The overlap between the leadership of major interest associations and both legislative and high executive office is likewise of relatively great importance in Colombia. Men who are themselves past or present officers of such organizations as the Federation of Coffee Growers, the National Sugar Growers Association, the ANDI, or the professional associations are frequently to be found in high government posts, including the presidency. A former Minister of Agriculture may well later become president of, say, the Cattlemen's Association. The point is not that leadership in interest associations is a primary basis of recruitment to governmental office. Rather, the patterns of Colombian society tend to produce such an overlap and to this degree to fuse the interests of major organized groups with those of government.

There is also a distinct inclination for Colombian interest groups to see themselves as petitioners for the redress of government decisions which adversely affect them, instead of as bargainers over policy before it is formulated.[8] There is considerable stress, in other words, on shielding the group from the consequences of the decisions of the administrative state. The accent is on protest and on the reversal of a ruling, or on the exception of a given group from its application. Relatively great emphasis is placed on preventing the implementation of a decreed rise in gasoline prices, or on demanding exemptions from price freezes or import restrictions. When such claims are denied, there is a further tendency for the group to take direct action in the form of a strike or the withholding of products from market. Though not necessarily *usual* procedure, protest actions of this kind have occurred with increasing frequency in recent years. They are by no means limited to the ranks of labor or students.

8. Cf. Pye, *Politics, Personality, and Nation Building*, for the concept of interest groups as protective associations.

Truck- and bus-line owners, cattlemen, sugar growers, coffee growers, teachers, and judicial employees have been among those resorting to such tactics. Although exceptional in its objectives and its consequences, the civic strike which helped to overthrow Rojas Pinilla, and which included the voluntary closing of many banks and businesses, was a notable example of direct political action on the part of some of the more powerful of Colombian interest associations.

The principal explanation for this kind of group behavior lies in the paucity for certain groups of alternative institutionalized ways of influencing the actions and policies of government. The administrative state, the restricted size of the ruling group, and the political culture generally produce a situation in which participation in decision-making is limited and is highly dependent on connections and deals. "If one does not agree with the decisions of the governing elite and does not have personal influence among them, the chief hope is confrontation of the decision makers with an uproar sponsored by those whom they fear or respect. For Latin Americans the available 'middle way' between submission and revolution is public demonstration." [9]

Implied in the whole pattern of the relationship of Colombian interest groups to government—and partly its cause, partly its effect—is the ineffectiveness of the parties as aggregators of group interests. Despite substantial overlap between officers of organized groups and the leadership of the parties, there is little effort to accommodate and adjust within the framework of the parties the claims on the political system of the various interest associations. As a matter of fact, there are legal prohibitions against the sending of official representatives of interest associations to political conferences and against their subsidization of political parties.[10] One result is that interest groups turn directly to government with claims unprocessed through the filter of the parties. Leaders of the parties have themselves lamented that, "The factors of real power, admirably organized for the defense of their particular interests, prevail over the government and over the parties." [11]

9. E. Wight Bakke, *Students on the March: The Cases of Mexico and Colombia*, Reprint No. 31 (Princeton, N.J., Inter-University Study of Labor Problems in Economic Development, 1964), pp. 209–10.

10. Cf. U.S. Department of Labor, *Labor Law and Practice*, p. 20.

11. El Presbítero Jerónimo (pseudonym for Laureano Gómez), cited in *El Tiempo*, Aug. 27, 1963, p. 2. See also *Plataforma del Frente Nacional*, p. 38.

A final point to be made concerning the behavior of Colombian interest associations is that in a few instances groups act as clients of the parties and are partly dependent on such a relation for the satisfaction of their political demands. The CTC is the leading example, although this is truer of the past than of the present. Generally speaking, this variety of corporatism—where groups replace individuals in the patron-client relationship —has not as yet developed very far in Colombia.[12] In fact, with the inauguration of the National Front, the Federación de Cafeteros amended its statutes to assure political parity in both its national and departmental committees.[13] Where such a relationship does occur, economic or occupational organizations are likely to be highly politicized and partisan. Rigidities are introduced into the processes of interest articulation and aggregation which hamper the evolution of a pluralistic, bargaining political culture.

The contrasts are notable, then, between the behavior of Colombian interest groups and those of a political system such as that of the United States, but they should not be overemphasized. For all the interpenetration of traditional with modern modes of articulating interests, the impressive extent to which those interests have been organized into secondary associations, as well as other of their characteristics, mark them as a significant departure from the more strictly particularistic behavior of the past.

ORGANIZED LABOR IN POLITICS

Organized labor, while an interest group with some attributes similar to those of the rest of the species, merits individual treatment for two reasons. The first is that the nature of its relationship to government, the parties, and the Church sets it off from most other groups in certain key respects. The second is that labor is the principal organized embodiment of a potential Colombian counter-elite. Its strengths, weaknesses, and orientations toward change are therefore important elements in any analysis and assessment of Colombia's political approach to modernization.

Societies of artisans had existed in nineteenth-century Colombia and

12. Not nearly so far as in Italian politics, for example. Cf. Joseph La Palombara, *Interest Groups in Italian Politics* (Princeton, N.J., Princeton University Press, 1964).
13. *Revista Cafetera, 15* (March 1959), 10.

even during colonial days. Politically, they played a part in impelling a series of mid-nineteenth-century reforms under the administration of General Hilario López, and their support helped to bring about a brief dictatorship under General Melo in 1854. For the most part, though, they were little more than mutual aid societies of brief and intermittent duration. By the early decades of this century, however, incipient industrialization was bringing with it the organization of a few genuine labor unions. Several important strikes took place, including that of the banana plantation workers in 1928; and one or two false starts were made on the organization of a national labor confederation, primarily under Communist and Anarcho-Syndicalist auspices. Still, by 1930 hardly 100 unions had been organized, there was no effective national labor organization, and the freedom to organize was not fully guaranteed by law until the following year.[14]

It was during the first administration of President Alfonso López that a permanent national labor confederation, the CTC, was founded. The codification of 1936 meanwhile elevated the right to strike to a constitutional canon and guaranteed to labor the special protection of the state. By December 1938 84,497 Colombians were affiliated with legally recognized unions.[15]

The current membership of the two major Colombian labor confederations, the CTC and the Union of Colombian Workers (UTC), is difficult to assess, since claims are notoriously exaggerated. Thus the CTC in August 1963 reported a total of 439,561 members,[16] probably two or more times the correct figure, particularly if one counts only dues-paying members. United States observers estimate the total Colombian union membership to be anywhere from 150,000 to 500,000, or from 3 to 10 per cent of the labor force (including those employed in agriculture, still a majority of the Colombian labor force). Perhaps the best (and admittedly quite arbitrary) estimate would place the effective (although not necessarily dues-paying) membership of Colombian unions at about 400,000, with the UTC having about 200,000, the CTC about 150,000, and unions not affiliated

14. Justiniano Espinosa, "Veinticinco Años de Sindicalismo," *Revista Javeriana, 51* (Apr. 1959), 112.

15. *Anuario de Estadística, 1938,* p. 143. The CTC was founded in 1936; however, it grew out of an organization formed the year before, the *Confederación Sindical de Colombia;* cf. Alexander, *Communism in Latin America,* pp. 247–48.

16. Cf. the statement of the CTC executive committee in *El Espectador,* Aug. 11, 1963, p. 8A.

with either an additional 50,000. Both the CTC and the UTC are sub-divided into a series of departmental and industrial federations. The strongest affiliates of the CTC are those of Cundinamarca (which includes Bogotá) and Atlántico (Barranquilla). Occupationally, the CTC has had considerable success in the organization of transport workers. The UTC federations with the most affiliates are those of the Valle and Antioquia. The UTC is also strong among textile workers.[17]

Not all Colombian labor has been affiliated to the two major confederations. The Communists formed the CTCI (the Independent CTC) in 1950, but it proved ephemeral. During the Rojas era a Peronist-inspired confederation appeared briefly. More recently, since the expulsion of a number of Communist-controlled unions from the CTC in December 1960, the Communists and their allies have attempted to found a new labor central, the Sindical Confederation of Workers of Colombia (*Confederación Sindical de Trabajadores de Colombia*—CSTC). Although it has succeeded in attracting some support, it has been denied legal recognition. There are in addition a number of independent unions and federations which are affiliated to no national confederation.

Union organization in general has progressed farthest among industrial, petroleum, textile, and transport workers, and among those employed in commercial agriculture, as on the sugar plantations of the Valle del Cauca. But it has not been restricted to industrial or plantation workers. As early as 1932 a National Confederation of Employees (white-collar workers) was founded, and a Central Committee of the Middle Class existed during the late 1950s. Bank clerks, teachers, insurance company employees, airline pilots, and some categories of government employees are among those middle-sector occupations organized into unions, and often quite militant ones. Their pronouncements and publications stress that the problems of their members differ from those of blue-collar workers. Recent years have also seen increased efforts to organize agricultural unions, particularly by the National Agrarian Federation (*Federación Agraria Nacional*—FANAL), a UTC affiliate. UTC organizers have worked in cooperation with government officials, parish priests, and Catholic lay organizations in this endeavor. Their hope is to compete for rural support with the *ligas campesinas* formed under the auspices of the far Left.

17. For an assessment of the strength of organized labor in Colombia by official U.S. sources see U.S. Department of Labor, pp. 22–23.

Although one FANAL spokesman claimed 300 affiliated unions in 1963, the federation is undoubtedly still quite weak and lacks strong leadership.[18] At present, the campesino is the most poorly organized and the least politically effective of anyone in Colombian society.

Feuds among Communists, leftist Liberals, moderate Liberals, and other political factions wracked the CTC from its inception. Yet all recognized their dependence on the Liberal governments of the 1930s and 1940s. The CTC was vociferous in its support of President López, and the unions used the strike weapon on behalf of his legislative program. For its part, the government regularly subsidized the congresses of the CTC, enacted social legislation for labor's benefit, and accorded labor other favors.[19]

When the Liberals lost power in 1946, the CTC went into a precipitate decline which was furthered both by government repression and its own internal dissension. It became evident that the CTC was not truly independent but for all practical purposes was the labor wing of the Liberal and Communist parties, who fought over its control. By the early 1950s the CTC had become a rather pale shadow of its former self, operating in a hostile environment which for a brief time in 1950 even deprived it of its legal status. Under the circumstances what was left of the CTC sought and obtained an accommodation with the Government of the Armed Forces after June 1953, continuing to adhere to this liaison even after most Liberals had broken with Rojas Pinilla.

With the collapse of the Rojas regime the CTC began to recover some of its former strength. However, while the national leadership of the CTC today is mainly Liberal in its political allegiances, and officers of the confederation occasionally run for election on the Liberal ticket or appear on Liberal party advisory committees (as individuals, not as official representatives of the CTC), the earlier ties with the Liberals have not been fully restored. There are no formal links between the two and on occasions

18. Interview with Father Miguel Angel González, Bogotá, Aug. 22, 1963. See also Eugenio Colorado, *El Sindicato y la Comunidad Rural* (Washington, D.C., Unión Panamericana, 1954).

19. Cf. Weiner, *Party Politics in India*, p. 13. "So long as these groups have not organized themselves, they provide a fertile ground for organization by party leaders who seek to direct protest in ways that will gain political benefit for their groups or themselves."

such as the one-day general strike called by the CTC in August 1963 the latter acted contrary to the wishes of the Liberal leadership. Under a bipartisan government the CTC must of course share favor with the UTC. Too close ties between the CTC and the Liberal party might offend the Conservatives. The current relationship also signals changed attitudes and greater confidence on the part of the CTC leadership, who appear reluctant to reinvoke the dangers of past dependence. A number of the officers of the CTC have been exposed in recent years to doctrines of apolitical collective bargaining propounded by the Interamerican Regional Organization of Workers (*Organización Regional Interamericana de Trabajadores*—ORIT) and other advisers associated with the international free trade union movement. At the same time, those currently in control of the Liberal party do not seem particularly anxious to see a revival of the militancy characteristic of the CTC in the years 1936–48. The CTC is therefore somewhat less political and obviously partisan than it once was, and is probably less dependent on the fortunes of the Liberal party.

Colombia's second labor confederation, the UTC, was formed in 1946. It had its origins in several earlier unions and regional federations founded under Church or Catholic lay auspices to combat Marxist and other leftist influences in the CTC.[20] Given favorable treatment by Conservative governments as a counterweight to the Liberal- and Communist-dominated CTC, the UTC flourished as the CTC declined. By the time of the advent of the military government in 1953 the UTC had far outdistanced the CTC to become Colombia's leading labor confederation, a position which it continues to hold despite the latter's revitalization.

The UTC long prided itself on being apolitical. It was looked on in some labor quarters as probably the chief exception in Latin America to the rule that organized labor is usually dependent on government or a particular political party. At least until very recently it asserted its overriding concerns to be economic rather than political; it had the good will of a number of employers who looked on the CTC as "Red" and hoped that the UTC would be less militant.

Such claims concerning the UTC can be partially substantiated. It has no direct ties with any political party; until recently its leaders refrained from running for political office; and it has not been subject to internecine

20. For the origins of the UTC see Espinosa, "Veinticinco Años de Sindicalismo"; and Nieto Rojas, *La Batalla contra el Comunismo,* pp. 262–69.

political disputes to the extent the CTC has. But in reality the UTC has been far from nonpolitical. Its very creation, and its rise to replace the CTC as Colombia's principal labor federation, was in itself a major political event, weakening an important arm of the Liberal party.

Furthermore, the UTC has had reasonably close ties to the Church, especially to the Jesuits. The UTC purports to follow the social doctrines of the Catholic Church. The Jesuits provide advisers to a number of the important unions and federations that comprise the UTC, as well as to the national organization itself. These advisers often serve in a dual spiritual and technical capacity. The Jesuits have been mainly responsible for the operation of a labor training center through which have passed most of the relatively few trained leaders of the UTC. Especially at the outset, Jesuit brothers also played a significant organizational role. An increasing sophistication and feeling of self-sufficiency on the part of the UTC leaders has led to a reduction in that role, although it apparently continues important in the field of rural labor organization. The precise degree of clerical influence on the UTC may be disputed, but both in its statements and its actions it is quite clear that from its inception the UTC has seldom gone counter to at least the broad social and political objectives of the Church, which in turn have often tended to be similar to those of important segments of the Conservative party. The latter, in fact, has explicitly endorsed the kind of "Christian, democratic, apolitical unionism . . . that has been carried on by the Union of Colombian Workers (UTC)." [21]

Again, the UTC has on certain occasions taken action which by any definition must be accounted political. According to the UTC's principal clerical adviser, Father Vicente Andrade, the collaboration of the UTC was crucial on at least two occasions—May 13, 1947, and November 25, 1949 —in breaking strikes, the former a planned national strike of a quasi-revolutionary character, and the second also having political overtones. More recently, in August 1963, the UTC opposed the CTC's call for a one-day work stoppage in protest against alleged government delay in solving certain economic and social problems. "Political strikes," said a UTC spokesman, "and work stoppages of a demagogic type, far from benefiting the workers actually prejudice their interests in that they prepare the way for anarchy and destroy the economy of the nation." [22] Indeed the pri-

21. Directorio Nacional Conservador, *Plataforma, 1957*, p. 30.
22. Cited in *El Espectador*, Aug. 25, 1963, p. 1.

mary role of the UTC as envisaged by Father Andrade is at bottom political: "The unions, besides their private function of regulating relations between workers and employers . . . have another, *much more important* function of social peace and of contributing toward the preparation of a more just social and economic order [based on Catholic principles].[23]

Finally, there is very recent evidence that the UTC is seeking a more openly political role than in the past. Early in 1964 it constituted a political advisory committee, composed of labor leaders, intellectuals, and political figures, which in turn helped the president of the UTC to draw up a May Day message highly critical of government policies. The UTC proclamation likewise affirmed the union's intention of exercising its influence on the selection of candidates for public office.[24] It followed this up in the 1966 congressional elections by sponsoring its own list of candidates (running, in different places, under Conservative and Liberal labels). The UTC has also shown signs of a new combativeness. In the threatened general strike of January 1965, for example, it was the UTC rather than the CTC which pressed hardest for its demands.

It is clear, then, that the UTC has come to have almost as intimate a relationship to politics as the CTC has long had, although the latter has been more directly partisan. Many leaders of both the Liberal and Conservative parties would have been satisfied if the prohibition on union participation in politics in a 1931 law had been strictly observed. However, the growth of unions and the actions of the first López administration made the law virtually a dead letter for many years.[25] In 1946 a decree was issued making it mandatory for a union official to have been actually employed at wages in the industry concerned in order to hold union office. This provision is still a part of the Labor Code. Aimed at Communist political organizers, it met at the time with only partial compliance.[26] Generally adhered to today, it can nevertheless be circumvented

23. My emphasis. Vicente Andrade Valderrama, S.J., "La U.T.C., realidad católica," *Revista Javeriana,* 37 (March 1952), 98–102. For other characterizations of the UTC see Justiniano Espinosa, "Unidad Sindical," *Revista Javeriana,* 52 (Oct. 1959), 302–10; and Espinosa, "Veinticinco Años de Sindicalismo."

24. Richard Eder, "Colombian Unions Seek Ruling Role," *New York Times,* May 3, 1964, p. 27.

25. Cf. Santos, *Una Política Liberal,* p. 29.

26. Cf. Serafino Romualdi, "Labor and Democracy in Latin America," *Foreign Affairs,* 25 (April 1947), 477–89.

to a degree by the device of legal advisers. Although not officers of unions, nor involved in day-to-day union operations, labor lawyers have sometimes played key roles in stimulating (or restraining) strikes with political implications. They provide linkage between the unions and other elements of the political system such as the parties and the Labor Ministry. Diego Montaña Cuellar, a Communist active off and on for two decades as legal adviser to important petroleum workers' unions, is an example of one such non-worker playing a leading role in union affairs. Politicians who are only incidentally labor leaders also occasionally continue to appear in actual union leadership positions.

While some persons who are not themselves workers thus play important roles in the Colombian labor movement, most actual union officers have risen from the ranks. Although the subtler ties of ideological and political loyalties to the Liberal party or to the Church remain strong, the organic links have become tenuous. The unions continue to be dependent on a favorable political climate for their effective functioning, and they are important political actors, but they are no longer mere instruments of the government, or the parties. Despite close links to politics, organized labor in Colombia today more nearly approaches autonomy than is the case in many other developing nations.[27]

Communist and other radical forces seeking to use the Colombian labor movement for revolutionary ends have had over the years some limited success. During most of the period prior to 1950 the Communists held a number of key posts in the CTC. The public positions of the CTC reflected their influence. An example was the resolution approved by the 1938 CTC congress which advocated the nationalization of foreign-owned mines, oil fields, railways, and utilities. During the years 1946–48 CTC militancy reached a peak under the combined influence of Communists and Gaitanistas, and a number of political protest strikes were undertaken which apparently had the ultimate objective of bringing about the collapse of the new Conservative regime.

Today Communist influence continues strong among a few labor groups: petroleum workers; sugar workers in the Valle; the gold miners of Segovia, Antioquia; in a few industrial unions of the Bogotá area; and

27. Cf. e.g. Bruce H. Millen, *Labor Unions and Politics in the Developing Countries* (Washington, D.C., The Brookings Institution, 1963).

elsewhere. Some bank employees' unions have also been subject to penetration by the far Left. But in the main, while there were indications of a
Communist resurgence in the labor movement in the years immediately
following the fall of Rojas, and although the resumed struggle with the
Liberals for domination of the CTC was for a time closely contested, Communist and other radical strength in Colombian labor is not at present
impressive. It does not compare with the halcyon days of two decades
ago.

Since organized labor is looked upon by the Communists as the core
of their potential strength, it is worthwhile speculating on some of the
reasons for their failure thus far to radicalize Colombian labor. It is just
such failure that has induced various revolutionary groups to turn to the
campesinos in their search for a mass base for the hoped-for revolution.

One factor that works against any radical assault on the current
regime is the bond that unites both the leadership and the rank-and-file
of the CTC to the elite-dominated Liberal party. It is noteworthy that only
during the late 1940s, when opposition to the existing social and political
structure was identified with Liberal opposition to a Conservative regime,
did the CTC come close to being revolutionary. Secondly, the rise of the
UTC and its orientation to the Church's approach to social justice has
dampened militancy among a substantial proportion of Colombian labor
and has at the same time divided it, making concerted action more difficult. Thirdly, attitudes persist which anticipate and look with favor upon
the paternalistic behavior of employers. One study of workers in a Medellín textile factory noted that most workers had a genuine regard for the
"great family" constituted by the company and its directors.[28] Since en-
lightened paternalism seems particularly characteristic of Antioqueños,
and since Antioquia has at least until quite recently been the industrial
heart of Colombia, this may have constituted an important brake on the
radicalization of the Colombian working class. Fourthly, workers in the
larger, more stable industries comprise a privileged group relative to the
rest of the lower class and are little inclined to pursue radical political
objectives. It is to them that the nation's social legislation is most effectively applied and their wages often compare favorably with the salaries
of lower middle-class employees. Fifth, there is still considerable dependence on government for continued legal recognition of the union, for

28. CIS, *Compañía Colombiana de Tejidos, S.A., Estudio sobre . . .*, pp. 1 and 153.
See also Savage, *Social Reorganization.*

subsidization of labor congresses, and as arbitrator of strikes. Moreover, several kinds of strikes, including those in the public services, are illegal and may be declared so by the Ministry of Labor.[29] Action by a Liberal government was instrumental in helping to break the Federation of River Transport Workers in 1946; Conservative governments effectively contained or broke unions during the 1950s; and the petroleum workers' federation, FEDEPETROL, was finally forced to retreat in the face of strong government action when a strike threatened damage to the nationalized installations of ECOPETROL in 1963. As long as the will of the government remains firm, it is difficult for the unions successfully to oppose it. Finally, the fact that most Colombian industry has been domestically owned and operated has perhaps made it harder for labor to cohere politically around a common set of nationalistic objectives.

The Colombian labor movement, perhaps as much as any other in Latin America, is oriented toward specific economic gains rather than toward diffuse political action. Collective bargaining and peaceful settlement, rather than industrial warfare for broad social and political goals, has on the whole been the object of the two main labor centrals in recent years.

The two principal Colombian labor organizations have supported the National Front coalition, both as a consensual political arrangement and as an instrument for the modernization of the country. Both the CTC and the UTC have been represented on numerous public bodies dealing with economic and social matters, including the commission which wrote the agrarian reform law of 1961. Their leaders took part in the "summit" conferences of the fuerzas vivas in August 1963 and January 1965. Both confederations have found it possible on occasion to bury political and ideological differences and take joint action for the general welfare. Such an instance was the CTC-UTC committee formed to process some of the housing loans from Alliance for Progress funds. The close ties which both labor centrals have with the ORIT and with the AFL-CIO help to strengthen

29. The definition of public services is a broad one. It includes government itself; all enterprises supplying the public with transportation, water, electric power, or telecommunication; hospitals; charitable and welfare establishments; dairies; markets; and slaughterhouses. The government has discretionary power to designate still other activities as public services. Jurisdictional and sympathy strikes are likewise unlawful. Penalties for breaking the law include suspension or dissolution of a union's legal recognition. Workers engaged in illegal strikes may be discharged under certain conditions. U.S. Department of Labor, pp. 26–27.

their adherence to the gradualist approach to change represented by the National Front. Their respective affinities for the Liberal party and the Catholic Church lead in the same direction.

It is true, however, that labor has become increasingly dissatisfied with the economic and social policies of the coalition government. Particularly since the devaluation of November 1962 and the subsequent rise in prices has this been the case. Both the CTC and UTC threatened a general strike in January 1965 to protest government inaction, while in its May Day message of 1964 the UTC assailed "A Government that cannot govern because all its effort is spent in agreements, consultations and bargaining among different political groups to the exclusion of the rest of the country." [30] More effective control of prices, improvement in various welfare and housing programs, increased stimulus to economic development, and fuller employment are at the heart of labor's demands. [31] Yet a UTC "Platform of Immediate Action" issued in June 1965 called additionally for constitutional reforms to amend the coalition arrangement, as well as for more positive social policies, including stepped-up agrarian reform. [32] Notwithstanding the growing feeling that the government's program of economic austerity is demanding disproportionate sacrifices of the lower classes, there is nonetheless little indication that Colombian labor sees itself as part of a potential ruling counter-elite. While it seems probable that labor will increasingly insist on a larger political voice, it is likely to view its role less as the spearhead of radical change than as a pressure group (or groups) acting both on the parties and on the government to produce candidates and programs more acceptable in its eyes. [33]

Besides, although its disparate parts sometimes cooperate, the labor movement is not unified. Sporadic attempts have been made to merge the UTC and the CTC but with no lasting success. The CTC failed to make much of an impression with its protest strike of August 9, 1963, for example, because the UTC's decision not to take part greatly diluted its impact. Re-

30. Quoted in Eder, "Colombian Unions Seek Ruling Role," *New York Times,* May 3, 1964, p. 27.

31. Cf. e.g. the 22-point memorandum presented jointly by the CTC and the UTC to the "summit meeting" of Aug. 19, 1963; *El Espectador,* Aug. 20, 1963.

32. *Justicia Social,* Primera Quincena, June 1965.

33. In the 1966 congressional elections leaders of both the CTC and the UTC appeared on tickets of the traditional parties; in addition there were independent UTC slates in some places, running under the rubric of one or the other party.

gional and political differences, as well as those between the aims of blue-collar and white-collar unions, further mute the voice of labor in political councils.

Labor remains weak in organization, in finances, in its ability to withstand the concerted pressure of a government that might seek to crush it, and in its failure so far to organize most of those Colombians who work in the agrarian sector and in non-industrial urban occupations.

At the same time, there is evidence of pressure from below on the leadership of organized labor to become more aggressive. The Colombian Left has long charged that both major national confederations have betrayed labor by their subservience to the Colombian elite and to their instruments: the parties, the Church, and the government. An indication that this view may be gaining some credence among workers is that rallies sponsored by the UTC and CTC in recent years have often evoked little response in terms of attendance or enthusiasm. The incidence of strikes likewise seems to have increased, and the rapid rise in the cost of living has stimulated labor protest. It was precisely in an earlier period of especially acute inflationary pressures (1946–48) that Colombian labor reached its previous high point of militance.

Whatever its weaknesses, and whatever its latent challenge to the incumbent elite, the Colombian labor movement is today a key instrument for mobilizing popular support for the National Front. More accurately put, both the outlook of its leadership and its modes of operation help to channel protest in directions quite harmless for the continued modernizing rule of the Colombian upper class. Yet if the UTC and the CTC appear in the eyes of their members and potential members too subservient to others not of the working class, too uninterested in providing an effective voice for those not now organized, too divorced from the aspirations of the rank-and-file, the consequences could ultimately be drastic. An apolitical stance is not necessarily the most appropriate one for the labor movement of a developing society. It may need to remain political both for its own good and for the stability of the political system.

STUDENTS IN POLITICS

Student organizations, like labor unions, have qualities and functions which set them apart from other groups. While they sometimes interest themselves in causes germane to student life and university administration, more prominent is their pursuit of broader social and political goals. In Colombia at least, they are more thoroughly and overtly political than most other voluntary associations. Students are especially sensitive to social, ideological, and political change and to the differences which set them off from their parents' generation. While rooted in universities which in themselves remain quite traditional, Colombian student groups have tended to become challengers of the established social and political systems. Not only the "conflict of generations," but the students' youthful idealism, their middle-sector origin, and their contact with books and ideas all help to make them peculiarly conscious of the gap between their own outlook and aspirations and the realities and opportunities in the society around them.

As of 1962 Colombia had 23 "universities," 14 of them national or departmental and 9 of them private (including religious), although some might more accurately be termed institutes or colleges.[34] Their total enrollment was 27,410, which represented more than a 100 per cent increase over 1950.[35] In addition, there were at least 3,000 students attending universities abroad, mainly in the United States, Europe, and other Latin American countries.[36]

A sample of students at the National University in Bogotá in 1961 reported their social class origins to be as follows:

Lower or lower middle	5.4%
Middle	80.3%
Upper middle	7.6%
Upper	6.7% [37]

34. Fals Borda, *Educación en Colombia*, p. 9n.

35. *Anuario de Estadística, 1962*, p. 362, and Fals Borda, *Educación en Colombia*, p. 23n. The 1950 figure was 10,672. Among the Latin American countries Colombia ranks sixth (after Argentina, Uruguay, Panama, Venezuela, and Costa Rica) in the proportion of university students to total population, with 296 students per 100,000 population; Russett et al., *World Handbook*, pp. 214–16 (based on 1960 figures).

36. Richard Eder, "Colombian Group Aids Higher Study," *New York Times*, Oct. 3, 1963, p. 37, cites figures of the Colombian Institute for Technical Specialization Abroad (ICETEX) which reported 2,477 studying abroad under its auspices. In addition, there are an undetermined number studying privately in other countries.

37. Williamson, *El Estudiante Colombiano*, p. 16. The total sample of 610 was as nearly as possible a random sample of the student population, except that nearly one

The same study indicated that, compared with the social origins and educational backgrounds of their parents, most of the students were upwardly mobile, that is, they were receiving more education and being trained for occupations with a higher social status than their parents, and even than their elder brothers and sisters.[38]

University and departmental student associations existed prior to the decade of the 1920s, and an unsuccessful effort had been made to found a national student federation as early as 1911. But it was in the wake of the University Reform Movement centered at Córdoba, Argentina, in 1918 that the first two Colombian national student congresses were held, in 1922 and 1924. Out of the first of these came the Federation of Colombian Students (*Federación de Estudiantes Colombianos*—FEC). Of primary concern during these years were student representation in university government and improvement in the curriculum, in the faculty, and in teaching methods. There was a marked disposition to eschew political and controversial matters for fear of disrupting the hard-won student harmony. Nevertheless, written into the federation's statutes adopted at the second congress was the exalted objective of "exercising an effective influence on the destinies of the Republic and the race." [39] Also infusing the spirit of these first two congresses was the desire to forge closer bonds with other Latin American students in order to resist the "aggressive imperialism of the northern power" (although this was not couched in Marxist terms and there is practically no Marxist ideological influence evident in the proceedings of these early congresses). The students saw themselves as renovators, as forgers of a "new fatherland." As one practical application of this conception of themselves they set out to establish a series of university extension courses for the "popular" classes.

By the time of the third congress, held at Ibagué in 1928, the student federation had taken on a more political and more radical cast. Student activism had increased in the interim. At the congress itself imperialism and dictatorships were explicitly and systematically attacked and the

half were first-year students. Students at National University are not necessarily representative of those at Colombian universities generally, as indicated by very small samplings of students at other universities reported in Williamson's appendix. National University is the largest Colombian university, however.

38. Ibid., pp. 13–15.

39. Federación de Estudiantes Colombianos, Comité Ejecutivo Nacional, *I y II Congresos Nacionales de Estudiantes* (Bogotá, Ediciones Colombia, 1926), p. 143.

congress called for the "effective nationalization of petroleum." When read closely, however, there was, again, little of a Marxist tone to such pronouncements; memories of the United States' involvement in the severance of Panama from Colombia were, after all, still fresh enough in Colombian minds to account for them.[40]

The trajectory of national student organizations over the course of the next 25 years or so is obscure. Student associations continued to function in various universities and something of a national federation continued to persist. Colombian delegates participated in the Latin American Student Conference held in Bogotá just prior to the bogotazo. But organized student activities on a national basis seem to have been at a low ebb during this period. It therefore appears reasonable to view the Rojas era as the beginning of the recent history of associations claiming to speak for Colombian students generally. Their renaissance was to be marked by a new political involvement and the influence within them of the revolutionary Left.

During the mid-1950s there existed two rival federations, both claiming to be the legitimate national representative of Colombian students. One was the FEC,[41] in which the Communists played an important role (whether it was a dominant one or not is less clear). It opposed the Rojas dictatorship. The other was the Federation of Colombian University Students (*Federación de Universitarios Colombianos*—FUC), which was Catholic-oriented and generally supported or at least accepted the Rojas regime. Following Rojas' fall, the FUC faded out of existence and the FEC evolved into the National Union of Colombian Students (*Unión Nacional de Estudiantes Colombianos*—UNEC). For several years there was an active, if sporadic, UNEC press. Although the UNEC was clearly left-of-center politically, its leadership appeared initially to represent a rather wide political spectrum and to be a genuine national voice for Colombian students. It was not long, though, before the UNEC had been captured by the Communists and their allies. Coupled with internal factionalism, this served to discredit UNEC's claim to be the true representative of Colombian students and by the early 1960s it was defunct.

40. See Federación de Estudiantes Colombianos, Comité Ejecutivo Nacional, *III Congreso Nacional de Estudiantes* (Bogotá, Editorial Minerva, 1930). Alcohol and syphilis, not economics or class relationships, were seen as the principal elements in the poverty and degradation of the lower classes.

41. It is not clear whether the FEC was a lineal, or a merely nominal descendant of the earlier Federation of Students.

Communist and other leftist students have since attempted to recreate a national student federation. At a convention in November 1963 they founded the National Federation of University Students (FUN). To counteract this move students from several universities formed the *Confederación de Estudiantes Universitarios* (CEU) in August 1964 with the professed objective of promoting student interests without ulterior political aims. They have not attracted as wide a following as the FUN, however.[42]

In addition to the national student federations most universities, and often each faculty within the university, have student councils or associations. Regional associations and ad hoc groups are common. Students, as well as non-student youth, also find political outlets through such organizations as the Communist Youth of Colombia (UJCC), the Juventudes del MRL, the MOEC, and the youth affiliates of the Liberal and Conservative parties.

Student organizations perform a variety of roles in the Colombian political system. For one, they act as spokesmen for student interests before the executive, the Congress, and in the press. Since the majority of universities depend on the national or departmental governments for funds and for appointment of their rectors, it is to government and public opinion that the students must ultimately turn for the solution of problems affecting the university and student life. Thus students have been among the principal advocates of university autonomy, that is, of student, faculty, and alumni control of university administration. As early as the 1920s the Federation of Colombian Students was accorded the right to represent students before the education committees of Congress, and both the executive and Congress have continued the practice of such student representation. As a rule, student organizations can expect governmental subsidies for national congresses and for travel to international student meetings.

Student groups often prepare their members for political careers. Through them a student may gain experience in organization and agitation and it is in student politics that he may first come to serve actively a particular party or ideology. Among the delegates to the 1928 student congress, for example, were Carlos Lleras Restrepo and Gilberto Alzate Avendaño, the late Conservative politician.[43] More recently, student politics has served as a recruiting ground for parties and political movements

42. *Actualidades*, Vol. IV, No. 10, pp. 4–5.
43. Federación de Estudiantes Colombianos, *III Congreso*, p. 38.

of the far Left. Here the link between student and national politics is closer than is the case with the traditional parties, especially for middle-class students who lack the alternative channel of political recruitment afforded by an upper-class social background.

Student political organizations are likewise something of a battle-ground, or testing-ground, for political groups, especially those of the far Left. Victory in student elections is an indicator of broader strength, and may bring prestige. Control of student groups also gives a party or politi-cal leader a tool which, properly manipulated, may be of great utility in staging demonstrations or in other forms of protest. A good example was the May 1965 student strike, directed largely by the FUN's revolutionary leadership. The students' concern for national political issues, and the direct effects of government policy on university affairs, help to create a climate propitious for such activity.

Furthermore, students are more prone than any other organized group in Colombian society to take direct protest action.[44] The *manifestación,* the strike with political overtones, and various forms of vocal, and some-times physical harassment, seem to be endemic features of student politi-cal involvement. Because student protests can so readily lead to a disruption of public order the government is especially sensitive concern-ing them, with the result that students frequently win at least partial victories out of proportion to their organizational strength. Thus in Au-gust 1963, when students at National University "kidnapped" a number of public service busses and held them inside the university grounds in protest against a proposed increase in bus fares for students, the govern-ment capitulated to the key student demands. The government's diffi-culties in such a case are compounded by the traditional immunity of university grounds from trespass by soldiers and police, the abridgement of which often has the effect of exacerbating the situation and winning

44. Cf. Bakke, *Students on the March,* for an excellent brief analysis of the role of students in Colombian society. Among the reasons he cites for their propensity to direct protest action are the image of the student in the society, that is, the expecta-tions held by students and others concerning their special status, their idealism, and their role as future leaders; the character of the university experience, which in many respects frustrates the student's desire for an effective education and fails to provide him with outlets for youthful enthusiasm and leadership; and the lack of channels for self-actualization outside the university, notably the gap between students' expecta-tions and ideals, on the one hand, and the career opportunities open to them in the larger society.

non-student sympathy for the strike. In any event, student strikes—even when originating in an intrauniversity controversy—have a way of escalating into disturbances outside university grounds and of taking on broader implications. Labor organizations, for instance, may strike in support of the students, as the petroleum workers threatened to do at the time of a 1964 strike called by the FUN. Similarly, student strikes are sometimes called to support the demands of nonstudent groups. Since the government is responsible for appointment of the rector, and for the adequacy of university facilities, even a student strike confined to university objectives necessarily has political overtones.

Finally, student groups in Colombia are among the principal spokesmen for change. As early as the 1920s student associations were exponents of Colombian nationalism and anti-imperialism; in recent years revolutionary groups and ideologies have had significant influence on Colombian students. 81.9 per cent of a sample of university students declared in 1961 that they favored "a radical change" in Colombian society.[45] Such attitudes seem to fit with the students' tendency to regard themselves as in some sense the conscience of the nation, as a group as yet untainted by the corrupting influences of a status-conscious society. Thus it was students who in 1954 raised the first significant protest against the Rojas regime, and it was again students who during the days of May of 1957 played a leading part in the demonstrations which helped to bring about the fall of the dictator.

On the basis of data currently available it is not possible systematically to compare the political behavior of Colombian students with that of students in other Latin American countries. Yet, in spite of the degree of organization, politization, and radicalization which has characterized Colombian students, on all three grounds they would probably rank behind the students in most other Latin American countries, at least until about 1964. Granted that as a rule only a minority of students in any country become actively involved in student politics,[46] Colombian national student federations have seemed particularly unrepresentative and have at times maintained only shadowy existences. Seldom has there been

45. Williamson, *El Estudiante Colombiano*, p. 24.
46. According to one investigation, only 8.8 per cent of Colombian students reported themselves as so involved; "La Universidad de Espaldas al Sistema," *Acción Liberal*, No. 1 (Aug. 1965), p. 80.

the kind of intense intrauniversity politicking among rival party slates that occurs in student elections elsewhere. When measured against the long-term effectiveness of Chilean student organizations, for instance, Colombian student groups appear inchoate.[47]

Compared with the influence of the far Left in Venezuelan and Peruvian student organizations, radical influence among Colombian students has been relatively small, again until very recently. Even the student sample which declared itself overwhelmingly in favor of "radical change" in Colombian society does not prove to be very radical when examined more closely. When asked to rank a number of world leaders, the following received accolades of good or very good in the indicated percentages:

President Kennedy	71.3
Chancellor Adenauer	70.3
President De Gaulle	63.4
Prime Minister Nehru	59.7
Premier Khrushchev	38.5
Fidel Castro	28.6

Among national leaders, Gaitán was by far the most popular, but López Michelsen and Gilberto Vieira, the secretary-general of the Communist party, received relatively small support.[48] The same student sample showed that, while a majority supported use of the strike weapon for tangible university-related goals, only about a quarter favored its employment to gain broad political objectives.[49]

Why Colombian student movements should differ from those of other Latin American nations invites an attempt to identify some of the factors that have influenced the Colombian experience. Colombia's regionalism doubtless is in some measure responsible for the contrast. Students frequently attend the universities in the capitals of their departments of origin. The National University in Bogotá may well be less dominant in

47. Frank Bonilla, "Students in Politics: Three Generations of Political Action in a Latin American University" (unpublished doctoral dissertation, Harvard University, 1959).

48. Williamson, *El Estudiante Colombiano,* pp. 24–25.

49. Ibid., pp. 19–20. A more recent sample presents a somewhat more radical picture of student opinion, though hardly a revolutionary one. Cf. "La Universidad de Espaldas al Sistema," *Acción Liberal,* pp. 74–91.

university life than are the national universities of other countries. Hence national student organizations have perhaps been more difficult to sustain and to direct toward common goals.

It is likely, too, that the depth of attachment to Colombia's traditional parties, and the failure of these parties to take a very active part in developing counterpart organizations within the universities, has dampened the tendency, often evident in Latin America, for student factions to act as virtual wings of the national parties and to serve them for purposes of political action or agitation. The fact that the channel for post-university political advancement must normally be that of identification with one of the two elite-dominated parties has been impressed on most students.[50] It is interesting in this connection to note that the principal political event in which Colombian students have taken a leading part was the overthrow of Rojas, that his fall was engineered mainly by the Colombian elite and the parties which represented that elite, and that the students who organized the demonstrations were in large part from among those who do not normally play an activist role.

Finally, the whole complex of factors which so far has kept the Left weak in Colombia has probably helped to restrain student political activism, at least of a very radical sort. The absence of a xenophobic nationalism is one such factor. Moreover, that students are optimistic about their professional prospects, and about their probable future incomes,[51] would seem related to an expanding economy where opportunities for social mobility are increasing and where the prospect of entering an intellectual proletariat has not so far loomed seriously for too many.

The increasing propensity for Colombian students to engage in strikes, both for university and extrauniversity objectives, indicates that significant change may be under way which will bring more effective and continuous student political involvement, and of a more radical kind, than heretofore. This may in turn be a symptom of a growing unrest among the Colombian middle sectors in particular. Much may depend on the ability of Colombian society to fulfill the somewhat overblown expectations of

50. The survey reported in *Acción Liberal* showed that barely 17 per cent of the students at National University identify with the official wings of one of the traditional parties. Almost a quarter of the sample named no party, or did not answer the question. At the same time, 88 per cent said that their parents were affiliated with either the Liberal or Conservative parties.

51. Williamson, *El Estudiante Colombiano*, p. 15.

students concerning their own futures. The student strike which resulted in some violence and served at least as the pretext for the government's declaration of a state of siege in May 1965 brought considerable prestige to the recently organized FUN and may be a harbinger of a growing militancy among Colombian university students.

On the other hand, there is at least one long-term counter-trend at work. This is the transformation beginning to take place in some of the Colombian universities themselves, often with international support, especially from United States government and foundation sources. The traditional emphasis on humanistic, abstract learning for a cultured elite is being supplemented by the serious research and investigation into national problems now being carried out at several universities, for example at the Faculty of Sociology at the National University and at the Center of Studies in Economic Development at the University of the Andes. National development through community service is leading the universities in unwonted directions. Thus the Medical School of the University of Valle runs a large rural health center and conducts medical care programs in several slums in the city of Cali. The School of Education of the same university has started a program to prepare and provide low-cost books and laboratory equipment to secondary schools in the region.[52] The establishment of the privately financed University of the Andes in Bogotá has given Colombia its first university tied neither to the government nor the Church.[53] There is now a School of Public Administration in Bogotá and a School of Business Administration in Medellín. To the extent that such changes begin to permeate the Colombian system of higher education—and they are still only in their initial stages—students may increasingly come to direct their concern for national development into channels other than those of protest and demonstration.

Nonetheless, for the immediate future, Colombian student associations —whether organized on a national basis, or by faculties, universities, or regions—will continue to exemplify the Colombian pattern of interest groups which impinge on government with raw, unprocessed claims and take direct action when those claims are thwarted. Students will continue

52. For a report on the Universidad del Valle see Richard Eder, "Pragmatic University Aids Colombia," *New York Times*, March 1, 1964, p. 32.
53. For a report on the Universidad de los Andes see Hunter, *Emerging Colombia*, chapter 7.

to be important beyond their numbers because of the central place of the intellectual in traditional Colombian life, and the need for educated persons in a rapidly developing nation. In a society where opposition to the elite is frequently coopted by that same elite, and where parties critical of the elite have generally been weak, Colombian students—or rather the politically articulate among them—stand out as critics of the traditional order. At the same time, their relative lack of politization and radicalization in the past compared to other Latin American students, as well as the new activist and radical trends, are indicative of much concerning both the past and present of Colombian society and politics.

INTEREST GROUPS AND POLITICAL CHANGE

President Alfonso López was among the first to comment that in Colombia the *"país económico"* was replacing the *"país político,"* that is, that a politics of pressure groups and of economic conflicts was beginning to supersede the traditional style of political and ideological warfare between the parties.[54] To the extent that this has occurred—and supplementing would be a more accurate term than replacing—interest associations have provided vehicles through which their members can act independently of one or the other party. The officers and membership of organizations such as the ANDI and the FENALCO are of mixed political lineage and tend to view the interests of the organization as something apart from their allegiances to Conservatism or Liberalism. Since the inauguration of the National Front some Colombian interest groups have even attempted to assure their partisan neutrality through the maintenance of at least approximate political parity among their leadership.

With increasing frequency specific, negotiable interests on matters of policy have cut across the traditional politics of the hereditary hatreds. In this sense pressure groups without doubt contributed to the growth of the degree of consensus within the Colombian elite that made the National Front possible. It is noteworthy that the businessmen of Antioquia were among the original proponents of the idea of a National Front, and organizations such as the ANDI have from time to time reiterated their support of the coalition arrangement. The growing diversity of interests in a modernizing society, and the fact that many members of the society,

54. *La Política Oficial,* 5, 44–45.

especially among the elite, have a stake in several organizations whose respective interests do not always coincide, presumably conduce to moderation and bargaining in matters political.

At the same time, there are characteristics of Colombian interest associations and aspects of their relationships to the political system which make their contribution to the evolution of consensus equivocal. Their autonomy from government, the parties, the Church, or even from other interest groups (for example, in the case of company unions) is often questionable. Hence, their ability to act as free agents in a process of political bargaining is sometimes quite limited. In a few cases, where membership in an interest group parallels loyalty to a political party, as has largely been the case with the CTC, such membership may even help to reinforce traditional political loyalties.

Moreover, the failure of the parties to aggregate the wide variety of interest group claims, means that the multiplication of interests and political demands may actually work to destroy the possibilities of any lasting consensus on crucial matters such as development policies. The rise of direct action gremio politics in turn further weakens the party system. It also bypasses and therefore weakens the legislature. By placing the government at the mercy of persistent demands from special interest groups, demands which must be allayed to prevent disruption of vital services and loss of confidence in the government, it sustains both the image and the reality of the weak state. Denunciations of the lack of concern for the public interest on the part of the fuerzas vivas have come from many quarters, including the parties and, not least, spokesmen for the military. President Valencia lamented the lack of "a common national denominator which makes possible general and satisfactory solutions" and declared that "I attribute such importance and gravity to this situation that I consider its possible modification of decisive importance for the future of the country, for if we continue divided into irreducible and irreconcilable economic interests it is very probable that there would have to be a *solution of force* to unify interests and points of view." [55]

The proliferation of interest groups cannot in itself promote consensus. Unless their conflicting claims are somehow conciliated and transformed into national policies which all groups can in large measure accept, the consequence will be political disruption. For a modernizing nation like

55. My emphasis. *El Espectador,* July 21, 1963, p. 10A.

Colombia, the consistency and predictability of public policies may be crucial to sustained development. The alternative prospect is stagnation and the possible advent of a government which can assure the strength which a more open political system has failed to provide.

The appearance of interest groups has other implications for Colombian development no less striking than those for evolving a political consensus. Otherwise restricted in their access to positions of political leadership and influence by such impediments as the class structure and the party system, the middle sectors, urban labor, and the campesino can through their organization into pressure groups create for themselves alternative channels for expression and political participation. It is no accident that labor unions were among the first groups in Colombia to organize for political action. Middle-sector groups have formed unions or associations to press their demands, and students have organized themselves for ends which are substantially political. Such groups have made their claims on government primarily through consultative and other semi-institutionalized relationships to the executive branch, by petition, and by means of strikes and similar protest actions. Some have attached themselves in varying degrees to a political party. There are recent signs, on the other hand, that the utc may begin consciously to pursue the classic North American pressure group strategy of trying to induce both major parties to nominate candidates acceptable to labor, under threat of loss of electoral support.

At any rate, thus far in Colombia it has been interest associations rather than parties that have been the primary vehicles for the attainment of political objectives on the part of non-elite groups. It may be that in the future pressure groups will play a significant role in forcing the internal transformation of Colombia's traditional parties. Alternatively, they may provide the stimulus for new parties. Clearly, the continued growth of associations representing middle-sector and lower-class interests, coupled with the modes of political expression they seek, will have a profound effect on the future of Colombia's politics. Hirschman has put it this way:

Political development could . . . be described in terms of the emergence of a wide diversity of mechanisms and leverages, from elections to lobbying by pressure groups, through which individuals and groups can compel policymakers to pay attention to their problems. Such multiplicity certainly does not assure *equal* access to the government for all groups and their problems, but it is likely to reduce the huge differences in access that exist when only those that can deliver a credible threat to the stability of the social and political order obtain a hearing.[56]

Those Colombian interest groups representative mainly of the elite also have been promotive of change, in keeping with a pattern of paternalistic modernization. Thus the communal action program has the participation not only of government, the Church, the military, and the Peace Corps but of various private associations as well. The Federation of Coffee Growers has been organizing and financing a number of community development programs in the country's coffee-growing regions. The National Federation of the Private Sector for Communal Action (*Federación Nacional del Sector Privado para la Acción Comunal*—FEPRANAL) has meanwhile been founded for the express purpose of mobilizing private assistance for programs of communal action. Some of the leading firms in the country have collaborated with FEPRANAL, as have organizations such as Catholic Action and Acción Cultural Popular.[57]

Some gremios have themselves undertaken programs in fields such as rural health, housing, education, and technical assistance. The Federation of Coffee Growers maintains five experimental stations for research in methods of increasing coffee yields and diversifying agricultural production in the coffee-producing regions. It also has more than 1,100 demonstration plots scattered throughout the country's twelve coffee-producing departments.[58] In a number of instances interest associations have been instrumental in bringing about government action on behalf of specific development programs. Thus it was the Cali branch of the ANDI which took the early initiative for the establishment of the Cauca Valley Corporation.[59]

56. Hirschman's emphasis. Hirschman, *Journeys toward Progress*, p. 230. It might be added, however, that for some groups access will depend in part precisely on their ability to deliver a credible threat to public order, or even political stability. Cf. Payne, *Labor and Politics in Peru*.

57. See FEPRANAL (*Federación Nacional del Sector Privado para la Acción Comunal*), Statement of goals and achievements (Bogotá, 196?).

58. Holt, *Colombia Today*, p. 114.

59. See International Bank for Reconstruction and Development, *The Autonomous Regional Corporation of the Cauca and the Development of the Upper Cauca Valley* (Washington, D.C., 1955), p. 1.

The Colombian business community has begun in a modest way to subsidize higher education. Some sixty per cent of the budget of the Colombian Institute for Technical Specialization Abroad (*Instituto Colombiano de Especialización Técnica en el Extranjero*—ICETEX) now comes from such sources, with most of the rest provided by the Colombian government.[60] Private philanthropy has also supported the University of the Andes, founded in 1948.

Recognizing that what they regard as "responsible" unionism may help to preserve labor peace and keep extremists out of the labor movement, several organizations, notably the Center of Social Studies and Action (*Centro de Estudios y Acción Sociales*—CEAS), the so-called Black Hand (Mano Negra), have supported training programs for labor leaders. Some individual employers have instituted substantial private welfare programs for their workers and employees, including in some cases subsidized housing. Some of the textile firms in Medellín and some of the foreign petroleum companies have been leaders in providing such benefits.

In their public statements officers of such organizations as the ANDI and the Coffee Federation stress the commitment of their groups to economic development and social justice. Lipman found relatively liberal attitudes among Bogotá businessmen toward such matters as agrarian reform and labor-management relations.[61] Also noteworthy are the efforts of some interest groups to educate their own members, and the Colombian elite more broadly, to their social responsibilities. Thus the Social Orientation of Colombian Employers (OSDEC) was founded in 1961 as a branch of the International Union of Christian Employers Associations to promote among its members the concept that business should be of service to the community and to ensure that Christian ideas constitute the foundation of contemporary social reform "through the influence of its members in the organs of government, in the employers and workers organizations, in the universities, etc." [62]

In all, the attempt on the part of organized interest associations to mobilize the influence and financial resources of powerful individuals and firms on behalf of economic and social development is a significant dimen-

60. Eder, "Colombian Group Aids Higher Study," *New York Times*, Oct. 3, 1963, p. 37.

61. Lipman, *El Empresario Industrial*, pp. 57–58.

62. *Anuario de la Iglesia, 1961*, pp. 1186–93.

sion of the process of elite-directed modernization which Colombia is currently undergoing.

At the same time, the proliferation of interest associations has in some ways strengthened the Colombian elite and enhanced opposition to reform. The most powerful associations represent primarily elite interests. Even though most of them include small farmers, merchants, or industrialists in their memberships, they generally are dominated by the larger owners or firms. Moreover, oligarchic tendencies in their internal organization are accentuated in some cases by provisions such as those of the Coffee Growers Federation which stipulate that half the members of the Federation's departmental committees be chosen by the national committee (the other half by municipal committees) and that half the members of municipal committees of the Federation be named by the relevant departmental committee.[63] One effect, then, of the creation of ANDI, FENALCO, the Federación de Cafeteros, and other associations of this nature has been to marshal certain elite interests more effectively for political action. The forms of organization and the techniques used have been modernized; the goal—that of the defense of elite interests—has remained essentially the same.

Interest groups have also opposed and resisted policies designed to effect specific kinds of change. For example, the Ninth National Congress of Cattlemen held in July 1963 approved a resolution which, while it supported Law 135 of 1961, called upon the government to consider a number of modifications both in the law and in the implementing decrees which would substantially affect the application of the agrarian reform in certain areas.[64] Some groups have been founded with the express purpose of limiting change, or of containing it within certain channels. Thus the defunct Employers' National Economic Association (APEN), formed in 1934 about the time of the inauguration of the revolución en marcha, set forth as one of its objectives: "To impede the triumph in Colombia of the doctrines of abolition of property and of the eradication of capital, industry, and agriculture as individual rights, for the purpose of converting them into the exclusive activity of organized collectivities controlled by the State." [65]

63. Federación Nacional de Cafeteros de Colombia, *La Federación Nacional de Cafeteros de Colombia*, Mimeo. (1963), p. 1.

64. *El Tiempo*, July 27, 1963, p. 31.

65. Nieto Rojas, p. 113; see also Fluharty, *Dance of the Millions*, p. 58.

Similarly the CEAS, founded in 1960 and financed largely by business firms whose presidents or directors are members, aims at educating selected publics such as students and labor in the dangers of Communism and in the virtues of democracy and free enterprise. For the purpose it subsidizes organizations and publications which stress such themes. It was apparently first dubbed Mano Negra by Alfonso López Michelsen who, along with others on the Left, accused the CEAS of McCarthyist tactics, including a conspiracy to withhold advertising from the leftist press. The CEAS denied the charge, but it may not be coincidental that several such publications at the time met serious difficulties in obtaining advertising.[66]

The growth of interest associations has thus had contradictory effects. Some groups have afforded access to the political process for previously excluded segments of the society. Others have served as vehicles for paternalistic reform. Still others—or in some cases the same ones—have acted as instruments of resistance to change. It is therefore uncertain to what degree an increased rate of interest articulation by organized groups will contribute to Colombia's political development.

In spite of certain characteristics which mark them as products of a still substantially traditional political system, Colombian interest groups do evince a number of modern attributes. To a considerable extent they are private, voluntary associations by no means wholly dependent on state, party, or Church. Nor are they merely more elaborate versions of family and personalistic alignments. Their continued growth and activity should presumably further the development of a pragmatic politics centered around concrete social and economic issues.

The existence of voluntary associations among non-elite social strata may provide an arena—heretofore lacking—for the development of a popular leadership which will be able to bypass or challenge previous patterns for the recruitment of political leaders. Their growth should also provide that infrastructure of private groups which Tocqueville believed so vital to a democratic politics. If such groups, as well as those comprised mainly of members of the elite, can achieve their goals by operating within a constitutional framework, it may give them a stake in its preservation. The pres-

66. For discussions of the Black Hand, see Norman A. Bailey, "The Black Hand," *Inter-American Economic Affairs* (Autumn 1962), pp. 79–85; "Acción Comunal para Evitar la Acción Comunista," *Sucesos*, Sept. 21–28, 1961; and "La Verdad sobre la Mano Negra," *Política, 1*, No. 27, 1 and 12.

ence and functioning of such groups may prevent the rise of a society characterized by an undifferentiated mass with no effective alternative but mob action to press its claims and express its dissatisfaction with things as they are. The multiplication of groups means that politicians are less likely to build their careers by seeking to satisfy only one. As Weiner puts it, "Equity becomes politically feasible in a society of many associations." [67] An important implication of the development of a network of interest groups in a nation such as Colombia may therefore be its making at least possible the growth of a genuinely pluralistic politics. It may be a significant straw in the wind that the National Front in its 1962 program affirmed the need to sitmulate the growth of associations of all kinds "to give better texture and solidity to Colombian society and enrich the possibilities for the progress and welfare of its members." [68]

On the other hand, the close relationship which many associations have to government, the attitudes and practices of paternalism or dependence which infuses many of them, and their propensity for making direct claims on government, argue against their gaining the requisite experience to evolve as independent bargaining mechanisms. Moreover, a modernizing state with overriding problems of national development is hard pressed to grant pressure groups free rein to make demands in open competition with each other. Rather, the central problem faced by such a country is how to harness the energies of its citizens to attain the ends of development. The growth of powerful associations representing, above all, elite interests and those of the labor "aristocracy" may also work against the development of an effective political voice for the great majority who remain unorganized. This may be especially pertinent in a nation where such things as the party system, the class structure, and the organs of public opinion have like effects. Meanwhile, the organization of groups for economic ends and the parallel weakening of some of the vertical linkages of the traditional patron-client relationships could, despite a new style paternalism, undermine the hereditary hatreds of the traditional political system only to repolarize Colombian politics along class lines and create a yet more fundamental kind of political instability than heretofore.

Associational groups in Colombia have not so far presented any very

67. Myron Weiner, *The Politics of Scarcity* (Chicago, University of Chicago Press, 1962), p. 232.
68. *Programa del Frente Nacional*, p. 4.

direct or fundamental challenge to the elite's direction of the modernizing process. In some ways—through the growth of powerful elite-dominated organizations such as the ANDI and the Federación de Cafeteros—their proliferation has even strengthened the elite's ability to confront change. In their efforts at paternalistic reform such groups have paralleled the actions of the National Front governments. In any case, the beginnings of an interest group politics in Colombia has not on balance contributed very much to cohering a counter-elite opposition. Instead, there has ensued a kind of anarchy of direct action which is closely related to the parties' incapacity to adapt to a new mode of politics.

13

LA VIOLENCIA

THE ORIGINS OF LA VIOLENCIA[1]

There remains one major aspect of Colombian political behavior to which we have so far only alluded and which is crucial to our analysis. This is the phenomenon called by Colombians la violencia. It arose out of the superimposition of Colombia's crisis of modernization on the patterns of the country's hereditary hatreds. At the same time, it has been an important determinant of the way the Colombian political system has responded to that crisis over the past decade and a half.

No other country of Latin America—and few nations of the world— have in the mid-twentieth century experienced internal violence and guerrilla warfare as has Colombia. The struggle in the Cuban mountains prior to Fidel Castro's ascent to power on January 1, 1959, pales in extent, if not in its consequences, compared to the virtual civil war which ravaged the Colombian countryside in the years after 1948. The number of combatants are difficult to estimate, but between twenty and thirty thousand at

1. The principal single source for this chapter has been the two-volume work by Guzmán et al., *La Violencia en Colombia.* Purporting to be a scientific and objective analysis, most of it more nearly resembles a compilation of undigested facts and quotations. It is replete with value judgments and sometimes makes highly questionable use of documents, interviews, and other source materials. It has been accused of being a political document directed against the Conservative party, and even against the army and the Church. Polemics in the Colombian press and elsewhere concerning the work have generally followed partisan lines. Nevertheless, used with caution, the work is indispensable to any study of la violencia. For a critique of the first volume, see Miguel Angel González, S.J., *"La Violencia en Colombia," Análisis de un Libro* (Bogotá, Centro de Estudios Colombianos, 1962). Father González' critique also appeared in the September 1962 (No. 288) issue of the *Revista Javeriana.*

the peak of the violence may not be too high a figure.[2] As Eric Hobsbawm has pointed out, "It represents what is probably the greatest armed mobilization of peasants (as guerrillas, brigands or self-defence groups) in the recent history of the western hemisphere, with the possible exception of some periods during the Mexican Revolution."[3]

Violence was of course no stranger to Colombia when it arrived in full force beginning about 1948. Civil war seemed almost endemic during much of the nineteenth century. Even in this century, during the period of the so-called forty-five year peace, some localized violence was a fairly normal concomitant of elections. Pursuant to the change of administrations in 1930, in particular, there were several years of rather serious political strife centered in the departments of eastern Colombia. Following the next alternation of the parties in power, in 1946, there were again complaints, this time from the Liberals, of violence perpetrated against their partisans by or with the connivance of the authorities. Another form of violence, especially prevalent in the early 1930s, involved land invasions by campesinos and, conversely, the forcible removal of squatters.

Nevertheless, between 1902 and 1948 violence was, in the main, sporadic and confined to a few localities. It became persistent and almost nationwide for the first time in almost half a century only in 1948 or 1949. It was also qualitatively different from the nineteenth-century civil wars with their caudillo-led "armies" engaged in open combat. Now there was widespread "official" violence directed against Liberal civilians, and on the other side guerrilla actions directed against both the authorities and Conservative civilians. Terrorism and mass murder ("genocides"), though

2. Monseñor Guzmán, principal author of *La Violencia en Colombia,* estimates the total at 30,000. Martz, *Colombia,* p. 177, accepts a *New York Times* figure of 20,000 (*New York Times,* Aug. 28, 1953, p. 5). Other estimates place the total number of guerrillas at 50,000 (*Rojas Pinilla ante el Senado,* p. 88) and at 80,000–100,000 Liberal guerrillas alone (Eduardo Franco Isaza, *Las Guerrillas del Llano* [Caracas, Editorial Universo, 1955], p. 24). The fluid nature of the guerrilla forces and their lack of any centralized organization make a judgment of their strength exceedingly difficult. There are few reliable statistics to go on. One reasonably authoritative indication is the 3,500 who laid down their arms in the eastern plains region within the space of a few days in September 1953, according to General Duarte Blum. The General claimed the total for the nation during the same period to be 6,500; cited in Guzmán et al., *1,* 100. As Hobsbawm notes, this is in itself a sizable figure for irregular forces; Hobsbawm, "The Revolutionary Situation in Colombia," *The World Today, 19* (June 1963), 248n.

3. Hobsbawm, "Anatomy of Violence," p. 16.

occasionally present in earlier periods, now occurred on an unprecedented scale.

Altogether, in the years between 1948 and 1964, la violencia took between 100,000 and 200,000 Colombian lives, perhaps more than in all of the country's nineteenth-century internal strife, and was responsible for an undetermined number of maimed and wounded.[4] Material losses are impossible to calculate accurately, but one estimate for the department of Tolima alone places them at almost one billion pesos. This is a sum almost equivalent to the entire Colombian budget for 1955.[5]

Geographically, the violence at one time or another affected most of the country, with the exception of the Atlantic and Pacific littorals, the extreme southwest (Nariño and much of Cauca) and the largely unpopulated jungle regions of the southwest. It was most widespread in its first phase, 1948–53, but was centered in the eastern plains and in the central and western departments. A truce effected by the Government of the Armed Forces in 1953 brought an intermission, but by 1955 violence had erupted once more, this time primarily in the central and western departments of Tolima, Caldas, and Valle, and the adjoining areas of neighboring departments. In its third, and reduced phase, since 1958, it has been concentrated again in that same region. Although the violence has been principally a rural phenomenon, urban areas have not been wholly immune from acts of terrorism. Cities have also served as bases of operation in a few cases, notably for the Conservative gunmen known as *pájaros* (birds).

It is a bit difficult to generalize about the causes of the violence that began in the late 1940s, since they have varied both by geographic region and over time. Initially, they were chiefly political. There was a climate of considerable political tension and some violence during 1947 and the

4. Once more, accurate statistics are elusive, making it doubtful that a truly reliable estimate of casualties will ever be forthcoming. 300,000, or even a higher figure, is often used but is almost certainly too high. The authors of *La Violencia* posit about 200,000, largely based on extrapolations from existing partial data (Guzmán et al., *1*, 287–93). The total is in any case high enough to place it above most internal wars and even many international ones.

5. The estimate was based on a sample; Guzmán et al., *1*, 293–94. Father González believes these figures to be considerably exaggerated; González, p. 20. Very roughly, eight pesos equalled one U.S. dollar at the time of the estimate.

early months of 1948 as a byproduct of the change in regimes, and in January 1948 a state of siege was declared in the department of Norte de Santander. However, it was the murder of Gaitán in April and the upheavals which immediately followed that marked the real turning point. Those events brought armed clashes between Liberal rebels and Conservative authorities, resulting in several thousand dead and great destruction of property. Beginning with the bogotazo both Liberals and Conservatives, especially in the countryside, came to feel that their political enemies were inexorably bent on their destruction. Particularly after the Liberal victory in the June 1949 congressional elections, the official violence grew in anticipation of the presidential elections scheduled to take place in May 1950 (later moved up and actually held in September 1949).[6]

The violence fed on the traditional partisan hatreds and on the political "law of the jungle" which stipulated that one's goods, one's honor, and even one's life depended on who controlled the government.[7] The flames were fanned by the sensationalism with which the Colombian press treated the subject and the partisanship with which it attributed responsibility for particular incidents.[8] Operations conducted by organized bands of Liberal guerrillas are perhaps best dated from November 1949, following the election of Laureano Gómez as president and an abortive Liberal plot to overthrow the government.[9] But given the nature of the confrontation, the development of the phenomenon called la violencia was probably inevitable at least from April 1948 on.

Explication cannot end here, however. Although la violencia was chiefly political in its origins, as time went on it drew on other motivations and other causal factors that exacerbated it or prolonged it long after the political causes had greatly diminished in importance. Furthermore, underlying conditions of social and economic change in the Colombian countryside led certain kinds of men to seek in la violencia an outlet for the frustrations of modernization. In the absence of such conditions it is doubtful that the old political calls to violence would have evoked the response

6. For a good presentation of the arguments concerning the origins of the violence from both the Liberal and Conservative sides see *La Oposición y el Gobierno*.

7. Laserna, *Estado Fuerte*, pp. 72–75 and passim, particularly stresses this point.

8. For comment on this factor see "La Publicidad de la Violencia," *Revista Javeriana*, 53 (Feb. 1960), 9–10; and Fluharty, *Dance of the Millions*, pp. 266–76 and 300. An examination of the daily press emphatically bears out these assertions.

9. Cf. Franco, passim.

they did. It is also doubtful that the impact of the violence on the Colombian political system would have been as far-reaching.

Almost from the start economic motives for violence were mixed with the political. Farms abandoned as the result of attack, or fear of attack, by partisans of the opposite band were often appropriated by the aggressors. In fact, it seems to have been common in some localities, long before the onset of la violencia, for a change of regime (which usually also brought corresponding changes at the local level) to entail dislodgement of the political losers from their properties, which were then reclaimed when the political winds shifted. The incidence of such dislocation merely increased after 1948 and led to subsequent claims and counterclaims which helped to perpetuate a climate of violence in some areas. In the process the despoiling of one's political enemy became in a sense legitimized, with political pretexts invoked to mask other ends.[10]

Particularly in the Quindío, a coffee-producing area in western Colombia, "entrepreneurs" hired gunmen to sow terror and destroy crops, thus inducing abandonment of farms or their sale at minimum prices. A variant involved forcing the owner off his land just before the coffee harvest in order to confiscate the crop. A species of protection racketeering also flourished, carried out by a *Cofradía de Mayordomos* (Brotherhood of Estate Managers), that has been compared to the Sicilian Mafia. The Cofradía was composed of estate administrators and middlemen who sold "protection" to landlords. In Hobsbawm's view, the violence was thus used to gain wealth and power by a rising rural middle class which otherwise found social ascent difficult in a quasi-feudal society.[11] Still others took economic advantage of the violence by trafficking in weapons and ammunition.[12]

Another, quite different factor which fed la violencia was the socialization into violence of boys (and sometimes girls, as well) who had grown up with it as a way of life. At early ages they saw fathers killed, sisters raped, and homes burned. An ever-present feature of their environment was violence, the threat of violence, or the consequences of violence. As Williamson notes, "Socialization was systematically devoted to aggression and

10. Guzmán et al., *1*, 275–76; and *2*, 387.

11. Ibid., *1*, 170, 213, 275; and *2*, 269; and Hobsbawm, "Anatomy of Violence," p. 17.

12. Guzmán et al., *2*, 395–96.

sadism over the larger part of a generation, at least for some thousands of males in relevant geographic areas." [13] Moreover, to join a guerrilla band might provide an escape from home for the adolescent, who saw the life of a guerrilla—with its opportunities for glory and an expression of his *machismo* (prowess)—as more exciting than the drudgery of agriculture. Motives of revenge, hard experience, and a yen for adventure and self-assertion of a kind not readily available in the life of a campesino all had their place in perpetuating a hard core of banditry and violence long after its political causes had receded.

The era of violence coincided with a growing mistrust in the institutions of authority. Gaitán's denunciations of the oligarchy, his defeat in 1946, and the reaction to his assassination which pinned the blame on the incumbent government and led to the sacking of buildings identified with both the government and the Church, played a major role in this disintegration. Professor Luis López de Mesa has pointed out that the violence which took place prior to 1946 occurred contrary to the wishes and orders of the national authorities whereas in the subsequent period, at least in his eyes and unquestionably those of most other Liberals as well, it obeyed the designs of the government itself.[14]

A related institutional factor was judicial impunity, a persistent complaint against the Colombian courts. The fact that those who were apprehended for acts of violence often went scot-free, or were released after short periods of confinement, was partly the consequence of the political and personalistic considerations which so often entered into judicial appointments or into the disposition of cases in the courts. Moreover, the backlog of cases was generally overwhelming, the jails overcrowded, bribery of guards fairly easily managed, and threats against the families of judges or prison officials not uncommon in some rural districts.

Underlying these more immediate causes of la violencia and its perpetuation were conditions of unrest and change which for many years had been eroding old social and economic patterns, as well as old attitudes, in the Colombian countryside.

Landholding in Colombia had always been replete with uncertainties for the minifundio owner, the squatter, the tenant. For many who owned

13. Robert G. Williamson, "Toward a Theory of Political Violence: The Case of Rural Colombia," *Western Political Quarterly, 18* (March 1965), 42.

14. Guzmán et al., 2, 382–83.

land, titles had never been properly settled nor boundaries officially confirmed. Pushed into debt because of illness, bad crops, or other emergencies, the small farmer often saw part or all of his land slip into other hands. The process of subdivision among heirs added to the instability of land ownership. And for the squatter, as for the tenant and the sharecropper, there was the perennial legal possibility of his eviction, especially if he planted crops to which the owner objected. The unsettled nature of propertyholding constituted a prime ingredient in the agrarian unrest of the late 1920s and early 1930s. Law 200 of 1936 alleviated part of the problem, especially for squatters. Nevertheless, in some cases the law apparently had the effect of encouraging evictions. It failed to touch still other problems. These remained to provide a propitious environment for later rural violence, especially when added to the continued press of a growing population on available land resources. It may not be at all a coincidence that two of the three Colombian departments most affected by la violencia, Caldas and Valle, have also experienced the highest rates of population increase. The third, Tolima, has also been well above the national median for population growth.[15]

Luis Duque Gómez, a student of Colombian agrarian problems, has noted another socioeconomic stimulus to rural violence. Writing in 1954 Duque observed:

It is curious to note that besides favorable topographical conditions, the zones affected by political violence coincide exactly with the fronts of modern colonizations which in recent years have been pushing ahead in the regions of the Carare, the northeast of the Department of Antioquia, the north of Tolima, the border zone between the latter department and the Valle del Cauca, some areas along the banks of the Magdalena and in the eastern plains.[16]

In fact, there was a high correlation between those departments (Valle, Caldas, and Tolima in that order) with the highest rates of immigration to rural areas and those most prone to incidents of violence.[17] Duque

15. Hobsbawm, "Anatomy of Violence," p. 16.

16. Luis Duque Gómez, "Los Problemas Antropogeográficos de Colombia y la Escuela Rural," *Ciencias Sociales* (Unión Panamericana), 5 (Oct. 1954), 205–06.

17. Cf. the table in Pérez, *El Campesinado*, p. 70. The rates of migration are taken from the census of 1951.

ascribed the parallel between frontier areas and the location of the violence to the fact they attracted those campesinos who had originally mi-
grated to the cities. Disillusioned with their opportunities there, they had
returned to their rural homes only to find themselves unable to readjust to
the old ways. They therefore gravitated to areas where new land was
being cleared or reclaimed. Hobsbawm has also noted that the independent pioneer breaking away from a traditional setting is often one of the
most potentially militant rural elements.[18]

The development of a cash-crop economy attuned to the world market,
and the attendant decline of semi-subsistence agriculture, has been another potent factor of change in rural Colombia. In the pre-1936 period,
the very attempts of tenants and squatters to plant coffee trees evoked a
reaction on the part of some landlords and led to violence. More recently,
the use of force for economic gain has found its greatest resonance in the
coffee region. The commitment of many small Colombian farmers to a
cash crop like coffee, which takes several years to mature and thereafter
makes them vulnerable to the vagaries of a market they cannot control,
constitutes a radical departure from patterns of subsistence farming. The
impact of such a change on the Colombian campesino is largely unstudied,
but it would seem to be great. Presumably its effect is to unsettle traditional attitudes by placing the peasant in contact with a world beyond his
patria chica and by exposing him to new economic possibilities based on
cash accumulation. At any rate, it seems notable that the area of Colombia
most persistently affected by violence since 1948 is also that region where
cash-crop farming by small operators has taken particular hold. The three
leading coffee-producing departments—Caldas, Tolima, and Valle—have
been those most affected by *la violencia*. On the other hand, Nariño, in
which the minifundio is prevalent but in which traditional modes of agriculture remain dominant, has been almost free from it.[19]

Perhaps curiously, at first glance, the violence does not correlate with
particularly low levels of education and property ownership. Although
the rural areas of Colombia have a rate of literacy generally much lower
than the urban, there is no appreciable difference in rates of literacy be-

18. In Brazil and elsewhere, and even at times in Colombia, the militance of the
pioneer has been expressed by joining leftist organizations, rather than by violence.
Cf. Hobsbawm, "Anatomy of Violence," p. 17; cf. also Guzmán et al., *1*, 414.

19. For this whole point see Hobsbawm, "Anatomy of Violence," pp. 16–18; and
Guzmán et al., *1*, 414.

tween those rural communities affected by la violencia and those which
have escaped it. There also appears to be little correspondence between
low levels of property ownership and areas of violence.[20] Regions of the
country where the latifundio is dominant have scarcely been touched by
it, which probably indicates that those with some property are more likely
to be subject to the currents of rural change than the landless laborer or
the sharecropper.[21] In fact, there is evidence that in the Colombian countryside changes are most readily adopted by those with higher than minimal economic and educational levels.[22] Agricultural wages have been
highest in those departments where cash cropping is particularly important and where, as already noted, the violence has taken strongest hold.[23]
It is not the desperately poor who have generated the violence but rather
those most directly involved in the social and economic changes that are
undermining the traditional patterns of quasi-feudal landownership and
subsistence agriculture. "The 'violence'," according to Fals Borda, "seems
to have been especially virulent in those human groups which by their contacts or their migratory origins had begun to aspire to a better condition." [24]

Some observers have suggested a relationship between family patterns
and sexual repression on the one hand and la violencia on the other. The
argument is that the principal areas of violence have been characterized
by a closer adherence to the norms of monogamy and the institution of
the Catholic marriage. The argument gains added force when it is noted
that regions where the violence was most noticeably absent, such as the
Atlantic and Pacific coastal regions, are those where sexual norms are most
permissive and free unions predominate. Obviously this is not a sufficient
argument for several reasons. It cannot explain why la violencia occurred
in 1950 but not in 1940. It cannot explain why a major portion of the violence should have had its locale in the llanos (not an area with the indicated family pattern) in the years 1949–53. And it cannot explain why

20. Guzmán et al., *1*, 139.
21. Land invasions, as distinct from la violencia, nonetheless seemed to occur more
often in latifundist zones (such as Nariño, Cauca, and the Atlantic coast region). They
tend to involve sharecroppers and tenants rather than landless laborers, according to
Hobsbawm, "The Revolutionary Situation in Colombia," pp. 254–55.
22. Cf. Deutschmann and Fals Borda, *La Comunicación*.
23. Pérez, *El Campesinado*, p. 54.
24. Guzmán et al., *1*, 414.

some portions of Antioquia and Caldas—the two departments where that family pattern is most prevalent—were relatively unaffected by the violence. It may, however, suggest why the violence assumed particular ferocity in certain areas.[25]

A somewhat different sociopsychological argument, with some of the same attractions and drawbacks, has been made by Fernando Guillén Martínez. He attributes the violence to "The inveterate struggle for 'honor' as an instrument of absolute social and economic dominion" which he sees as a corruption of traditional Hispanic culture. Presumably, areas where that culture was most nearly preserved would be most susceptible to political violence.[26]

Social, economic, and psychological changes in the countryside, and the ensuing disorganization of traditional structures and values, gave the violence a fertile soil in which to take root, as did poverty, lack of education, and the frustrations created in a society where all material goods, all justice, all honor, all opportunity, in short, all advantage, went to a very small group in the population. Indeed, beyond all the particular reasons for the violence, and contributing to its perpetuation once begun, was a growing, if largely unarticulated, feeling among lower-class Colombians that somehow the governing elite and the traditional institutions had failed. Aspirations, once aroused, found scant echo among those responsible for the governance of society. Once authority and traditional ways were questioned, what some Colombians have described as a general moral breakdown or spiritual disorientation set in.[27] A kind of anarchy, which perhaps tends to be the antithesis of hierarchical authority patterns in a political culture like the Colombian, took the place of the accustomed deference and reverence.

The violence cannot, then, be understood solely in terms of those more direct causes in which it had its origins and which have sustained it. For it has also been intimately tied to social dislocations with which, for the moment at least, the nation's leadership was unable to cope.

25. For this argument see Williamson, "Toward a Theory of Political Violence," p. 38. For the categorization of Colombian family patterns see *Anuario de la Iglesia, 1961*, pp. 956–58.

26. Guillén Martínez, *Raíz y Futuro de la Revolución*, p. 187 and passim.

27. This point was stressed by Father Miguel Angel González in an interview with the author (Bogotá, Aug. 22, 1963).

THE DYNAMICS OF LA VIOLENCIA

The nature and dynamics of the violence, no less than its causes, have had profound implications for the Colombian political system. Accordingly, it is necessary to examine what la violencia was—and just as important what it was not—in terms of the objectives of those who took part in it, their links to the parties, their organization, and their modes of operation.

One of the principal points to be made in this connection is that the guerrillas who fought to vindicate Gaitán or Gaitanismo, or to defend themselves from the repression carried out by the police and by civilian partisans of the Conservative regime, never came to constitute a coherent national revolutionary movement. To qualify as genuinely revolutionary, violence must be centralized, and must attack the seats of political and administrative power, as well as the established social order.[28] This the Colombian guerrillas never did. On the whole, the guerrilla bands were spontaneous in origin, restricted in their range of operation, and limited in their goals—which were often those of self-defense, or revenge against local political enemies or local officials.

Attempts were indeed made to establish a national guerrilla command with headquarters in Bogotá, while supplies, ammunition, and political guidance did sometimes emanate from Liberal leaders in the capital or other urban centers. But for practical purposes the guerrilla bands were quite localized, with some minimum of regional coordination. It cannot be said, therefore, that the rebels were part of a single force with clearly defined objectives. Most of them were Liberals, but the national Liberal directorate often ignored or even disowned them. Guerrilla successes might strengthen the hand of the Liberals in negotiations with the Conservatives at the national level. Yet at the same time the republican traditions to which the Liberal leaders adhered, as well as a fear of what uncontained guerrilla violence might mean for social stability, caused them to vacillate.[29]

There were attempts on the part of individual guerrilla leaders, and by

28. Hirschman, *Journeys toward Progress*, p. 257.
29. Cf. esp. Franco, *Las Guerrillas*, passim, on these points.

the Communists, to make of the guerrillas a genuine mass organization or revolutionary movement. In 1952 Communists and a number of Liberal bands participated in a National Conference of Guerrillas, which tried to inject such goals as agrarian reform into the guerrilla resistance.[30] Such efforts in general proved abortive. They were hampered by the absence of effective leadership, by continuing ties to the hierarchy of authority within the Liberal party, and, among the Liberal guerrillas at least, by the lack of a real ideology or objective beyond a vague desire for revenge against the *godos* (Conservatives). The formation of a single guerrilla movement also had to contend with ancient habits of *caudillismo* and *caciquismo* that led to rivalries among guerrilla chieftains and their bands at the expense of cooperation in a common struggle.

The proposition was taken quite seriously by some that the guerrillas were Communist-led and were about to sweep over the country in the style of Mao Tse-tung.[31] This was not simply an attempt to brand all Liberal rebels as Communists for purposes of political obfuscation, though it was that in part; there was at least some evidence to support such a claim. The Communists had exercised more or less effective control of the Viotá area near Bogotá since at least the early thirties, and during the early years of la violencia they gained control over several other small mountainous districts. Communist propaganda and translations of works of Mao Tse-tung found in certain guerrilla areas lent added weight to this contention.

In all, perhaps ten or fifteen per cent of the guerrillas and rural "self-defense" groups were Communist-led. The Liberal guerrillas, both for political reasons and because of the personal antipathies of their leaders, were often bitter enemies of their Communist counterparts. This in itself went far to contain Communist inroads. Besides, the Communists themselves sometimes proved narrowly sectarian. On the whole they were unable to do much beyond ensuring their own survival. In obvious recognition of the party's weakness, Communist policy in the countryside was generally one of self-defense, rather than of aggressive revolutionary

30. Comité Central, *Treinta Años*, pp. 95–96.
31. For this view see Nieto Rojas, *La Batalla contra el Comunismo*, chapters 2 and 9; and Roberto Urdaneta Arbeláez, *El Materialismo contra la Dignidad del Hombre* (Bogotá, Editorial Lucros, 1960), pp. 335–52.

action.[32] While the potential for Communist organization among the campesinos cannot be entirely discounted for the future, the violence in the years after 1948 can only to a minimal degree be attributed to Communist activity.

There were also guerilla bands of Conservative affiliation. A distinct minority of civilians-in-arms, these groups were formed to fight the Liberal guerrillas, often in alliance with the police or the army. Some of them, along with some Liberals and Communists, continued to terrorize the countryside even after the conclusion of political peace between the traditional parties in 1957.

Significantly, the Colombian guerrillas were seldom inspired by conscious class goals. Instead of campesino against hacendado, la violencia above all pitted the Liberal campesino against the Conservative campesino and against the local government official and policeman. The social inconformity that underlay much of the violence was channeled not along class lines, but along those of the hereditary hatreds of Colombia's poly-class parties.

To be sure, elements of class warfare infused the violence as time went on but were never dominant. Proclamations of guerrilla bands on occasion spoke of fighting "for the liberation of the exploited people of Colombia." [33] In the llanos a war led by Liberal ranchers and ranch foremen against the Conservative government began to develop into a war of cowhands and peons against their bosses and employers. It may well have been this circumstance that caused the cattlemen of the llanos to make peace with the Rojas government in 1953, a peace which endured even after la violencia resumed in other parts of the country.[34] There is evidence that after the violence was renewed in late 1954 or early 1955 in Tolima the Communists were more influential than previously in the active guerrilla groups and that their propaganda, which portrayed the guerrilla struggle in class terms, was making some headway. There were

32. The tactic of self-defense *(auto-defensa)* entailed the organization, arming, training, and indoctrination of campesino groups in anticipation of possible enemy attack. For assessments of self-defense as a tactic see M. Torres, *La Naturaleza de la Revolución,* pp. 106–13; and Comité Central, *Treinta Años,* pp. 95 and 123. See also Guzmán et al., *1,* 57–60.

33. Guzmán et al., *2,* 146.

34. Cf. Hobsbawm, "The Revolutionary Situation in Colombia," p. 251.

also Liberal guerrillas who from the beginning had been motivated by more than the traditional party hatreds, who had seen their party as the party of Gaitán, as the party of social and political change. It is clear besides that a diffuse agrarian unrest with significant social content had fed the violence, or had served as one of its preconditions. In a few cases, campesinos used the political cover of the violence to despoil their landlords of their properties.

Such class overtones to the violence as did exist, and more important, the *potentialities* for class warfare that la violencia seemed to embody, partly accounted for the increasing desire of the Colombian elite to bring it to an end. Nonetheless such motives as political rivalries, revenge, and protection racketeering, rather than any deep-felt or articulate desire to overthrow the established social order, continued to be the primary spurs to violence. Thus the Communists lamented that the program approved by the Guerrilla Conference of 1952 was "above the real level of consciousness and alien to the very character of the Colombian guerrilla movement." [35] Most of the Liberal guerrillas saw their actions in the traditional terms of Colombian politics and regarded the Communists' appeal to class motivations as opposed to the mores of Colombians. "They are bandits who say that everything belongs to all and that things do not belong to the owner but to him who has need of them." [36]

Many of the factors already reviewed contributed to the failure of the widespread rural unrest to take the form of revolutionary opposition to the existing social and political order. They include the partisan origins of violence and the nature of Colombia's hereditary hatreds, personal and regional rivalries, and failures of leadership and organization on the part of those who would have turned it in such a direction. Furthermore, the guerrillas lacked effective ties to urban groups who might have given them both allies and ideological leadership. The economic and social organization of the Colombian countryside may also have played a role. It may be that when traditional social patterns begin to disintegrate, the minifundio owner or the squatter is more inclined to embrace anarchical forms of action than to join a mass movement. In contrast to the wage-earning plantation laborer the Colombian campesino is an individualist. And in contrast to some of the Indians of the Bolivian highlands who have tended to

35. Comité Central, *Treinta Años*, p. 96.
36. Quoted in Guzmán et al., *1*, 161.

respond to change collectively, preserving rural organizational patterns while at the same time becoming acculturated to new ways of life, the Colombian rural dweller has again been the individualist.[37]

Whatever the reasons, la violencia more nearly resembled anarchism than a "war of national liberation."

The guerrillas' own forms of organization and styles of action denote still other significant characteristics of the violence. Of especial interest was the creation by the various guerrilla bands of their own fairly elaborate social and political subsystems, as a substitute for the severing of those bonds which had tied the guerrillas as individuals to the larger society. Noteworthy, too, was the ferocity, or better, sadism, that marked the violence.

Almost all the guerrillas were rural in origin and most were young, between the ages of 14 and 35.[38] Most of their leaders were campesinos as well, although some, particularly in the llanos, were ranch owners or ranch foremen. This contrasts with Castro's guerrilla forces in Cuba which were led by intellectuals and professional men of urban origin. According to Fals Borda, there were two principal stages in the evolution of Colombian guerrilla leadership. In the first, they were usually informal leaders of the traditional society. Gradually, though, there appeared younger leaders, themselves "children of the violence," with a somewhat different scale of values. Although many clearly had criminal and pathological tendencies, they represented to the campesino a symbol of rebellion against the past injustices of the social order, an identification which went beyond the traditional political hatreds.[39] In general, leaders were chosen by the guerrilla band itself, or were individuals who were able to win a following because they were considered particularly brave or pitilessly cruel toward their enemies.

The ideal-type of guerrilla organization included a hierarchy of units, from the "division" to the "squad," and of ranks, from "colonel" or "general" down. Most guerrilla leaders were known, both to their comrades and to the public at large, by their rank, plus a nickname or pseudonym adopted less to hide identity than to designate a particular quality and,

37. See Richard S. Patch, "Peasantry and National Revolution: Bolivia," in Silvert, ed., *Expectant Peoples*, chapter 3.
38. Guzmán et al., *1*, 143.
39. Fals Borda, "El Liderazgo," pp. 8–9.

perhaps, to point up the adoption of a new way of life by the individual concerned. Among the prominent guerrilla nicknames were *Triunfo* (Triumph), *Sangre Negra* (Black Blood), *Media Vida* (Half Life—descriptive of his extensive wounds), *Venganza* (Vengeance), and *Tiro Fijo* (Sure Shot).

Again ideally, the guerrillas lived by a set of stringent internal rules. Justice was administered by the group's commanders, with penalties ranging from the requirement to repay stolen items, or to work without pay on the lands of a poor farmer, to execution. In one or two cases at least penal colonies were maintained by the guerrillas for their own delinquents. Traitors and dissidents were either liquidated or banished. Alcoholic beverages were sometimes prohibited, presumably in the interest of discipline and order.[40] Other regulations might deal with robbery, murder, rape, violence against members of the group, and other common crimes.

Some of the guerrilla bands developed a real mystique, including in some cases the wearing of a kind of uniform (often made from captured military stores) and insignia (some Liberal guerrillas in southern Tolima used a cross above a heart with the motto "God and Mother"). Poems were recited or songs sung recounting the heroics, the ideals, the sufferings, and the longings of the guerrillas. There were even guerrilla hymns. No matter how senseless or barbaric their actions sometimes were, the guerrillas seemed to themselves at least to be fighting for a better future and for a just cause, however vaguely that cause might be defined.[41]

A final aspect of the dynamics of la violencia which commands our attention was its savagery and sadism. Much of the killing took the form of indiscriminate massacres of whole families, or of groups of campesinos, often including women and children. Victims were preferably of the opposite political coloring, which was used at least as a pretext, but these "genocides" often made little or no attempt to single out specific political enemies or particular targets of revenge. Such terrorism might be functional to the guerrilla band, it is true, in the sense that the latter's survival depended on the complicity of the local population, a complicity which might in turn be extorted by terror. But in the manner of the killings it becomes obvious that such "rational" considerations do not fully explain

40. Guzmán et al., 2, 158.
41. For expansion on the points made above concerning the guerrillas' organization and mystique see Guzmán et al., 1, chapters 5–8; and 2, Part I.

the actions. For the victims were not merely killed but were often cut to pieces, decapitated, disfigured. Among the refinements were scalping, a symbolic placing of the decapitated head on the chest of the deceased (the so-called *corte de mica,* or monkey's cut), several varieties of throat-cutting, and tortures which produced a slow and painful bleeding to death. Most barbaric of all was the practice of *"no dejar ni una semilla"* (not leaving even a seed). It signified such acts as the tearing of the foetus from pregnant women, the castration of males, and the murder of infants. Eric Hobsbawm has summed up the implications of such brutality as follows:

> One cannot escape the impression that the killers know that their ac-
> tions . . . are not merely savage, but wrong and immoral by the stand-
> ards of their traditional society. There are isolated examples of delib-
> erately anti-social initiation rituals or other practices. There are
> chieftains whom close observers frankly describe as mentally un-
> hinged, or whose killings plainly exceed even the norm of outlawry,
> such as Teofilo Rojas (*"Chispas"*) [Sparks], killed a few weeks ago,
> who is held responsible for an average of two murders a day for the
> past five years. But even without such direct evidence, it is difficult to
> see the pointless sadism of so many bands as anything except a symp-
> tom of deep social disorganization.[42]

La violencia did not in the main signify social revolution, but the feroc-ity and psychopathology which attended it were symptoms of profound social illness. It is true that many campesinos were led to seek in the guer-rillas new forms of organization and action to replace a world whose norms and structures were in process of disintegration. Yet the guerrilla warfare on the whole led nowhere; it had most of the drawbacks and few of the possibilities for change for the better which social revolution entails.

THE NATIONAL FRONT AND LA VIOLENCIA

Although the Colombian army made concerted efforts to bring the vio-lence to an end in the years between 1949 and 1957, the obstacles of

42. Hobsbawm, "Anatomy of Violence," p. 18. See also Guzmán et al., *1,* chapter 9. Williamson, "Toward a Theory of Political Violence," pp. 38–39, notes an isolation from society's norms during the process of socialization on the part of the leaders of the violence and points to the fact that many of them were parentless.

topography, the guerrillas' ability to live off the land, and the support they received from the noncombatant *campesino* made its complete suppression impossible. Nor was the army by training or inclination really prepared to wage a war against guerrillas. An interval of peace had been attained in the early stages of the Rojas regime by means of an amnesty, rehabilitation measures, and the aura of political compromise and popular backing that at first surrounded the military government. However, it was not until the political truce of the National Front that the permanent eradication of rural violence became possible through the elimination of at least its political causes and rationale.

One of the prime motives in the formation of the National Front had been to put an end to violence. The Pact of Sitges, signed on July 20, 1957, by Drs. Gómez and Lleras, pledged the Conservative and Liberal parties to a two-pronged campaign of pacification: one, firmness on the part of the respective party leaderships toward those within their ranks who sought to promote violence for their own ends under the cover of political sectarianism; and second, a program of "reconciliation of spirits." [43] In addition, the entire institutional structure of the National Front, including *paridad* and *alternación*, was designed to do away with the partisan roots of civil strife.

In May 1958 the government of the military junta created by decree an Investigating Commission Concerning the Present Causes of Violence, composed of representatives of the two traditional parties, the army, and the Church. The Commission spent eight months conducting interviews and collecting documents. Its members also helped to arrange for the signing of peace pacts between the guerrillas and the authorities, and between rival armed bands, setting forth the terms of their mutual coexistence. As a result of the recommendations of this commission President Lleras set up an Office of Rehabilitation headed by José Gómez Pinzón, a man high in the President's personal confidence. It continued the peace efforts of the commission, and created relief and rehabilitation teams to assist the victims of violence in various localities. It also provided loans to former guerrilla leaders for the purpose of reestablishing themselves and their men on the land, and sponsored public works projects to give employment to former combatants. The government meanwhile granted a virtually complete amnesty.

Such efforts met with only partial success. Limitations on funds, inexpe-

43. *Por qué y cómo se Forjó*, pp. 36–37.

rienced personnel, and administrative problems created their own difficulties. The greatest difficulty, however, was political. Many Conservatives criticized actions of the office as pay-offs to Liberal criminals and as a particularly obnoxious form of conferring legal immunity for political motives. The Rehabilitation Office therefore functioned effectively for only a year or so before its work was terminated.

There still remained small groups of bandits, plus districts where former guerrillas, though now at peace, retained their arms, organization, and virtual autonomy.[44] A number of measures in the years that followed were aimed at eliminating such foci, and potential foci, of violence. The Church, with the benign eye and often the material assistance of the government, has sent missions into some of the violence areas, using combined social welfare and religious appeals. They have been well received and are given credit in some quarters for a substantial assist in pacification and even for undermining the degree of loyalty which the campesinos of some regions continued to hold toward certain former guerrilla leaders.[45] Both the civic-military action program of the army and the communal action programs of various agencies, public and private, have worked to the same general ends.

The army, in the meantime, has taken action of a different sort. With United States assistance it has trained and equipped some of its elite units in antiguerrilla warfare. It has placed substantial rewards on the heads of bandit leaders. And it has pursued the outlaws into their mountain strongholds. In many cases the army seems to have adopted a policy of preferring to kill outlaws rather than bring them to the bar of an undependable justice. At any rate, the results of the army's campaign since about late 1962 have been impressive. A number of bandit gangs have been destroyed or decimated and many bandit leaders killed, including the infamous "Chispas." More recently, the army has combined programs of civic-military action with the attempted reduction of some of the remaining semiautonomous areas ruled by former guerrilla leaders.

44. At the time of Lleras' accession there were reputedly 10,000 men in arms; *Semana*, No. 625, p. 37. The Minister of War claimed in early 1961 that there were only some 300 bandits remaining but that they received help from as many as 30,000 persons "who practice terrorism for a variety of reasons"; *New York Times*, Feb. 14, 1961, p. 3.

45. Cf. Guzmán et al., 2, 424 and 435; and *El Siglo*, July 30, 1963, p. 3, and Aug. 1, 1963, p. 4.

Some of the broader National Front legislation, such as agrarian reform, has had as one goal the eradication of the violence and of the conditions that might foster its renewal. Certain judicial reforms have permitted the government to move more effectively against guerrilla activity. Thus a decree issued in October 1963 raised the penalties for multiple crimes by either a person or a group. The decree also made it possible to convict for criminal association. Previously it had not been enough to apprehend bandits near a mound of corpses; it was legally necessary to prove which bandit was responsible for which corpse.[46]

None of these measures, singly or in combination, has been sufficient to eliminate the violence entirely. After a decline of almost a third in the number of civilian victims of the violence between 1958 and 1959, the rate more or less stabilized at slightly more than 200 a month through 1962. However, 1963 saw a marked reduction to almost half the previous year's rate; by 1965 the yearly figure had dropped to 544 deaths.[47]

Several factors accounted for the persistence of the violence—albeit on a much reduced scale—even after the conclusion of the National Front agreements.

Shorn of any real political justification for their actions, some of the former guerrillas continued to engage in banditry, either as a way of life to which they knew or accepted no alternative, or for profit. Many of the underlying social causes of rural unrest likewise remained. In 1960 the military governor of Caldas claimed that the proliferation of the minifundio, combined with a rapid increase in population, were principal causes of the failure to pacify that department completely.[48] Furthermore, many of those who had abandoned properties during the years of violence were

46. Richard Eder, "Colombia Seeks to Speed Justice," *New York Times*, Oct. 27, 1963, p. 36.

47. The figures for 1958–62 are from Guzmán et al., 2, 283, and are in turn based on national police statistics. 300 municipios in 13 of the 17 Colombian departments were the scene of incidents of violencia during 1962 (Guzmán et al., 2, 284). The figures for 1963 are from Holt, *Colombia Today*, p. 186. The 1964 figures were supplied by the Colombian Embassy in Washington; the 1965 figures were reported by the Associated Press. These figures do not include the deaths of bandits or guerrillas ("*antisociales*"), or of soldiers or police. Thus, during 1964 bandit deaths numbered 341 and those of soldiers and police 43 compared to 727 civilians killed through the actions of antisociales.

48. Colonel Jaime Durán Pombo, in an interview in *El Espectador*, April 29, 1960.

now reclaiming them, creating bitter and sometimes violent disputes which the intervention of the Rehabilitation Office could only partly assuage. Nor had the promised agrarian reform as yet had much effect. Invasions of public and private lands were still quite frequent. They did not necessarily issue in violence, even when countered by use of the army or police, but they did contribute to a continuing atmosphere of rural tension.

Political causes of the violence also remained. National party leaders were not always able to control their partisans in the countryside. This was true even of the supposedly more highly disciplined Communists, who as a party called for support of national pacification and a return to "bourgeois democracy." Moreover, the intraparty factional squabbles which had largely superseded competition between the parties sometimes erupted in violence. Early in 1960 intraguerrilla rivalries, apparently exacerbated by the approaching election campaign which pitted official Liberals against the MRL, caused incidents in Tolima which finally led to military occupation of one area in the south that had lacked direct governmental authority for more than ten years.

There have been other political sources of violence. Possibly it was not a mere coincidence that in October 1961, just four days after the former dictator, Gustavo Rojas Pinilla, delivered a speech declaring that only a revolution "in which little blood would be shed" was sufficient to reestablish social justice in Colombia, two army lieutenants, one of whom had been implicated in the affair of May 2, 1958, led a mutiny against the government. The plan was to create a rebel nucleus in the eastern plains. Though crushed within hours, this "uprising" was enough, along with other indications of an upsurge in political violence, for a nationwide state of siege to be reinstated for the first time since January 1959.[49]

Guerrilla groups of a designedly revolutionary nature, such as the Revolutionary Armed Forces of Colombia (FARC) have also been formed. In other instances groups such as the MOEC have apparently attempted to

49. For this episode see *New York Times*, Oct. 12, 1961, p. 5; and Oct. 13, 1961, p. 11; and *Hispanic American Report*, Dec. 1961, pp. 912–13. The state of siege which had been in effect continuously since November 1949 was lifted by President Lleras at the time of his inauguration in August 1958, with the exception of those five departments in central and western Colombia where foci of violence remained. In December 1958 it was reimposed nationwide in face of the alleged Rojista conspiracy; it was lifted the following month, again with the exception of the five departments.

win existing bandit groups to their political purposes. At least a few Colombian youth associated with radical political groups have received training in Cuba for the purpose of "turning the Andes into the Sierra Maestra of South America," and propaganda and even arms of Cuban origin have reportedly been introduced into some rural regions.[50] It is further suggested by the authors of *La Violencia en Colombia*, as well as by Eric Hobsbawm, that as the old justification of fighting for one of the two traditional parties has faded in recent years, those men remaining under arms have increasingly come to see themselves as champions of the poor.[51]

In early 1963 still another dimension was for a time added to the violence, that of urban terrorism. It consisted mainly of occasional bombings in Bogotá and other cities. Presumably responsible were persons associated with the Fidelista Left and/or the Rojistas. A series of kidnappings also began during 1964, usually carried out by bandits or thugs for purposes of ransom. Several prominent Colombians were victims of kidnappings and in some cases met with death.

Finally, there remain the so-called "independent republics." The authors of *La Violencia* identified some eleven of them as of about 1958. Among them at least two, Viotá (the "Republic of the Tequendama") and Sumapaz, dated from well before the onset of the post-1948 violence. The others were organized in the following years as semiautonomous areas where the legal authorities were refused entry by the guerrillas, or in areas settled by campesinos displaced from the areas of violence. Some of them have since been occupied by the army or have acquiesced in the restoration of governmental authority. Except for one or two, the several that still exist are not foci of violence, though they may retain caches of arms. In the case of the Communist "republics" they serve as centers for antigovernment agitation in the countryside.[52]

Although ancient partisan hatreds continue to feed acts of violence in a

50. For the activities of one such group see Richard Eder, "Colombia Hunts Guerrilla Band," *New York Times*, Jan. 17, 1965, p. 28; for another, see Young, "Revolutionary Parties in Colombia," p. 19. The latter band has since been broken up, however.

51. Guzmán et al., 2, 267–68 and 346; and Hobsbawm, "Anatomy of Violence," p. 17.

52. Guzmán et al., 2, 284 and 286; see chapter 4 for a report on an organizational meeting of a Liberal "republic" in southern Tolima in 1957.

few places, the National Front has largely solved, for the time at least, the problem of interparty ferocity. Under its auspices, most of the former combatants have turned to peaceful pursuits, the army has adopted new and efficacious tactics to combat the remaining vestiges of violence, and since 1962 the violence itself has diminished considerably. Its incidence has not approached the quasi-civil war proportions of the past at any time since the inauguration of the National Front. By 1966 most of what remained of the violence could be attributed, not to banditry or factional fights within the traditional parties, but to the genuinely revolutionary action of guerrilla groups inspired by the far Left.

THE IMPLICATIONS OF VIOLENCE

It remains to summarize some of the implications of the years of violence for Colombian society and politics.

Psychologically, the effects of the violence have been profound, according to a study conducted by Professors Havens and Lipman which contrasted the attitudes and opinions of a group of refugees from the violence with those of a control group, comparable in other respects, whose members had had no direct contact with the violence. On the attitude scales, the former manifested much more insecurity than the control group.[53] This was true even though they had moved to Bogotá, away from the source and locale of the original insecurity. The first group also evidenced a much higher degree of anomie, and of distrust toward the social order and toward authority. As Fals Borda suggests, the consequence of the violence has been to speed the undermining of traditional norms without substituting a coherent set of modern values, thus producing a transitional, anomic value pattern.[54] Havens and Lipman found the first group to be more oriented to the past, toward "things as they used to be," than the control group, which tended to have greater confidence in the future. The years of violence seemed to have made life meaningless for those most affected by it and left them with a feeling that their environment was unpredictable and uncontrollable.

In their opinions of governmental and social institutions, most individuals in both groups agreed with the statement, "Because of the violence

53. See Lipman and Havens, "The Colombian Violencia," for this point and those that follow.
54. Guzmán et al., *1*, 414–15.

the majority of people have lost confidence in the government." The majority (with little difference between the two groups) also believed that it was impossible to expect justice from judges, and that the government would not be able to end the violence. The majority of the entire sample likewise agreed that "Because of the violence, the people have lost confidence in the Church." [55] Although of course there is no comparison in the study with the pre-violence period, and although the persons less touched by the violence had about the same opinions on these questions as those more directly affected, these findings nonetheless seem significant. Other causes are probably involved, including increasing dissatisfaction with the social order generally, but it seems reasonable to conclude that la violencia has played an important role in undermining the trust of many rural Colombians (and of many formerly rural Colombians now living in urban areas) in some of the major authoritative institutions of their society. There are other indications that confidence in the police has been seriously damaged by their involvement in political sectarianism and their failure to act the neutral instrument of authority. Popular confidence in the army was diminished as well, although to a lesser and more ambiguous degree.

The effects of la violencia have not been entirely disintegrative. In some ways civil strife may paradoxically have contributed to the modernizing process in Colombia, although obviously at very great cost in human suffering. Thus the hastening of the breakdown of traditional institutions and traditional values is in some sense an integral part of development. The violence has also been an important factor in inducing traditional institutions and groups to take stock of themselves in the interest of their own survival. The Liberal and Conservative parties were led, in part by the violence, to seek means to supersede the politics of the hereditary hatreds and to seek solutions to the underlying problems to which la violencia gave witness. The military, too—its tactics, its arms, its training, and its very conception of itself proven inadequate to the challenge that the violence posed—has taken some giant steps toward modernization.

Surprisingly, the violence does not appear to have interrupted the pace of rapid economic growth experienced by Colombia during most of the postwar period. In the coffee areas at least, when farms and crops were abandoned they were usually taken over at once by others and exploited economically. Sometimes coercive or terrorist tactics were invoked for

55. This was despite the differences in feelings toward the Church evidenced on the attitude scales.

the purpose of precipitating such a transfer. But as a rule the harvest was not lost to the national economy and to its balance of payments. Secondly, as Hirschman has suggested, the violence in the countryside may have helped to stimulate industrialization and the growth of the larger cities, much as the enclosure movement did in 17th and 18th century England. The violence was not of course the prime cause of migration to urban centers—a similar process was occurring all over Latin America at the same time—but it may have augmented its rate. Additionally, rural violence may have lessened the propensity of Colombians to invest savings in land and may have led them to seek alternatives in industry and commerce. On the other hand, it is impossible to tell what the country's rate of economic growth might have been in the absence of la violencia.[56]

The experience of the violence has also generated in many Colombian campesinos a greater awareness of their own potential strength, a feeling that they have a right to be heard on policies and decisions which affect them, and a more skeptical attitude toward those who would manipulate them by demagogic promises which are never fulfilled. Many rural dwellers have as the result of the years of guerrilla warfare learned either by observation or direct participation what organization can do to make their voices effective, or merely how to defend themselves against the repressive action of the government. The violence similarly brought to the fore a new kind of leader, younger and less inclined to act in terms of traditional rural categories and preconceptions. It appears to have stimulated in some parts of the Colombian countryside a greater inclination to see social and political issues in class terms, to demand some real attention to such matters as agrarian reform from the historic parties to which the campesino has heretofore given his unquestioning loyalty. The extent to which such changes in perspective have taken place is impossible to judge, but those who have studied most closely the Colombian of the violence areas believe it to be considerable. The subject political culture and the traditional patterns of party rivalries are far from dead in those areas or elsewhere in Colombia. But it does seem probable that la violencia has worked to loosen their hold.[57]

There is even evidence from the Havens and Lipman study that the

56. See Hirschman, p. 116.

57. For these points see Guzmán et al., *1*, 297–300 and chapter 13. A report on acción comunal notes that the precedent of organizing for a common purpose, such as self-defense against la violencia, assisted the *equipos polivalentes* in stimulating community cooperation; cf. *Acción Comunal en Colombia*, p. 45.

violence may have contributed in a measure to national integration. It is true that the deep division of the country along partisan lines and the challenge to national authority posed by the formation of guerrilla bands and rural "republics" suggest the opposite. The impact of the violence in its early years was undoubtedly almost wholly in this direction. However Havens and Lipman found that despite the fact that the refugees from the violence whom they studied felt it was more important to be from a particular region or department than to be a Colombian, they had a greater subjective awareness than the control group that whatever happens to or in Colombia would inevitably affect them as persons. More generally, Colombians of all categories and political persuasions condemn the violence and seem to see it as a social and political problem which demands a remedy. It may be, therefore, that out of the crisis of la violencia will come that greater social cohesion and national solidarity which is both a condition and criterion of political development.

Violence has deep cultural, social, and political roots in rural Colombia. It did not begin with the late 1940s. Yet its renewal at that time had a number of qualities which made it in many ways unique: its extent, its ferocity, the degree of social decomposition which it both evidenced and caused, the nature of the nonpolitical motivations which attached themselves to it, the institutional crisis which it evidenced, and the overtones of class warfare which it sometimes had. What was at first largely political violence after the fashion of the early 1930s snowballed into the phenomenon of la violencia.

This was of an entirely different order than anything that had gone before (and not *merely* an extended version of it) because Colombian society and politics had become different. It revealed a deep political and social crisis which expressed itself at a distinct but related level in the rise of Gaitán, and the instability of the '40s and '50s. Above all, the years of violence, channeling social unrest and political discontent into riverbeds marked Liberal and Conservative, may have prevented an explosion of a social revolutionary nature. It oversimplifies to view Colombian history since 1948, and in particular the role of la violencia in that history, solely in the light of an aborted social revolution.[58] Too many other factors, including the strength of traditional institutions such as the army, the

58. This is essentially Hobsbawm's view, as expressed in "Anatomy of Violence," and "The Revolutionary Situation in Colombia."

Church, and the parties; the fundamental weakness of the Left; and the lack of class consciousness on the part of lower-class Colombians, suggest that social revolution was not necessarily the alternative to anarchic violence. Moreover, the violence has in some ways actually stimulated class consciousness in rural Colombia. It would nevertheless seem fair to speculate that the violence, as an exaggerated and perverse outpouring of the traditional hatreds between Colombia's two polyclass parties, has been at least a major reinforcing factor in preventing the emergence of a full-blown class politics in Colombia and, perhaps, the occurrence of social revolution. It may be here that lies its ultimate significance for Colombia's political development. Precipitated by the initial social and political shocks of modernization, la violencia has been a major factor in conditioning the country's political response to the resulting crisis.

PART V

Conclusion

14

MODERNIZATION
BY AN ELITE—
SUMMARY
AND IMPLICATIONS

PROCESS AND PROBLEMS

In contrast to most other Latin American countries in the same period, Colombia has by and large adhered to a political route to development which we have called that of a modernizing elite, functioning within the forms of republican government. Though it has by no means remained wholly closed to new recruits or new ideas, the Colombian upper class has retained in its hands most of the power resources of the society, including economic dominion, highly disproportionate access to education, and control of the mass media and the major political parties. Its approach to change has on the whole been that of palliative, paternalistic reform, designed to alleviate severe stresses in the system and to respond to certain cues (such as anarchic rural violence) or to certain demands on the part of counter-elite groups, without at the same time yielding up any real share of effective control over the major power resources. It might of course be contended that violence, or the threat of disruption of public services, is an important political resource in the hands of non-elite groups and in a sense it assuredly is.[1] But while direct action or "political bargaining" of this sort has at times served to signal dissatisfaction in certain segments of the society, or to obtain special dispensation for a particular

1. Cf. e.g. Payne, *Labor and Politics in Peru.*

group with respect to a given law or policy, it has seldom led to any very measurable permanent realignment in the distribution of economic, social, or political power.

The Colombian polity's first concerted attempt to confront the challenges posed by twentieth-century change was President Alfonso López' revolution on the march. It was termed a revolution by its authors, and there were elements (in its agrarian reform law, for example) which bespoke genuine reform (that is, an effective granting of a share of economic, social, or political power to new groups). These elements were in the end few and in any case more striking in word and on paper than in their lasting imprint. Still, it was during the mid-1930s that a substantial segment of the traditional Colombian upper class did adopt a modernizing orientation and attempt to use government for modernizing ends. Although the main thrust of the revolution on the march was spent by the end of López' first administration—partly because of the resistance of nonmodernizers, partly because some of the modernizers themselves became frightened by what they had wrought—the spirit of the modernizing "Liberal Republic" continued in modified form until 1946.

The politics of the next dozen years can in large part be explained as a reaction to the previous dozen. The short-lived Gaitanista movement, with its strains of both democratic reformism and authoritarian populism, was led by a man not himself of the elite and reflected disillusionment with the "revolution's" failure to fulfill its initial promise. Yet even Gaitán did not escape the embrace of the Liberal party. Despite his assumption of its leadership, the party did not, at least in the brief time allotted to him, lose its essential character as an elite-controlled polyclass party.

The Conservative reaction to the Liberal Republic, as personified by Presidents Ospina and Gómez, took steps to freeze, or even to reverse earlier reforms in the social and political orders. Especially under Gómez, this took the political form of a quasi-dictatorship. Though holding the allegiance of most of the traditionalist landed elite, the Conservatives also represented important industrial and commercial interests, notably in Antioquia. They sought to advance economic growth while at the same time seeking to preserve the essence of traditional values and traditional society.

In effecting a pale imitation of a populistic authoritarianism, the regime that followed bore distinct overtones of a challenge to the incumbent elite's exclusivist rule. Yet, again, most of the country's leaders had supported Rojas' accession to power, viewing it as an interim necessity for the restoration of intra-elite harmony. When Rojas sought to slip the confines of the mediator's role he was brought down with relative ease, the military showing little heart for a contest with the country's civilian leadership.

Today there waits in the wings an array of political groups advocating various alternative solutions to rule by a modernizing elite: the PCC and a myriad of small direct action groups, all presumably promoting the eventual establishment of a regime of totalitarian mobilization; the mainstream of the MRL, as well as the PSDC, both advocating broader reforms and something more nearly resembling full constitutional democracy; and the ANAPO and the MDN seeking the advent of a regime of authoritarian populism.

Yet other than for a moment coinciding with the years immediately following World War II, and in a highly qualified sense during the Rojas years, the country has not had a truly strong movement or party of either the Left or the non-Left which was opposed to the pattern of upper-class rule. Parties or movements seeking the support of potential counter-elites in the middle or lower social strata have existed in some profusion. But almost without exception they have remained small and rather insignificant; or as factions of one of the traditional parties they have been reabsorbed into the old party structures; or their challenge to elite rule has in the end proved spurious. In general, Colombia has lacked the kind of strong revolutionary or reformist political organization, based mainly on middle-sector leadership, which in the last several decades has appeared in many other Latin American countries (for example, the American Popular Revolutionary Alliance [APRA] of Peru, the Institutional Revolutionary Party [PRI] of Mexico, the National Revolutionary Movement [MNR] of Bolivia, the Christian Democrats, Socialists, and Communists of Chile, the Peronistas of Argentina, and the Castro movement in Cuba).

With the overthrow of Rojas in 1957 and the inauguration in the following year of the first government under the National Front dispensation, Colombia reverted to the posture toward change that it had maintained under López—paternalistic and limited reform under the auspices of the modernizing segments of the elite. In its efforts at paternalistic reform there is a parallel between the National Front and Alfonso López' *revolución en marcha*. The agrarian reform, the extension and modernization of education, the increased reliance on direct and graduated taxation, the efforts to promote industrialization, the spirit in which reform has been undertaken, and the social sectors which have assumed its leadership, suggest a close resemblance. There are many differences in detail between the two, and the lessons of the Gaitanista and Rojista challenges to elite rule, and of la violencia, have intervened. But the fundamental distinction is that the reforms of the thirties were effected under the hegemonic rule of the Liberal party. The National Front, on the other hand, entails reform on the basis of political agreement between Liberals and Conservatives. It reflects a conversion to limited modernization (going beyond the purely economic to include a measure of the social and political) on the part of many Conservatives. It also reflects a new Liberal strategy—that of sharing power with the country's minority party in order to coopt its leadership into the modernizing strategies of the majority. This strategy bears the defect that the need to achieve mutual accord on such programs as agrarian reform may so dilute them as to bring them in the end to nought. Yet it seems reasonable to see the major difference between the National Front and the earlier experiment with "reform from above" as one between the presence and absence of a consensus within the Colombian elite on the broad outlines, if not always on the specifics, of the pace and nature of modernization.

A. F. K. Organski has distinguished four stages of development: the politics of primitive unification; the politics of industrialization; the politics of national welfare; and the politics of abundance.[2] There are in turn three alternative types of political regimes which may prevail during the stage of industrialization. They are: bourgeois politics, by which Organski means industrialization under the aegis of an industrial elite at the expense of the agricultural sector, with mass participation or any concern for mass welfare largely excluded or irrelevant and with government playing more of a permissive than a directive role; stalinist politics, or rapid forced-draft industrialization using extensive repression; and "syncratic" politics. The latter entails a compromise between antagonistic industrial and agricultural elites whereby the latter is protected in its own domain and industrialization proceeds essentially at the expense of the urban workers. Both elites under syncratic regimes are protected from the

2. Organski, *The Stages of Political Development.*

"threat from below"; indeed, this is a primary motive for the alliance of the two elites in the first place. At the same time, syncratist regimes tend to occur in societies where the politicization of the masses has *preceded* idustrialization to a substantial degree. In contrast to bourgeois regimes they therefore feel called upon to pacify the masses with at least some welfare measures. Still another criterion for a syncratic regime, according to Organski, is that it tends to occur at a time when earlier economic gains are followed by a period of slower growth, which in turn creates social unrest. The three leading historical examples of syncratist regimes (often labeled fascist in popular terminology) have been Mussolini's Italy, Franco's Spain, and Perón's Argentina. (Nazi Germany was not syncratist since it was a product of Organski's next stage of development, the politics of national welfare in an already industrialized society.)

Without much doubt Colombia fits Organski's second developmental stage, the politics of industrialization.[3] It also, since at least the mid-1940s, has borne a considerable resemblance to Organski's syncratic politics. This might seem reasonably obvious in the case of the Gómez regime. Not only was it quasi-Falangist in its ideology and in many of its political actions, but it followed a period of popular unrest marked by the rise of Gaitán and by the bogotazo. This unrest had in turn been preceded by a slowing down or seeming reversal of many of the economic, social, and political gains (though not of the rate of economic growth) which had been heralded by the revolution on the march. The Rojas regime preserved many of the characteristics of its predecessor, and of syncratism, in keeping with its imitative Peronism. In fact, Organski specifically classifies Perón's rule as syncratist, notwithstanding its populistic aspects (although he is not entirely successful in depicting the true nature of the Peronist regime and tends to underplay the role of its mass base).

Yet it seems reasonable to suggest that the National Front likewise fits the essence of syncratism, even though in its political *form*—and especially in its adherence to many of the norms of republican government—it is in many ways far different from Organski's historic examples. It may

3. Organski's rule-of-thumb indicator for a society's move from the industrializing to the industrialized stage is that it has passed the fifty per cent mark in the proportion of its population engaged in non-agricultural pursuits. Colombia passed this mark about 1960. The utility of this indicator in the case of countries like Colombia is open to serious question, however, in view of the rapid urbanization which places many in non-agricultural, but also non-industrial, marginal occupations.

well be an instance of the new forms of syncratism which Organski pre-
dicts will evolve in the developing nations, particularly since the fascism
of the past has gone out of political fashion.

Thus, despite Law 135 of 1961, the National Front governments have
not on the whole sought to advance industrialization at the expense of
agriculture. The agrarian reform's provisions for land distribution have
had rather minimal application while other aspects of the law such as
credit expansion and land reclamation have in fact aided the agricultural
sector. In this respect the Colombian elite's approach to modernization
would appear to fit the syncratic model rather than the bourgeois model
of the countries of nineteenth-century Europe, or even of López' efforts
to advance modernization in the absence of a compromise between Colombia's Liberal and Conservative leaderships. In still another way contemporary Colombia more nearly resembles syncratic than bourgeois politics. Its government is forced to deal with a historical situation in which
the masses have been substantially politicized *before* industrialization is
very far advanced. Government must therefore, at least in some minimal
way, enact a series of social welfare measures, even while it takes care
not to spend on welfare any very substantial share of potential investment
funds (a goal obtained by taxing luxury items, or even the workers themselves).

It is in its political form that the National Front diverges markedly
from Organski's typical syncratic regime. For the National Front is led
by the Colombian elite itself, not by a non-elite party that wins elite
acquiescence (as in the cases of the Spanish Falange, the Italian Fascists,
and the Peronistas); in fact, it is a coalition mechanism for the leadership
of the two traditional parties. Moreover, the procedures of a modified
constitutionalism are maintained, including the continued existence of an
opposition.

Even so, some of Organski's political criteria do apply. In certain ways
the National Front is much like a one-party system. There is, after all, but
a single presidential nominee chosen together by the official wings of both
parties. The electorate does not have an opportunity to vote one party in
and the other out. Furthermore, joint declarations of the coalition partners are quite common. Thus late in 1961 the two official party directorates appointed a commission which drew up a "Program of the National
Front" which both could support during the election campaigns of March

and May 1962. The formal creation of a Bipartisan Commission of National Transformation to support the 1966 presidential candidacy of Carlos Lleras is yet another instance of coalescence. Above all, despite alternation, the two parties—together—remain in power. In a sense the former hegemonies of one or the other traditional party have been replaced by a hegemony of the official leaderships of both.

Moreover, the opposition is faced with some peculiar handicaps under such an institutional arrangement. To exorcise competition between the two historic parties, and to exclude third parties from disruptive access to government, were the essence of the original agreement. Yet even factions *within* the major parties that are opposed to the government are placed in an equivocal position. It would, of course, be possible to have an opposition which called merely for a change of personnel and policy without attacking the system. To a degree, this has been the case among the factions of the Conservative party. But the tendency is strong for the intraparty opposition to couch its challenge in terms of an attack on the structure of the Front as well, or at the very least to criticize undue concessions made to the other party in the coalition. Opposition to the particular government in office therefore readily becomes, or is seen as becoming, an attempt to subvert the constitutional order itself.

To term the National Front a one-party system goes too far. It is more accurate to view the National Front as a truce designed to mark out a field of neutral action between the parties, rather than as a fusion of them which seeks to suppress all opposition. Leaders of both historic parties are very insistent and explicit on the point that the parties do and will remain distinct entities, with important differences in matters of ideology, program, and tradition. Certainly the National Front was conceived as an armistice only, with competitive party politics to resume after 1974. Even the factionalism that grips each party takes some of its meaning from the fact that it occurs in the context of a bipolar party situation. The latter circumstance marks the limit of factional conflict, while relations with the other party are a principal issue among the factions in both parties.

Yet if the National Front cannot be called truly a one-party system, it may nevertheless possess some of the attributes of such a system. And, to the degree that it serves to mute intra-elite conflict, while at once protecting the elite from outside challenge and carrying out those welfare and reform measures necessary in a society where mass politicization precedes or accompanies industrial growth, the National Front may be the functional equivalent of Organski's syncratism. If this is the case, it suggests that syncratic politics may take a variety of unanticipated political forms in the developing nations. It further suggests that our comprehension of recent Colombian politics can be enhanced by relating it to a particular configuration of problems and attributes which tends to recur in many nations, and especially in many Latin American nations, during a particular phase of their development.

It is as an interim consensual mechanism for Colombia's warring elites and their respective partisans that the National Front has best served its purpose. The coalition has likewise helped to preserve stability by guaranteeing during a key transitional period the status of those in society who stand prospectively to lose by change.[4] It has also had some limited success in its economic and social programs. It has not wholly succeeded, however, in moving the economy to a sustained level of growth; it has done relatively little to alter social relationships or opportunities and to use governmental policy to redistribute income; and it has failed to give the nation a dynamic "sense of itself."

Above all, the Great Coalition has done little to develop institutionalized channels for the expression of popular aspirations and to incorporate ambitious persons and groups into positions of influence and leadership. It is precisely here that the principal opposition criticism of the National Front is focused, namely, that the kind of consensus it embodies, by requiring the majority Liberal party to enter into transactions with the Conservative party, necessarily brakes the processes of change and government's responsiveness to the popular will.

The political consensus on which the National Front was founded may have made its prospects for success greater than earlier efforts at elite-directed reform. It has mitigated, if by no means wholly resolved, the intra-elite conflict that put an end to the earlier efforts of the Liberal Republic. Yet there are several questions which must be raised concerning the feasibility of any regime like that of the National Front successfully accomplishing its self-imposed task of tutelary modernization.

4. Cf. Lipset, *Political Man*, pp. 65–67.

The first is whether a "transaction coalition," as its enemies sometimes derisively refer to it, can really make the hard decisions, can really establish the priorities necessary to a developing society. Can the executive count on the necessary cooperation of the majority wings of two political parties that are at the same time jealous of each other and challenged by rival factions within their own parties? President Valencia's need to request extraordinary powers to carry out fiscal and judicial reforms in the face of congressional reluctance to enact the government's program, and his ultimate resort to decree powers under a state of siege when in 1965 the Congress failed to enact further proposed reforms, illustrate the dilemmas of coalition politics. Likewise, the government's lack of a firm popular or party base, and the urgency of holding together diverse groups and factions in some kind of consensus, have made it highly vulnerable to the protests and threatened direct action of important interest groups. Under the rules of the game which the coalition arrangement itself imposes, the governments of the National Front have often lacked the political strength to pursue a consistent policy of even relatively limited and gradual modernization.

The second fundamental query concerning the viability of the reformist posture of a government like that of the National Front is still more serious, even if less immediate. It is whether the attempts of an upper class to adapt to change in order to maintain the system of its own rule will arouse expectations beyond its capacities, or its willingness, to satisfy. A great deal will depend on the rate of economic growth and upon the continuance of at least an illusion of progress or hope for improvement. There is, as former President Lleras has said, both a demand and a determination at every economic level to see the nation prosper.[5] And Colombia, more than many developing nations, does have entrepreneurial skills among its elite. The first years of the 1960s appeared to indicate that Colombia might soon reach the stage of self-sustaining and rapid growth. More recent evidence offers a less encouraging picture of the nation's economic performance under the National Front. Perhaps most significant has been the seemingly endemic series of strikes and threatened strikes, involving not only obreros, but also groups identified

5. Cited in Philip S. Cook, "Colombia's Objective: To Grow Realistically," *New York Herald Tribune Magazine,* April 10, 1960, p. 22.

with the middle sectors such as teachers, bank clerks, and insurance company employees. The implication would seem to be that aspirations are already beginning to outrun real economic and social advance among important elements of the population.

A related question is whether the modernizers among a nation's political leadership can somehow reach the masses and involve them either vicariously or through a more direct form of participation in the attainment of development objectives. In an era of an increasingly urbanized and articulate population, popular support must be built even for tutelary reforms. The older modes of authoritarian political control, now in decline, must be replaced, or at any rate supplemented, by a new basis of authorization and legitimacy for government. Presumably, too, those who experience economic advance and upward social mobility as the consequence of development will eventually come to demand a share in political decision-making. The incorporation of some aspirant members of the middle sectors into the expanding development apparatus of the Colombian state is a step in this direction. But electoral abstention and the waves of direct action protest argue that there is a very long way to go in establishing effective linkages between the political and technocratic modernizers, and the mass of Colombians. If the National Front is unable to surmount this difficulty, which seems probable, it will continue to appear to many as merely a new form of hegemony—this time not the dominance of one party but of a social class, now united within itself in defense of its economic interests and social privileges.

Finally, there is the predicament that an elite like Colombia's has in certain senses been deprived of that deference which it presumably needs to carry out its role as modernizer. It is undoubtedly true that among most Colombians "subject" orientations toward politics and government still prevail. Yet the bogotazo, the years of la violencia, the direct action behavior of numerous interest groups, the continued "independence" of certain rural enclaves, and the persistent abstention of many voters from the polls, are all indications that there has been a very serious undermining of authority, both governmental and in social relationships, in recent years. The supremacy of the state as a substantially neutral, secular arbiter has not as yet been established, despite the efforts of the National Front. The state itself remains quite weak in its ability to enforce compliance with its decisions. Furthermore, the Colombian elite has so far not been able to create a mystique of development which might provide, through identification with a broad national goal, a functional substitute for deference. (Thus there is evidence to suggest that in Mexico an identification with the Revolution and with the presidents who successively have become its leaders has helped to free the revolutionary elite from the need to produce immediate results for the masses.) In any case, the Colombian elite seems increasingly to lack the sort of deference which the British aristocracy, for example, was able to evoke while it played the part of modernizer during the nineteenth century.

Sustained and successful modernization by an elite may have been feasible in nineteenth-century England. Given such factors as the higher level of mass politicization at a comparable stage of economic development, and the much higher "load" of demands on the political system, the endeavor in countries like contemporary Colombia would appear doomed to ultimate failure.

CAUSES

When one turns from the nature of the process of modernization by an elite, and from its achievements and shortcomings, to deal with cause the problems are manifold. Fundamentally, we seek the reasons why the Colombian elite has succeeded in retaining the direction of the modernization process essentially in its own hands, and why counter-elite groups have failed to pose as meaningful a challenge to elite rule as they have elsewhere in Latin America.

The difficulties in analysis are, broadly speaking, two. Most important is that our propositions are not really provable. We treat the case of but a single country, while we are concerned with the kinds of questions of historical cause and effect which often do not admit of quantitative or strictly documented verification. Secondly, the categories of causation earlier set forth themselves overlap. This makes it not always possible, for example, to distinguish causes rooted in social structure from those founded in the nature of the traditional party system. Recognizing such limitations, and employing the categories outlined in the Introduction, let us nevertheless proceed with the analysis.

Ecological Factors

Seymour M. Lipset has suggested that the propensity of the members of a lower class to develop common class attitudes is related to their concentration in a given social environment.[6] Colombia would seem, in a negative sense, to add weight to this hypothesis. The fact that potential counter-elites among the middle and lower classes are divided among four geographically separated major urban centers, as well as among several lesser but important cities or industrial regions, may have militated against the crystallization of a common class or group consciousness. It might also be hypothesized that such dispersion has created the logistical problem for any groups attempting to capture the centers of authority of concentrating their strength. Too, even should another bogotazo result in insurgents seizing the capital, several principal economic and population centers would remain outside their control and hence a focus for a comeback by the government. The *relative* lack of dominance of Bogotá in Colombia, compared to Lima, Buenos Aires, or Caracas in their respective countries, may thus be an important factor conditioning counter-elite cohesion.

Apart from the very traditionalism of the Colombian campesino, the structure of land ownership and labor relations in the countryside may bear on the failure of the rural lower class to develop a consciousness of class, despite several decades of unrest and violence. Minifundio owners, squatters, tenants, and sharecroppers predominate. Plantation "factories on the land," congenial to the growth of a wage-earning rural proletariat, are few; where they are prevalent, as in the sugar industry in the Valle del Cauca, unionization and political radicalism have both made some progress. There are also few communal holdings to serve as a foundation for class- or group-based revolution. Landownership, either legal or de facto, is fairly widespread. On the whole, individualism prevails in the Colombian countryside. This spirit has undoubtedly been further enhanced by the existence of an internal frontier—notably in the region of the Quindío but elsewhere as well—which has served as something of an

6. Seymour Martin Lipset, "The Changing Class Structure and Contemporary European Politics" (Paper prepared for delivery at the 1963 annual meeting of the American Political Science Association, New York, Sept. 1963), passim.

outlet for population pressures and the restless rural dweller. The hypothesis here is that where individualistic holdings and attitudes prevail, the stimuli of modernization will tend, at least initially, to produce a kind of anarchism (whose victims may well be intraclass) rather than class consciousness and effective "horizontal" organization.

Colombia has also had a reasonable availability of economic resources, and of elements within the elite who have been possessed of entrepreneurial and other economic skills. Potentially productive land is in fairly good supply (though not always in the right location), while other resources have been sufficient for the emergence of a modest industrial base. Economic growth, though erratic, has been quite consistently upward for several decades. Real wages have on the whole tended to rise over time; most Colombians are probably no worse off materially than they were five, ten, or twenty years ago; and many are in modestly better circumstances. Recovery from the depression of the '30s was fairly rapid, and even the bouts of intense inflation characteristic of some Latin American countries have so far been brief. All this says nothing in itself, of course, of *expectations* in relation to progressive material improvement. It merely suggests that, if the stability of a social and political order in part depends on its economic performance, Colombia has had certain advantages among the countries of the developing world.[7]

A final ecological consideration is that, unlike many other Latin American countries, foreign business enterprise has not been central to the development of Colombia's economy. One might hypothesize that this would make it much more difficult for workers, or for that matter small merchants or white-collar employees, to express their opposition to large businesses or large landholdings in terms of nationalistic emotions and ideologies. Moreover, it is presumably easier to call for government ownership of an industry or a resource if it is in foreign hands. It is interesting to note in this connection that among the principal centers of successful leftist activity in Colombia, either past or present, have been the banana plantation of the Atlantic coast, the oil fields, and the gold mines at Segovia in the department of Antioquia—all of them foreign-owned.[8]

7. For the long-term relevance of successful economic performance for politics see Lipset, *Political Man,* p. 70. It would be far removed from reality, however, to suggest that Colombia is characterized by *abundance;* for the latter's effects on political development see *Political Man,* pp. 50–53.

8. The point should not be exaggerated, though. Communist inroads in rural areas

Social Factors

Although class lines are not easily crossed in Colombia, the elite has been open to the entry of ambitious individuals into its ranks, especially through the avenue of economic achievement. Those two crucial modernizing groups, the entrepreneurs and the technocrats, are to a significant degree being absorbed into the ruling elite, or into their service, thus acquiring a stake in stability and the existing system. At the same time, some of the very members of traditional elite families are themselves capitalists or have otherwise become modernizers. As Millikan and Blackmer note, "Historically, the social conflicts inherent in modernization have been reduced when the large landowners have begun to raise the productivity of their own land or when they have shifted their interests to commerce and industry." [9] In one case the dynamic entrepreneurs of a whole region—Antioquia—have become an effective part of the elite under circumstances which preserved both their loyalty to the old order and even many of the mental sets of traditionalism. A major reason for the longevity of old political patterns may well be that the new industrialists have not found it necessary to challenge those patterns to achieve their ends. In sum, the very facility with which the Colombian elite has integrated the modern with the traditional has probably helped to postpone or mitigate the need for more far-reaching changes in social, economic, and political relationships. [10]

The values and goals of the middle sectors would likewise seem particularly relevant to an analysis of the stability of elite rule. For it is precisely from this social group that the push, and the leadership, for change has come in a number of other developing societies. Unfortu-

such as Viotá cannot be ascribed to an anti-foreign reaction. It might also be noted that in 1958 labor relations on the remaining United Fruit properties were described as "very good"; cf. May and Plaza, *The United Fruit Company,* p. 204.

9. Max Millikan and Donald W. Blackmer, eds., *The Emerging Nations* (Boston, Little, Brown, 1961), p. 128.

10. By the same token, adaptation in some ways may have inhibited adaptation in others, e.g. with regard to the admission of the lower classes to participation as a group or stratum. For the classic case of "fusion" see Harry Eckstein, "The British Political System," in Beer and Ulam, eds., *Patterns of Government.*

nately, comparative evidence concerning the attitudes and aims of the middle sectors of various societies is lacking. Even solid information on the Colombian middle sectors alone is scarce. Yet we would suggest that the Colombian middle sectors have been particularly prone to the "aristo-cratizing" orientations characteristic of many of that class in most countries of Latin America. We would further speculate that contributing to such a presumed state of affairs are: the strength and permanence of the elite itself; the cooptation of the potential leadership cadres of a middle class into the elite; the influence of the Catholic Church (greater in Colombia than in many countries of Latin America); and the channeling of middle-class political aspirations into two traditional, elite-dominated political parties. Moreover, the arrival of the Colombian middle sectors on the stage of history at roughly the same time as a politicized working class may lead them to seek their political allies from among the elite before the latter is politically defeated, and before the middle class has attained a real consciousness of its own independent strength and objectives.

Finally, it may be crucial (though it is also true of other Latin American countries) that a relatively small, but key, segment of the working class— notably those in the larger industrial firms and in foreign enterprises— has received most of the benefits of the welfare state without much struggle. Wages may still be low. But the fact that the state and the firm have replaced the former patrón-peón relationship of the hacienda with a kind of welfare paternalism may be highly significant in tempering the workers' sense of identification with their fellows over against the employer or the government. A corollary consideration is that such welfare privileges are not in practice (and often not in law) extended to the majority of the rural and urban lower classes. There is thus created a privileged stratum within the lower class which may be quite uninterested in organizing those in less favored occupations, or in uniting with them for political action.

The Colombian social order is therefore interlaced by a series of attitudes and relationships which arranges groups and classes in a fairly rigid hierarchical order and leads them to seek, not a restructuring of that order, but a consolidation of their own position within it. Though the pattern is a common one in Latin America, we advance the proposition that it has had a special hold in Colombia.

Political Culture

Several aspects of Colombian political culture have helped to perpetuate elite rule. One of these is the continued predilection of most Colombians to "look up" for decisions and largesse and to feel that there is little they can or should do to influence the policy making process. This "subject" orientation common to most Latin Americans is reinforced in the Colombian case by the dominance in the political system of two elite-controlled parties and the relative weakness of class-organized alternatives. This pattern is in turn related to the hereditary hatreds which have constituted the primary basis of political cleavage in the country. The hereditary hatreds have both strengthened the elite's hold on the traditional parties and made it difficult to align Colombians' political emotions in a manner which would oppose the interests of counter-elites to those of the elite.

It is also true that there tends to be a certain deprecation of the national self among Colombians at all social levels. Derived in part from the "foreignizing" ways of the elite itself, in part, perhaps, from the absence of a visible national goal or external enemy, it expresses itself in many ways: a talking-down of one's own country; a hardly disguised scorn for one's fellow nationals; the hope that one might somehow escape one's own country; the imitation of foreign ways and foreign ideas.[11] For our immediate purposes, this deprecation of the national (and personal) self has meant that it has been that much more difficult to organize political movements focused on nationalist aspirations of counter-elite groups.

Traditional Institutions

That history has bequeathed to the country two polyclass parties deeply rooted in the Colombian psyche and controlled by members of the upper class is surely central to any analysis of the inability of counter-elite groups to find effective independent channels of political expression. The

11. Lipman notes that in one small sample survey only eleven per cent of Colombians disagreed with the statement, "All countries have their rights and wrongs, but Colombia is almost always wrong." Lipman, "Perception of the Colombian Agrarian Reform," p. 2.

violence which has often accompanied the rivalry between these two parties has served further to rigidify traditional loyalties and to prevent political realignment. Since potential class conflicts cut across partisan lines of division, the likelihood of political polarization along Right-Left lines is materially diminished.

At the same time, the Liberal party in particular has been able to talk in language which sounded reformist enough, and to point to sufficient achievements on behalf of the popular welfare, to prevent its following from going elsewhere. Even Gaitán, who experimented briefly in the early '30s with the UNIR, thereafter strove to carry out his program within and in the name of the Liberal party, under which designation he received wide support. The historical circumstance that the Liberals came to power in 1930 to effect a supposed "revolution" at the precise moment when new parties were forming elsewhere in Latin America, that the party carried Colombia successfully through the depression years, and that it launched the revolution on the march at the time it did, undoubtedly gave a major assist to the Liberals in neutralizing forces which might otherwise have proven insurgent. In contrast, then, to Liberal parties of some of the other Latin American nations, the Colombian Liberal party has been able to adapt sufficiently to the new to prevent its displacement by another party or the permanent defeat of its old-line leadership from within. One should also not overlook the presence of the strong Conservative half of Colombia's party system. Had the Liberal party split or been challenged by a significant party on the Left the victor in the 1930s would have been neither the Left nor the old Liberals, but the Conservatives, as occurred in 1946.

With the advent of the National Front the pattern of paternalistic reform has been repeated, this time embracing both traditional parties. The very fact that the parties, and the state, have adopted such a posture toward change is one element that must be taken into consideration in explaining the failure of counter-elite movements to gain strength. That the National Front has forged a degree of intra-elite harmony over the issues of modernization—precisely at a time when intra-elite conflict had imposed a tentative counter-elite solution in the form of the Rojas regime —is also of considerable import. For among the historic preconditions of the decline and fall of a ruling group is said to be its own internal division in the face of external threat.

Meanwhile both the Colombian military and the Catholic Church have in the main supported the elite road to modernization. Despite the direct military intervention of the years 1953–57, the Colombian armed forces entered politics at the time precisely to bring about a cessation of conflict within the elite, not to supplant its rule. There were features of the Rojas regime which suggested otherwise. But for the most part, including during the year of junta rule, and since under the National Front, the Colombian military has played a role essentially supportive of elite rule. The army has not thrown its considerable weight behind men like Ruiz Novoa and the renascent Rojas Pinilla. At least as yet there seems to be little inclination in the military to take over the job of modernization itself or to serve as a prop for a populistic authoritarianism. Its dominant approach is to enforce institutional stability and to employ its personnel and facilities in tasks which will increase its own, and the regime's, popularity. The recruitment over the years of much of the officer corps from rural and Conservative families, and the very lack of a tradition of political intervention, have probably contributed to such a stance. Most important, however, may have been the strength (and currently the relative cohesion) of the civilian elite itself. The military has therefore not been forced to fill a political vacuum (other than during the Rojas years); nor has it been induced to enter politics to exclude from the political arena powerful counter-elite groups which might threaten its own institutional prerogatives.[12]

It may also be that a strongly entrenched religion works against the victory (although not necessarily the rise) of a political religion such as Communism.[13] The influence of the Church, and of a traditional Catholic social philosophy of paternalistic charity, in the important industrial region of Antioquia, as well as in many rural areas, has probably helped to reduce the number of potential recruits to counter-elite political movements. Moreover, in recent years the Church has associated itself quite closely with the modernizing elite's approach to change. Its priests and

12. This would seem to have occurred, for example, in Argentina on various occasions since 1955, in Brazil in 1964, and in Peru in 1962. Cf. Edwin Lieuwen, *Generals vs. Presidents: Neomilitarism in Latin America* (New York, Praeger, 1964).

13. This factor seems to exercise particular influence on women in a Catholic society. It has not, however, prevented the simultaneous rise of strong Marxist parties in such Catholic countries as Chile and Italy. It may be that Communism acts as a surrogate religion once Catholicism has been discredited by its association with the social and political status quo, especially among men of the lower classes.

bishops have more or less openly campaigned for National Front candidates; and the Church's participation in such actions as the drawing up of Law 135 of 1961 has made it a kind of legitimizer of some of the principal programs of the National Front governments.

In sum, both the peculiar strength (compared to other countries of Latin America) of some of Colombia's traditional institutions—notably the traditional parties and the Church (plus, perhaps, the historic political weakness of the military)—as well as the common modernizing stance adopted by them all, has played one of the crucial roles in conditioning Colombia's political path to modernization.

Counter-Elite Groups

The relative weakness of organized counter-elite groups in Colombia, and the relative non-radicalness of the more important among them, owes much to the very strength and malleability of traditional institutions and of traditional values and social patterns. Nevertheless there are several points worth emphasizing regarding Colombian counter-elites that are not entirely subsumed under other causal categories.

One is the sectarianism, the organizational weaknesses, the general lack (with the notable exception of Gaitán) of strong or charismatic personalities among the leadership of opposition political groups. Some of these problems are frequent ones in Latin American organizational life. Insofar as their Colombian versions do differ in degree from those of other countries (and comparative data are lacking to confirm that they do), circumstances such as the untimely death of Gaitán may have played a part. Yet it may also be that the propensity of sons of the elite or men of upper-middle-class status to assume the leadership of opposition groups (e.g. Alfonso López Michelsen, Alvaro Uribe) has militated against their effective organization of the masses and has led to an intellectualizing of politics remote from its hard realities.

Nor have the conditions been ripe for the masses to follow a counter-elite opposition leadership. Samuel Huntington has suggested that intellectuals in developing societies tend to be inherently revolutionary. The question of whether a polity will undergo social revolution then depends on whether the intellectuals can forge a mass base. According to Huntington, the bulk of the urban middle class tends to grow conservative as it increases in size, while urban labor, for some of the reasons already suggested, is also likely to be nonrevolutionary. The key is then the campesino.[14] In Colombia several groups of the revolutionary Left have turned their hopes in the campesino's direction, but as yet there is little evidence that significant numbers of Colombian rural dwellers have joined their ranks. Links between urban intellectuals and the guerrilla partisans of the traditional parties also remained very weak throughout the years of la violencia. In fact, the violence helped to channel the frustrations of agrarian change along the lines of interparty (intra-elite) conflict instead of those of social revolution.

Finally, Colombian counter-elite groups have lacked a focus around which an opposition coalition might be built. Nationalism and "anti-imperialism" are of course invoked by the Left, and by the non-Left as well. But tangible targets in the form of major foreign enterprises are for the most part not available (in contrast to the salience of the foreign oil companies in Venezuela, for example, or of the copper mines in Chile, or of the pre-revolutionary tin industry in Bolivia, or of the sugar industry in pre-Castro Cuba). Furthermore, the rape of Panama is by now ancient history and Colombia has no recent experience of the political overlordship of a colonial power against which to inveigh. Nor has a search for national self-identification and pride as yet impelled Colombians to seek out a foreign enemy in order to help construct it. Hence there has not taken place in Colombia a merging of the socioeconomic with nationalist issues, and the association in the popular mind of foreign "imperialism" with their own foreignizing elites, a fusion which has nourished so many of the revolutionary movements of the modern era (including those of Mexico, Bolivia, and Cuba in Latin America).[15] Indeed, we would hypothesize that an identification with nationalist symbols is a necessary, though not sufficient, condition for a counter-elite to mount an effective challenge to an incumbent elite in the developing nations.

Nor has the long-term oppression of a tyrant served as a focus of opposition unity (at that, the short-lived Rojas regime united the elite rather

14. Professor Samuel Huntington of Harvard University, in a lecture delivered at Yale University, New Haven, Conn., January 12, 1966.

15. In an interview with the author on Aug. 29, 1963, Alvaro Uribe Rueda, leader of the Línea Dura, acknowledged that in the absence of an obvious U.S. presence in Colombia which could serve as a target for nationalistic attack, the alleged anti-democratic nature of the National Front would have to serve as a surrogate focus of cohesion for an opposition movement.

than the counter-elite opposition). Colombia's political system, for all its exclusiveness, has remained in certain important ways an open one. If, as Celso Furtado affirms, social revolution occurs in politically closed societies, Colombia is not a candidate for upheaval.[16] Again, the elite's aristocratic republicanism has served it well.

External Influences

Foreign influences on Colombia's particular political approach to modernization began perhaps with former President López' admiration for England and its style of pragmatic politics, and with his knowledge of and interest in the New Deal in the United States. In Britain the upper class had continued to play a leading political role while at the same time proving its adeptness at adjustment to changed circumstances. The New Deal represented the attempt of an established system (though not of an elite in the British or Colombian sense) to save itself by reforming itself.

More recently, the 1960s have been the era of Castro, of new attitudes emanating from Rome, of the Alliance for Progress. The Cuban Revolution has quite evidently stimulated something of a defensive reaction on the part of the Colombian elite (it seems, for example, to have been in the minds of a number during the course of passage of Law 135 of 1961). A new spirit within the Vatican with regard to social and political change has had a significant impact on one of the major institutions of Colombian society, the Roman Catholic Church. And Colombia was to have been one of the showcases of the Alliance for Progress, even though the initial enthusiasm has diminished somewhat with time and with disappointment over Colombia's economic performance. The Alliance, in fact, is a practically unique attempt by a foreign power to induce changes within other societies in return for aid, both financial and technical. And there is fairly clear evidence of instances in which pressure exerted by the United States was instrumental in the enactment of certain of the National Front reforms.[17] More intangible, but possibly more important, is that a power

16. Celso Furtado, "Brazil: What Kind of Revolution?" *Foreign Affairs* (April 1963), pp. 526–35.

17. Cf. *El Espectador,* Aug. 14, 1963, p. 10. According to one United States official the tax reforms of 1963 and 1965 would not have gone through, at least in the form that they did, if the U.S. had not exerted pressure by means of the threatened withholding of aid allocations.

generally assumed in Latin America to be supportive of the status quo has committed itself to measured change. Colombian government officials have indeed sometimes publicly defended their actions on the grounds that they were the result of an "international commitment" and an essential quid pro quo for aid received under the Alliance for Progress.[18] In any case, the United States has through its aid program helped both to legitimize (in the eyes of conservative groups) and to support materially a political approach to change which is that of a modernizing elite.

The Management of Historic Crises

The most significant feature of the Colombian political system's management of the several historic crises that tend to confront nations in the course of modernization is that the crisis of integration—in this case the forging of a sense of community among the traditional adherents of Conservatism and Liberalism—has remained unresolved well into the era in which the system has been faced with a new political awareness on the part of previously excluded strata of the population. Put another way, the cleavages characteristic of the hereditary hatreds have persisted into a time when the conditions and pressures are potentially present for an expanded participation of the masses in politics on behalf of their own class interests, for the more effective "penetration" of the government's administrative arm into various areas of Colombian life, and for a larger governmental role in the distribution of the society's material and psychic rewards. The result, in terms of our analysis, has been to strengthen abnormally the hand of those who owe their leadership to the traditional pattern of politics and to make more difficult the consolidation of counter-elites around new socioeconomic banners.

Secondly, one of the key counter-elite groups—urban labor—was not forced to struggle for an alteration in political arrangements in order to win the right to organize and to strike, and to benefit from welfare legislation.[19] Rather, these things were granted, along with fuller political participation, by a paternalistic elite, mainly during the years of the revo-

18. Cf. Minister of Agriculture Virgilio Barco, as quoted in *El Tiempo,* July 27, 1963, p. 31.
19. Cf. Lipset, *Political Man,* p. 67.

lución en marcha.[20] The majority of Colombia's working population, especially the large number of campesinos, were largely unaffected by the
new unionism and the new welfare laws, and even the gains of organized
urban labor were far from princely. But a protected stake in the system
was afforded the latter, beyond indeed the power of labor, acting on its
own, to effect. This may be one reason why Colombian labor has remained fairly conservative, and only mildly inclined to pursue diffuse
political goals. The hypothesis is that the way in which a group is accorded a stake in the ongoing system is an important conditioner of its
subsequent political behavior.

Short of systematic examination of other instances of modernizing elites
it is impossible to be sure which of the various factors we have mentioned
bear most closely on our intended explanation of the Colombian development pattern. Even then, there would be obvious limits on the use of
comparisons of a large number of countries as the equivalent of a laboratory experiment. Certainly, the points we have raised regarding Colombia
can only suggest, not prove or validate. We are inclined, however, to
emphasize three things, which to some extent crosscut the categories we
have employed above.

The first is the strength and nature of the traditional linkages between
the Colombian elite and the mass of the population. Most striking among
these, and most distinctive of Colombia, is the party system of the hereditary hatreds and the interparty violence which it has helped to foster.
Another is the role of the Roman Catholic Church in Colombian society.
The tenacity of such linkages has helped to maintain traditional leadership patterns during a period of rapid change.

The second is the adaptability of the elite and its major institutions.
Subsumed here are the fusion of the traditional and the modern within
the elite itself and the elite's willingness and ability to coopt ambitious
individuals (though not whole groups) into its own ranks. The modernizing role assumed in the 1930s by the Liberal party (a role conditioned
by its urban orientation and social composition and its doctrinal devotion
to nineteenth-century liberalism), and subsequently by both parties in the

20. The measure of participation was of course limited. It did include the vote, the
right to strike, and a new paternalistic concern on the part of the elite. It only
marginally entailed effective inclusion in the decision-making process.

National Front, is also highly relevant in this connection. That the military and the Church have accepted the imperatives of change is important as well.

Lastly, there is the inability of counter-elites to cohere around a sustained challenge to the elite. It has been conditioned by such factors as regionalism, the actual or apparent opportunities for individual advancement in existing Colombian society, the entry of labor into the political system under paternalistic auspices, the desire on the part of important elements of the lower and middle classes to maintain acquired stakes in the system, the traditional partisan divisions which rend all groups in Colombian society, and the absence of a nationalistic focus for anti-elite frustrations.

THE ROAD AHEAD

What has sustained elite rule in the past, and what has induced the Colombian elite to assume a modernizing role, will of course not necessarily remain true of the future. There are several trends at work on which a supposition of imminent alterations in the pattern of rule by a modernizing elite might be predicated. One of these is fragmentary evidence of a long-term radicalization of the countryside. Partly responsible have been the destructive effects of la violencia on traditional authority patterns, and on the propensity of the campesino to organize for action and to develop his own, nontraditional leadership. Community development, the radiophonic schools of Radio Sutatenza, and the promises and beginnings of agrarian reform are producing changes in values and attitudes whose ultimate impact is hard to predict but certain to be disruptive of traditional outlooks. There are indications, too, that the Colombian student movement has entered a more radical and activist phase, suggesting that there may be developing a significant sector among youth which is failing to find opportunities that fulfill its expectations in society as it is now structured. Among the ranks of organized labor, the UTC, once self-confessedly apolitical, has shown some signs of greater militancy.

Colombia's rapid rate of urbanization, considerably outrunning the ability of industry and commerce to absorb the migrants into productive and remunerative employment, or of government to provide such facilities as housing, transportation, or water, meanwhile suggests an increasing gap between aspiration and achievement. One study of the social correlates of political instability in fact placed Colombia high on an "index of social frustration." [21] Moreover, Colombia has for long been characterized by a strong emphasis on distinctions of social status; the isolation of the lower class from the activities, issues, and organizations of the rest of the social system; and fairly rapid industrialization, all, according to Lipset, tending toward a radicalization of the lower class.[22] The fact that the recent writings of a number of Colombian intellectuals— men like Alfonso López Michelsen, José Gutiérrez, and Fernando Guillén Martínez—are replete with calls for "authenticity," and with the urgency of the rediscovery of the real roots of the nation and of the creation of a healthy nationalism, further suggests that a nationalist focus for counter-elite action may be in its germinating stage.

For all the impressive skills and adaptability of the Colombian upper class, it would also be misleading to overestimate the effectiveness and success of its response to change. Economically, and in the political short-run, the success of the elite has been modestly impressive. Yet it has so far failed to cope, and may in the future well be unable to cope, with the deeper social and political implications of modernization. In particular, the system has failed to solve the crisis of participation, other than at the formal level of voting (and even so, with some qualification). The traditional parties have failed effectively to adjust their own internal structures and patterns of recruitment to a politics where socioeconomic issues are central and the lower and middle classes are at least potentially participant. The regime of the modernizing elite continues to lack the institutional channels through which participation of non-elite groups in the political process can effectively take place. Social mobilization, now much farther advanced than in the days of the revolution on the march, has far outrun the development of the institutional instruments both of participation and administration.

The principal exception to our contention that there has been an absence in Colombia of a strong party or movement opposed to continued upper-class rule—the rise of Gaitanismo in the years 1944–48—is instruc-

21. Ivo Feierabend, Rosalind Feierabend, and Betty Newbold, "Correlates of Political Stability" (Paper prepared for delivery at the annual meeting of the American Political Science Association, New York, Sept. 1963), p. 17.

22. See Lipset, *Political Man*, chapters 2–4 passim; and Lipset, "Changing Class Structure," passim.

tive in this connection. Gaitán's rise, and the bogotazo that followed his death, were the consequence of the post-war dislocations produced by inflation and industrialization, of the failure of the second administration of Alfonso López to fulfill its promise, and of the electoral victory of the Conservatives in 1946. Insofar as a pre-revolutionary situation prevailed in the Colombia of those years (and, among other reasons, this is doubtful in view of the staunch ties of non-elite groups, and even of Gaitán, to the traditional parties) the proposition would seem to hold that "Revolutions are most likely to occur when a prolonged period of objective economic and social development is followed by a short period of sharp reversal." [23] Except that, in the Colombian case, the sharp reversal was as much political as it was economic or social. The parallel cannot be extended too far, but there are some distinct similarities between the "reversal" of the late forties, and the failure of the National Front to meet expectations of more rapid change.

Finally, if there is anything to the point that a system's stability is in part dependent on its success in managing a series of historical crisis-problems in some sequence which permits one to be resolved before the system is forced to confront others, the survival of the current system would appear to be open to considerable doubt. Actually, no one of such crises—those of identity, legitimacy, integration, participation, penetration, and distribution—has been truly resolved in Colombia. All today impinge concurrently on the system. Thus, for example, the masses have entered, or are seeking to enter, the political arena before Colombians have reached agreement on the aims and nature of the state, or come to view it as promotive of the general rather than particular interests. The strain may eventually prove too great for a governing class such as the Colombian, and for a system which seeks to modernize within the forms of representative government.

The fact that rule by a modernizing elite continues to prevail in Colombia, despite the presence of a number of factors—some of them long-standing—which would seem to undermine it, is all the more testimony to the strength and significance of those causes which have helped to sustain elite rule. Moreover, if economic growth can be accelerated, it might provide just enough of a margin of expanding opportunities for the most

23. James A. Davies, "Toward a Theory of Revolution," *American Sociological Review,* 27 (Feb. 1962), 6.

ambitious among the non-elites to prevent their attempting to remove the incumbent leadership from its commanding position. Some modifications of the National Front agreements to improve its representativeness and mitigate its immobilism may also be in the offing. Thus President Lleras Restrepo has proposed an end to the two-thirds rule for the approval of legislation by Congress, and the granting of proportional representation in Congress to all parties and factions (while still preserving the Liberal-Conservative alliance).

Indeed, despite indications that the Colombian polity is at its most radicalized point since 1948, the prospects of a true social revolution—that is, the more or less wholesale destruction of the old configuration of power and its replacement by a new—seem rather dim. The residues of traditional linkages between the elite and the masses, the very adaptiveness of the elite, the continued vitality of institutions such as the military and the Church, the partial openness of the society (the existence of a meaningful opposition is an example), and the disarray of the very advocates of revolution, are among the factors militating against it. Furthermore, despite the gradual emergence of class-oriented issues and political groupings in the countries of Latin America, it seems unlikely that exclusivist ideological movements based on appeals to a single class, and seeking to destroy other classes, will come to dominate the political scene in the near future. For, crosscutting the tendency of political cleavage to align itself along a class-versus-class dimension are cleavages which pit against each other modernizers and traditionalists, and modernizers who differ on the desirable degree and manner of change.

Broadly speaking, there are two potential sequels to rule by a modernizing elite in the context of contemporary Latin America. One resembles what Samuel Huntington has called political decay, that is, an actual *decline* in the ability of government to deal with change through the failure of institutions such as parties to provide effective links between the elites and the increasingly politicized mass of the population.[24] This gap between mobilization and institutionalization produces a politics of direct action on the part of groups whose interests are imperfectly aggregated by parties and the legislature. It is a politics which leads to outbreaks of

24. For an extended discussion of the concept of political decay see Samuel P. Huntington, "Political Development and Political Decay," *World Politics,* 27 (Apr. 1965), 386–430.

anomic and quasi-anarchic violence. It is a politics which brings frequent military intervention, or threatened intervention. There is thus created a *new* instability, quite distinct from the instability of the past which fed on personal ambition for prestige or material gain and merely entailed changes in the persons of those who governed. The new instability is more profound and has an intimate connection with the failure of elite groups fully to meet the challenge of change, and in particular to confront forthrightly the crisis of participation.

The other possible sequel is for the emergence of a coalition that embraces the modernizers (and quite possibly some traditionalists as well, for varying reasons) within a wide spectrum of groups and classes. Such coalitions may vary in their form—from the Christian Democrats of Chile operating within a regime of constitutional democracy, to the current version of Mexico's democratic one-party mobilization regime. They may similarly include authoritarian populisms like those of Perón and Vargas. The common threads are that each represents a broad coalition of classes and groups, including many with a substantial existing stake in the system; that each has a leadership (usually of middle-sector origin) committed to substantial modernization—including its social and political dimensions; and that each has built some kind of effective link (through such means as party organization and charisma) between the new governing group and the mass of the population. Their approach—despite certain ideological façades—tends to resemble a politics of pragmatic modernization rather than a politics of intense ideological and class warfare. Helping to cement the coalition is usually an element of self-conscious nationalism. An essential difference from earlier European developments is that the tasks of modernization tend to enlist the interests of many groups and classes simultaneously, including some of the very groups who in a different time and place bitterly resisted the effort or were remote from it.

This is not precisely the kind of incremental change depicted by Hirschman, however. His reformmonger is the leader of a minority of modernizers who must seek to construct different coalitions on different issues from among those, on the Right or Left, who essentially oppose particular reforms but are induced by persuasion or political legerdemain to support them.[25] The modernizing coalitions of which we speak, on the other hand,

25. See Hirschman, *Journeys toward Progress.*

are politically dominant, at least for the time being, or are on their way to becoming so. Though at given moments they may well employ the tactics of the reformmonger, they are also to some extent willing and able to *override* the opposition of both traditionalists and revolutionaries to achieve their goals. They are more inclined to modify structures than is the reformmonger, who tends to be content to work within the existing order.

There is, in fact, a potential bond that might be forged between the modernizers within the Colombian elite and many in the middle and popular classes. If the traditional parties were willing to utilize their poly-class composition to give genuine representation in party councils to non-elite groups, the potential might be made actual. The reunion of the warring factions of the Liberal party on the basis of compromise between the oficialistas and the insurgents of the MRL, and a reorientation of the Conservative party in a genuinely social Christian direction, would be steps to this end. Yet the likelihood of such fusions or reorientations, and any real participation in the parties' leadership for groups currently excluded, appear to be remote. The apparent failure of the Liberal party reforms of 1963 here seems indicative.

To date, there is only faint evidence of the emergence of the kind of modernizing coalition—including a major role for non-elite groups—that will rescue the country from what appears to be a fairly advanced state of political decay. In the end, as Organski notes, syncratic regimes (and we have so characterized the National Front) are necessarily only interim solutions. In his view they are generally succeeded by some form of parliamentary regime rooted in the new era of mass politics which accompanies the shift from industrializing to industrialized societies. In today's Latin America, where the transition may well be prolonged, the alternatives would seem rather to be the accentuation of political decay or the forging of a broadly based modernizing coalition, infused with the spirit of a new nationalism, as a substitute for the eroded bonds of traditional authority.

BIBLIOGRAPHY

The following bibliography consists of those items relating to Colombia which were consulted and found useful in writing this book. Those items consulted but not made use of and references not concerning Colombia have been omitted.

BOOKS

Aguilera Camacho, Alberto, *Derecho Agrario Colombiano*, Bogotá, Ediciones Tercer Mundo, 1962.

Alexander, Robert J., *Communism in Latin America*, New Brunswick, Rutgers University Press, 1957.

American University (Washington, D.C.), Foreign Areas Studies Division, *Special Warfare Area Handbook for Colombia*, U.S. Department of the Army, 1961.

Andrade, Raúl, *La Internacional Negra en Colombia y Otros Ensayos*, Quito, Editora Quito, 1954.

Arciniegas, Germán, *The State of Latin America*, trans. Harriet de Onís, New York, Alfred A. Knopf, 1952.

Azula Barrera, Rafael, *De la Revolución al Orden Nuevo: Proceso y Drama de un Pueblo*, Bogotá, Editorial Kelly, 1956.

Bedoya Cardona, Ernesto, ed., *De Desterrado a Presidente*, Medellín, Tipografía Estilo, 1950.

Belmonte, Pedro Luis, *Antecedentes Históricos de los Sucesos del 8 y 9 de Junio de 1954*, Bogotá, Imprenta Nacional, 1954.

Betancur, Belisario, *Colombia Cara a Cara*, Bogotá, Ediciones Tercer Mundo, 1961.

Blandón Berrío, Fidel, *Lo Que el Cielo no Perdona*, Bogotá, Editorial Minerva, 1955.

Burnett, Ben G., "The Recent Colombian Party System: Its Organization and Procedure," unpublished Ph.D. dissertation, University of California at Los Angeles, 1955.

Bushnell, David, *The Santander Regime in Gran Colombia*, Newark, Delaware, University of Delaware Press, 1954.

Caicedo, Daniel, *Viento Seco*, Bucaramanga, Imprenta Meridiano, 1955.

419

Canal Ramírez, Gonzalo, *El Estado Cristiano y Bolivariano del 13 de Junio*, Bogotá, Editorial Antares, 1955.

———, *Del 13 de Junio al 10 de Mayo en las Fuerzas Armadas*, Bogotá, Editorial Antares, 1958.

——— and Jaime Posada, *La Crisis Moral Colombiana*, Bogotá, Editorial Antares, 1955.

Cárdenas García, Jorge, *El Frente Nacional y los Partidos Políticos (Análisis e Interpretación de una Política)*, Tunja, Boyacá, Imprenta Departamental, 1958.

Comité Central del Partido Comunista de Colombia, *Treinta Años del Partido Comunista de Colombia*, Bogotá, Ediciones Paz y Socialismo, 1960.

Consuegra, José, *Apuntes de Economía Política*, 2d. ed., Bogotá, Ediciones Tercer Mundo, 1964.

Córdoba, José María, *Jorge Eliécer Gaitán, Tribuno Popular de Colombia*, Bogotá, 196(?).

Crist, Raymond E., *The Cauca Valley, Colombia: Land Tenure and Land Use*, Baltimore, Waverly Press, 1952.

Cuéllar Vargas, Enrique, *13 Años de Violencia*, Bogotá, Editorial SIPA, 1960.

Cultura y Economía en: Colombia, Ecuador, Venezuela, Bogotá, Oliverio Perry, 1956.

Currie, Lauchlin, *Ensayos sobre Planeación*, Bogotá, Ediciones Tercer Mundo, 1963.

Díaz, Antolín, *A la Sombra de Fouché; Pequeño Proceso de las Izquierdas en Colombia*, Bogotá, Editorial ABC, 1937.

Eder, Phanor James, *Colombia*, London, T. Fisher Unwin, 1913.

Fals Borda, Orlando, *El Hombre y la Tierra en Boyacá*, Bogotá, Editorial Antares, 1957.

———, *Peasant Society in the Colombian Andes: A Sociological Study of Saucío*, Gainesville, Fla., University of Florida Press, 1955.

Fluharty, Vernon Lee, *Dance of the Millions*, Pittsburgh, University of Pittsburgh Press, 1957.

Franco Isaza, Eduardo, *Las Guerrillas del Llano*, Caracas, Editorial Universo, 1955.

Gaitán, Jorge Eliécer, *Las Ideas Socialistas en Colombia*, Bogotá, Editorial América Libre, 1963.

———, *Las Mejores Oraciones de Jorge Eliécer Gaitán 1919–1948*, Bogotá, Editorial Jorvi, 1958.

Galbraith, W. O., *Colombia: A General Survey*, London, Royal Institute of International Affairs, 1953.

García, Antonio, *Gaitán y el Problema de la Revolución Colombiana*, Bogotá, 1955.

García, José Berardo, *La Explosión de Mayo*, Cali, Imprenta Departamental, 1957.

García Calderón, Francisco, *Latin America: Its Rise and Progress*, trans. Bernard Miall, New York, Scribner's, 1917.

Gibson, William Marion, *The Constitutions of Colombia*, Durham, N.C., Duke University Press, 1948.

Gómez, Laureano, *Comentarios a un Régimen*, Bogotá, Editorial Minerva, 1934.

Gómez Hurtado, Alvaro, *La Revolución en América*, Bogotá, Compañía Grancolombiana de Ediciones S.A., 1959(?).

———, *El Cuadrilátero*, Bogotá, Editorial Centro, 1935.

Guillén Martínez, Fernando, *Raíz y Futuro de la Revolución*, Bogotá, Ediciones Tercer Mundo, 1963.

Gutiérrez, José, *La No-Violencia en la Transformación Colombiana*, Bogotá, Ediciones Tercer Mundo, 1964.

———, *De la Pseudo-Aristocracia a la Autenticidad*, Bogotá, Ediciones Tercer Mundo, 1961.

———, *La Rebeldía Colombiana*, Bogotá, Ediciones Tercer Mundo, 1962.

Guzmán, Monseñor Germán, Orlando Fals Borda, Eduardo Umaña Luna, *La Violencia en Colombia*, Bogotá, Ediciones Tercer Mundo, I, (2nd ed. 1963), II (1964).

Hagen, Everett E., *On the Theory of Social Change*, Homewood, Illinois, The Dorsey Press, 1962.

Henao, Jesús María and Gerardo Arrubla, *History of Colombia*, trans. and ed. J. Fred Rippy, Chapel Hill, N.C., University of North Carolina Press, 1938.

Hernández Rodríguez, Guillermo, *La Alternación ante el Pueblo*, Bogotá, Editorial América Libre, 1962.

———, *De los Chibchas a la Colonia y a la República*, Bogotá, Universidad Nacional, 1949.

Hirschman, Albert O., *Journeys toward Progress*, New York, The Twentieth Century Fund, 1963.

Holt, Pat M., *Colombia Today—And Tomorrow*, New York, Frederick A. Praeger, 1964.

Hunter, John M., *Emerging Colombia*, Washington, D.C., Public Affairs Press, 1962.

James, Preston E., *Latin America*, 3rd ed., New York, Odyssey Press, 1959.

Jaramillo, Francisco de Paula, *La Democracia Cristiana: Una Nueva Perspectiva para Colombia*, Bogotá, Ediciones Caribe, 1962.

Johnson, John J., *The Military and Society in Latin America*, Stanford, Cal., Stanford University Press, 1964.

Lanao Loaiza, José Ramón, *Mirando las Izquierdas*, Manizales, 1935.

Lannoy, Juan Luis de and Gustavo Pérez, *Estructuras Demográficas y Sociales de Colombia,* Bogotá, Centro de Investigaciones Sociales, 1961.

Laserna, Mario, *Estado Fuerte o Caudillo,* Bogotá, Ediciones Mito, 1961.

Lieuwen, Edwin, *Arms and Politics in Latin America,* New York, Frederick A. Praeger, 1960.

Liévano Aguirre, Indalecio, *Rafael Núñez,* Bogotá, Compañía Grancolombiana de Ediciones, 1959(?).

Linke, Lilo, *Andean Adventure: A Social and Political Study of Colombia, Ecuador and Bolivia,* London, Hutchinson, 1945.

Lleras Camargo, Albert, *Sus Mejores Páginas,* Bogotá, Compañía Grancolombiana de Ediciones, 1959(?).

Lleras Restrepo, Carlos, *De la República a la Dictadura,* Bogotá, Editorial ARGRA, 1955.

Londoño, General Julio, *Geopolítica de Colombia,* 2nd ed., Bogotá, Ministerio de Guerra, 1949.

————, *Nación en Crisis,* Bogotá, Ministerio de Educación Nacional, 1955.

López, Alejandro, *Idearium Liberal,* Paris, Ediciones La Antorcha, 1931.

López de Mesa, Luis, *Escrutinio Sociológico de la Historia Colombiana* (Academia Colombiana de Historia) 2nd ed., Bogotá, Biblioteca Eduardo Santos, Vol. 10, 1956.

————, *Cuestiones Colombianas (Ensayos),* Mexico, D.F., Impresiones Modernas, 1955.

————, *Los Elegidos,* Mexico, Editorial Guaranía, 1953.

López Michelsen, Alfonso, *Colombia en la Hora Cero,* 2 vols. Bogotá, Ediciones Tercer Mundo, 1963.

Maffitt, Peter C., "Colombia, The Revolution on March 1934–1938," unpublished manuscript, New Haven, Conn., Scholars of the House Program, Yale University, 1963.

Martz, John D., *Colombia, A Contemporary Political Survey,* Chapel Hill, N.C., The University of North Carolina Press, 1962.

May, Stacy and Galo Plaza, *The United Fruit Company in Latin America,* New York, National Planning Association, 1958.

Mecham, J. Lloyd, *Church and State in Latin America,* Chapel Hill, N.C., University of North Carolina Press, 1934.

Misión "Economía y Humanismo" (Louis J. Lebret O.P., Director), *Estudio sobre las Condiciones del Desarrollo de Colombia,* Bogotá, Aedita, 1958.

Molina, Felipe Antonio, *Laureano Gómez, Historia de una Rebeldía,* Bogotá, Librería Voluntad, 1940.

Morales Benítez, Otto, *Revolución y Caudillos,* Medellín, Editorial Horizonte, 1957.

La Nación ante la Universidad, Curso Académico Organizado por la Universidad Nacional de Colombia, Bogotá, Fondo Universitario Nacional, 1957(?).

Nieto Arteta, Luis Eduardo, *Economía y Cultura en la Historia de Colombia*, 2nd ed., Bogotá, Ediciones Tercer Mundo, 1962.

Nieto Rojas, José María, *La Batalla contra el Comunismo en Colombia*, Bogotá, Empresa Nacional de Publicaciones, 1956.

Niño H., Alberto, *Antecedentes Secretos del 9 de Abril*, Bogotá, Editorial Pax, 1949(?).

Núñez, Rafael, *Los Mejores Artículos Políticos de Rafael Núñez*, Bogotá, Ministerio de Educación Nacional, 1936.

Osorio Lizarazo, J. A., *Gaitán: Vida, Muerte y Permanente Presencia*, Buenos Aires, Ediciones López Negri, 1952.

Ospina Vásquez, Luis, *Industria y Protección en Colombia 1810–1930*, Medellín, 1955.

Parsons, James J., *Antioqueño Colonization in Western Colombia*, Berkeley, Cal., University of California Press, 1949.

Los Partidos en Colombia, Bogotá, 1922.

Patiño B., Abelardo, "The Political Ideas of the Liberal and Conservative Parties in Colombia During the 1946–1953 Crisis," unpublished Ph.D. dissertation, Washington, D.C., American University, 1954.

Pérez Ramírez, Gustavo, *El Campesinado Colombiano*, 2nd ed., Bogotá, Centro de Investigaciones Sociales, 1962.

———, *El Problema Sacerdotal en Colombia*, Bogotá, Centro de Investigaciones Sociales, 1962.

Plata Uricoechea, Fernando, *El Régimen Constitucional en Colombia y en los Estados Unidos*, Bogotá, Editorial Cromos, 1943.

Puentes, Milton, *Historia del Partido Liberal Colombiano*, Bogotá, Talleres Gráficos Mundo al Día, 1942 (2nd ed. Editorial Prag, 1961).

Quimbaya, Anteo, *Cuestiones Colombianas*, Bogotá, Ediciones Suramérica, 1958.

———, *Los Tres Partidos Colombianos*, Bogotá, Ediciones Suramérica, 1959.

Ramírez Moreno, Augusto, *Una Política Triunfante*, Bogotá, Librería Voluntad, 1941.

Reichel-Dolmatoff, Gerado and Alicia, *The People of Aritama*, Chicago, University of Chicago Press, 1961.

Rippy, J. Fred, *The Capitalists and Colombia*, New York, Vanguard Press, 1931.

Rodríguez, General Amadeo, *Caminos de Guerra y Conspiración*, Barcelona, Gráficas Claret, 1955.

Rodríguez Piñeres, Eduardo, *Diez Años de Política Liberal, 1892–1902*, Bogotá, Librería Colombiana, 1945.

Rojas Pinilla ante el Senado: El Gobierno Militar ante la Historia, Bogotá, Editorial Excelsior, 1959.

Rueda Vargas, Tomás, *El Ejército Nacional,* Bogotá, Editorial Antena, 1944.

Ruiz Novoa, Alberto, *El Gran Desafío,* Bogotá, Ediciones Tercer Mundo, 1965.

Salamanca, Guillermo, *Los Partidos en Colombia,* Bogotá, Editorial "El Voto Nacional," 1961.

————, *La Républica Liberal,* 2 vols. Bogotá, Editorial Centro, 1937.

Samper, José M., *Los Partidos en Colombia,* Bogotá, 1873.

Sánchez Gómez, Gregorio, *Sociología Política Colombiana,* Cali, Sánchez Gómez Hnos., 194(?).

Santa, Eduardo, *Nos Duele Colombia,* Bogotá, Ediciones Tercer Mundo, 1962.

Santos, Eduardo, *Una Política Liberal para Colombia,* Bogotá, Editorial Minerva, 1937.

Santos Forero, Julio Enrique, *Yo Sí Ví Huir al Verdadero Asesino de Jorge Eliécer Gaitán,* Bogotá, Gráficas Atenas, 1959.

Sarría, Eustorgio, *La Democracia y el Poder Militar,* Bogotá, Editorial Iqueima, 1959.

Serrano Blanco, Manuel, *La Vida Es Así,* Bucaramanga, Imprenta del Departamento de Santander del Sur, 1953.

Sierra Ochoa, Colonel Gustavo, *Las Guerrillas de los Llanos Orientales,* Manizales, Imprenta Departamental (Caldas), 1954.

Sus Pacheco, Colonel Carlos, *Presente y Futuro ante el Nuevo Orden,* Bogotá, Editorial Antares, 1956.

Szulc, Tad, *Twilight of the Tyrants,* New York, Henry Holt, 1959.

Tierra: 10 Ensayos sobre la Reforma Agraria en Colombia, Bogotá, Ediciones Tercer Mundo, 1961.

Torres, Camilo and Berta Corredor, *Las Escuelas Radiofónicas de Sutatenza-Colombia,* Bogotá, Centro de Investigaciones Sociales, 1961.

Torres, Mauricio, *La Naturaleza de la Revolución Colombiana,* Bogotá, Editorial Iqueima, 1959.

Urdaneta Arbeláez, Roberto, *El Materialismo contra la Dignidad del Hombre,* Bogotá, Editorial Lucros, 1960.

Whitaker, Arthur P., *The United States and South America: The Northern Republics,* Cambridge, Mass., Harvard University Press, 1948.

Whiteford, Andrew H., *Two Cities of Latin America,* Beloit, Wisconsin, Beloit College, 1960.

ARTICLES, MONOGRAPHS, AND OCCASIONAL PAPERS

Adams, Dale W., "Landownership Patterns in Colombia," *Inter-American Economic Affairs* (Winter 1964), pp. 77–86.

Aguirre de Jaramillo, Fabiola, "Por Qué en Colombia Son Dos los Partidos Políticos," *Cuadernos Americanos* (Mexico) *44* (Mar.–Apr. 1949), 24–30.

Alderfer, E. Gordon, "The People, Sí," *Americas, 13* (May 1961), 2–9.

Andrade Valderrama, S.J., Vicente, "El País Político y el País Nacional," *Revista Javeriana, 51* (May 1959), 213–14.

———, "La U.T.C., Realidad Católica," *Revista Javeriana, 37* (March 1952), 98–102.

Antequera Stand, Miguel A., *Ocupación y Desocupación en Bogotá,* Monografía No. 14, Bogotá, Universidad de los Andes, Centro de Estudios sobre Desarrollo Económico, 1962.

Arciniegas, Germán, "La Dictadura en Colombia," *Cuadernos Americanos* (Mexico), *49* (Jan.–Feb. 1950), 7–33.

Bailey, Norman A., "The Black Hand," *Inter-American Economic Affairs* (Autumn 1962), pp. 79–85.

Bakke, E. Wight, *Students on the March: The Cases of Mexico and Colombia,* Reprint No. 31, Princeton, N.J., Inter-University Study of Labor Problems in Economic Development, 1964.

Beals, Ralph, "Social Stratification in Latin America," *American Journal of Sociology, 58* (1952–53), 327–39.

Centro de Investigaciones Sociales (CIS), *Compañía Colombiana de Tejidos S.A. (Coltejer). Estudio sobre las Condiciones Sociales y Económicos de los Trabajadores de la Compañía y Posibilidades de Mejoramiento,* Bogotá, CIS, 1962.

———, *Estudio sobre las Condiciones del Desarrollo de la Región de Tibú* (Catatumbo), *Cúcuta,* Bogotá, CIS, 1960.

———, *Estudios sobre Desarrollo, Informe No. 7, Condiciones de Desarrollo y Reconstrucción en el Municipio de Sonsón (Ant.),* Bogotá, CIS, 1963.

Colorado, Eugenio, *El Sindicato y la Comunidad Rural,* Washington, D.C., Unión Panamericana, 1954.

Culhane, Eugene K., "Red Pocket in Colombia," *America, 102* (March 12, 1960), 701–04.

Currie, Lauchlin, "Operación Colombia," *La Nueva Economía* (Bogotá), *1* (Aug. 1961), 395–510.

Deutschmann, Paul J., and Orlando Fals Borda, *La Comunicación de las Ideas entre los Campesinos Colombianos,* Monografías Sociológicas No. 14, Bogotá, Universidad Nacional, Facultad de Sociología, 1962.

Dozer, Donald Marquand, "Roots of Revolution in Latin America," *Foreign Affairs, 27* (Jan. 1949), 274–88.

Duque Gómez, Luis, "Los Problemas Antropogeográficos de Colombia y la Escuela Rural," *Ciencias Sociales* (Unión Panamericana), *5* (Oct. 1954), 194–206.

————, "Los Problemas del Minifundio en Colombia," *Economía Colombiana*, 3 (Jan. 1955), 577–85.

Espinosa S., Justiniano, "Unidad Sindical," *Revista Javeriana*, 52 (Oct. 1959), 302–10.

————, "Veinticinco Años de Sindicalismo," *Revista Javeriana*, 51 (Apr. 1959), 112–19.

Estructura y Organización Social, unpublished papers, Bogotá, Universidad Nacional, Facultad de Sociología, 1961.

Fals Borda, Orlando, *Acción Comunal en una Vereda Colombiana*, Monografías Sociológicas No. 4, Bogotá, Universidad Nacional, Departamento de Sociología, 1961.

————, *La Educación en Colombia, Bases para su Interpretación Sociológica*, Monografías Sociológicas No. 11, Bogotá, Universidad Nacional, Facultad de Sociología, 1962.

————, *Facts and Theory of Sociocultural Change in a Rural Social System*, 2d ed., Monografías Sociológicas No. 2 Bis., Bogotá, Universidad Nacional, Facultad de Sociología, 1962.

————, "El Liderazgo Rural y la Reforma Agraria," Paper prepared for First National Seminar on Agrarian Reform, Bogotá, Nov. 1962.

————, *La Transformación de la América Latina y sus Implicaciones Sociales y Económicas*, Monografías Sociológicas No. 10, Bogotá, Universidad Nacional, Facultad de Sociología, 1961.

Fitzgibbon, Russell H., "Colombian Gadfly," *The Inter-American*, 4 (Feb. 1945), 15, 18 and 35.

Gilmore, Robert Louis, "Nueva Granada's Socialist Mirage," *Hispanic American Historical Review*, 36 (May 1956), 190–210.

Goff, Fred, *Colombia: The Pre-Revolutionary Stage*, Mimeo., Stanford, Cal., Stanford University, Institute of Hispanic American and Luso-Brazilian Studies, 1963.

González, S.J., Miguel Angel, *"La Violencia en Colombia": Análisis de un Libro*, Bogotá, Centro de Estudios Colombianos, 1962.

Havens, A. Eugene, *Critique of "Proposal for an Evaluation of Acción Comunal as an Instrument of Agricultural Modernization and National Economic Development in Colombia,"* Mimeo., 1963.

———— and Michael Romieux, *A Socio-Economic Survey of Cereté, Córdoba: An Area of Latifundio*, Typescript draft, Bogotá, Universidad Nacional, Facultad de Sociología, 1963.

Helguera, J. León, "The Changing Role of the Military in Colombia," *Journal of Inter-American Studies* (July 1961), pp. 351–57.

Hobsbawm, E. J., "The Anatomy of Violence," *New Society* (London), April 11, 1963, pp. 16–18.

————, "The Revolutionary Situation in Colombia," *The World Today*, 19 (June 1963), 248–58.

Holguín Holguín, Carlos, "Los Partidos Políticos," *Universidad Nacional de Colombia*, 2nd epoch, No. 17, 1953.

Holt, Pat M., "Constitutional Development in Colombia," Paper prepared for delivery at the 1963 annual meeting of the American Political Science Association, New York, Sept. 1963.

Johnson, Kenneth, "Political Radicalism in Colombia: Electoral Dynamics of 1962 and 1964," *Journal of Inter-American Studies* (Jan. 1965), pp. 15–26.

Land Reform and Social Change in Colombia, Discussion Paper No. 4, Madison, Wis., University of Wisconsin, Land Tenure Center, November 1963.

Lipman, Aaron, *El Empresario Industrial en América Latina. 4. Colombia*, Naciones Unidas, Consejo Económico y Social, 1963.

————, "Perception of the Colombian Agrarian Reform as a Value," Typescript of paper presented at the annual meeting of the Rural Sociological Society Los Angeles, Cal., August 1963.

———— and A. Eugene Havens, "The Colombian Violencia: An Ex Post Facto Experiment," Mimeo., Madison, Wis., University of Wisconsin, Land Tenure Center, 1965.

López de Mesa, Luis, "Exegesis de la Novísima Reforma Constitucional Colombiana," *Universidad de Antiquia, 134* (July–Sept. 1958), 519–23.

López Michelsen, Alfonso, "Influencia del Capital Extranjero en la Economía Colombiana," *Revista Bolívar, 51* (March–April–May 1959), 491–95.

Madrid Malo, Nestor, "Génesis e Ineficacia de la Reforma sobre Tierras," *Universidad Nacional de Colombia, 1* (Oct. 1944), 399–420.

McGann, Thomas F., "The Assassination of Sucre and its Significance in Colombian History, 1828–48," *Hispanic American Historical Review, 30* (Aug. 1950), 269–89.

Mendershausen, Horst, "Economic and Fiscal Problems of a Colombian Department," *Inter-American Economic Affairs, 6* (Spring 1953), 49–89.

Pearse, Andrew and Salomón Rivera, *La Tenencia de la Tierra y sus Implicaciones Socio-Económicas en Tenza, Colombia. Un Estudio de Minifundio*, Typescript draft, Bogotá, Universidad Nacional, Facultad de Sociología, 1963.

Pineda Giraldo, Roberto, *El Impacto de la Violencia en El Tolima: el Caso de El Líbano*, Monografías Sociológicas No. 6, Bogotá, Universidad Nacional, Departamento de Sociología, 1960.

Powelson, John P., "The Land-Grabbers of Cali," *The Reporter* (January 16, 1964), pp. 30–31.

Prospects for Political Stability in Colombia with Special Reference to Land Reform, Madison, Wis., University of Wisconsin, Land Tenure Center, 1962.

428 Bibliography

Reichel-Dolmatoff, Gerardo, "Notas sobre la Clase Media en Colombia," *Ciencias Sociales* (Unión Panamericana) 3 (Feb. 1952), 2–4.

Romualdi, Serafino, "Labor and Democracy in Latin America," *Foreign Affairs*, 25 (April 1947), 477–89.

Sarría, Eustorgio, "Naturaleza Jurídico-administrativa de la Federación Nacional de Cafeteros," *La Nueva Economía* (Bogotá) 1 (June 1961), 321–47.

Savage, Jr., Charles H., *Social Reorganization in a Factory in the Andes,* Ithaca, N.Y., Cornell University, 1964.

Serna Vélez, Ivan, "Origen, Desarrollo y Futuro de FENALCO," *Universitas*, No. 14 (1958), 147–53.

Shaw, Jr., Carey, "Church and State in Colombia, as Observed by American Diplomats, 1834–1906," *Hispanic American Historical Review, 31* (Nov. 1941), 577–613.

Torres Restrepo, Camilo, *La Proletarización de Bogotá,* Monografías Sociológicas No. 9, Bogotá, Universidad Nacional, Facultad de Sociología, 1961.

United States Department of Labor, Bureau of Labor Statistics, *Labor Law and Practice in Colombia,* Washington, D.C., 1962.

Universidad Nacional de Colombia, Facultad de Sociología, *Factores Sociales Que Indicen en el Desarrollo Económico de la Hoya del Río Subachoque,* Typescript draft, Bogotá, 1963.

Wiesner Durán, Eduardo, *Barreras Artificiales a la Inversión Extranjera en la Industria Nacional,* Bogotá, Universidad de los Andes, Centro de Estudios sobre Desarrollo Económico, 1960.

———, *Control Personal de la Economía Colombiana, Monografía No. 6,* Bogotá, Universidad de los Andes, Centro de Estudios sobre Desarrollo Económico, 1960.

Williamson, Robert C., *El Estudiante Colombiano y sus Actitudes,* Monografías Sociológicas No. 13, Bogotá, Universidad Nacional, Facultad de Sociología, 1962.

———, "Toward a Theory of Political Violence: The Case of Rural Colombia," *Western Political Quarterly, 18* (March 1965), 35–44.

Young, Allen, *Revolutionary Parties in Contemporary Colombia,* Mimeo., Stanford, Cal., Stanford University, Institute of Hispanic American and Luso-Brazilian Studies, 1963.

OFFICIAL DOCUMENTS

Corporación Autónoma Regional de los Valles del Magdalena y del Sinú (CVM), *Informe,* Bogotá, Editorial Antares, 1962.

Cuentas Nacionales, 1950–, Bogotá, Banco de la República.

En Defensa de la Democracia Colombiana, Bogotá, Imprenta Nacional, 1944.

Documentos Relacionados con la Renuncia del Señor Presidente de la República, Bogotá, Imprenta Nacional, 1937.

Economic Commission for Latin America, *Analyses and Projections of Economic Development. III. The Economic Development of Colombia,* United Nations Department of Economic and Social Affairs, Geneva, 1957.

Economic Commission for Latin America (ECLA), Division of Social Affairs, *Some Aspects of Population Growth in Colombia,* ECLA, 1960.

Escuela Superior de Administración Pública (ESAP), *Organización Constitucional del Estado Colombiano,* Bogotá, Editorial Bremen, 1962.

————, *Realizaciones del Primer Gobierno del Frente Nacional,* Bogotá, Publicaciones ESAP, 1963.

El Gobierno, El Ejército y las Medidas del Estado de Sitio, Bogotá, Imprenta Nacional, 1944.

Gómez, Laureano, *Los Efectos de la Reforma de 1953,* Bogotá, Imprenta Nacional, 1953.

Inter-American Development Bank, *Institutional Reforms and Social Development Trends in Latin America,* Washington, D.C., March, 1963.

International Bank for Reconstruction and Development, *The Autonomous Regional Corporation of the Cauca and the Development of the Upper Cauca Valley,* Washington, D.C., 1955.

————, (Report of a Mission headed by Lauchlin Currie), *The Basis of a Development Program for Colombia,* Baltimore, Johns Hopkins Press, 1950.

Memorias del Señor Ministro de Gobierno al Congreso Nacional, Bogotá, Imprenta Nacional, 1945.

Mensajes del Presidente López al Congreso Nacional, 1934–1938, Bogotá, Imprenta Nacional, 1939.

La Oposición y el Gobierno, Del 9 de Abril de 1948 al 9 de April de 1950, Bogotá, Imprenta Nacional, 1950.

La Política Oficial. Mensajes, Cartas y Discursos del Presidente López, 5 vols. Bogotá, Imprenta Nacional, 1935–38.

Por Qué y Cómo se Forjó el Frente Nacional, Bogotá, Imprenta Nacional, 1959.

Progress Report, Techo, March 31, 1963, Memorandum from Housing Adviser, Agency for International Development (AID), Bogotá, to Acting Director, AID, Mimeo., May 1, 1963.

República de Colombia, *La Opinión Nacional ante la Reforma de la Constitución,* Bogotá, Imprenta Nacional, 1936.

————, Cámara de Representates, *Informe de la Comisión que investigó los sucesos sangrientos de Paquilo, Municipios de Pandi y San Bernardo, y estudió el problema de los colonos de Sumapaz,* Bogotá, Imprenta Nacional, 1932.

————, Consejo Nacional de Política Económica y Planeación, Departamento Administrativo de Planeación y Servicios Técnicos, *Colombia, Plan General de Desarrollo Económico y Social,* 2 vols. Bogotá, 1961–62.

————, Consejo Nacional de Política Económica y Planeación, Departamento Administrativo de Planeación y Servicios Técnicos, *Colombia, Plan Quatrenial de Inversiones Públicas Nacionales 1961–1964,* Bogotá, 1960.

————, Departamento Administrativo Nacional de Estadística, *Anuario General de Estadística, 1962,* Bogotá, 1964.

————, Departamento Administrativo Nacional de Estadística, *Directorio Nacional de Explotaciones Agropecuarias (Censo Agropecuario), 1960. Resumen Nacional,* Bogotá, 1960.

————, Ministerio de Gobierno, División de Acción Comunal, Sección de Investigación y Planeamiento, *Informe Nacional sobre el Desarrollo de la Comunidad en Colombia Presentado a la Secretaría del Consejo Interamericano Económico y Social de la Unión Panamericana,* Mimeo., Bogotá, 1963.

————, Ministerio de Gobierno, *Estudios Constitucionales,* 2 vols. Bogotá, Imprenta Nacional, 1953.

————, Registrador Nacional del Estado Civil, *El Sufragio y la Identificación Ciudadana en Colombia, 1959 a 1961,* 2 vols. Bogotá, Imprenta Nacional, 1962.

————, Registraduría Nacional del Estado Civil, *Organización y Estadísticas Electorales, Marzo y Mayo de 1962,* Bogotá, 1962.

————, Registraduría Nacional del Estado Civil, *Organización y Estadísticas Electorales, Marzo 15 de 1964,* Bogotá, 1965.

Revista de la Controlaría de la República, Separato de Anales de Economía y Estadística, Supl. to Nos. 17 & 18, Bogotá, May–June, 1946.

Ruiz Novoa, Major General Alberto, *La Acción Cívica en los Movimientos Insurrecionales,* Bogotá, Imprenta de las Fuerzas Militares, 1963.

PAMPHLETS, TRACTS, AND MISCELLANEOUS

Acción Comunal en Colombia, Bogotá, CARE and Federación Nacional de Cafeteros de Colombia, 1962.

2 Años Despues. Colombia Adelante, Bogotá, USIA, 1963.

Anuario de la Iglesia Católica en Colombia. 1961, 1962, Bogotá, Centro de Investigaciones Sociales, 1961, 1962.

La Asociación Nacional de Industriales de Colombia, *ANDI—Industria,* Bogotá, 1963.

Colección Jorge Eliécer Gaitán, Documentos para una Biografía, I, Bogotá, Consejo Municipal de Bogotá, 1949.

Colombia en Cifras, Bogotá, Librería Colombiana–Camacho Roldán, 1963.

Convención Nacional del Partido Republicano, Bogotá, 1915.

Convención Nacional de Veteranos Liberales, Bogotá, Imprenta Nacional, 1938.

Directorio Nacional Conservador, *Plataforma de Acción Política y Social, 1957,* Bogotá(?), 1957.

Directorio Nacional Conservador(?), *La Unión Conservadora,* Bogotá(?), 1963.

Documentos del Octavo Congreso del Partido Comunista de Colombia, Bogotá, Editorial Diario Jurídico, 1958.

Estatutos del Partido Conservador, Draft proposals, Bogotá, 1964.

Estatutos del Partido Liberal, 1963, Bogotá, Directorio del Partido Liberal, 1963.

Estatutos y Doctrina Política del Movimiento Socialista Colombiano, Bogotá.

Federación de Estudiantes Colombianos, Comité Ejecutivo Nacional, *I y II Congresos Nacionales de Estudiantes,* Bogotá(?), Ediciones Colombia, 1926.

————, *III Congreso Nacional de Estudiantes,* Bogotá, Editorial Minerva, 1930.

Federación Nacional de Cafeteros de Colombia, *La Federación Nacional de Cafeteros de Colombia,* Mimeo., 1963.

FEPRANAL (Federación Nacional del Sector Privado para la Acción Comunal), (Statement of goals and achievements), Bogotá, 196(?).

El Frente Nacional. Síntesis Doctrinal e Histórica, Bogotá, Ediciones Laguram, 1958.

Institute for the Comparative Study of Political Systems, *Colombia: Election Factbook,* Washington, 1966.

Juventudes del M.R.L., *Plataforma Política,* Bogotá, Ediciones "Voces Libres," 196(?).

Laureano Gómez y La Jerarquía Eclesiástica, Bogotá, Ediciones "La Unidad," 1954(?).

Leyva, Jorge, *Los Siete Pecados Capitales,* Bogotá, 1959.

Liga de Acción Política, *Manifiesto al País: La Izquierda ante el Presente y el Porvenir de Colombia,* Bogotá, Ediciones Políticas "El Común," 1943(?).

Liga de la Juventud Liberal, *Insurgencia Nacional,* Bogotá, 1963.

López Michelsen, Alfonso, *Conceptos Fundamentales del M.R.L. No. 3,* Discurso de Alfonso López Michelsen ante la Convención de Ibagué, Noviembre de 1962, Bogotá(?), 1962.

————, *Consideraciones sobre la Reforma Constitucional por Medios de la Cual se Establece la Alternación Forzosa de los Partidos en la Presidencia de la República,* 1958.

Partido Social Demócrata Cristiano (Pamphlet containing the party's platform), Bogotá, Ediciones Caribe, 1961(?).

Programa del Frente Nacional, 1962, Bogotá, Editorial ARGRA, 1962.

Los Programas Conservadores, Bogotá, Directorio Nacional Conservador, 1952.

Quién es Quién en Colombia, 3rd ed., Bogotá, Oliverio Perry, 1961.

Quién es Quién en Venezuela, Panama, Ecuador, Colombia, Bogotá, Oliverio Perry, 1952.

Russett, Bruce M. and Hayward R. Alker, Jr., Karl W. Deutsch, Harold D. Lasswell, *World Handbook of Political and Social Indicators,* New Haven, Conn., Yale University Press, 1964.

Smith, T. Lynn, "Observations on the Middle Classes in Colombia," in *Materiales para el Estudio de la Clase Media en la América Latina, 6,* Washington, D.C., Unión Panamericana, 1951, pp. 1–14.

El Socialismo Colombiano y el Plebiscito, Bogotá, 1957.

The South American Handbook, 1963.

Statistical Abstract of Latin America, 1963, Los Angeles, Cal., University of California, Los Angeles, Center of Latin American Studies, 1963.

Uribe, Alvaro, *El Nacionalismo, Motor de Nuestro Tiempo,* Bogotá(?), Colección "Sol Naciente," No. 1, 1964.

Valencia, Luis Emiro, *El Nuevo Socialismo y Antonio García,* Bogotá, 1955.

NEWSPAPERS AND PERIODICALS
(all published in Bogotá unless otherwise noted)

Acción Liberal, left-of-center Liberal magazine.

Actualidades, newssheet for youth and students published by the Instituto de Asuntos Internacionales de la Juventud, New York.

Alianza Nacional Popular, Rojista weekly.

ANDI, Carta Mensual de la Asociación Nacional de Industriales.

Boletín de Información Económica, bulletin of the Cali branch of the Institute of Social and Economic Studies—the so-called "Black Hand."

Boletín Mensual de Estadística, monthly publication of the National Statistical Department (DANE).

La Calle, weekly organ of MRL, subsequently of Línea Dura.

El Campesino, weekly published by Acción Cultural Popular.

El Catolicismo, semi-official weekly of the Roman Catholic Church.

El Colombiano, Medellín daily; Ospinista Conservative.

Contrapunto, biweekly non-partisan journal of opinion.

Cromos, weekly feature magazine.

DECE (Santiago de Chile), formerly *Boletín Informativo Demócrata Cristiano* (New York).

Documentos Políticos, theoretical journal of the Colombian Communist party.

El Espectador, Liberal daily.

Gaitán, leftist revolutionary weekly.

Hispanic American Report, Stanford, California.

El Independiente, temporary substitute for *El Espectador,* 1956–58.

Intermedio, temporary substitute for *El Tiempo,* 1956–57.

Izquierda, weekly organ of Línea Blanda, faction of MRL.

Justicia Social, biweekly newspaper of the Union of Colombian Workers (UTC).

Land Tenure Center Newsletter, Land Tenure Center, University of Wisconsin, Madison, Wis.

The New York Times.

La Nueva Prensa, weekly news magazine published by Alberto Zalamea Borda.

Nuevo Orden (Cali), Christian Democratic newspaper, published sporadically.

El País (Cali), Conservative daily.

La República, Ospinista Conservative daily.

Revista del Banco de la República, publication of the quasi-official Banco de la República.

Revista Cafetera de Colombia, publication of the Federación Nacional de Cafeteros de Colombia.

Revista Javeriana, Jesuit monthly.

Semana, weekly news magazine.

El Siglo, Laureanista Conservative daily.

El Tiempo, Liberal daily.

Vanguardia del MRL, sporadically published newspaper of the Juventudes del MRL.

El Voto Nacional, magazine of Christian Democratic orientation.

Voz de la Democracia, Communist weekly newspaper, now *Voz Proletaria.*

Voz Proletaria, Communist weekly, formerly *Voz de la Democracia.*

INDEX

Italicized page numbers refer to tabular material

Abolengo, 45 ff., 56, 60, 246
Acción, cívica-militar. *See* Civic-military action
Acción comunal. *See* Community development
Acción Cultural Popular, 316 f., 354
Action Française, 81
Adenauer, Konrad, 348
Administrative Department of Planning and Technical Services, 195 f.
Administrative state (tradition), 171–77 passim, 179, 184–93 passim, 195, 202, 216, 326, 328 f. *See also* Presidency
AFL-CIO, 339
Agrarian Credit Bank, 178, 327
Agrarian reform, 82, 88, 122, 154–58, 196, 234, 253, 260, 287 f., 316, 318 f., 320 n., 356, 371, 379 f. *See also* Landownership patterns; Law 100 of *1944;* Law 135 of *1961;* Law 200 of *1936*
Agriculture, 22, 24–27, 30, 82; foreign ownership, 24 f.; commercialization and mechanization, 26, 49 f., 155; employment, 32. *See also* Agrarian reform; Cash-crop agriculture; Coffee
Alessandri, Arturo, 82 f.
Alfonsistas. *See* Liberal Revolutionary Movement
Alianza Nacional Popular. *See* National Popular Alliance
Alliance for Progress, 149, 195, 261, 267, 318, 339, 409 f.
Alternation (*alternación*), 135 f., 139–46 passim, 165 ff., 192; MRL critique, 260, 264, 268. *See also* National Front; Parity; Presidency
Alvaristas, 140, 142, 145 f. See also *Laureanistas*
Alza-Ospinistas, 137–45 passim, 165

Alzate Avendaño, Gilberto (*Alzatistas*), 112, 137, 145, 163, 345
American Popular Revolutionary Alliance (APRA), 83, 102, 291, 391
American Voter, The, 239
ANAC. *See* National Constituent Assembly
ANAPO. *See* National Popular Alliance
Anarcho-Syndicalism, 331
ANDI. *See* National Association of Manufacturers
Andrade Valderrama, S.J., Vicente, 335 f.
Antioquia (department of) (*Antioqueños*), 21 f., *23,* 30, 51–54, 59, 214, 258, 286 f., 307, 313 f., 332, 337 f., 351, 366, 369, 390, 402, 406; voting patterns, 240 f., *243, 263. See also* Regionalism
Aparcero, 64 f.
APEN. *See* Employers' National Economic Association
APRA (*Apristas*). *See* American Popular Revolutionary Alliance
Apter, David, 6
Aramburu, General Pedro, 128
Archbishop of Bogotá, 307 f., 310, 313
Argentina, 11 f., 26 n., 37, 63, 78, 82, 128, 130, 298, 342 n., 343, 406 n. *See also* Buenos Aires; Perón
Aritama, community study of, 67, 180 n.
Armed Forces of National Liberation (Venezuela), 266
Armenia (Caldas-Quindío), *243,* 244
Army (Armed Forces). *See* Military
Army of National Liberation (ELN), 277, 280
Arrendatario, 64
Article 121 (of Constitution of *1886*), 173, 192
Artisans, 70 f., 246, 256, 330 f.

Asociación Colombiana Popular de Industriales (ACOPI). See Popular Colombian Association of (Small) Manufacturers

Asociación de Ganaderos. See Cattlemen's Association

Asociación Nacional de Industriales (ANDI). See National Association of Manufacturers

Asociación Patronal Económica Nacional (APEN). See Employers' National Economic Association

Association of Liberal Veterans, 210

Atlántico (department of), 23, 262, 332; voting patterns, 240, *243*, *263*

AVIANCA, 118

Balance of payments, 24, 33 f., 84, 94, 148, 150, 155, 160. See also Economic development

Barrancabermeja (Santander), 244, 300 f.

Barranquilla, 21 f., *23*, 34, *243*, 262, *263*, 332

Batalla del Pueblo, 278 n.

Batlle y Ordóñez, José, 84

Bavaria Brewery, 31

Benidorm, Declaration of, 114, 132

Bipartisan Commission of Institutional Readjustment, 133

Bipartisan Commission of National Transformation, 395

Black Hand (*Mano Negra*). See Center of Social Studies and Action

Blackmer, Donald W., 402

Blandón Berrío, Fidel, 313

Bogotá, 21 f., *23*, 27, 31, 34, 103, 105, 178, 181, 209, 240, *243*, 245, *263*, 264, 274 f., 279, 286 f., 332, 337, 381 f., 400. See also *Bogotazo*

Bogotá Committee of Commerce, 325

Bogotazo, 72, 103 ff., 107, 114, 177, 224, 298, 308, 363, 393, 398, 400, 414. See also Gaitán

Bolívar (department of), 240

Bolívar, Simón, 117, 123, 125

Bolivia, 10, 68, 373 f., 408

Bolshevik Revolution, 81, 269

Boyacá (department of), 22, 25, 27, 46, 178, 214; voting patterns, 241 f., 245

Brazil, 11, 26 n., 37, 51, 78, 82, 278, 367 n., 406 n. See also Goulart; Vargas

British Commonwealth, 221 f.

Brotherhood of Estate Managers, 364

Bucaramanga (Santander), 21, *243*, 244, *263*

Buenos Aires, 400

Bureaucracy, 90, 180 ff., 192, 197 ff., 323, 325 ff. See also Civil service; Spoils system

Burnett, Ben G., 190, 250

Cabinet, 134, 173, 195

Cacique (*caciquismo*), 40, 189, 213, 371

Calarcá (Caldas-Quindío), 244

Caldas (department of), 21, 30, 59, 362, 366–69 passim, 379; voting patterns, 240 f., *243*, *263*

Cali (Valle del Cauca), 21 f., *23*, 34, 40, *243*, *263*, 264, 350

Calle, Diego, 195

Calle, La, 258, 264 f.

Campesino, El, 316

Campesinos, 30, 38, 40, 64–70; political role, 83 f., 176, 204, 213 ff., 223, 384, 400 f., 408, 412; support of Gómez, 109; and community development, 152 ff.; and agrarian reform, 154–57; and political parties, 155, 207; relationship to government, 179; and Conservative party, 234 f.; voting behavior, 239; and Communist party, 274 f., 277; and civic-military action, 302 f.; and Church, 312 f., 316 f.; organization, 332 f. See also Agrarian reform; Agriculture; Civic-military action; Community development; Lower class; Violence

Caquetá (intendancy of), 245, 275

Caracas, 400

Carare, 366

Cárdenas, Lázaro, 82

Cartagena (Bolívar), 21, 46 n.

Cash-crop agriculture, 24 ff., 31, 45; political and social effects, 25, 67, 80, 367 f. See also Agriculture; Coffee

Castro, Fidel, 154, 265 f., 348, 360, 374, 391, 409

Catholic Action, 157, 324, 326, 354. *See also* Church

Catolicismo, El, 312

Cattlemen's Association, 50, 157, 326, 328, 356

Cauca (department of), 25, 214, 240, 362, 368 n.

Cauca Valley Corporation (CVC), 50, 118, 149, 178, 354

Caudillo (*caudillismo*), 77, 292, 295 f., 371

Cédula (cedulazation), *162 n.,* 187, 189, 200 ff. *See also* Electoral system

Census of *1928,* 14 n.

Center of Colombian Studies (*Centro de Estudios Colombianos*), 210

Center of Social Studies and Action (*Centro de Estudios y Acción Sociales*) (CEAS), 355, 357

Central Committee of the Middle Class, 63, 332

Centralization, administrative, 175 f., 181 f., 194 f. *See also* Administrative state

Centro de Investigación y Acción Social (CIAS), 317

Centro de Investigaciones Sociales (CIS), 317

Cereté (Córdoba), community study of, 42, 56

Chamber of Representatives, 138 n., 193; voting qualifications, 86. *See also* Congress; Elections

Chambers of Commerce, 325

Chile, 7, 11, 78, 82 ff., 172, 254, 278, 289, 296 n., 306, 348, 408. *See also* Christian Democrats (Chile); Communists (Chile); Radical party (Chile)

China (Communist), 275 ff.

"*Chispas.*" *See* Rojas, Teofilo

Chocó (department of), 240

Christian Democrats (Chile), 391, 416

Christian Social Democratic party (PSDC), *140 n.,* 145, 257, 280, 284–89, 291 f.; bases of support, 286 f.; organization and membership, 286 f.; program, 287 f.; and Church, 285–89, 318

Church, Roman Catholic, 178, 221, 294, 315, 318, 385 f., 403, 409; in Antioquia, 53, 307; social origins of clergy, 56, 311, 316, 319; as political issue, 78, 212, 251 ff.; and revolution on the march, 85 ff., 92; and education, 86, 89, 233, 311; political role, 93, 239, 246 f., 280, 284 f., 320 f., 411 f.; and Gómez, 109 f., 115, 321; and Ospina, 110; and Rojas Pinilla, 115, 117–20, 122, 124 f., 321; and National Front, 134, 314 f., 318–21, 406 f.; and agrarian reform, 155; and Conservative party, 233 f., 241, 253, 306–11, 313 ff.; and Liberal party, 235 f., 239, 306–11, 314 f., 318, 321; and PSDC, 285–89; historical role, 305–13; bases of power, 306 f., 311 ff.; and *campesinos,* 312 f.; and political consensus, 313 ff.; and violence, 313 f., 365, 377 f., 383; and modernization by an elite, 315–21, 406 f.; and MRL, 315; internal diversity, 320 f.; and labor, 332–41 passim; and students, 344; and community development, 354. *See also* Vatican

Chusma, 120

Civic-military action, 196, 302 f., 317, 378. *See also* Military

Civil Front. *See* National Front

Civil liberties, 172, 175

Civil service, 134, 192, 198 ff. *See also* Bureaucracy; Spoils system

Civil wars, 45, 77, 203, 210, 213 f., 247 f., 295, 361. *See also* Violence; War of the Thousand Days

Coalitions, 129 f., 218–21, 237, 248. *See also* National Concentration; National Front; National Union; Republican Union

Cocorná (Antioquia), 214

Coffee, 24 f., 27, 31, 59, 79 f., 84, 110, 150, 324, 327, 364, 367, 383 f. *See also* Cash-crop agriculture; Colombian Federation of Coffee Growers

Cofradía de Mayordomos. See Brotherhood of Estate Managers

Coleman, James, 6, 8

Colombian Federation of Coffee Growers, 24, 43 f., 323 f., 326 ff., 330, 354 ff., 359. *See also* Coffee

Colombian Institute of Agrarian Reform (INCORA), 156 f., 195 f., 260, 316, 326

Colombian Institute for Technical Specialization Abroad (ICETEX), 342 n., 355

Colombian Popular Socialist party (PPSC), 115, 270 f., 278 f., 290

Colombian Socialist Movement, 270

Colombiano, El, 209

Colonos. See Squatters

"Colony" vs. "republic," 245–48, 251 f.

Comisarías, 240

Communication, political and social, 67 n., 312 f. *See also* Press

Communism, 92, 309, 406

Communist parties (Latin America), 277

Communist party of Colombia (PCC), 11, 81, 115, 121, 140 n., 145, 250, 269–81, 285, 291 f., 302, 315, 391, 401 n.; and MRL, 259, 261 n., 264–67 passim, 277; and revolution on the march, 271 f.; illegality, 272, 290; factionalism, 272, 276 f.; strength, 272 f., 277 f., 280 f.; and National Front, 273; and labor, 273 f., 331–38 passim; and *campesinos,* 274 f., 277; and students and intellectuals, 275, 277, 344 f., 348; program, 276; and violence, 276 f., 371 ff., 380 f. *See also* Union of Colombian Communist Youth

Communist party of Colombia-Marxist-Leninist, 277

Communist Workers' party (*Partido Comunista Obrero*), 272 n.

Communists (Chile), 391

Community development, 195, 228 f., 287, 318, 354, 378, 384 n.; under National Front, 151–54

Compadrazgo, 65, 191. *See also* Political culture

"*Comuneros*" revolt, *1781,* 256

Concordat of *1887,* 306, 308; revision of *1942,* 307 f., 310, 314. *See also* Church

Confederación de Estudiantes Universitarios (CEU), 345

Confederación Latinoamericana de Sindicalistas Cristianos (CLASC). *See* Latin American Confederation of Christian Union Members

Confederación Sindical de Colombia, 331 n.

Confederación Sindical de Trabajadores de Colombia (CSTC). *See* Sindical Confederation of Workers of Colombia

Confederación de Trabajadores de Colombia (CTC). *See* Confederation of Colombian Workers

Confederation of Colombian Workers (CTC), 111, 119, 272 ff., 323, 330–41 passim, 352; and Liberal party, 210, 333 ff., 338; and López, 333; and Rojas Pinilla, 333; and Communist party, 337 f. *See also* Labor

Confederation of Colombian Workers (Independent) (CTCI), 332

Congress, 99, 134, 178, 194, 200, 250, 326, 345, 352; opposition to president, 91, 93, 103, 112, 138, 172 ff., 192 f.; *1949* closing, 110, 298; proposed reform, 112; and constitutional reform, 135 f.; political composition (*1958–66*), *142;* and INCORA, 157; and National Front, 163–66, 172, 192 f., 397, 415; role in political system, 172 ff., 181, 187, 191 f.; method of election, 185 f.; qualifications for office, 186; and civil service, 198 f.; and Liberal party, 228; control over military, 295 f. *See also* Chamber of Representatives; Elections; Electoral system; Proportional representation; Representative state; Senate

Consensus, political, 78 f., 98, 164–68 passim, 253, 392, 394–97; and interest groups, 351 ff. *See also* Coalitions; National Front

Conservative Committee of Economic and Social Action, *1957* program, 233 f.

Conservative party, 43, 53, 77 f., 81, 83 ff., 91, 95, 98–124 passim, 128–46 passim, 158, 163, 192, 203, 231, 392, 394 ff., 405, 414, 417; social bases, 62, 83 f., 221, 226, 246 f.; opposition to López, 91–94, 98, 100 f.; and Gómez, 108 f., 111, 113; attitudes toward Liberal opposition, 108; republican traditions, 109, 112 f.; factionalism, 112 ff., 116, 137–46, 160 f., 163, 237 f., 253, 282, 286, 310, 395; and Ospina, 113; and Rojas Pinilla, 115–18 passim; and violence, 123, 361 ff., 370 ff., 377–80 passim, 383, 385 f.; coalitions with Liberals, 129 ff.; and *campesinos,* 155, 234 f.; and electoral fraud, 188 f.; and parity, 197; organization and statutes, 204–11, 229; press, 209; leadership, 225; and youth, 229, 345; changes in, 229, 254, 417; and education, 233; and Church, 233 f., 253, 306–11, 313 ff.; ideology, 233–39 passim, 246 ff., 285 f., 288 f.; and agrarian reform, 234; and labor, 234, 334–40 passim; regional strength, 239–42; urban-rural strength, 242–45; origins, 246 ff.; and students, 249; and Communist party, 272; and army, 296–99 passim. *See also* Coalitions; Congress; Elections; Factionalism; Gómez; "Hereditary hatreds"; National Front; Ospina; Rojas Pinilla; Violence

Constitutional democracy: as modernizing regime, 10 f., 309 f.

Constitutions, 171, 184 ff.; amendments of *1910,* 79; codification of *1936,* 86 ff., 92, 307, 315, 331; reforms proposed by Gómez, 112; National Front reforms, 133–36; codifications, 171; Constitution of *1886,* 173, 306 f.; Constitution of *1832,* 295 f.; Constitution of *1863,* 296; codification of *1945,* 297. *See also* Article 121; Plebiscite of *Dec. 1, 1957;* Representative state

Contrapunto, 226

Cooperatives, 152, 229, 287

Córdoba (department of), 42, 240

Corinto (Cauca), 214

Corporación Autónoma Regional de los Valles del Magdalena y del Sinú (CVM), 199 n.

Corporatism, 237, 330

Corruption, 125, 180

Costa Rica, 11, 15, 342 n.

Council of State, 174 f., 193 f.

Counter-elites (Colombia), 11, 96, 183,

225, 229 f., 251, 330, 340 f., 351, 353, 358 f.; weaknesses, 266, 289–93, 389–417 passim; leadership, 290 f. See also *Campesinos;* Labor; Oppositions, political; Students

Coup of *June 13, 1953,* 113, 115 f., 123 f. *See also* Government of the Armed Forces; Rojas Pinilla

Coup of *May 2, 1958,* 127 f., 380. *See also* Rojas Pinilla

Crises, historical, 9 f., 414

Crisis of integration, 410

Crisis of participation, 413. *See also* Political participation

"Critical" elections, 217 f.

CTC. *See* Confederation of Colombian Workers

Cuba, 6, 10, 262, 271, 275, 278 f., 280, 381, 408. *See also* Castro

Cúcuta (Norte de Santander), *243*

Cundinamarca (department of), 22, *23,* 27, 66 ff., 80, 103, 214, 274, 332; voting patterns, 240, *243, 263*

Currie, Lauchlin, 26, 111, 196 n.

Cvc. *See* Cauca Valley Corporation

"Days of May" (*1957*), 119 ff., 126. *See also* Government of the Armed Forces; Rojas Pinilla

De Gaulle, Charles, 348

Democratic party (U.S.), 219, 237

Democratic single-party mobilization regimes, 10, 416

Democratic Societies, 256

Department of Planning, 199

Departmental assemblies, 111, 134, 175, 186

Designado: definition, 95 n.; Lleras Camargo as, 94 f.; Urdaneta Arbeláez as, 111

Devaluation (of peso), 148, 340

Díaz, Porfirio, 30

Dictatorship: as modernizing regime, 7

"Direct action," 256, 269, 328 f., 346, 350, 352, 358 f., 391, 398. *See also* Interest associations

Documentos Políticos, 277

Dollfus, Chancellor Engelbert, 110

Duque Gómez, Luis, 366 f.

Durán, Augusto (*Duranistas*), 272 n.
Duverger, Maurice, 248

Echandía, Darío, 115
Economic Commission for Latin America (ECLA), 39, 59
Economic development: process, 22 f., 31–36; causes, 38 ff., 51–54; and López, 84 f.; state role in, 86, 89, 165, 234, 236 f., 253, 322; under Gómez, 109 ff.; under Ospina, 111; under National Front, 147–50, 152, 397; planning, 195 f.; political effects, 200, 400, 414 f.; MRL proposals, 260 f.; and violence, 383 f.
Economic Society of Friends of the Nation, 210
ECOPETROL, 118, 300 f., 339
Ecuador, 15, 82, 306
Ediciones Caribe, 286
Ediciones Tercer Mundo, 226
Education, 178, 355; levels, 43, 48, 65, 71 f.; and social status, 43, 46 ff.; and Church, 86, 89, 233, 306–09, 311, 316 ff.; López' reforms, 88 ff.; and National Front, 134, 150 f.; and Conservative party, 233; and Liberal party, 235. See also Literacy; Students; Universities
Ejército de Liberación Nacional (ELN). See Army of National Liberation
Elections, 204 f.; presidential, of *1922*, 14; of *1930*, 14, 77 f., 107 f., 307 f.; of *1934*, 14 n.; of *1942*, 92, 189; of *1946*, 95, 103, 107 f., *162*, 188, 242; of *1949*, 110, *162*, 363; of *1958*, 127 f., *162*; of *1962*, 141–44, *162*, 201; of *1966*, 145 f., *162*; congressional, of *1937*, 91; of *1947*, 108, *162*; of *1949*, 108, *162*, 189, 309, 363; of *1951*, 162 n.; of *1953*, 162 n.; of *1958–66*, *140*, *142*; of *1958*, 135, 137, *162*; of *1960*, 138 f., *162*; of *1962*, 140–43, 161, *162*, 201, 242–45, 281 f.; of *1964*, 144, 161, *162*, 222, 243 n., 282; of *1966*, 145, 161, *162*, 222, 282, 340 n.; functions, 191 f.; role of army, 296; and violence, 361. See

also Political participation; Voting patterns
Electoral abstention, 239; and National Front, 161–64, 201, 222, 224, 227 f., 243 n., 262, 290, 293; as counter-elite tactics, 266, 279, 288. See also Elections; Political participation
Electoral Court, 144
Electoral fraud and intimidation, 188 ff., 201, 242
Electoral quotient, 130, 185 ff., 200, 208, 249 ff.; in Liberal party elections, 228
Electoral system, 184–91; reform, 82, 86, 89, 189 f., 200; voter registration, *162*, 187 f., 201; voting qualifications, 185, 201, 297; and National Front, 200 f.; political effects, 249–52. See also Electoral fraud and intimidation; Electoral quotient; "Incomplete vote"; Plurality elections; Proportional representation
Elegidos, Los, 259
Elite, 42–55, 58, 60 f., 72 f., 180, 411, 413; political role and orientation, 78 f., 105 ff., 109, 113, 172, 191, 287; and political parties, 203 f.; 219 f., 222 f., 231–39 passim, 253 ff.; and army, 295 f., 303, 305; and Church, 311; and violence, 372 f., 389. See also Modernizing elite; Oligarchy
El Salvador, 7, 11
"Empathic," 84
Empleados, 58, 332. See also Middle sectors
Employers' National Economic Association (APEN), 323, 356
Employment, non-agricultural, 15, 23, 31 f., 70, 393 n. See also Unemployment
Entreguismo, 292
Equipos polivalentes, 152 f., 384 n.
Espectador, El, 197, 209 n.
Export-Import Bank, 111

Fachada, 61
Factionalism, 220, 223, 248, 250 f., 253 f.; under National Front, 136–47, 165 ff., 197, 395; causes, 216, 232; consequences, 217 f.; ideological aspects of,

237 f.; in MRL, 264 ff., 268 f.; in PCC, 276 f.; in MDN, 285; of counterelites, 291; and violence, 380. *See also:* for Conservative party, *Alvaristas; Alza-Ospinistas; Alzatistas; Laureanistas; Leyvistas;* National Popular Alliance; *Ospinistas;* for Liberal party, *Gaitanistas;* Liberal Revolutionary Movement; *Oficialistas*

Falangism, 81, 109, 112, 394

Fals Borda, Orlando, 66 ff., 153, 213, 318 f., 368, 374

Family patterns, 368 f.

Family-sized farms, 27, 30

Fascism, 92, 394

FEDEPETROL (petroleum workers' federation), 339

Federación Agraria Nacional (FANAL). *See* National Agrarian Federation

Federación de Cafeteros de Colombia. See Colombian Federation of Coffee Growers

Federación Nacional de Comerciantes (FENALCO). *See* National Federation of Merchants

Federación Nacional del Sector Privado para la Acción Comunal (FEPRANAL). *See* National Federation of the Private Sector for Communal Action

Federación Universitaria Nacional (FUN). *See* National Federation of University Students

Federalism, 21, 235, 251 ff.

Federation of Colombian Students (*Federación de Estudiantes Colombianos*) (FEC), 275, 343 ff.

Federation of Colombian University Students (*Federación de Universitarios Colombianos*) (FUC), 344

Federation of River Transport Workers, 339

Federation of Workers of the Valle (*Federación de Trabajadores del Valle*) (FEDETAV), 274

Fidelistas, 279 f., 292, 302, 381

First Conference of Revolutionary Forces, 278 f.

Florencia (Caquetá), 245

Fluharty, Vernon, 54, 62

Foreign investment, 31, 35 f., 84 f., 89 f., 110 f., 339, 355, 401, 408; in agriculture, 24 f. *See also* Nationalism

Forero, Lt. Col. Hernando, 127

France, 171, 212

Franco, Francisco, 12, 109 f., 113, 393

Frente Unido de Acción Revolucionario (FUAR). *See* United Front of Revolutionary Action

Frente Unido del Pueblo (FUP). *See* People's United Front

Front of National Liberation, 266

Front of National Transformation (*Frente de Transformación Nacional*) (FTN), 145. *See also* National Front

"*Fuerzas vivas,*" 161, 326, 339, 352. *See also* Interest associations

Furtado, Celso, 409

Fusagasugá (Cundinamarca), 245

Gaitán, 278 n.

Gaitán, Jorge Eliécer (*Gaitanistas; Gaitanismo*), 43, 68, 82, 85, 95, 99–108, 114, 224, 253, 257, 271, 278, 291 ff., 296, 298, 348, 363, 365, 370, 373, 385, 390, 392 f., 405, 407, 413 f.; sources of support, 62 f., 102 f.; background, 100; program, 102; assassination, 103 f.; and Liberal party, 103, 105 ff.; characterized, 105 ff.; and Rojas Pinilla, 124; and Communist party, 272; and labor, 337. See also *Bogotazo;* Counter-elites; UNIR

Gaitán de Valencia, Gloria, 279 f.

Gamonal, 204 f., 207, 213, 223, 226, 228

García, Antonio, 79, 190, 270 f.

García Calderón, Francisco, 232, 238

General Economic and Social Development Plan for *1961–70,* 149

Germani, Gino, 11, 77

Germany, 37, 393

Gillin, John, 57

Gómez, Juan Vicente, 82, 290

Gómez, Laureano, 92 f., 108–15, 119, 128, 145, 209, 272, 298, 363; as president, 12, 110–14, 125, 172, 238, 390, 393; authoritarianism, 99, 111 f., 114,

Gómez, Laureano (continued)
233 f., 390; characterized, 108 ff.,
113 f.; support, 109 f.; and Church,
110, 112, 309 f., 321; and labor, 111 f.;
and constitutional reform, 112; and Na-
tional Front, 132 f., 135, 137–41 pas-
sim, 377. See also Conservative party;
Laureanistas; National Front
Gómez Hurtado, Alvaro, 112, 145, 225.
See also Alvaristas
Gómez Pinzón, José, 377
Goulart, João, 11
Government of the Armed Forces, 115–
27, 271, 290, 298 ff., 362; failures,
121 ff.; accomplishments, 123, 126. See
also "Days of May"; Military; Rojas
Pinilla
Governors, 175
Gran Colombia, 295
Great Britain, 37, 171, 218, 220 f., 252,
399, 409
Great Coalition. See National Front
Gremio, 224, 326
Gross domestic product, 32 f., 79, 111,
149 f.
Gross national product, 31; per capita, 15,
34
Grupo Comunista, 269
Guerrillas: strength, 360 f., 378 n.; organ-
ization, 363, 370 f., 374 ff., 378, 381;
political affiliation, 370 ff. See also
Violence
Guianas, 306
Guillén Martínez, Fernando, 52, 369, 413
Gutiérrez, José, 413

Hacendados, 47, 62, 65 f., 69, 204, 246,
402. See also Elite; Oligarchy
Hacienda, 26 f., 30, 45, 50, 65, 122, 155;
and violence, 368. See also Agrarian
reform; Landownership patterns
Hagen, Everett, 51
Havens, A. Eugene, 382, 384 f.
Health: National Front programs, 151
Health, Ministry of, 151
"Hereditary hatreds," 211–16, 222–25,
360, 363, 384, 404 f., 410 f. See also
Political culture; Political parties

Herrera, General Benjamín, 115, 220
Herring, Pendleton, 249
Hirschman, Albert O., 26, 30, 35, 62, 86,
164, 353 f., 384, 416 f.
Hispanidad, 109
Hitler, Adolf, 110, 124
Hobsbawm, Eric, 361, 364, 367, 376, 381
Holguín Holguín, Carlos, 249, 251
Holt, Pat M., 173, 187 f.
Hombre y la Tierra en Boyacá, El, 213
Housing: National Front programs, 151
Huila (department of), 240, 275
Huntington, Samuel, 407, 415

Ibagué, 243, 343
Immigration, 37 f., 49
"Incomplete vote," 130, 185, 187. See
also Proportional representation
INCORA. See Colombian Institute of
Agrarian Reform
Independent Conservatives. See Leyvistas
"Independent republics," 378, 381, 385.
See also Violence; Viotá
Indians, 36 ff., 46, 213
Industrialists (businessmen, entrepre-
neurs): attitudes, 40, 50; as social
group, 43 f., 48 f.; Antioqueños, 51–54,
402; political role, 84 f., 93, 241, 390,
402
Industry, 31–36, 82; concentration of, 22.
See also Economic development; For-
eign investment; Employment, non-
agricultural
Inflation, 34 f., 94, 148, 150, 155, 160,
163, 340 f., 401. See also Devaluation;
Economic development; Wages, real
Institute of Industrial Development, 178
Institute of Municipal Development, 178
Institute of Political Diffusion, 229
Institute of Territorial Credit (Instituto
de Crédito Territorial) (ICT), 151
Institutional Revolutionary party (PRI)
(Mexico), 391
Instituto Colombiano de Especialización
Técnica en el Extranjero (ICETEX). See
Colombian Institute for Technical Spe-
cialization Abroad
Instituto Colombiano de Reforma Agrar-

ia (INCORA). *See* Colombian Institute of Agrarian Reform

Intellectuals: social status, 46 ff., 56; political role, 83 f., 91, 210, 226, 246, 269, 287, 291, 407 f.; and Communist party, 275 ff.

Intendencias, 240

Interamerican Regional Organization of Workers (ORIT), 334, 339

Interest aggregation, 222 f., 229, 329 f., 352 f.

Interest associations, 161, 163, 301, 351–59; and government, 322–30, 352 f., 358; origins, 323 ff.; methods, 325–30; and political parties, 329 f., 352 f. *See also* "Direct action"; *"Fuerzas vivas";* Interest aggregation

Interior, Ministry of, 117

"Internal frontier," 25, 30, 52, 400 f. *See also* Antioquia

International Bank for Reconstruction and Development, 111, 149

International Office of Social Research, 317

International Union of Christian Employers Associations, 355

Investigating Commission Concerning the Present Causes of Violence, 377

Italy, 124. *See also* Mussolini

Izquierda, 265

Jaramillo Giraldo, José, 145 f., 282

Jesuits, 287, 310, 315, 317 f., 335; expulsions, 235, 306

John XXIII, Pope, 316

Jornalero, 64 f.

Judiciary, 174 f., 177; rural, 65; reform, 193 f.; and violence, 365, 378 f.

Juventud Comunista Colombiana, 276 f.

Juventud Revolucionaria Demócrata Cristiana, 287 f.

Juventudes del MRL (JMRL). *See* MRL Youth

Kennedy, John F., 348

Key, V.O., Jr., 251

Khrushchev, Nikita, 348

Korean War: Colombian forces in, 114, 299

La Dorada (Caldas), 244

Labor, Ministry of, 272, 337, 339

Labor, organized, 35, 96, 355; during first López administration, 82, 87, 89 f., 227, 331; political role and orientations, 83 ff., 91, 106, 108, 403, 410 f.; and Conservative party, 111 f., 206 f., 229, 234–40 passim; and Rojas Pinilla, 119, 125; and National Front, 161, 339 ff.; and Liberal party, 206 f., 236, 333–41 passim; and MRL, 260 f.; and Communist party, 273 f., 331–38 passim; and PSDC, 286; early organization, 323, 331; rural, 326, 332 f., 335, 400; union membership, 331 f.; and government, 331–40 passim; and Church, 332–41 passim; and *Gaitanistas,* 337. *See also* CTC; Lower class; Strikes; UTC

Labor Code, 336

Labor party (Great Britain), 254

Landownership patterns, 26 f., 30, 45, 56. See also *Hacienda; Minifundio*

Larrazábal, Vice-Admiral Wolfgang, 128

Laserna, Mario, 199, 249

Latifundio. See Hacienda

Latin American Confederation of Christian Union Members (CLASC), 286

Latin American Student Conference, 344

Laureanistas, 134 f., 137–45 passim, 163, 165 f., 253; criticism of agrarian reform, 157. See also *Alvaristas;* Conservative party; Factionalism

La violencia. See Violence

Law 100 of *1944,* 94. *See also* Agrarian reform

Law 135 of *1961,* 154–58, 194, 227, 234, 316, 319, 339, 356, 394, 407, 409; effects, 68; *Laureanista* criticism of, 157; MRL criticism of, 260 f. *See also* Agrarian reform; National Front

Law 200 of *1936,* 88, 90, 94, 97, 156 f., 260 f., 366; effects, 68. *See also* Agrarian reform; Revolution on the march

League of Liberal Youth (*Liga de la Juventud Liberal*), 228

League of Political Action (*Liga de Acción Política*) (LAP), 270

Lebret mission, 33, 44, 56, 66

Legitimacy, governmental, 191

Leiserson, Avery, 239 f.

"Leopards," 81

Lerner, Daniel, 5, 10, 41

Leyva, Jorge (*Leyvistas*), 128, 137 f., *140, 142,* 143, *144. See also* Conservative party; Factionalism

Liberal, El, 209

Liberal Left Movement (*Movimiento de Izquierda Liberal*) (MIL), *140, 142,* 144 n.

Liberal party, 43, 77 f., 81–87 passim, 89, 91–123 passim, 128–46 passim, 154, 158, 163, 192, 203, 231, 269 f., 272 f., 390, 392, 394, 396, 405; social bases, 62, 83 f., 221, 225 f., 246 f.; factionalism, 91 ff., 137–46, 217 n., 228, 237 f., 253, 258, 262 ff., 268, 380, 417; and Ospina, 107 f.; and Gómez, 110; and Rojas Pinilla, 115, 120 f.; and violence, 123, 361, 363, 370–73 passim, 375, 377–80 passim, 383, 385 f.; coalitions with Conservatives, 129 ff.; and *campesinos,* 155; and electoral fraud, 188 f.; and parity, 197; organization and statutes, 204–11, 227 ff.; press, 208 f.; and labor, 210, 236, 333–41 passim; leadership, 225; modernization of, 227 ff., 254, 264 f., 411, 417; affiliated organizations, 227 ff.; and women, 228; ideology, 234–39, 246 ff.; and Church, 235 f., 239, 306–11, 314, 318, 321; and education, 235; and agrarian reform, 236; regional strength, 239–42; urban-rural strength, 242–45; origins, 246 ff., 249, 256; as majority party, 260; and ANAPO, 282 f.; and army, 296–99 passim; youth affiliates, 345; and students, 349. *See also* Coalitions; Congress; Elections; Factionalism; "Hereditary hatreds"; López; National Front; Revolution on the march; Violence

Liberal Recovery Movement (*Movimiento de Recuperación Liberal*) (MRL). *See* Liberal Revolutionary Movement

Liberal Republic, 78, 87, 99, 390, 396. *See also* López; Revolution on the march; Santos

Liberal Revolutionary Movement (MRL), 137–46 passim, 154, 163, 166, 217 n., 218, 253, 257–69, 290, 293, 380, 391, 417; social bases, 62, 262 ff., 267; and middle sectors, 62, 268; and agrarian reform, 157, 260 f.; and youth, 217 n., 268; and labor, 260 f.; critique of National Front, 260, 264, 268; program, 260 ff., 267 f.; voting patterns, 262 ff.; factions, 264 ff., 278; and Communist party, 264–67, 277; leadership, 268; assessment, 268 f.; and Church, 315. *See also* Factionalism; Liberal party; López Michelsen; National Front

Liberal Unionists (Great Britain), 218

Lieuwen, Edwin, 299 f.

Ligas de campesinos. See Peasant leagues

Lima, 400

Línea Blanda (of MRL), *140, 142,* 265 f. *See also* MRL

Línea Dura (of MRL), *140, 142,* 265 f., 268 f., 284 f., 304. *See also* MRL

Lipman, Aaron, 44, 355, 382, 384 f.

Lipset, Seymour M., 180, 400, 413

Lipson, Leslie, 221

Literacy: rates, 15, 47 f.; correlation with voting, 190; and army program, 301; and Church programs, 316 f.; and violence, 367 f. *See also* Education

Llanos (eastern plains), 302, 362, 368, 372, 374, 380

Lleras Camargo, Alberto, 99, 127, 145 f., 164, 225, 230, 397; presidency (*1945–46*), 94 f.; and creation of National Front, 127 f., 131 f., 135 ff., 168; *1958* election, 128, 273; as president (*1958–62*), 149, 160, 192 f., 195, 304, 377, 380 n.; characterized, 158 f.; and military, 300. *See also* National Front; National Union

Lleras Restrepo, Carlos, 44, 113, 145 f., 154 f., 164, 225, 345, 395, 415; as Liberal party leader, 227 f.

López, General Hilario, 249, 331

López de Mesa, Luis, 365

López Michelsen, Alfonso, 62 f., 137, 139, 143, *144*, 145 f., 225, 257–68 passim, 348, 357, 407, 413; *1962* presidential candidacy, 166; characterized, 259, 265, 267, 292. *See also* MRL

López Pumarejo, Alfonso, 14, 44, 62 f., 100, 113, 137, 209, 253, 259, 268, 351, 394, 409; first administration (*1934–38*), 82–92, 96; characterized, 84 f.; second administration (*1942–45*), 93 ff., 414; and National Front, 131 f.; as president, 172, 189 f., 208 n., 236, 238, 322; and Communist party, 272 f.; and army, 297 f.; and labor, 331, 333, 336. *See also* Liberal Republic; Revolution on the march

Lopistas. *See* Liberal Revolutionary Movement

Lo Que el Cielo no Perdona, 313

Lower class: rural, 63–73, 366 ff., 384, 400 f.; urban, 70–73; political orientations, 103, 226, 283, 289, 353 f., 369. See also *Campesinos;* Labor

MacIver, Robert, 123

Magdalena (department of), 240

Manizales, *243*, 244, *263*

Mano Negra (Black Hand). *See* Center of Social Studies and Action

Manzanillo, 204 n., 228

Mao Tse-tung, 371

March 20, 1957, Pact of, 133, 314

Marquetalia, 275

Martz, John D., 107

Marxism, 92, 254, 259, 270, 343 f.

Maurras, Charles, 81

Mecham, J. Lloyd, 305, 307

Medellín (Antioquia), 21 f., *23*, 34, 209, *243*, 244, *263*, 264, 338, 350, 355

"Mediterranean syndicalism," 12

Melo, General José María, 331

Merchants: political orientations, 246

Mestizos, 36 f.

Meta (department of), 240, 275

Mexico, 26 n., 30, 51, 62; one-party system, 7, 10, 416; Revolution, 81 ff., 361, 399, 408

Middle sectors: rural, 30, 56, 59, 241, 364; composition and values, 45, 47, 49, 55–63, 70, 72 f., 180, 343; political role and orientations, 61 ff., 84, 264, 280, 283, 285 ff., 289, 346, 349, 353 f., 391, 398, 402 f., 416; organization, 63, 332; support of Gaitán, 103; and army, 303; and Church, 311

Migration, rural, 38 ff., 69 ff., 80; effect on political loyalties, 225 f. *See also* Urbanization

Military, 127, 383; social origins, 56, 303; political role and orientations, 77, 85, 104, 113 f., 116, 125–28, 160, 167, 224, 246, 266, 292, 300–05, 320 f., 352; and public order, 80, 300 f., 305 n.; modernizing role, 89 f., 196, 301–05, 383, 406, 412; and Conservative party, 116, 296–99 passim, 406; and Rojas Pinilla, 118, 120, 281, 283 ff.; and National Front, 139, 301, 320 f., 406; and agrarian reform, 157; and electoral process, 188; and violence, 280, 298 ff., 302 f., 372, 377–82 passim; historic role, 294–99; functions, 294 f.; coups, 295; and political parties, 295; internal diversity, 320 f.; and community development, 354. *See also* Civic-military action; Government of the Armed Forces; Military junta

Military junta (*1957–58*), 126 ff., 134, 377. *See also* Government of the Armed Forces

Military rule: as modernizing regime, 7, 11

Millikan, Max, 402

Minifundio (*minifundista*), 27, 30, 59, 64 f., 156; and violence, 367, 373 f., 379

Minuto de Dios, 317

Modernizing coalitions, 285, 416 f.

Modernizing elite (Colombia), 7, 11–16 passim, 84 f., 91, 97 f., 202, 354–59, 389–417; and army, 301–05, 320 f.; and Church, 315–21. *See also* National Front; Revolution on the march

Modernizing regimes: typology, 6 f.; Latin America, 11

Molina, Gerardo, 259

Mompós (Bolívar), 46 n.

Montaña Cuellar, Diego, 337

Mosquera, General Tomás C., 129

Movimiento Democrático Nacional (MDN). *See* National Democratic Movement

Movimiento Obrero Estudiantil Campesino (MOEC). *See* Peasant-Student-Worker Movement

Movimiento Revolucionario Liberal (MRL). *See* Liberal Revolutionary Movement

MRL. *See* Liberal Revolutionary Movement

MRL Youth, 266, 268 f., 279 f., 345

Municipal government (*municipio*), 134, 175 f., 186, 194, 214; under Gómez, 111; PSDC proposals, 287. *See also* Administrative state; Centralization, administrative

Mussolini, Benito, 12, 102, 110, 393

Nariño (department of), 25, 27, 362, 368; voting patterns, 240, 243

Nasser, Gamal Abdel, 124, 266, 285

National Agrarian Federation (FANAL), 332 f.

National Association of Manufacturers (ANDI), 50, 324 f., 328, 351, 354 ff., 359

National Christian Movement of the *13th of June*, 117

National Committee of Revolutionary Action of the MRL. *See Línea Dura*

National Concentration (*1930–34*), 129, 219. *See also* Olaya Herrera

National Confederation of Employees, 332

National Conference of Guerrillas, 371, 373

National Constituent Assembly (ANAC), 112, 119, 123, 134 n., 172, 185, 273 n.

National Council on Economic Policy and Planning, 195

National Democratic Front, 259, 278

National Democratic Movement (MDN), 284 f., 289, 304, 391

National Federation of Merchants (FENALCO), 324 f., 351, 356

National Federation of the Private Sector for Communal Action (FEPRANAL), 354

National Federation of University Students (FUN), 275, 345 ff., 350

National Front (*Frente Nacional*), 127–68; goals, 121, 130 f., 168, 220; precedents, 129 f.; origins, 130–36; and modernization, 131, 147–58, 168, 359, 391 f., 414; factionalism, 136–47, 154 f., 160 f., 163, 165 ff., 216; *1962* program, 150, 194 f., 314 f., 358, 394; leadership, 158–64; popular support, 161 ff., 167 f., 196, 397 ff.; achievements, 167 f., 396; and Congress, 172, 192 f.; and violence, 177, 377–82; and spoils system, 182 ff.; and presidency, 192 f.; and economic planning, 195 f.; and electoral reform, 200 ff.; and political parties, 225, 252–55 passim; critiques of, 258 ff., 265, 288; and role of opposition, 290, 394 f.; and military, 301, 406; and Church, 314 f., 318–21, 406 f.; and labor, 339 ff.; as consensual mechanism, 330, 351, 394–97, 405; as syncratic regime, 393–96, 417; weaknesses, 397 ff.; proposed changes in, 415. *See also* Coalitions; Elections; Factionalism; Lleras Camargo; Modernizing elite (Colombia); Valencia

National integration, 13, 21 ff., 25, 37 f., 55, 68, 89 f., 179, 196, 312 f., 384 f.; role of army in, 297

National Liberal Gaitanista Movement (*Movimiento Nacional Liberal Gaitanista*) (MNLG), 278

National Popular Alliance (ANAPO), 163, 166, 281–85, 289 f., 293, 391; electoral strength, *140, 142*, 143 ff., *146*, 281 ff.; platform, 282; and Liberal party, 282 f.; assessment, 284. *See also* Factionalism; Rojas Pinilla

National Popular Gaitanista Movement (*Movimiento Nacional Popular Gaitanista*) (MNPG), 278 f.

National Popular Union (*Unión Popular Nacional*) (UPN), 278

National Revolutionary Movement (MNR) (Bolivia), 391

National Secretariat of Social Assistance (SENDAS), 119, 123

National Sugar Growers Association, 328

National Union, 95 f., 99, 108, 129, 131, 220. *See also* Lleras Camargo; Ospina

National Union of Colombian Students (UNEC), 275, 344

National University (Bogotá), 44, 88, 280, 342 f., 346, 348 ff. *See also* Education; Universities

Nationalism, 35 f., 55, 89, 102, 299, 319, 339, 347, 349, 401, 404, 408, 413, 416 f.; and MRL, 261, 267 f.; and counter-elites, 289 f.; and military, 304 f.

Nationalist Bloc (*Bloque Nacionalista*), 265

Nationalist party, 218, 220, 271

Nationalization: proposals for, 102, 261, 265, 270, 287

Near East, 37

Negroes, 36 f.

Nehru, Jawaharlal, 348

Neumann, Sigmund, 210

New Deal, 83, 409

Norte de Santander (department of), 22, 27, 363; voting patterns, 241 f., 243

Nueva Granada, vice-royalty of, 46 n., 295, 307

Nueva Prensa, La, 284

Núñez, Rafael, 129, 200, 218, 220, 232, 306

Obreros. See Labor

Office of Planning, 195

Office of Rehabilitation, 377 f., 380

Oficialistas ("official" Liberals), 139–45 passim, 154, 253, 265, 417. *See also* Factionalism; Liberal party; National Front

Olaya Herrera, Enrique, 81 f., 107, 210, 219

Oligarchy (*oligarquía*), 43 ff., 54, 77, 95, 101 ff., 119, 122 f., 126, 271. *See also* Elite

Oligarchy, Peruvian, 45

Opposition, political, 11; attitudes toward, 78 f.; Right, 81; Left, 81, 105 ff., 257–81, 290–93 passim, 391; institutionalization of, 130, 164–68 passim, 200; factionalism as equivalent of, 217; non-Left, 257, 281–89, 290–93 passim, 391; reformist, 257–69, 281–89; revolutionary, 257, 269–81; failures, 289–93, 399–412; suppression, 290 f.; internal divisions, 291; and National Front, 395, 415. *See also* Counter-elites; Gaitán; Gómez; Revolution on the march; Rojas Pinilla

Organización Regional Interamericana de Trabajadores (ORIT). *See* Interamerican Regional Organization of Workers

Organization of American States, 158, 261

Organski, A. F. K., 6, 12, 392–96 passim, 417

Ospina Pérez, Mariano, 44, 95, 99, 104 f., 107 f., 110 ff., 128, 131, 172, 225, 298 f., 390. *See also* National Union; *Ospinistas*

Ospinistas (*Unionistas*), 113, 134 f., 137–46 passim, 155, 163, 253; and Rojas Pinilla, 116, 120; press, 209. *See also* Conservative party; Factionalism; National Front

País económico, 351

País político, 351

Pájaros, 362

Palabra del Pueblo, 272 n.

Palancas, 180, 191

Palmira, 243

Panama, 15, 31, 342 n., 344, 408

Panama Canal, 31

Paraguay, 15

Parity, 134 ff., 146, 192, 196–200, 202, 254. *See also* Alternation; National Front

Partido Comunista de Colombia (PCC). *See* Communist party of Colombia

Partido Popular Socialista Colombiano (PPSC). *See* Colombian Popular Socialist party

Partido Social Demócrata Cristiano (PSDC). *See* Christian Social Democratic party

Partido Socialista Revolucionario (PSR). *See* Revolutionary Socialist party

Passing of Traditional Society, The, 41

Pasto (Cauca), 243 f.; military coup (*1944*), 298

Paternalism, 49 f., 53, 152 ff., 171 ff., 176, 234, 236, 286, 318, 338, 358, 406. See also *Patrón*-client relationship; Political culture

Patria chica, 179 f., 225, 367. *See also* Political culture

Patrón-client relationship, 40, 45, 57, 66, 69, 190, 204 f., 211, 213, 215 f., 223, 225, 232, 239, 322 f., 330, 358, 403. *See also* Paternalism; Political culture

Paulistas (São Paulo), 51

Paz del Río (steel mill), 178

Pcc. *See* Communist party of Colombia

Peace Corps, 354

Pearse, Andrew, 46, 67, 213

Peasant leagues, 274, 332. See also *Campesinos*

Peasant Society in the Colombian Andes, 213

Peasant-Student-Worker Movement (MOEC), 279 ff., 345, 380 f.

Peelites (Great Britain), 218

Peking line, 266, 276 f.

People's United Front (FUP), 280

Perdomo, Ismael, 307 f.

Pereira (Caldas), *243, 244, 263*

Pérez Jiménez, Marcos, 7, 290 f.

Permanent Committee of Productive Associations, 323

Perón, Juan D. (*Peronistas*), 7, 10 ff., 63, 119, 122, 289, 332, 391, 393 f., 416

Personalism, 57, 216, 231, 245, 248, 253, 291 f., 322 f. See also *Caudillo;* Political culture

Peru, 11, 22, 82, 178, 291, 297, 298 n., 348, 406 n. *See also* APRA

Petroleum industry, 22, 31, 35, 178, 265, 355. *See also* ECOPETROL

Plan de SET, 260 ff.

Plebiscite of *December 1, 1957,* 133 f.,
136, 168, 193 f., 196, 198, 272 f., 314. *See also* National Front

Plural executives, 126. *See also* Military junta

Plurality elections, 249 f. *See also* Electoral system; Proportional representation

Police, 65, 177, 380, 383; nationalization of, 89, 297; and violence, 116, 298, 370, 372; political role, 117, 127, 297; and public order, 300

"Political bargaining," 179 n., 389 f. *See also* "Direct action"

Political culture, 46 f., 57 f., 66, 78 f., 171–77 passim, 179 ff., 184, 191, 203 f., 211–16, 312, 318, 322, 329, 358, 382–85 passim, 403 f.; *Antioqueños,* 51–54 passim; changes in, 67 ff., 202; and National Front, 131, 136, 165, 167, 198; and community development, 152 ff., 195; and two-party system, 223 f.; and violence, 369. *See also* "Hereditary hatreds"; Paternalism; *Patria chica; Patrón*-client relationship; Personalism; Political socialization

Political decay, 415 ff.

Political Modernization in Japan and Turkey, 8

Political participation, 11 f., 14 f., 40 f., 78 f., 161 ff., 176 f., 201–11 passim; 216, 222 f., 353, 356 ff., 398, 402 n., 410, 413, 416 f.; women, 118, 134; civil service employees, 134; obstacles to, 189 ff., 225. *See also* Elections; Electoral abstention; Electoral system; Political recruitment

Political parties, traditional: organization and finances, 183, 203–11, 213, 215, 223; party lists, 187, 208; social bases of, 203 ff., 231–48; as polyclass, 222, 229, 254; changes in, 225–30, 234, 236 f., 252–55; origins, 231; ideological conflict, 253–55. *See also* Coalitions; Conservative party; Factionalism; "Hereditary hatreds"; Interest aggregation; Liberal party; National Front; Two-party system

Political recruitment, 43 f., 328, 346, 353,

357. *See also* Elite; Oligarchy; Political participation
Political socialization, 16, 231, 251, 364 f. *See also* "Hereditary hatreds"; Political culture
Political stability, 41, 54, 77, 224, 396, 413–16
Popayán, 21, 159, 293; social classes in, 44 n., 46, 56 f., 62, 71 f., 183, 226, 229, 308 f.
"Popular" classes. *See* Lower class
Popular Colombian Association of (Small) Manufacturers (ACOPI), 63
Popular Front, 267, 271
Popular Nationalist Movement (*Movimiento Nacionalista Popular*) (MNP), 266
Population growth, 38 ff., 80, 379
Populistic authoritarianism (Colombia), 125, 257, 289, 390 f., 406. *See also* National Democratic Movement; National Popular Alliance; Rojas Pinilla
Populistic authoritarian regimes, 7, 10, 416
"Post-war generation," 81, 84
Power, concentration of, 43–50. *See also* Oligarchy
Presidency: voting qualifications for, 86; proposed changes in, 112; powers, 173 ff., 179; qualifications for office, 184; method of election, 185, 250; and party system, 248, 252. *See also* Administrative state; Alternation; Centralization, administrative; Congress
Press: readership, 15; restrictions on, 111 f., 117 f., 172, 357; partisanship, 208 f., 212, 363
Principal, 46
Promotor, 152 f. *See also* Community development
Property, social function of, 83, 87 ff., 234, 236 f., 287 f.
Proportional representation, 130, 134, 165 f., 185–88, 249–52 passim. *See also* Electoral quotient; Electoral system; "Incomplete vote"
Protestants, 309
Puerto Wilches (Santander), 244 f.

Pye, Lucian, 215

Querétaro (Mexico), 62
Quién es Quién, 44
Quindío (department of), 21, 30, 244, 364, 400 f.

Racial composition of population, 36 ff.
Radical party (Argentina), 82
Radical party (Chile), 91
Radio: political role, 209. *See also* Radio Sutatenza
Radio Sutatenza, 316–19 passim, 412
"Reformmongering," 91 n., 164
"Regeneration," 220
Regional development, 149
Regionalism, 21 ff., 157, 178; political effects, 21 ff., 251 f., 348 f., 400; Antioquia, 51–54
Reichel-Dolmatoff, Gerardo and Alicia, 67
Representative state (tradition), 171–77 passim, 179, 184–92 passim, 202
"Republic of Tequendama." *See* Viotá
República, La, 209
Republican party, 198 n., 218, 220, 271
Republican party (U.S.), 219
Republican Union (*1909*), 129
Resguardos, 213, 236, 246
Revolution on the march (*revolución en marcha*), 83–98 passim, 178, 268, 390 ff., 405, 410 f.; origins, 83–86 passim; achievements, 86–89, 91; failures, 89 f.; opposition to, 91 ff.; and Communist party, 271 f. *See also* Liberal Republic; López
Revolutionary Armed Forces of Colombia (*Fuerzas Armadas Revolucionarias de Colombia*) (FARC), 280, 380
Revolutionary Leftist National Union (UNIR), 82, 85, 270, 405. *See also* Gaitán
Revolutionary Socialist Party (PSR), 269 ff.
Reyes, General Rafael, 130, 296
Rionegro (Antioquia), 314
Rivera, Salomón, 46, 67, 213
Rojas Pinilla, General Gustavo (*Rojistas*),

Rojas Pinilla, General Gustavo (*cont.*)
113, 115–28, 141, 167, 281–84, 329,
391 f.; as president, 12, 132 f., 148,
172, 185, 393, 405 f., 408 f.; support,
115, 258, 271; and Conservative party,
115 f.; and violence, 115, 117 f., 121 ff.,
372, 377, 380 f.; program and ideology,
117; and Church, 117–20, 122, 124 f.,
321; and military, 118, 122, 304; and
students, 118, 120 f., 344, 347, 349;
and labor, 119, 332 f.; characterized,
124 f., 292, 303; trial, 127, 133, 144 n.,
281 f.; election of *1962*, 143, *144*, 281;
and Communist party, 272 f. *See also*
Coup of *June 13, 1953;* "Days of May";
Government of the Armed Forces; National Popular Alliance
Rojas, Teofilo (*"Chispas"*), 376, 378
Roosevelt, Franklin D., 83
Ruiz Novoa, General Alberto, 160, 284 f.,
301, 406. *See also* National Democratic
Movement
Rustow, Dankwart, 8

Sáenz Peña Law (Argentina), 130
Salazar, Antonio de Oliveira, 110
Salcedo, Father José Joaquín, 316
San Carlos, Pact of, 135 n.
Santander (department of), 22, 27, 197,
214; voting patterns, 241–44, *263*
Santos, Eduardo, 91, 94, 208 f.
Saucío (Cundinamarca), community
study of, 66 ff., 214, 318 f.
Savage, Charles, 52
School of Business Administration (Med-
ellín), 350
School of Public Administration, 199, 350
Secretariado Nacional de Asistencia Social
(SENDAS). *See* National Secretariat of
Social Assistance
Segovia, 337, 401
Semi-autonomous agencies, 175
Senate, 112, 138 n., *142 n.*, 184. *See also*
Congress; Elections
Shils, Edward, 6
Siglo, El, 209
Silvert, K. H., 12

Sindical Confederation of Workers of
Colombia (CSTC), 332
Sino-Soviet bloc, 261
Sitges, Pact of, 133, 182, 198, 377
Slavery, 236, 246 f.
Social classes, 42–73, 402 f.; ethnic bases
of, 37 f., 46. *See also* Elite; Lower
class; Middle sectors
Social Democratic party (*Partido Social
Democrático*) (PSD), 271 n.
Social mobility, 38, 44 ff., 49, 66, 71, 180,
316, 343, 349, 364, 398, 402
Social Orientation of Colombian Employ-
ers (*Orientación Social de Dirigentes
de Empresas Colombianos*) (OSDEC),
318, 355
Social Security Institute, 175, 178
Socialism, 83, 102
Socialists (Chile), 391
Sociedad de Agricultores. See Society of
(Large) Farmers
*Sociedad Económica de los Amigos del
País. See* Economic Society of Friends
of the Nation
Society of Engineers (*Sociedad de In-
genieros*), 323
Society of (Large) Farmers, 157, 323,
326
Socorro (Santander), 197
Sogamoso (Boyacá), 245
Sonsón (Antioquia), 214
Soviet Union, 79, 275 f.
Spain, 12, 83, 109, 308; Civil War, 92;
empire of, 171, 306. *See also* Franco
Spoils system, 90, 179–84; political ef-
fects, 183 f., 212, 231 f., 251; and Na-
tional Front, 196 ff. *See also* Bureau-
cracy
Squatters (*colonos*), 64, 80, 88, 96 f.,
155, 157, 361, 366 f.; and violence,
373 f., 380
State of siege, 128, 163, 172, 177 f., 363,
380; constitutional provisions, 173,
192 f. *See also* Administrative state
Steel industry, 22, 178
Strikes, 35, 62 f., 105, 160 f., 163, 179,
260 f., 296, 300 f., 305 n., 318, 331,
333–41 passim, 346–50 passim, 397 f.;

of banana workers (*1928*), 80, 296. *See also* Labor

Students: social origins and aspirations, 40, 56, 342 f.; and Rojas Pinilla, 118, 120 f., 344, 347, 349; political role and orientations, 163, 277, 279, 286, 341–51, 412; and political parties, 209 f.; and government, 345 ff. *See also* Universities

Subachoque (Cundinamarca), 68 ff.

Sub-proletariat, 70 f.

Sukarno, Achmed, 266

Sumapaz, 274, 317, 381

Superintendent of Banking, 327

Suplentes, 174, 186 f.

Supreme Court, 134, 174 f., 192 ff.

"Swing" vote, 215, 223

"Syncratism," 12, 392–96, 417

Szulc, Tad, 267

Tariffs, 82; internal, 89

Tax reform: of revolution on the march, 87, 89; of Rojas regime, 118, 122 f.; of National Front, 150

Technocrats, 47, 183, 199, 402

Tenza (Boyacá), community study of, 46, 67, 181 f., 213 f.

Third Force, 119, 125, 281. *See also* Government of the Armed Forces; Rojas Pinilla

Third International, 269

Third parties, 186 ff., 203, 218, 249 f., 254 ff., 271, 273, 288, 395; and National Front, 290, 415

Tiempo, El, 118, 208 f., 259

Tocqueville, Alexis de, 175, 181, 322, 357

Tolima (department of), 80, 122, 274 f., 362, 366 ff., 372, 380; voting patterns, 240, *243*

Torres, Camilo, 280

Totalitarian mobilization regimes, 6, 10, 391

Transportation network, 23, 87, 89

Tropical Oil Company, 80

Turbay, Gabriel, 95, 103, 272

Turbay, Julio César, 259

Two-party system (Colombia), 221–24; causes, 231–52; changes, 252–55

Two-party systems, 248–52 passim; criteria, 221

Unemployment, 31, 34. *See also* Labor; Wages, real

UNESCO, 317

Union of Colombian Communist Youth (*Unión de la Juventud Comunista de Colombia*) (UJCC), 275 ff., 279, 345. *See also* Communist party of Colombia

Union of Colombian Workers (UTC), 111, *140 n.*, 145, 273 f., 286, 288, 331–41 passim, 353, 412; and Church, 111, 309, 312, 317, 334–41 passim; and Conservative party, 111, 309, 334 ff.; and Liberal party, 336, 340 n. *See also* Labor

Unión Nacional de Estudiantes Colombianos (UNEC). *See* National Union of Colombian Students

Unión Nacional Izquierdista Revolucionaria (UNIR). *See* Revolutionary Leftist National Union

Unión de Trabajadores de Colombia (UTC). *See* Union of Colombian Workers

United Front of Revolutionary Action (FUAR), 278–81 passim

United Fruit Company, 25, 80, 401 n.

United States, 31, 35 ff., 173 ff., 181, 195 f., 199, 220, 249, 252, 261, 273, 279, 299, 328, 330, 342 ff., 350, 378, 409 f.; two-party system, 217, 222; and military aid, 302 f. *See also* Alliance for Progress

Universidad Libre (Bogotá), 275

Universities, 342 f., 345 f., 350. *See also* Education; Students

University of the Andes (Bogotá), 350, 355

University of Valle (Cali), 350

University Reform Movement (Argentina), 343

Upper class. *See* Elite; Oligarchy

Urbanization, 15, 22; rates, 38 f.; effects, 39 ff., 412 f. *See also* Migration, rural

Urdaneta Arbeláez, Roberto, 111 ff., 313

Uribe Rueda, Alvaro, 265 f., 268, 304, 407, 408 n. See also *Línea Dura*
Uribe Uribe, General Rafael, 81, 212
Uruguay, 26 n., 37, 130, 342 n. *See also* Batlle y Ordóñez

Valencia, Guillermo León, 225; arrest, 120; *1958* candidacy, 135; *1962* presidential election, 141, *144;* as president, 146, 149, 159–64 passim, 195, 198, 326, 352, 397; characterized, 159 f. *See also* Conservative party; National Front; *Ospinistas*
Valencia, Luis Emiro, 278 f.
Valle (del Cauca) (department of), 21, *23,* 27, 80, 214, 332, 337, 362, 366 ff., 400; voting patterns, 240, *243, 263*
Vanguardia Socialista, 270
Vargas, Getulio, 10 f., 82, 289, 416
Vatican, 306, 308, 316, 409. *See also* Church; Concordat
Venezuela, 7, 11, 22, 36 f., 82, 128, 278, 290 f., 295, 342 n., 348, 408. *See also* Pérez Jiménez
Vieira, Gilberto, 348
Violence (*la violencia*): effects, 33, 226, 251, 382–85, 392, 398, 408, 412; urban, 72, 113, 163, 177, 362, 381; pre-*1948,* 77, 80; location, 77, 122, 362; in elections, 77, 242; and agrarian reform, 88, 154 f.; partisan basis of, 108, 110, 203, 215; and Gómez, 110, 113 f.; and economic development, 111, 382 f.; and military, 113, 295, 298 f., 302; and Rojas Pinilla, 115, 117 f., 121 f., 125; under National Front, 152, 160, 177, 196; and spoils system, 182 f.; causes, 224, 362–69, 372 ff.; advocacy by

counter-elites, 266, 278 ff., 282–85 passim, 288; and Communist party, 274, 276 f.; and Church, 309 ff., 313 f.; casualties, 362, 379; savagery of, 375 f.; and class warfare, 381 f., 384 ff. See also *Bogotazo;* Guerrillas; "Hereditary hatreds"; "Independent republics"
Violencia en Colombia, La, 360 n., 381
Viotá (Cundinamarca), 274 f., 371, 381, 401 n. *See also* Communist party of Colombia; "Independent republics"
Voting patterns, 214, 222; Liberal party, 222, 262 ff.; regional differences, 240 ff.; urban-rural differences, 242–45, 262 ff.; MRL, 262 ff. *See also* Elections; Electoral abstention
Voz Proletaria (*Voz de la Democracia*), 277

Wages, real, 34 f., 401. *See also* Lower class; Unemployment
Wahl, Nicholas, 212
War, Ministry of, 295 n., 296 f., 299, 301
War of the Thousand Days, 77 f., 81, 84, 115, 129, 205, 296
Ward, Robert, 8
Wars of Independence, 246, 306
Weak state, 177 ff., 183, 249, 352
Weber, Max, 106, 203
Weiner, Myron, 358
Whiteford, Andrew H., 45 f., 56 f., 62, 64, 71 f., 183, 226, 293, 308 f.
Williamson, Robert G., 44, 56, 364 f.
Women: political participation, 118, 134, 201 f.; and political parties, 206 f., 209 f., 228 f.; social role, 233

Zalamea, Alberto, 284 f.

YALE STUDIES IN POLITICAL SCIENCE

1. Robert E. Lane, THE REGULATION OF BUSINESSMEN
2. Charles Blitzer, AN IMMORTAL COMMONWEALTH: THE POLITI-
   CAL THOUGHT OF JAMES HARRINGTON. Out of print.
3. Aaron Wildavsky, DIXON-YATES: A STUDY IN POWER POLITICS
4. Robert A. Dahl, WHO GOVERNS? DEMOCRACY AND POWER IN AN
   AMERICAN CITY
5. Herbert Jacob, GERMAN ADMINISTRATION SINCE BISMARCK:
   CENTRAL AUTHORITY VERSUS LOCAL AUTONOMY
6. Robert C. Fried, THE ITALIAN PREFECTS: A STUDY IN ADMINIS-
   TRATIVE POLITICS
7. Nelson W. Polsby, COMMUNITY POWER AND POLITICAL THEORY
8. Joseph Hamburger, JAMES MILL AND THE ART OF REVOLUTION
9. Takehiko Yoshihashi, CONSPIRACY AT MUKDEN: THE RISE OF THE
   JAPANESE MILITARY
10. Douglas A. Chalmers, THE SOCIAL DEMOCRATIC PARTY OF GER-
    MANY: FROM WORKING-CLASS MOVEMENT TO MODERN PO-
    LITICAL PARTY
11. James D. Barber, THE LAWMAKERS: RECRUITMENT AND ADAP-
    TATION TO LEGISLATIVE LIFE
12. William J. Foltz, FROM FRENCH WEST AFRICA TO THE MALI
    FEDERATION
13. Fred I. Greenstein, CHILDREN AND POLITICS
14. Joseph Hamburger, INTELLECTUALS IN POLITICS: JOHN STUART
    MILL AND THE PHILOSOPHIC RADICALS
15. Hayward R. Alker, Jr., and Bruce M. Russett, WORLD POLITICS IN
    THE GENERAL ASSEMBLY
16. Richard L. Merritt, SYMBOLS OF AMERICAN COMMUNITY, 1735–
    1775
17. Arend Lijphart, THE TRAUMA OF DECOLONIZATION: THE DUTCH
    AND WEST NEW GUINEA
18. David P. Calleo, COLERIDGE AND THE IDEA OF THE MODERN
    STATE
19. Ronald C. Nairn, UNITED NATIONS FIELD OPERATIONS IN THAI-
    LAND
20. Robert H. Dix, COLOMBIA: THE POLITICAL DIMENSIONS OF
    CHANGE